THE SOCIAL FABRIC

American Life from 1607 to 1877

FIFTH EDITION

Editors

JOHN H. CARY   *Cleveland State University*

JULIUS WEINBERG   *Formerly of Cleveland State University*

LITTLE, BROWN AND COMPANY   *Boston   Toronto*

Library of Congress Cataloging-in-Publication Data

The Social fabric.

  Includes bibliographies.
  Contents: v. 1. American life from 1607 to 1877 —
v. 2. American life from the Civil War to the present.
  1. United States — Social conditions. I. Cary,
John H. (John Henry), 1926–   . II. Weinberg,
Julius, 1922–1984.
HN57.S623 1987   306'.0973   86–18617
ISBN 0–316–13070–2 (v. 1)
ISBN 0–316–13071–0 (v. 2)

Library of Congress Catalog Card Number 86–18617

ISBN 0-316-13070-2

10 9 8 7 6 5 4 3

MV

Published simultaneously in Canada
by Little, Brown & Company (Canada) Limited

Printed in the United States of America

IN MEMORY OF

Julius Weinberg (1922–1984)

Dedicated Teacher of

American Social History

Preface

I know histhry isn't thrue Hinnessy, because it ain't like what I see ivry day in Halsted Sthreet. If any wan comes along with a histhry iv Greece or Rome that'll show me th' people fightin', gettin' dhrunk, makin' love, gettin' married, owin' the grocery man an' bein' without hard-coal, I'll believe they was a Greece or Rome, but not befure.

The sentiment of Mr. Dooley, Finley Peter Dunne's comic Irish philosopher, expresses the attitude of many people toward history. Young Americans, especially, question the relevance of a history that deals only with politics, diplomacy, governments, and famous leaders, and ignores the daily life of average men and women. Two recent trends, however, are doing much to remedy this neglect. One is increased popular interest in the forgotten mass of men and women who tilled our fields, built our cities, and fought our wars, but who achieved no particular fame and left very little record of their lives and thought. The second development is the renewed concern of historians with social history.

This kind of history has more meaning for us, and touches our lives more directly, than any other aspect of our past. In an age seeking "relevance" nothing is more relevant than American social history. Each of us has direct experience, or an intimate awareness, of being part of a family, of falling in love and marrying, of poverty and pain, of suffering in war, of earning a living, of social oppression and reform. By understanding the social life of an earlier age, we can gain an understanding of ourselves and of others.

This is an anthology of American social history for college history courses. It began with our belief that college students would find more meaning in the kind of history described by Mr. Dooley than in political, diplomatic, or constitutional history. This and the companion volume of

The Social Fabric, which covers the period from 1865 to the present, touch upon marrying and making love, fighting and getting drunk, owing the grocer, and going without heat. Covering the time from the earliest settlement of America to Reconstruction, this volume contains descriptions of what it was like to cross the ocean in an immigrant ship and the Great Plains in a covered wagon, what marriage and the family were like in the seventeenth century and what farm life was like in the nineteenth, what life was like for workers in New England factories and for slaves on southern plantations, and how people behaved in a frontier revival meeting or in an austere Shaker community.

No single book can treat every aspect of our history, but these volumes examine American life in much of its diversity. There are essays on women as well as men, on Indians and blacks as well as whites, and on the poor and the oppressed as well as the rich and powerful. The sectional, class, racial, and religious differences among our heterogeneous people have created serious strains that at times threatened to tear the nation apart. But with all their diversity, the American people have also shared many common attitudes and traditions that provided a common social fabric to bind them together.

We have selected the readings from some of the most interesting writing on the American past. We have prefaced each reading with an introductory note, explaining the relation of the subject to broader developments in American history of the period. Each selection is also accompanied by an illustration, which provides a visual commentary on the topic under consideration. The study guide that follows the selection will help you review the special aspects of the reading, and may suggest issues for class discussion. The bibliographical note will help you find further material, should you wish to read more on the topic.

The Fifth Edition

Six articles have been changed in this new edition of volume I of *The Social Fabric.* We have been assisted by the questionnaires, printed at the end of each volume, which many student readers have sent to the publisher, as well as the suggestions and criticisms of teachers who have used the book. Several suggested that the section on the colonial period include an article on the South. We have introduced a selection from Daniel Blake Smith's highly regarded study of the southern family, which contrasts nicely with the picture of women in New England presented by Lyle Koehler. Because the article on Eli Whitney seemed to many teachers to be somewhat marginal, we have substituted a broader study of nineteenth-century industrialization by C. Joseph Pusateri. Some users felt that the volume should have at least one article directly on agriculture. The selection from John M. Faragher's book describes farm life in the Midwest, with special attention to the lives and work of farm women. An earlier article on houses of refuge for children has been replaced by an article, by Christine Stansell, that captures the experience of street children in New York and the efforts of a group of reformers who attempted to restructure their lives. A new article by Mark Wyman on immigration gives more attention to conditions in the old country that led millions of poor and homeless people to venture across the Atlantic. Finally, once again responding to a suggestion made by several teachers, we have included a selection from Barbara M. Tucker that represents the "New Labor History."

The response of students and teachers in both four-year colleges and community colleges to this anthology has been most gratifying. A number of teachers who used the earlier editions of *The Social Fabric* in introductory courses have indicated that these volumes rank with the most successful supplementary materials they have ever used. We hope that the revisions in the fifth edition make the volumes even more useful in American history courses.

Contents

The Social Fabric

I COLONIAL AMERICANS

All Americans are descended from ancestors who came to the western hemisphere from other parts of the world in what was to be the largest migration of people in recorded history. For some 15,000 years, the land we know as the United States was inhabited by Indian peoples who had crossed from northern Asia to Alaska and made their way across both American continents. When Jamestown, Virginia, was founded in 1607, the Indian population of North America may have numbered 500,000 to 1,500,000 people, thinly scattered in tribes from the warlike Iroquois hunters of the Northeast to the pueblo dwellers of the Southwest.

During the next two centuries, one tribe after another encountered invaders from England and other European countries who brought with them very different social values, technological developments, agricultural traditions, governmental institutions, and diseases. The Europeans also brought hundreds of thousands of African slaves to the New World, and the encounter of these three peoples makes up much of the sometimes tragic and occasionally brutal history of early North America. People of English descent comprised half of the population of newcomers by the end of the eighteenth century, and the colonies had been under the English government. Thus, English influences were naturally predominant in shaping colonial institutions and social life. However, Africans and continental Europeans comprised the other half of the population, and their language, religion, and social attitudes modified English institutions and contributed significantly to the rich variety of North American society.

The first article in this section depicts the life and culture of the Seneca Indians in the eighteenth century, by which time all of the eastern Indian tribes had suffered serious consequences from the European invasion of their lands. The selection describes the power of women in Seneca society, the way in which parents raised their children, and their attitudes toward crime, war, and other social questions. The second reading treats the conditions of slavery in Virginia, the complex relationship that existed between master and slave, and the ways in which slaves rebelled at their enslavement. It would seem that Europeans of the seventeenth and eighteenth centuries had some peculiar ideas about their own superiority and the inferiority of other peoples to be able to self-righteously dispossess the Indians from their homelands and to enslave millions of Africans. The third essay may provide some indirect evidence of this sort of thinking, for it concerns the New England male's assumption of his own superiority and the divine law of women's submissiveness. The final essay describes a very different family life that developed in the eighteenth-century South.

*Bertoli's 1796 portrait of Cornplanter (Ki-on-twog-ky) reflects
European influence on the clothing and weapons of the Seneca.*

1

ANTHONY F. C. WALLACE

Indian Life and Culture

In order to understand the history of the United States, we must look to two remote cultures — the European world in the fifteenth century, on the eve of the discovery of the Western Hemisphere, and the ancient Indian culture that existed on this side of the Atlantic. The red man has lived on this continent for about 15,000 years and has been in contact with Europeans and Africans for nearly five hundred years. Yet most Americans know little about Indian life and culture. The movie image of a treacherous savage and the trinket purchased at a souvenir shop have left the real character of the Indian as invisible to the white majority as that of the black man has been for more than three hundred years.

Oliver La Farge has suggested that the Indian has always been unknown to his more recently arrived fellow countrymen, because of a number of myths that whites found it convenient to believe. The earliest of these myths — picturing the Indian as a noble, uncorrupted child of nature — survived in distant Europe longer than it did in the British colonies. Here, as settlers pushed inland and came into conflict with the Indian over land, the more convenient myth of the brutal, treacherous savage supplanted it. Eventually, as industrialized America pushed the Indian tribes onto reservations, a third myth, that of a drunken, irresponsible dependent, became popular.

Anthropologists and historians have been devoting serious attention to the American Indian since Lewis Henry Morgan published a path-breaking study of the Iroquois in 1851. Yet, much of the writing has necessarily been based on a record left by whites, has dealt mostly with Indian–white relations, and leaves one wondering what Indian life looked like from the inside. In fact, Indian life was somewhat different in different historical periods, and it varied considerably from the warlike tribes of the Northeast to the buffalo hunters of the Plains and the pueblo peoples of the Southwest.

Anthony F. C. Wallace is one of the leading students of the Iroquois. His book, *The Death and Rebirth of the Seneca,* is a remarkable study of the devastating effects of European influences on this Iroquois tribe and of the attempt of the prophet Handsome Lake to renew the spirit of his people. The following selection is a general introduction to the Seneca in the eighteenth century. Wallace describes their farming, hunting, warfare, marriage, and training of children, and thus conveys a sense of the fierce independence and loyalty of these earliest Americans.

. . . The traditional Iroquois dwelling unit was called a longhouse. It was a dark, noisy, smoke-filled family barracks; a rectangular, gable-roofed structure anywhere from fifty to seventy-five feet in length, constructed of sheets of elm bark lashed on stout poles, housing up to fifty or sixty people. The roof was slotted (sometimes with a sliding panel for rainy days) to let out some of the smoke that eddied about the ceiling. There was only one entrance, sometimes fitted with a wooden or bark door on wooden hinges, and sometimes merely curtained by a bearskin robe. Entering, one gazed in the half-light down a long, broad corridor or alleyway, in the center of which, every twelve or fifteen feet, smoldered a small fire. On opposite sides of each fire, facing one another, were double-decker bunks, six feet wide and about twelve feet long. An entire family — mother, father, children, and various other relatives — might occupy one or two of these compartments. They slept on soft furs in the lower bunks. Guns, masks, moccasins, clothing, cosmetic paint, wampum, knives, hatchet, food, and the rest of a Seneca family's paraphernalia were slung on the walls and on the upper bunk. Kettles, braided corn, and other suspendable items hung from the joists, which also supported pots over the fire. Each family had about as much room for permanent quarters as might be needed for all of them to lie down and sleep, cook their meals, and stow their gear. Privacy was not easily secured because other families lived in the longhouse; people were always coming and going, and the fires glowed all night. In cold or wet weather or when the snow lay two or three feet deep outside, doors and roof vents had to be closed, and the longhouses became intolerably stuffy — acrid with smoke and the reeking odors of leftover food and sweating flesh. Eyes burned and throats choked. But the people were nonetheless tolerably warm, dry, and (so it is said) cheerful.

The inhabitants of a longhouse were usually kinfolk. A multifamily longhouse was, theoretically, the residence of a maternal lineage: an old woman and her female descendants, together with unmarried sons, and the husbands and children of her married daughters. The totem animal of the clan to which the lineage belonged — Deer, Bear, Wolf, Snipe, or whatever it might be — was carved above the door and painted red. In this way directions were easier to give, and the stranger knew where to seek hospitality or aid. But often — especially in the middle of the eighteenth century — individual families chose to live by themselves in smaller cabins, only eighteen by twenty feet or so in size, with just one fire. As time went on, the old longhouses disintegrated and were abandoned, and by the middle of the century the Iroquois were making their houses of logs.

Around and among the houses lay the cornfields. Corn was a main food. Dried and pounded into meal and then boiled into a hot mush, baked into dumplings, or cooked in whole kernels together with beans and squash and pieces of meat in the thick soups that always hung in kettles over the fires, it kept the people fed. In season, meats, fresh fruits, herb teas, fried grasshoppers, and other delicacies added spice and flavor to the diet. But the Iroquois were a cornfed people. They consumed corn when it was fresh and stored it underground for the lean winter months. The Seneca nation alone raised as much as a million bushels of corn each year; the cornfields around a large village might stretch for miles, and even scattered clearings in the woods were cultivated. Squash, beans, and tobacco were raised in quantity, too. Domesticated animals were few, even after the middle of the century: some pigs, a few chickens, not many horses or cattle. The responsibility for carrying on this extensive agricultural establishment rested almost entirely on the women. Armed with crude wooden hoes and digging-sticks, they swarmed over the fields in gay, chattering work bees, proceeding from field to field to hoe, to plant, to weed, and to harvest. An individual woman might, if she wished, "own" a patch of corn, or an apple or peach orchard, but there was little reason for insisting on private tenure: the work was more happily done communally, and in the absence of a regular market, a surplus was of little personal advantage, especially if the winter were hard and other families needed corn. In such circumstances hoarding led only to hard feelings and strained relations as well as the possibility of future difficulty in getting corn for oneself and one's family. All land was national land; an individual could occupy and use a portion of it and maintain as much privacy in the tenure as he wished, but this usufruct title reverted to the nation when the land was abandoned. There was little reason to bother about individual ownership of real estate anyway: there was plenty of land. Economic security for both men and women lay in a proper recognition of one's obligation to family, clan, community, and nation, and in efficient and cooperative performance on team activities, such as working bees, war parties, and diplomatic missions.

If the clearing with its cornfields bounded the world of women, the forest was the realm of men. Most of the men hunted extensively, not only for deer, elk, and small game to use for food and clothing and miscellaneous household items, but for beaver, mink, and otter, the prime trade furs. Pelts were the gold of the woods. With them a man could buy guns, powder, lead, knives, hatchets, axes, needles and awls, scissors, kettles, traps, cloth, ready-made shirts, blankets, paint (for cosmetic purposes), and various notions: steel springs to pluck out disfiguring beard, scalp, and body hair; silver bracelets and armbands and tubes for coiling hair; rings to hang from nose and ears; mirrors; tinkling bells. Sometimes a tipsy hunter would give away his peltries for a keg of rum, treat his friends to a debauch, and wake up with a scolding wife and hungry children calling him a fool; another might, with equal improvidence, invest in a violin, or a horse, or a gaudy military uniform. But by and large, the products of the commercial hunt — generally conducted in the winter and often hundreds of miles from the home village, in the Ohio country or down the Susquehanna River — were exchanged for a limited range of European consumer goods, which had become, after five generations of contact with beaver-hungry French, Dutch, and English traders, economic necessities. Many of these goods were, indeed, designed to Indian specifications and manufactured solely for the Indian trade. An Iroquois man dressed in a linen breechcloth and calico shirt, with a woolen blanket over his shoulders, bedaubed with trade paint and adorned with trade armbands and earrings, carrying a steel knife, a steel hatchet, a clay pipe, and a rifled gun felt himself in no wise contaminated nor less an Indian than his stone-equipped great-great-grandfather. Iroquois culture had reached out and incorporated these things that Iroquois Indians wanted while at the same time Iroquois warriors chased off European missionaries, battled European soldiers to a standstill, and made obscene gestures when anyone suggested that they should emulate white society (made up, according to their information and experience, of slaves, cheating lawyers with pen and paper and ink, verbose politicians, hypocritical Christians, stingy tavern keepers, and thieving peddlers).

Behavior was governed not by published laws enforced by police, courts, and jails, but by oral tradition supported by a sense of duty, a fear of gossip, and a dread of retaliatory witchcraft. Theft, vandalism, armed robbery, were almost unknown. Public opinion, gently exercised, was sufficient to deter most persons from property crimes, for public opinion went straight to the heart of the matter: the *weakness* of the criminal. A young warrior steals someone else's cow — probably captured during a raid on a white settlement — and slaughters it to feed his hungry family. He does this at a time when other men are out fighting. No prosecution follows, no investigation, no sentence: the unhappy man is nonetheless severely punished, for the nickname "Cow-killer" is pinned to him, and he must drag it rattling behind him wherever he goes. People call him a coward behind his back and snicker when they tell white men, in his presence, a story of an unnamed Indian who killed cows when he should have been killing men. Such a curse was not generalized to the point of ostracism, however. The celebrated Red Jacket, about whom the "Cow-killer" story was told, vindicated his courage in later wars, became the principal spokesman for his nation, and was widely respected and revered. But he never lost the nickname.

Disputes between people rarely developed over property. Marital difficulties centering around infidelity, lack of support, or personal incompatibility were settled by mutual agreement. Commonly, in case of difficulty, the man left and the woman, with her children, remained with her mother. A few couples remained together for a lifetime; most had several marriages; a few changed mates almost with the season. Men might come to blows during drunken arguments over real or fancied slights to their masculine honor, over politics, or over the alleged mistreatment of their kinfolk. Such quarrels led at times to killings or to accusations of witchcraft. A murder (or its equivalent, the practice of witchcraft) was something to be settled by the victim's kinfolk; if they wished, they might kill the murderer or suspected witch without fear of retaliation from his family (provided that family agreed on his guilt). But usually a known killer would come to his senses, admit himself wrong, repent, and offer retribution in goods or services to the mourning family, who unless exceptionally embittered by an unprovoked and brutal killing were then expected to accept the blood money and end the matter.

Drunkenness was perhaps the most serious social problem. Two Moravian missionaries who visited the Iroquois country in 1750 had the misfortune to reach the Seneca towns at the end of June, when the men were just returning from Oswego, where they had sold their winter's furs, and were beginning to celebrate the start of summer leisure. Hard liquor was dissolving winter's inhibitions and regrets. At Canandaigua, the missionaries, who were guests at the house of a prominent warrior, had just explained the friendly nature of their errand when the rum arrived. "All the town was in a state of intoxication, and frequently rushed into our hut in this condition," complained the white men. "There was every reason to think that fighting might ensue, as there were many warriors among those who were perfectly mad with drink." After a sleepless night the missionaries traveled on, reaching the outskirts of Geneseo on the second of July. "The village," said the observers in surprise, "consisted of

40 or more large huts, and lies in a beautiful and pleasant region. A fine large plain, several miles in length and breadth, stretches out behind the village." But the kegs of rum had anticipated them. "When we caught sight of the town we heard a great noise of shouting and quarreling, from which we could infer that many of the inhabitants were intoxicated, and that we might expect to have an uncomfortable time. On entering the town we saw many drunken Indians, who looked mad with drink. . . ."

Alas, poor Christians! They had to hide in a stuffy garret, without food or water. David, their devoted Indian convert and servant, stole out toward evening with a kettle to fetch his masters some water and was seen. "A troop of drunken women came rushing madly toward him. Some of them were naked, and others nearly so. In order to drive them away he was obliged to use his fists, and deal blows to the right and left. He climbed up a ladder, but when he had scarcely reached the top they seized it and tore it from under his feet." David barely managed to escape "in safety" from these playful Amazons. The missionaries decided not to wait the two days until the liquor ran out to meet the chiefs in council; they bent their prayers to an early departure. They finally managed to escape at dawn by jumping down from an opening in the gable and tiptoeing away. "The Lord watched over us in such a manner that all the drunken savages were in their huts, not a creature to be seen. Even the dogs, numbering nearly 100 in the whole village, were all quiet, wonderful to relate, and not a sound was heard. A dense fog covered the town, so that we could not see 20 steps before us. A squaw stood at the door of the last hut, but she was sober and returned our greeting quietly."

But such drunken debauches were only occasional rents in a fabric of polite social behavior. Other missionaries were more favorably impressed than the Moravians. The Seneca, said a Quaker scribe, "appear to be naturally as well calculated for social and rational enjoyment, as any people. They frequently visit each other in their houses, and spend much of their time in friendly intercourse. They are also mild and hospitable, not only among themselves, but to strangers, and good natured in the extreme, except when their natures are perverted by the inflammatory influence of spirituous liquors. In their social interviews, as well as public councils, they are careful not to interrupt one another in conversation, and generally make short speeches. This truly laudable mark of good manners, enables them to transact all their public business with decorum and regularity, and more strongly impresses on their mind and memory, the result of their deliberations."

During the seventeenth and eighteenth centuries Iroquois men earned a reputation among the French and English colonists for being the most astute diplomatically and most dangerous militarily of all the Indians of the Northeast. Yet at the same time the Iroquois were famous for the "matriarchal" nature of their economic and social institutions. After the colonial era came to an end with the victory of the United States in the Revolutionary War, the traditional diplomatic and military role of the Iroquois men was sharply limited by the circumstances of reservation life. Simultaneously, the "matriarchal" character of certain of their economic, kinship, and political institutions was drastically diminished. These changes were codified by the prophet Handsome Lake. As we shall see later in more detail, the changes in kinship behavior that he recommended, and which to a considerable degree were carried out by his followers, amounted to a shift in dominance from the mother–daughter relationship to that of the husband–wife. Handsome Lake's reforms thus were a sentence of doom upon the traditional quasi-matriarchal system of the Iroquois.

The Iroquois were described as matriarchal because of the important role women played in the formal political organization. The men were responsible for hunting, for warfare, and for diplomacy, all of which kept them away from their households for long periods of time, and all of which were essential to the survival of Iroquois society. An expedition of any kind was apt to take months or even years, for the fifteen thousand or so Iroquois in the seventeenth and eighteenth centuries ranged over an area of about a million square miles. It is not an exaggeration to say that the full-time business of an Iroquois man was travel, in order to hunt, trade, fight, and talk in council. But the women stayed at home. Thus, an Iroquois village might be regarded as a collection of strings, hundreds of years old, of successive generations of women, always domiciled in their longhouses near their cornfields in a clearing while their sons and husbands traveled in the forest on supportive errands of hunting and trapping, of trade, of war, and of diplomacy.

The women exercised political power in three main circumstances. First, whenever one of the forty-nine chiefs of the great intertribal League of the Iroquois died, the senior women of his lineage nominated his successor. Second, when tribal or village decisions had to be made, both men and women attended a kind of town meeting, and while men were the chiefs and normally did the public speaking, the women caucused behind the scenes and lobbied with the spokesmen. Third, a woman was entitled to demand publicly that a murdered kinsman or kinswoman be replaced by a captive from a non-Iroquois tribe, and her male relatives, particularly lineage kinsmen, were morally obligated to go out in a war party to secure captives, whom the bereaved woman might either adopt or consign to torture and death. Adoption was so frequent during the bloody centuries of the beaver wars and the colonial wars that some Iroquois villages were preponderantly composed of formally adopted war captives. In sum, Iroquois women were entitled formally to select chiefs, to participate in consensual politics, and to start wars.

Thus the Iroquois during the two centuries of the colonial period were a population divided, in effect, into two parts: sedentary females and nomadic males. The men were frequently absent in small or large groups for prolonged periods of time on hunting, trading, war, and diplomatic expeditions, simultaneously protecting the women from foreign attack and producing a cash crop of skins, furs, and scalps, which they exchanged for hardware and dry goods. These activities, peripheral in a geographic sense, were central to the economic and political welfare of the Six Nations. The preoccupation of Iroquois men with these tasks and the pride they took in their successful pursuit cannot be overestimated. But the system depended on a complementary role for women. They had to be economically self-sufficient through horticulture during the prolonged absences of men, and they maintained genealogical and political continuity in a matrilineal system in which the primary kin relationship (not necessarily the primary social relationship) was the one between mother and daughter.

Such a quasi-matriarchy, of course, had a certain validity in a situation where the division of labor between the sexes required that men be geographically peripheral to the households that they helped to support and did defend. Given the technological, economic, and military circumstances of the time, such an arrangement was a practical one. But it did have an incidental consequence: It made the relationship between husband and wife an extremely precarious one. Under these conditions it was convenient for the marital system to be based on virtually free sexual choice, the mutual satisfaction of spouses, and easy separation. Couples chose one another for personal reasons; free choice was limited, in effect, only by the prohibition of intraclan marriage. Marriages were apt to fray when a husband traveled too far, too frequently, for too long. On his return, drunken quarreling, spiteful gossip, parental irresponsibility, and flagrant infidelity might lead rapidly to the end of the relationship. The husband, away from the household for long periods of time, was apt in his travels to establish a liaison with a woman whose husband was also away. The wife, temporarily abandoned, might for the sake of comfort and economic convenience take up with a locally available man. Since such relationships were, in effect, in the interest of everyone in the longhouse, they readily tended to become recognized marriages. The emotional complications introduced by these serial marriages were supposed to be resolved peacefully by the people concerned. The traveling husband who returned to find his wife living with someone else might try to recover her; if she preferred to remain with her new husband, however, he was not entitled to punish her or her new lover, but instead was encouraged to find another wife among the unmarried girls or wives with currently absent husbands.

The basic ideal of manhood was that of "the good hunter." Such a man was self-disciplined, autonomous, responsible. He was a patient and efficient huntsman, a generous provider to his family and nation, and a loyal and thoughtful friend and clansman. He was also a stern and ruthless warrior in avenging any injury done to those under his care. And he was always stoical and indifferent to privation, pain, and even death. Special prominence could be achieved by those who, while adequate in all respects, were outstanding in one or another dimension of this ideal. The patient and thoughtful man with a skin "seven thumbs thick" (to make him indifferent to spiteful gossip, barbed wit, and social pressures generally) might become a sachem or a "distinguished name" — a "Pine Tree" chief. An eloquent man with a good memory and indestructible poise might be a council speaker and represent clan, nation, even the confederacy in far-flung diplomatic ventures. And the stern and ruthless warrior (always fighting, at least according to the theory, to avenge the death or insult of a blood relative or publicly avowed friend) might become a noted war-captain or an official war-chief. The war-captain ideal, open as it was to all youths, irrespective of clan and lineage or of special intellectual qualifications, was perhaps the most emulated.

In the seventeenth century an Onondaga war-captain named Aharihon bore the reputation of being the greatest warrior of the country. He realized the ideal of autonomous responsibility to virtually pathological perfection. Let us note what is told of Aharihon in the *Jesuit Relations*.

Aharihon was a man of dignified appearance and imposing carriage, grave, polished in manner, and self-contained. His brother had been killed about 1654 in the wars with the Erie, a tribe westward of the Iroquois. As clansman and close relative, he was entitled — indeed obligated — either to avenge his brother's death by killing some Erie people or by adopting a war captive to take his place. Aharihon within a few years captured or had presented to him for adoption forty men. Each of them he burned to death over a slow fire, because, as he said, "he did not believe that there was any one worthy to occupy his [brother's] place." Father Lalemant was present when another young man, newly captured, was given to Aharihon as a substitute for the deceased brother. Aharihon let the young man believe that he was adopted and need have no further fear, and "presented to him four dogs, upon which to hold his feast of adoption. In the middle of the feast, while he was rejoicing and singing to entertain the guests, Aharihon arose, and told the company that this man too must die in atonement for his brother's death. The poor lad was astounded at this, and turned toward the door to make his escape, but was stopped by two men who had orders to burn him. On the fourteenth of February, in the evening, they began with his feet, intending to roast him, at a slow fire, as far up as the waist, during the greater part of the night. After midnight, they were to let him rally his strength and sleep a little until daybreak, when they were to finish this fatal tragedy. In his torture, the poor man made the whole village resound with his cries and groans. He shed great tears, contrary to the usual custom, the victim commonly glorying to be burned limb by limb, and opening his lips only to sing; but, as this one had not expected death, he wept and cried in a way that touched even these Barbarians. One of Aharihon's relatives was so moved with pity, that he advised ending the sufferer's torments by plunging a knife into his breast — which would have been a deed of mercy, had the stab been mortal. However, they were induced to continue the burning without interruption, so that before day he ended both his sufferings and his life." Aharihon's career of death continued without interruption, and by 1663 he was able to boast that he had killed sixty men with his own hand and had burned fully eighty men over slow fire. He kept count by tattooing a mark on his thigh for each successive victim. He was known then as the Captain General of the Iroquois and was nicknamed Nero by the Frenchmen at Montreal because of his cruelty.

The French finally captured him near Montreal, but even in captivity his manner was impressive. "This man," commented Father Lalemant, "commonly has nine slaves with him, five boys and four girls. He is a captain of dignified appearance and imposing carriage, and of such equanimity and presence of mind that, upon seeing himself surrounded by armed men, he showed no more surprise than if he had been alone; and when asked whether he would like to accompany us to Quebec, he deigned only to answer coldly that that was not a question to ask him, since he was in our power. Accordingly he was made to come aboard our Vessel, where I took pleasure in studying his disposition as well as that of an Algonquin in our company, who bore the scalp of an Iroquois but recently slain by him in war. These two men, although hostile enough to eat each other, chatted and laughed on board that Vessel with great familiarity, it being very hard to decide which of the two was more skillful in masking his feelings. I had Nero placed near me at table, where he bore himself with a gravity, a self-control, and a propriety, which showed nothing of his Barbarian origin; but during the rest of the time he was constantly eating, so that he fasted only when he was at table."

But this voracious captain was not renowned among the Onondaga as a killer only. He was, on the contrary, also a trusted ambassador, dispatched on occasion to Montreal on missions of peace. He was, in a word, a noted man. He was a killer, but he was not an indiscriminate killer; he killed only those whom it was his right to kill, tortured only those whom he had the privilege of torturing, always as an expression of respect for his dead brother. And although his kinfolk sometimes felt he was a little extreme in his stern devotion to his brother's memory, they did not feel that he was any the less a fine man, or that they had a right to interfere with his impulses; they were willing to entrust the business of peace, as well as war, to his hand.

A century and a half later Mary Jemison, the captive white woman who lived for most of her life among the Seneca on the Genesee River, described her Indian husband in not dissimilar terms. "During the term of nearly fifty years that I lived with him," she recalled, "I received, according to Indian custom, all the kindness and attention that was my due as his wife. — Although war was his trade from his youth till old age and decrepitude stopt his career, he uniformly treated me with tenderness, and never offered an insult. . . . He was a man of tender feelings to his friends, ready and willing to assist them in distress, yet, as a warrior, his cruelties to his enemies perhaps were unparalleled. . . . In early life, Hiokatoo showed signs of thirst for blood, by attending only to the art of war, in the use of the tomahawk and scalping knife; and in practising cruelties upon every thing that chanced to fall into his hands, which was susceptible of pain. In that way he learned to use his implements of war effectually, and at the same time blunted all those fine feelings and tender sympathies that are naturally excited, by hearing or seeing, a fellow being in distress. He could inflict the most excruciating tortures upon his enemies, and prided himself upon his fortitude, in having performed the most barbarous ceremonies and tortures, without the least degree of pity or remorse. . . . In those battles he took a number of Indians prisoners, whom he killed by tying them to trees and then setting small Indian boys to shooting at them with arrows, till death finished the misery of the sufferers; a process that frequently took two days for its completion! . . . At Braddock's defeat he took two white prisoners, and burnt them alive in a fire of his own kindling. . . ."

With this sort of man serving as an ego-ideal, held up by sanction and by praise to youthful eyes, it is not remarkable that young men were ambitious to begin the practice of war. All had seen captives tortured to death; all had known relatives lost in war whose death demanded revenge or replacement. The young men went out on practice missions as soon as they were big enough to handle firearms; "infantile bands, armed with hatchets and guns which they can hardly carry, do not fail to spread fear and horror everywhere." Even as late as the middle of the eighteenth century, Handsome Lake and his brothers and nephews were still busy at the old business of war for the sake of war. Cornplanter became a noted war-captain; Blacksnake, his nephew, was one of the official war-chiefs of the Seneca nation; and Handsome Lake himself took part in the scalping-party pattern as a young man. But Handsome Lake became a sachem and later a prophet, and he never gloried in the numbers of men he killed as his brother Cornplanter (somewhat guiltily) did. "While I was in the use of arms I killed seven persons and took three and saved their lives," said Cornplanter. And Blacksnake, in later life, told with relish of his exploits as a warrior. "We had a good fight there," he would say. "I have killed how many I could not tell, for I pay no attention to or kept [no] account of it, it was great many, for I never have it at all my Battles to think about kepting account what I'd killed at one time. . . ."

The cultivation of the ideal of autonomous responsibility — and the suppression of its antinomy, dependency — began early in life. Iroquois children were carefully trained to think for themselves but to act for others. Parents were protective, permissive, and sparing of punishment; they encouraged children to play at imitating adult behavior but did not criticize or condemn fumbling early efforts; they maintained a cool detachment, both physically and verbally, avoiding the intense confrontations of love and anger between parent and child to which Europeans were accustomed. Children did not so much live in a child's world as grow up freely in the interstices of an adult culture. The gain was an early self-reliance and enjoyment of responsibility; the cost, perhaps, was a lifelong difficulty in handling feelings of dependency.

The Seneca mother gave birth to her child in the privacy of the woods, where she retired for a few hours when her time came, either alone or in the company of an older woman who served as midwife and, if the weather was cold, built and tended a fire. She had prepared for this event by eating sparingly and exercising freely, which were believed (probably with good reason) to make the child stronger and the birth easier. The newborn infant was washed in cold water, or even in snow, immediately after parturition and then wrapped in skins or a blanket. If the birth were a normal one, the mother walked back to the village with her infant a few hours afterwards to take up the duties of housewife. The event was treated as the consummation of a healthful process rather than as an illness. The infant spent much of its first nine months swaddled from chin to toe and lashed to a cradle-board. The child's feet rested against a footboard; a block of wood was placed between the heels of a girl to mold her feet to an inward turn. Over its head stretched a hoop, which could be draped with a thin cloth to keep away flies or to protect the child from the cold. The board and its wrappings were often lavishly decorated with silver trinkets and beadwork embroidery. The mother was able to carry the child in the board, suspended against her back, by a tumpline around her forehead; the board could be hung from the limb of a tree while she hoed corn; and it could be converted into a crib by suspending it on a rack of poles laid horizontally on forks stuck in the ground. The mother was solicitous of the child's comfort, nursed it whenever it cried, and loosened it from the board several times a day to change the moss that served as a diaper and to give it a chance to romp. The children, however, tended to cry when released from the board, and their tranquility could often be restored only by putting them back. Babies were seldom heard crying.

The mother's feeling for her children was intense; indeed, to one early observer it appeared that "Parental Tenderness" was carried to a "dangerous Indulgence." Another early writer remarked, "The mothers love their children with an extreme passion, and although they do not reveal this in caresses, it is nevertheless real." Mothers were quick to express resentment of any restraint or injury or insult offered to the child by an outsider. During the first few years the child stayed almost constantly with the mother, in the house, in the fields, or on the trail, playing and performing small tasks under her direction. The mother's chief concern during this time was to provide for the child and to protect it, to "harden" it by baths in cold water, but not to punish. Weaning was not normally attempted until the age of three or four, and such control as the child obtained over its excretory functions was achieved voluntarily, not as a result of consistent punishment for mistakes. Early sexual curiosity and experimentation were regarded as a natural childish way of behaving, out of which it would, in due time, grow. Grandparents might complain that small children got into everything, but the small child was free to romp, to pry into things, to demand what it wanted, and to assault its parents, without more hazard of punishment than the exasperated mother's occasionally blowing water in its face or dunking it in a convenient river.

The years between about eight or nine and the onset of puberty were a time of easy and gradual learning. At the beginning of this period the beginnings of the differentiation of the roles of boys and girls were laid down. The girls were kept around the house, under the guidance of their mothers, and assigned to the lighter household duties and to helping in the fields. Boys were allowed to roam in gangs, playing at war, hunting with bows and arrows and toy hatchets, and competing at races, wrestling, and lacrosse. The first successes at hunting were greeted with praise and boasts of future greatness. Sometimes these roaming gangs spent days at a time away from the village, sleeping in the bush, eating wild roots and fruits, and hunting such small game as could be brought down by bow and arrow, blowgun, or snare. These gangs developed into war parties after the boys reached puberty. Among themselves, both in gangs and among siblings of the same family, the children's playgroups were not constantly supervised by parents and teachers, and the children governed themselves in good harmony. Said one close observer, "Children of the same family show strong attachments to each other, and are less liable to quarrel in their youthful days than is generally the case with white children."

The parents usually tried to maintain a calm moderation of behavior in dealing with their children, a lofty indifference alike to childish tantrums and seductive appeals for love. Hardihood, self-reliance, and independence of spirit were sedulously inculcated. When occasion presented itself, fathers, uncles, or other elder kinfolk instructed their sons in the techniques of travel, firemaking, the chase, war, and other essential arts of manhood, and the mothers correspondingly taught their daughters the way to hoe and plant the cornfields, how to butcher the meat, cook, braid corn, and other household tasks. But this instruction was presented, rather than enforced, as an opportunity rather than as a duty. On occasion the parent or other responsible adult talked to the child at length, "endeavoring," as a Quaker scribe gently put it, "to impress on its mind what it ought to do, and what to leave undone." If exhortation seemed inadequate in its effect, the mentor might ridicule the child for doing wrong, or gravely point out the folly of a certain course of action, or even warn him that he courted the rage of offended supernatural beings. Obedience as such was no virtue, however, and blows, whippings, or restraints of any kind, such as restriction to quarters, were rarely imposed, the faults of the child being left to his own reason and conscience to correct as he grew mature. With delicate perception the adults noted that childish faults "cannot be very great, before reason arrives at some degree of maturity."

Direct confrontation with the child was avoided, but when things got seriously out of hand, parents sometimes turned older children over to the gods for punishment. A troublesome child might be sent out into the dusk to meet Longnose, the legendary Seneca bogeyman. Longnose might even be impersonated in the flesh by a distraught parent. Longnose was a hungry cannibal who chased bad children when their parents were sleeping. He mimicked the child, crying loudly as he ran, but the parents would not wake up because Longnose had bewitched them. A child might be chased all night until he submitted and promised to behave. Theoretically, if a child remained stubborn, Longnose finally caught him and took him away in a huge pack-basket for a leisurely meal. And — although parents were not supposed to do this — an unusually stubborn infant *could* be threatened with punishment by the great False Faces themselves, who, when invoked for this purpose, might "poison" a child or "spoil his face." "I remember," recalled a Cayuga woman of her childhood, "how scared I was of the False-faces; I didn't know what they were. They are to scare away disease. They used to come into the house and up the stairs and I used to hide away under the covers. They even crawled under the bed and they made that awful sound. When I was bad my mother used to say the False-faces would get me. Once, I must have been only 4 or 5, because I was very little when I left Canada, but I remember it so well that when I think of it I can hear that cry now, and I was going along a road from my grandfather's; it was a straight road and I couldn't lose my way, but it was almost dark, and I had to pass through some timber and I heard that cry and that rattle. I ran like a flash of lightning and I can hear it yet."

At puberty some of the boys retired to the woods under the stewardship of an old man, where they fasted, abstained from any sort of sexual activity (which they had been free to indulge, to the limit of their powers, before), covered themselves with dirt, mortified the flesh in various ways, such as bathing in ice water and bruising and gashing the shinbones with rocks.

Dreams experienced during such periods of self-trial were apt to be regarded as visitations from supernatural spirits who might grant *orenda*, or magical power, to the dreamer, and who would maintain a special sort of guardianship over him. The person's connection with this supernatural being was maintained through a charm — such as a knife, a queerly shaped stone, or a bit of bone — which was connected with the dream through some association significant to the dreamer. Unlike many other tribes, however, the Iroquois apparently did not require these guardian-spirit visions for pubescent youths. Many youths were said not to have had their first vision until just before their first war party. Furthermore, any man could have a significant dream or vision at any time. Girls too went through a mild puberty ritual, retiring into the woods at first menstruation and paying particular attention to their dreams. With the termination of the menstrual period the girl returned to the household; but hereafter, whenever she menstruated, she would have to live apart in a hut, avoiding people, and being careful not to step on a path, or to cook and serve anyone's food, or (especially) to touch medicines, which would immediately lose their potency if she handled them.

The Europeans who observed this pattern of child experience were by no means unfavorably impressed although they were sometimes amazed. They commented, however, almost to a man, from early Jesuit to latter-day Quaker, on a consequence that stood out dramatically as they compared this "savage" maturation with "civilized." "There is nothing," wrote the Jesuit chronicler of the Iroquois mission in 1657, "for which these peoples have a greater horror than restraint. The very children cannot endure it, and live as they please in the houses of their parents, without fear of reprimand or chastisement." One hundred and fifty years later, the Quaker Halliday Jackson observed that "being indulged in most of their wishes, as they grow up, liberty, in its fullest extent, becomes their ruling passion." The Iroquois themselves recognized the intensity of their children's resentment at parental interference. "Some Savages," reported Le Mercier of the Huron, "told us that one of the principal reasons why they showed so much indulgence toward their children, was that when the children saw themselves treated by their parents with some severity, they usually resorted to extreme measures and hanged themselves, or ate of a certain root they called *Audachienrra*, which is a very quick poison." The same fear was recorded among the Iroquois, including the Seneca, in 1657. And while suicides by frustrated children were not actually frequent, there are nevertheless a number of recorded cases of suicide where parental interference was the avowed cause. And *mutatis mutandis*, there was another rationalization for a policy of permissiveness: that the child who was harshly disciplined might grow up, some day, to mistreat his parents in revenge.

This theory of child raising was not taken for granted by the Seneca;

on the contrary, it was very explicitly recognized, discussed, and pondered. Handsome Lake himself, in later years, insisted that parents love and indulge their children.

STUDY GUIDE

1. Be prepared to discuss European influences on Indian social life, housing, clothing, weapons, and values.

2. What was the role of the Seneca woman in the family, economic life, and government affairs, and how was her position different from that of a European or American woman?

3. Review the introduction to this selection, in which certain myths held by Europeans are discussed. Considering Seneca government, the personality of the Iroquois, and attitudes toward loyalty and war, how does the picture presented by Wallace differ from the myths La Farge noted?

4. Different societies have varied views on child-rearing, marriage, and divorce, and have different ways of controlling such antisocial behavior as crime. How did Seneca practices in each of these areas differ from the patterns in modern America?

5. Like Mary Jemison, who is mentioned in this selection, a great many colonists were adopted as full-fledged members of Indian tribes, remained with them, and rejected opportunities to return to English society. What explanations can you think of for their finding Indian tribal life so attractive?

BIBLIOGRAPHY

One should keep in mind that in this selection Wallace is portraying only one of many Indian societies. Generally, we have tended to see Indian culture as a monolithic system and to ignore important differences among the various tribes. Many people think of all Indians as wearing colorful headdresses, living in tepees, using horses and canoes for transportation, and depending on the bow and arrow for their livelihood. Dress, housing, economy, marital customs, burial rites, and agricultural patterns varied in different regions. Your library may have some of the specialized studies of these aspects of Indian life or books on individual tribes through which you can extend your knowledge of these first Americans.

Wallace's essay on the Iroquois replaces an essay by the distinguished anthropologist Ruth Underhill on the Southeastern tribes that was used in the first edition of this volume. Her book, *Red Man's America* (1953), is one of the best general studies of the various Indian societies. Another very well written, general study of most tribes is Peter Farb, *Man's Rise to Civilization as Shown by the Indians of North America from Primeval Times to the Coming of the Industrial State* (1968). The following are also excellent studies, utilizing both anthropological and historical knowledge: Harold E. Driver, *The Indians of North America*, 2nd ed. (1969); William T. Hagan, *American Indians* (1961); Alvin M. Josephy, Jr., *The Indian Heritage of America* (1968); and Clark Wissler, *Indians of the United States*, rev. ed. (1966).

There are many volumes that deal more directly with topics mentioned in the selection by Wallace. Richard Drinnon, *Facing West: The Metaphysics of Indian-Hating and Empire Building* (1980) describes colonial attitudes toward Indians and examples of white cruelty that equaled that of Aharihon. A book by James Axtell, *The European and the Indian: Essays in the Ethnohistory of Colonial North America* (1981), is a series of fascinating essays on such subjects as scalping, colonists who lived with Indian tribes, and the cultural interaction of Indian and European.

In much historical writing, the American Indian has been treated merely as a "problem" or an obstacle in the path of the more highly advanced civilization of Europe. A very different perspective is given in Francis Jennings, *The Invasion of America: Indians, Colonialism, and the Cant of Conquest* (1975), which treats the European colonists as invaders. Another work which gives a more balanced, and less European-oriented, view of early American history is Gary B. Nash, *Red, White, and Black: The Peoples of Early America* (1974).

*The painting "The Old Plantation" shows a slave wedding and the
survival of African culture in customs, headties, and the musical
instrument.*

2

GERALD W. MULLIN

Life Under Slavery

The attitude of British colonials — and later, of American whites — toward blacks, who first landed at Jamestown in 1619, was shaped by myths and stereotypes. Influenced by sexual anxieties, economic self-interest, physical distinctions, and other factors, whites found it impossible to view blacks unemotionally. The first blacks in Virginia were bound to a limited term of service, just as were white indentured servants, but by the 1660s slave codes provided permanent enslavement of African laborers.

The serious study of black history began well before 1900. A number of circumstances limited such study, even by thoughtful scholars who tried to be objective. Black Americans had left some written records and a substantial oral tradition, but most of the sources from which black history was written were left by whites. An equally important limitation was that historians were most interested in those aspects of black history that shed light upon general American history. Thus, their attention was concentrated on slavery. Some understanding of slavery was essential for studying the history of American agriculture, presidential and congressional politics before the Civil War, westward expansion, or the upsurge of social reform after 1830.

Aspects of black life and culture that were only marginally related to white concerns went unstudied. African influences on American culture, black religion, the slave trade, even the impact of slavery on the American black's personality, received scant attention. With the exception of slavery, black history before the Civil War was not considered worthy of intensive study. The mainstream of American social and cultural life clearly came from Europe, as had the ancestors of most Americans, and little note was taken of the early origins of the Afro-American minority.

23

Yet many black Americans today can assume that their ancestors were in this country before 1800, and most of them can also be certain that those ancestors came in chains. They were rugged pioneers who cherished freedom, but, like no other people, they suffered harrowing hardships involuntarily, helping to establish the foundations of American agriculture under the lash. Disagreement remains concerning some aspects of slavery, but historians have reached a large measure of agreement concerning the life of the slave. By the use of more representative records and new approaches to the study of slavery, they have drawn a graphic portrait of the slaves' family life, housing, food, legal status, rewards and punishments, their work in the fields and in the cities, and their reaction to enslavement.

Gerald W. Mullin's *Flight and Rebellion* is a sensitive study of how African people adapted to, and resisted, enslavement. Mullin deals with slavery in Virginia at the end of the eighteenth century. On one question — whether slaves were contented with their lot or fundamentally rebellious — his work may be more informative than studies of the era just before the Civil War. He writes of a time before the antislavery movement, with its tracts, newspapers, and underground railroad. In the eighteenth century, the slaves reached their own decision. This selection gives a vivid picture of slave life and the determination to gain freedom of a group of our forebears who happened to be black.

The field slave "is called up in the morning at daybreak, scarcely allowed time to swallow three mouthfuls of homminy," wrote the English traveler J. F. D. Smyth. Brief notations like this in travelers' and plantation accounts and record books must suffice for data on the field slave's material condition. Although the records are sketchy, his diet, although probably adequate in bulk, was scarcely nourishing. "Homminy," Indian corn, was the slaves' staple food.

Random accounts of quantities of corn allotted suggest that provisions were sometimes based on the worker's productivity. During the Revolutionary War, "Councillor" Carter asked that "the stronger Shears [shares] men & women" be given one peck of corn per week, "the Remainder of the Black People they to have ¼ Peck per Week each." By 1787 Carter, who was one of the least oppressive slave masters, increased this slightly. He ordered 44 pecks of shelled Indian corn as two weeks' allowance for

From *Flight and Rebellion: Slave Resistance in Eighteenth-Century Virginia* by Gerald W. Mullin. Copyright © 1972 by Oxford University Press, Inc. Reprinted by permission. (Footnotes omitted.)

26 slaves, less than a full peck per week per laborer. (One peck equals 14 lbs. of Indian corn.)

Meat was seldom given to slaves. Smyth said slaves ate hoecakes and little else; unless their master "be a man of humanity the slave eats a little fat, skimmed milk, and rusty bacon." La Rochefoucauld-Liancourt said that on large plantations the slave subsisted on corn and sometimes on buttermilk. They were given meat 6 times a year. Robert "Councillor" Carter estimated that the common allowance for wheat per hand per year was 15 bushels for those "negroes, who are not fed with animal food" (e.g., meat). These slaves only received meat on special occasions. Joseph Ball wrote his steward that slaves were to "have ffresh meat when they are sick, if the time of the year will allow it." The cuts were to be the least desirable, although not necessarily the least nutritious. When calves were slaughtered, Ball ordered him to give the field hands the "head and Pluck"; the "ffat backs, necks, and other Coarse pieces" of hogs were also to be reserved for the slaves. James Mercer directed his steward to give the slaves the innards of chickens unless he sold them to the local Negro chicken merchants.

Plantation slaves wore clothing usually cut from a heavy, coarse cloth of flax and tow originally manufactured in Osnabrück, Germany. Following the non-importation agreements of the late 1760's, coarse-textured cotton wool weave, "Virginia plains," "country linen," replaced "Osnabrugs." Unlike the colorful variety of many of the artisan's clothing, the notices for runaways after 1770 indicate that field laborers wore uniform pants and trousers. "They are well clothed in the usual manner for Negroes"; "clothed as usual" and "the usual winter clothing for corn field negroes" are representative descriptions from advertisements of that period.

Black women who worked on the quarter wore clothing of the same weight and texture as the men. They usually dressed in a loose-fitting smock or shift, often tied at the waist; a short waistcoat was fitted over this dress. A Dutch blanket used for a sleeping robe and shoes and stockings completed the plantation Negroes' clothing allowance.

Housing for slaves varied widely. But there are frequent references in travelers' accounts to clusters of slave cabins that looked like small villages, and, in plantation records, numerous directions from masters indicating a concern for warm, dry houses with floors, lofted roofs, and on occasion, fireplaces. Slave quarters, however, may have been a late development. Subscribers who used advertisements to sell plantations frequently mentioned "negro quarters," but usually only in those notices published in the last quarter of the century. The plantation's size, location, and wealth were not factors; nearly all had slave quarters. It is likely that the smaller planter's field hands may have slept in the lofts of barns, in tobacco houses, and other outbuildings before the war. Joseph Ball told his nephew that the slaves "must ly in the Tobacco house" while their quarters, 15 by

20 feet with fireplace and chimney, were "lathed & fitted." However, several planters, including George Washington, used a less substantial, pre-fab arrangement. These shacks were small, temporary, and were moved from quarter to quarter following the seasonal crop.

J. F. D. Smyth was forced to take shelter one evening in a "miserable shell" inhabited by six slaves and their overseer. Unlike many slaves' houses "it was not lathed nor plaistered, neither ceiled nor lofted above . . . one window, but no glass in it, not even a brick chimney, and, as it stood on blocks about a foot above the ground, the hogs lay constantly under the floor, which made it swarm with flies."

On the home plantations, "servants," like the crop hands, usually slept in their own quarters. A planter who moved to the valley in 1781 asked his steward to place the "house Servants for they have been more indulged than the rest" with the overseer and his family, "till Such Time as Warehouses can be provided for them." Slaves evidently rarely slept in the great house. . . .

Some idea of a slave's yearly expenses is provided by James Madison's remark to a British visitor earlier in the nineteenth century. "Every negro earns annually, all expenses being deducted, about $257," wrote John Foster. "The expense of a negro including duty, board, clothing, and medicines, he [Madison] estimates from $12–$13."

The lean, spare character of the field slave's material condition was a function of his place in the servile work hierarchy. Most plantation slaves worked in the fields where their tasks were tedious, sometimes strenuous, and usually uninspiring. Although tobacco is a difficult and challenging crop, field laborers — especially the "new Negroes" — were forced into the most routine tasks of transplanting seedlings, weeding, suckering, and worming. Following the harvest their work days extended into the night, when they sorted, bundled, and pressed the tobacco into hogsheads for shipment.

The slave jobber's work assignments were not as routine as the field laborer's chores. Armistead was hired out by his master to "act as a jobber, *viz.* to cut firewood, go to [the] Mill, work in your garden, and occasionally to work in your Corn-field." Jobbers also mended stone and wood fences, patched and whitewashed the plantation's outbuildings, dug irrigation and drainage ditches, and the like. "Councillor" Carter hired John McKenney to "overlook" his jobbers in 1777. Their agreement read:

> the sd Jobbers to make a Crop of Corn Pumpkins, Irish Potatoes, at my plantation called Dickerson's Mill, that is, a full crop fr about 4 Shares —
> the sd Jobbers to raise Stone to build a tumbling Dam at Dickerson's Mill, they to make ye dirt Dam sufficient, there, and to do several Jobs at Nomony Hall in the course of this year.

McKenney's wages indicate that this type of work was not well paid: he was "to receive f[o]r his services at the rate of 25s/6 per month, [is] to find himself, Board, lodging, Washing &c."

But jobbers were scarcely better off than the field laborers, because they too did not travel outside the plantation. Nor did their menial tasks spur assimilation and a corresponding change in their view of slavery. Regardless of the specific nature of their tasks, the horizons and expectations of most plantation slaves were sharply limited by the plantation environment.

Their tiresome routines in the meager setting of reserve land, in meadow and woods, monotonous rows of tobacco, and temporary, ramshackle buildings, made the quarter a world of its own. But the isolation and work routines of the quarter provided slaves with a convenient means of expressing their unhappiness, so it was also a constant, nagging source of trouble for the planter. Blacks and whites alike knew that the plantation's efficiency and profitability could be seriously impaired simply by a "little leaning" on the slaves' part. "My people seem to be quite dead hearted, and either cannot or will not work"; "my people are all out of their senses for I cannot get one of them to do a thing as I would have it and as they do it even with their own time they have it to do again immediately." These words are Landon Carter's. A tough and competent man, Carter did not bend easily, but this note of resignation is heard early in his diary.

Accounts of the field slave's performance are rare, but one of the best can be found in Jack P. Greene's fine edition of Landon Carter's Diary which tells a dreary story of the crop laborers' quiet and persistently non-cooperative actions. Slaves reported ill every day but Sunday when there were no complaints because they considered this "a holy day"; men treading wheat slept while their "boys," left to do the job, "neglected" it; the "crop people," forced to stem tobacco in the evening hours, retaliated "under the guise of semi-darkness [by] throwing away a great deal of the saleable tob[acco]"; men whom Carter harassed about weeding a corn patch feigned stupidity and leveled thousands of hills of corn seedlings. Carter's slaves, in fact, were so rebellious that he came to question the profitability of slavery. "It is the same at all my plantations," he complained:

> Although I have many to work and fine land to be tended, I hardly make more than what cloaths them, finds them tools, and pays their Levies. Perhaps a few scrawney hogs may be got in the year to be fattened up here. If these things do not require the greatest caution and frugality in living I am certain nothing can do.

William Strickland, an Englishman who visited colonial America in 1800, concurred. As well as any traveler, he succinctly defined the character of the plantation slaves' rebelliousness in a letter to the Board of Trade:

> Any slave that I have seen at work, does not appear to perform half as much, as a labourer in England; nor does the business under which the master sits down contented, appear to be half of what we require to be

performed by one. . . . If to this be added the slovenly carelessness with which all business is performed by the slave, the great number of useless hands the slave owner is obliged to maintain, the total indifference to, and neglect, not to say the frequent wilful destruction, of whatever is not immediately committed to his care. . . . And also the universal inclination to pilfering shown by them, I cannot do otherwise than acquiesce in the received opinion of the country, that slave labor is much dearer than any other.

Lazy, wasteful, and indifferent work was a chronic problem on eighteenth-century plantations. Slaves understood that there was a great deal of time to waste, and little hope of improving their lot. "It will be better to have more eyes than one over such gangs," Landon Carter noted. Following another inspection he complained, "the old trade, take one hour from any job and it makes a day loss in work." Most plantation slaves desired challenging tasks, but once they had them, they dragged out the job as long as possible. Herdsman Johnny, charged with breaking up the quarter patch at Sabine Hall, "does not intend to finish," Carter wrote, "by contriving that all his lambs should get out of the yard that he may be trifling about after them."

Careful planters habitually spot-checked their slaves' productivity. Planters like Landon Carter and George Washington who demanded from their slaves punctiliousness, order, and a high output, were convenient and effective targets for the slaves' piddling laziness and wasteful procedures. A 1760 entry in Washington's diary noted that four of his sawyers hewed about 120 feet of timber in a day. Dissatisfied with this rate of production, and determined to apply gentle pressure, Washington stood and watched his men. They subsequently fell to work with such energy and enthusiasm that he concluded that one man could do in one day what four had previously accomplished in the same length of time.

How many seemingly routine plantation practices were actually concessions to the unreliability of slave labor? For years Landon Carter refused to introduce plows and carts onto his quarters since he felt that these technological innovations would only serve "to make Overseers and people extremely lazy . . . wherever they are in great abundance there is the least plantation work done."

Feigned illness was another remarkably simple but effective ruse. When a slave asked to "lay-in," his master often suspected he was faking, but could never be certain. Too many had stood helplessly by while a strange and lethal "distemper," or "ague," suddenly swept through their slave quarters and carried off numbers of workers. Plantation records are filled with notes on these epidemics: "The mortalities in ties in my families are increased. . . . The number of my dead is now fifteen working slaves. I thank God I can bear these things with a great deal of resignation," or "a grievous mortality of my familys hath swept away an abundance of my people"; and, "we kept the plantations on James River to try to make

Crops, but there broke out a malignant fever amongst the Negroes & swept off most of the able Hands; this threw all into Confusion & there has been little or no thing made since."

Women who feigned illness were usually more effective than men. "As to Sall," James Mercer wrote his steward, "I believe her old complaint is mere deceit, if it is not attended with a fever it must be so unless it is owing to her monthly disorder & then can only last two days, and exercise is a necessary remedy." Washington complained of women who "will lay up a month, at the end of which no visible change in their countenance, nor the loss of an ounce of flesh, is discoverable; and their allowance of provision is going on as if nothing ailed them." Exasperated and uncertain about the health of a black woman, Betty Davis, he explained that "she has a disposition to be one of the most idle creatures on earth, and besides one of the most deceitful." When two of his slave women approached clutching their sides, Landon Carter told them to work or be whipped. He observed that they had no fever (the test of whether or not slaves were ill). "They worked very well with no grunting about pain." But Sarah, one of the women who had pretended to be pregnant for eleven months earlier in the year, soon ran off. When Wilmot used the same stratagem, Carter noted: "it cost me 12 months, before I broke her." This lesson was not satisfactory; for a third woman "fell into the same scheme," and "really carried it to a great length." So Carter whipped her severely; and she was "a good slave ever since only a cursed thief in making her Children milk Cows in the night."

Plantation slaves who "hid out" in the woods and fields as runaways represented a more serious breach of plantation security. They often returned to the quarter in the evening for food and shelter and were an invitation to others to follow their example. But truancy was also inward rebelliousness: it was sporadic, and it was directed toward the plantation or quarter. Unlike the real fugitives, truants had no intention of leaving the immediate neighborhood and attempting to permanently change their status. Truancy was so common that most planters either did not make it a matter of record or simply referred to it in a random manner in their correspondence. "King" Carter actually viewed it as part of his "outlandish" slaves' learning process: "Now that my new negro woman has tasted the hardships of the woods," he observed to an overseer, "she'll stay nearer to home where she can have her belly full." Planters accepted the fact that absenteeism, particulary in the evening hours, was scarcely controllable. In response to Landon Carter's complaint that his pet deer were straying in the Sabine Hall fields, John Tayloe wrote:

Dear Col
. . . Now give me leave to complain to you, That your Patroll do not do their duty, my people are rambleing about every night, . . . my man Billie was

out, he says he rode no horse of Master & that he only was at Col. Carter's, by particular invitation, so that the Entertainment was last night at Sabine Hall, & may probably be at Mt Airy this night, if my discoverys do not disconcert the Plan, these things would not be so I think, if the Patrollers did the duty they are paid for.

Plantation slaves probably "rambled" to the "entertainment" in the neighborhood several nights of the week; as long as they reported for work the following day few efforts were made, or could be made, to curtail this practice.

Truants habitually remained very close to the quarter or plantation; but this did not make it much easier for the planter to recapture them. Evidently they were sufficiently clever (and the other plantation slaves were sufficiently secretive) to keep themselves in hiding until they decided to return on their own. Sarah ran off because Carter refused to let her "lie-in" as ill. She spent a week in the woods and ate during the evening hours while visiting the slave quarters. Simon, an ox-carter, also hid beneath the vigilant Carter's very nose. He "lurked" in Johnny's "inner room," and in the "Kitchen Vault."

The outlaw, a far more dangerous type of runaway, used his temporary freedom to inflict punishment on his tormenters. Outlawing a slave was a legal action, placing the runaway beyond the law, making him a public liability, and encouraging his destruction by any citizen. Those who killed outlaws did so without fear of legal prosecution; they also collected a fee from the public treasury and a reward from the slave's owner. The master's advertisements usually did not encourage the slave's preservation: George America was worth forty shillings if taken alive; five pounds if destroyed.

Some slaveowners only threatened to outlaw truants. Recognizing the effective communication between slaves who remained on the quarter and their "outlying" brother, masters used outlawry as a warning for slaves to come in or suffer the consequences. Many did not return, nor were they satisfied with merely "lurking" about and "tasting the hardships of the woods" until hunger brought them back to the quarter. Outlaws destroyed. The omnibus slave codes of the century (four were passed from 1705 to 1797) described these desperate, courageous and "incorrigible" slaves in language which changed only slightly during the ninety years:

WHEREAS many times slaves run away and lie hid and lurking in swamps, woods, and other obscure places, killing hogs, and committing other injuries to the inhabitants . . . upon intelligence, two justices (*Quorum unus*) can issue a proclamation . . . if the slave does not immediately return, anyone whatsoever may kill or destroy such slaves by such ways and means as he . . . shall think fit. . . . If the slave is apprehended . . . it shall . . . be lawful for the county court, to order such punishment to the said slave, either by dismembering, or in any other way . . . as they in their discretion shall think fit, for the reclaiming any such incorrigible slave, and terrifying others from the like practices.

Newspaper advertisements provide a glimpse of why a few runaways were outlawed: John Smith outlawed Mann because he threatened to burn Smith's house; and John Tayloe's manager at the Occoquan Furnace reported that "Leamon's obstinacy in not delivering himself up when lurking a considerable time about the ironworks, and doing mischief, Induced me to have him outlawed; in which condition he now stands and remains." Other explanations were not as clear as these. Moses and his wife were "harboured" by some "ill disposed" persons in Williamsburg. His master advertised "such notorious offences are not to be borne with any degree of patience." Edward Cary's explanation for outlawing Ben and Alice was even more cryptic. Cary was the chairman of the House of Burgesses committee that reimbursed masters whose slaves were outlawed as public liabilities. "As neither of those slaves have been ill used at my hands, I have had them outlawed in this county and for their bodies without hurt, or a proper certificate of their death, a proper reward will be given."

Some potentially explosive outlaws stayed on the quarters and physically assaulted their overseers. One of Landon Carter's supervisors, Billy Beale, chastised a slave who was weeding a corn patch. Told that his work was "slovenly," the slave replied "a little impudently" and Beale was "obliged to give him a few licks with a switch across his Shoulders"; but the slave fought back, and he and Beale "had a fair box." Subsequently, the laborer was brought before his master; and Carter noted that "it seems nothing scared him." Direct confrontations such as these, between comparatively unassimilated slaves and whites, seem to have been rare; a few, however, are described in detail in the advertisements for runaways. Two fugitives, for example, a husband and wife, were recaptured by an overseer while crossing a field, and were "violently" taken from the overseer and set free by field workers. Another runaway, also a field hand, escaped by "cutting his Overseer in Several Pieces [places?] with a Knife." John Greenhow of Williamsburg lost a slave who "laid violent hands" on him; this man ran off with another field slave who had also beaten his overseer.

Murders, small and unplanned uprisings, and suicides are instances of rebelliousness that was clearly inward-directed in a psychological sense as well as directed against the confines of the plantation. A September 1800 newspaper story graphically illustrates how even the most calculating, courageous, and murderously violent action could be, in a fashion, internalized violence: for after this slave methodically stalked and killed his master he simply "went home."

Captain John Patteson, a tobacco inspector at Horsley's warehouse in Buckingham County, punished his slave for "some misdemeanor"; and from that time, the slave told the court, "he ever after meditated [Patteson's] destruction."

> On the evening to which it was effected, my master directed me to set off home . . . and carry a hoe which we used at the place. . . . I concluded to way-lay him. . . . after waiting a considerable time, I heard the trampling of horses' feet. . . . I got up and walked forwards — my master soon overtook me, and asked me (it being then dark) who I was: I answered Abram; he said he thought I had gone from town long enough to have been further advanced on the road; I said, I thought not; I spoke short to him, and did not care to irritate him — I walked on however; sometimes by the side of his horse, and sometimes before him. — In the course of our traveling an altercation ensued; I raised my hoe two different times to strike him, as the circumstance of the places suited my purpose, but was intimidated. . . . [W]hen I came to the fatal place, I turned to the side of the road; my master observed it, and stopped; I then turn'd suddenly round, lifted my hoe, and struck him across the breast; the stroke broke the handle of the hoe — he fell — I repeated my blows; the handle of the hoe broke a second time — I heard dogs bark, at a house which we passed, at a small distance; I was alarmed, and ran a little way, and stood behind a tree, 'till the barking ceased; in running, I stumbled and fell — I returned to finish the scene I began, and on my way picked up a stone, which I hurl'd at his head, face, &c. again and again and again, until I thought he was certainly dead — and then I went home.

The most violent reactions to slavery were small, unorganized uprisings. A newspaper account written in 1770 reported a battle between slaves and free men, which suddenly erupted during the Christmas holidays on a small plantation quarter in New Wales, Hanover County. The reporter's explanation for the uprising was a familiar one. "Treated with too much lenity," the plantation slaves became "insolent and unruly." When a young and inexperienced overseer tried to "chastise" one of them by beating him to the ground and whipping him the man picked himself up and "slash[ed] at the overseer with an axe." He missed, but a group of slaves jumped on the white and administered such a severe beating that the "ringleader," the slave whom the overseer had whipped, intervened and saved his life. The overseer ran off in search of reinforcements; and instead of fleeing or arming themselves, the slaves tied up two other whites and "whipped [them] till they were raw from neck to waistband." Twelve armed whites arrived, and the slaves retreated into a barn where they were soon joined by a large body of slaves, "some say forty, some fifty." The whites "tried to prevail by persuasion," but the slaves, "deaf to all, rushed upon them with a desperate fury, armed solely with clubs and staves." Two slaves were shot and killed, five others were wounded, and the remainder fled.

Some slaves took their own lives. The journals of the House of Burgesses contain 55 petitions from slaveowners who sought reimbursement from public funds for slaves who committed suicide. Most of these men were outlawed runaways who, since they feared trial and conviction for capital crimes, hanged or drowned themselves. Since few petitioners reported the circumstances of a slave's death, the journals are not too informative. But one suicide, William Lightfoot's Jasper, was also described in a runaway notice:

> [A] well set Negro Man Slave, much pitted with the Small-pox; he was lately brought from *New-York*, but was either born or lived in the *West-Indies*, by which he has acquired their peculiar Way of speaking, and, seems to frown when he talks; he carried with him different Sorts of Apparel.

If indeed Jasper was a suicide his decision to "dash his brains out against a rock" must have been sudden, for he took a change of clothing with him.

But the field slaves' rebelliousness was not typically violent, self-destructive, or even individualistic. In fact they were much more inclined to attack the plantation in a quietly cooperative and effective way than were the slave artisans. Pilferage was a particularly rewarding and often organized action. "I laughed at the care we experienced in Milk, butter, fat, sugar, plumbs, soap, Candles, etc." wrote Landon Carter. "Not one of these enumerations lasted my family half the year. All gone, no body knows how . . . thievish servants . . . Butter merely vanishing." Washington estimated that his servants stole two glasses of wine to every one consumed by the planter's visitors. His slaves made a practice of stealing nearly everything they could lay their hands on. Washington had to keep his corn and meat houses locked; apples were picked early, and sheep and pigs carefully watched. . . .

The slaves' traffic in stolen goods was extensive, relatively well organized, and carried on virtually with impunity. The problem was of such proportions that by the 1760's it led to several letters to newspaper editors and to a series of laws. "I suppose every family must have so sensibly felt this evil," noted one letter writer to the *Virginia Gazette*. He observed that in every part of the country, henhouses, dairies, barns, granaries, gardens, and even patches and fields were "robbed in every convenient moonshiny night." Another contributor noted that, in his travels about the country, he had heard "frequent and various complaints" of this "pernicious evil." There was "hardly a family that was not full of enjuries they had received from the numerous thefts of servants and slaves."

Many slaves were fences for stolen goods; they had licenses from "over-tender" masters to sell produce. Whites, too, cooperated with the plantation slaves; they were referred to in the newspapers as "common proprietors of orchards," "liquor fellers," and "idle scatter lopping people." One writer made the interesting observation that some slaveowners, with "a modest blush," were so ashamed to sell certain farm products that they gave them to their slaves to dispose of. "Pray why is a fowl more disgraceful," he asked, "in the sale of it at market, than a pig, lamb, a mutton, a veal, a cow or an ox?"

Additional evidence of organized thievery as an outgrowth of the plantation slaves' culture and community is preserved in the Richmond County court records. Between 1710 and 1754 the justices tried and passed sentence in 426 cases. In 1750, although blacks made up 45 per cent of the population and there were nearly twice as many black tithes (1,235) as white (761), only 26 of these 426 actions involved slaves. (It should also be remembered that all slave criminals — with the exception of insurrectionists and murderers who were supposed to be tried by the General Court — were tried by county justices.) Only two trials concerned serious crimes. These were murder trials and both defendants were slave men. One was convicted of stabbing a black woman to death; the other, who later died in jail under very unusual circumstances, was charged with killing his master's young daughter. After his death, the court ordered his body to be quartered and displayed. Most slave crimes in this forty-four year period were petty thefts of the kind described earlier; that is, the charge was nearly always breaking and entering, and the slaves usually took a few shillings' worth of cider, liquor, bacon, cloth, or hogs. One typical case involved a slave who stole five sheets, a fishing line, and a bottle of brandy. Nearly all of these robberies were committed by one person; but the largest theft was conducted by a man and a woman. They took forty gallons of rum and fifty pounds of sugar. Evidently these thefts were well organized; the slaves usually selected such vulnerable targets as the homes of widows, ministers, warehouses, and slave quarters. Only on one occasion did a slave rob his master (who was Landon Carter!). The usual punishment for these crimes was between ten and thirty-nine lashes. For more serious crimes (including a conviction of perjury) slaves lost one or both ears. For capital crimes, slaves were often allowed to plead benefit of clergy.

The plantation slaves' organized burglaries were similar to the rebellious styles of the mobile, comparatively assimilated slaves. These crimes required planning; they took the slaves outside the plantation, and evidently compensated them with money and goods which could be exchanged for articles they needed.

Most field slaves, however, never acquired sufficient literate and occupational skills to move away from the quarter and into the society beyond it. Most were Africans and they remained "new Negroes" all of their lives. There are, then, two possible aspects to the personal dimension of slave life on the quarter. First, from an outsider's point of view, the quarter was a stultifying experience which slowed and restricted the slave's rate of acculturation. Second, from the slave's point of view, life on the quarter was perhaps preferable to daily contact with his captors, because it allowed him to preserve some of his ways.

Household slavery entwined the lives of whites and blacks. In the household more than anywhere else, there were direct and personal encounters that intensified the meaning of slavery for slaves and free alike. For the black servant these situations were often harrowing experiences which threatened to expose a nature sharply divided between enervating fear and aggressive hostility. His inward styles of rebelliousness and such related neurotic symptoms as speech defects were often manifestations of a profound ambiguity about whites and his own "privileged" status. For the white master the intimate presence of so many blacks subtly influenced domestic affairs, particularly his behavior toward his wife and children. The roles developed in household slavery restricted the master's actions toward his servants too. Once a style of discipline and correct order had been established, the master's reactions were often determined by what the slaves had come to expect of him. Highly sensitive to the patriarch's role, servants were quick to exploit any weakness in his performance. If the master was insecure, so were his dependents; but they also kept him that way by their persistent and petty rebelliousness. Household slavery then was the epitome of Professor Tannenbaum's dynamic view of human relationships in slave societies in which slavery was "not merely for blacks, but for the whites [and] . . . Nothing escaped, nothing, and no one."

The greatly enlarged situational (or interpersonal) dimension of slavery in the household is fundamentally important for another reason. Our limited understanding of slave behavior is based almost exclusively on interpretations of these personal encounters. These interpretations, which argue that slaves became the characters they played for whites, that their masters' view of them as infants or Sambos became their self-view, must be used with extreme caution. The interpersonal encounter was only a fragment of slavery's reality for both whites and blacks. When slaves were among their own and using their own resources as fugitives and insurrectionists, it is abundantly clear that much of their true character was concealed or intentionally portrayed in a dissembling manner in the presence of whites.

STUDY GUIDE

1. Differences between black slaves and poor white farmers with respect to freedom are obvious. How would their lives compare with respect to the following: housing; the actual labor they performed; food; health and medical care?

2. What were the various kinds of violent resistance that slaves used to protest enslavement? What were the techniques of "quiet resistance" that they used?

3. How might the following factors have influenced the slave's choice of violent or passive resistance: the master or conditions on the plantation; the slave's personality and character; the slave code and attitudes of a particular region, such as South Carolina as compared to Virginia?

4. How did the household slave's relationship to whites differ from that of the field slave? What were the relative advantages of each position?

5. Though Mullin's selection focuses on the life of the slave, he mentions several times that the institution of slavery influenced every aspect of life in the South for both blacks and whites. How do you think black slavery might have influenced each of the following aspects of southern life: education of whites; relations between whites of different classes; the relative slowness of the South in industrial development; southern politics? Can you think of specific evidence to support your arguments on these points?

BIBLIOGRAPHY

Mullin's book is a study of slavery in eighteenth-century Virginia. The work, the slave code, and the conditions of slave life differed somewhat in other colonies such as New York or South Carolina. Wherever the slave ended up — on a southern plantation or in a port city, as a farmer or a craftsman — the slave's experience began with his or her capture and sale to the captain of a slave ship in Africa. The ghastly conditions aboard such vessels are described in Daniel P. Mannix and Malcolm Cowley, *Black Cargoes: A History of the Atlantic Slave Trade* (1962). Philip D. Curtin, *The Atlantic Slave Trade: A Census* (1969) is a careful study of the number of slaves brought to various parts of North and South America.

Unlike most Europeans who came to the colonies, Africans brought virtually no personal property with them — no jewelry, no utensils, no tools, no musical instruments, no clothes. They did, however, bring their traditions and values — their dances and music, their folklore and religion, and their sense of family and personal relations. Since Melville J. Herskovits published his study of the subject, *The Myth of the Negro Past* (1941), scholars have devoted much energy to identifying African influences upon American Negro culture. The first chapter of John Blassingame, *The Slave Community: Plantation Life in the Ante-Bellum South* (1972) discusses the cultural shock of enslavement, as well as the question of the survival of African culture in the New World. John B. Boles, *Black Southerners, 1619–1869* (1983) is a recent study that treats nearly all aspects of slave life and culture during an extended period.

Another important question is whether racism or slavery developed first in the British colonies. In the very early seventeenth century, Africans were treated as indentured servants and were freed after a number of years of service. Did English colonials force Africans into slavery because of white racism, while allowing Europeans to continue in temporary servitude? Or was it the economic advantage of a wageless, hereditary labor force that led to enslavement, with racism following as a rationalization of white guilt? Anyone interested in this question should read Winthrop Jordan's lengthy study *White Over Black: American Attitudes toward the Negro, 1550–1812* (1968) and Edmund S. Morgan, *American Slavery, American Freedom: The Ordeal of Colonial Virginia* (1975). The various forms of slave resistance are described in the later chapters of Peter H. Wood, *Black Majority: Negroes in Colonial South Carolina from 1670 through the Stono Rebellion* (1974).

About half of the people who came to the colonies in the colonial period were of English descent; Africans were the second largest group, making up nearly 20 percent of the population by 1790. Many other nationalities came in smaller numbers, and your college library is likely to have some of the studies of the Germans, the Scots-Irish, and the other groups that settled the New World. The origins, voyages, and New-World conditions of the European group that most closely paralleled the enslaved Africans are studied in Abbot E. Smith, *Colonists in Bondage: White Servitude and Convict Labor in America, 1607–1776* (1947).

An artist known as the Pollard Limner managed to portray the indomitable spirit of the elderly Puritan woman Ann Pollard.

3

LYLE KOEHLER

Husbands and Wives

As children, most of us take marriage and the family very much for granted — as part of the natural order of things. Eventually, we may come to wonder just how natural matrimony is, whether it exists because of love or social necessity, and what the role of parents and children in the family is and should be. Several factors account for the heightened skepticism about marriage and the family in recent years. One, of course, is the rising divorce rate, and another may be the lessened economic dependence of both women and children upon the father of the family.

In recent years, historians have turned their attention to the makeup of the family and household in earlier times, and have examined how our views have changed with respect to the relationships between men and women. Some historians believe that women were more highly valued members of the family and had greater equality in earlier centuries, when they were vital to the economy of the household, than in the period since industrialization. Children in the colonial period tended to be treated as "little adults," dressed like their fathers and mothers, from the age of six or seven. There was no recognized period of adolescence, and advice to parents emphasized discipline rather than love and support of children. Fathers, most of whom were farmers or home craftsmen, spent their day in the household, rather than away in factories and offices.

Most of the colonists' views, including those of marital relationships and child-rearing, were heavily influenced by English and continental European traditions. But these customs — like their language, government, and class attitudes — slowly and subtly changed in the

New World. The following selection by Lyle Koehler emphasizes the continuity of English traditions in Puritan New England and the pervasive influence of Calvinism upon family life. Koehler argues forcefully that the colonial period was far from being a golden age for women. He views men as striving for male dominance and women as being forced into abject submission.

Other historians might well question these conclusions. Some scholars have suggested that one cannot get a reliable view of the day-to-day life of average people by studying the sermons and laws written by a small elite. Others have suggested that we cannot really speak of a monolithic, New England, Calvinist society. Some students believe that men and women were closer to having an equal status in the colonial period than in the nineteenth century. In any case, Koehler's article cannot be assumed to give a clear portrait of the family in the middle or southern colonies.

Calvinists in England and in America expected each person to keep his or her proper place in God's social design. They placed virtually everyone on a grid of inferiority and superiority — servant before master, non-church-member before church member, idler before working man, wife before husband, child before adult. Such a system facilitated supervision, because each master was legally accountable for overseeing the behavior of designated subordinates.

Crucial to the maintenance of religious and social order was the Puritans' attention to proper child-rearing. Godly parents were to make sure that their "unstaid and young" charges did not become addicted to the "greasy sensuality" of play — to "rattles, baubles, and such toyish stuff." Pilgrim pastor John Robinson described the difficulty of such a task:

> ... surely there is in all children ... a stubborness, and stoutness of mind arising from natural pride, which must, in the first place, be broken and beaten down; that so the foundation of their education being laid in humility and tractableness, other virtues may, in their time, be built thereon. . . . For the beating and keeping down of this stubborness parents must provide carefully. . . . Children should not know, if it could be kept from them, that they have a will in their own, but in their parents' keeping; neither should these words be heard from them, save by way of consent, "I will" or "I will not."

Reprinted with permission from Lyle Koehler, *A Search for Power: The "Weaker Sex" in Seventeenth-Century New England* (Urbana, Chicago, and London: The University of Illinois Press). © 1980 by the Board of Trustees of the University of Illinois.

As Robinson indicated, the parent was to crush the child's drive or desire for self-assertion or independence, for such feelings might advance the child's "natural pride." Instead, adults were to inculcate in youngsters a sense of virtual helplessness before parental whim and God's authoritarian will. . . .

. . . If children cursed or struck their parents — except "to preserve themselves from Death or Maiming" — Puritan law specified the death penalty. New Hampshire and Connecticut also prescribed hanging for any son who refused to heed his mother's or father's voice after chastisement. The authorities neglected to prosecute youngsters under such capital laws, but they did use the laws to inspire fear. In 1647 the authorities also expended some time and effort attempting to revive "the ancient practice in England of children asking their parents' blessing upon their knees," which would presumably symbolize the child's "Obedience unto the commands" of his or her parents. Ipswich minister Thomas Cobbett went still further, explaining that children "should rise up and stand bare [headed] before their Parents when they come to them, or speak to them. . . . It stands not with Parents' Honour for children to sit and speak, but rather they should stand up when they speak to Parents." . . .

The archetypal Puritan patriarch kept his children in a state of repressive bondage. He was a classic example of what clinical psychologist Diana Baumrind calls the authoritarian parent, who

> values obedience as a virtue and favors punitive, forceful measures to curb self-will at points where the child's actions or beliefs conflict with what he or she thinks is right conduct. He or she believes in keeping the child in his place, in restricting his autonomy, and in assigning household responsibilities in order to inculcate respect for work. This parent regards the preservation of order and traditional structure as a highly valued end in itself. He or she does not encourage verbal give and take, believing that the child should accept the parents' word for what is right.

Such a parent believed that "too much doting affection" distracted children from thoughts of God, or led them to consider themselves their parents' equals. Minister Thomas Cobbett warned that "fondness and Familiarity breeds . . . contempt and irreverence in children." Robert Cleaver believed "cockering" children with affection could only ruin them: "For as the Ape doth with too much embracings, well neer kill her young whelpes: so likewise some indiscrete parents, through immoderate love and over-much pampering and cherishing do utterly despoil and mar their children. Therefore, if parents would have their children live, they must take heed that they love them not too much."

Puritans stressed discipline more than affection. In English Puritan households, according to one scholar, "the rod was most favored" as a punitive device. In America, the Massachusetts *Body of Liberties* (1641) prohibited "unnaturall severitie" toward the young, but did not specify when punishment became "severe" or "unnatural." The adult faced prosecution when he broke a child's bones, endangered the child's life, or delivered a cudgeling with "a walnut tree plant, big enough to have killed a horse" — but only three of nearly three dozen such offenders received more than an admonition or a very small fine. Still, New England Puritans did not oppose the use of the "Rod of Correction"; in fact, they considered it "an ordinance of God," suitable to inspire "love and fear." Cotton Mather stated it simply: "Better whipt, than Damn'd." . . .

Growing up in a Puritan home was certainly painful. Strict control through the family and all other social institutions often created a feeling of profound helplessness in children. This phenomenon had wide-ranging impact, for, as psychologist Martin Seligman has shown, repeated and sustained perceptions of an inability to control one's outcomes can lead to a state of chronic despair. Many boys and girls, in true Puritan fashion, lamented their own despicability and great sinfulness. Elizabeth Butcher, aged two and one-half, purportedly asked herself often from the cradle "the question, What is my corrupt Nature? and would make answer to herself, It is empty of Grace, bent into Sin, and only to Sin, and that continually." Jerusha Oliver, "While her infancy was hardly yet expired," professed many sins. Depressed by her backsliding, at age twelve she began sequestering herself for entire days, so that she could repent. Sarah Derby "set up almost all night, crying to the Lord, that he would please apply unto her, by His own Holy Spirit, a Promise, which might Releive the Disconsolations of her Soul." Recurrent melancholia assailed Samuel Sewall's daughter Elizabeth between the ages of seven and fifteen. One minister's son, Nathaniel Shrove, hoped for death, that he might avoid sin — and then decided he was too despicable to deserve even that.

These were anxiety-ridden, insecure, unhappy children — the products of a culture which devalued independent thought, self-satisfaction, exuberance, and real closeness. A consideration of their anguish and preoccupations can help us understand the Puritan psyche, particularly as it affected attitudes toward the female sex. . . .

Like so many of their European contemporaries, New England's male Puritan leaders assumed that the obvious physical differences between the sexes had important social consequences. Throughout the seventeenth century these authorities argued and acted as if they believed anatomy alone determined destiny. In virtually all avenues of behavior Puritans affirmed the differences and deemphasized the similarities between the sexes — a practice which usually worked to the disadvantage of women. Because Puritan men had a high need to prove that they wielded some sort of power, in the face of the impotence inculcated in childhood and a theology of man's ultimate powerlessness before God, they tended to exaggerate prevailing notions of male superiority. While such men referred to themselves as the "Magnanimous, Masculine, and Heroicke sexe," every woman became a "poor fraile" creature — the "weaker sex." As Elnathan Chauncy scrawled in his commonplace book, "Y^e soule consists of two portions inferior and superior[;] the superior is masculine and aeternal. Y^e inferior foeminine and mortal." Custom meshed with psychological need for Puritans and non-Puritans alike — with sometimes bizarre results.

Beginning with conception and birth, profound developmental differences were assumed between male and female infants. Some physicians hypothesized that the male child was conceived earlier than the female because the male, as a higher, more sophisticated form of life, needed more time to develop in the womb. On the other hand, some religious leaders asserted that the male embryo, in recognition of its ultimate superiority, received his soul on the fortieth day, while the female embryo had to wait until the eightieth day before she acquired hers. When a woman had conceived twins of each sex, those twins supposedly occupied segregated uterine chambers to breathe into them the "laws of chastity." When the twins or a single child was ready to enter the outside world, the birth of a male was easier, according to the English obstetrical expert Thomas Raynalde. The reason for this was simple: babies were presumed to find their way into the outer world under their own power, and boys, being more vigorous than girls, got out faster. After delivery, the attending midwives cut a girl's navel string shorter than a boy's, "because they believe it makes . . . [females] modest, and their [genital] Parts narrower, which makes them more acceptable to their husbands."

Daughters were "less long'd for" than sons, perhaps in part because English obstetrical guides asserted that mothers who were carrying boys enjoyed fair complexions, red nipples, and white milk, while girls gave them "a pale, heavy, and swarth[y] countenance, a melancolique eye," black nipples, and watery bluish milk. At birth Puritan daughters, in particular, often received names which providentially reminded them of the limitations of their feminine destiny: Silence, Fear, Patience, Prudence, Mindwell, Comfort, Hopestill, and Be Fruitful. No Calvinist girl would ever bear an impressive name such as Freeborne, Fearnot, or Wrestling.

Puritan males, like so many of their English contemporaries, valued those characteristics in women which would insure submissiveness. The ideal woman blushed readily and chose "to be seen rather than Heard whenever she comes." She held her tongue until asked by her father or husband to speak; then only good, comforting words flowed from her mouth. "The greatest Nuisance in Nature," Joseph Beacon unequivocatingly wrote, "is an immodest impudent Woman." The ideal female displayed "an Eminence in Modesty, reserve, purity, temperance, humility, truth, meekness, patience, courtesie, affability, charity, goodness, mercy,

[and] compassion," taking special care to avoid the "monstrous" decorative habit of painting the face with "varnish." Tender, consoling, and in need of careful direction, she was viewed as a defenseless creature, "that naked Sex that hath no arms but for imbraces."

In Puritan terms, women needed men, not only for physical protection and financial support but also to prevent themselves from going intellectually astray. Since the woman was presumed less able to ground her spiritual development in the cold logic of reason, Puritan divines told her to consult her father, her husband, or a minister whenever she wished to comprehend a theological issue. In fact, too much intellectual activity, on a theological or any other plane, might overtax her frail mind and thereby debilitate her equally weak body. In 1645 Emmanuel Downing claimed his wife, Lucy, made herself sick "by trying new Conclusions"; he suggested riding as a cure. In the same year Downing's brother-in-law, Massachusetts Governor John Winthrop, asserted that Ann Hopkins, the wife of the Connecticut governor, had lost her understanding and reason by giving herself solely to reading and writing. This statesman commented that if she "had attended her household affairs, and such things as belong to women, and had not gone out of her way and calling to meddle in such things as are proper for men, whose minds are stronger etc., she had kept her wits, and might have improved them usefully and honorably in the place God had set her." . . . Thomas Parker, the Newbury pastor, reacted to his own sister's writing with particular sharpness. "Your printing of a Book," he wrote, "beyond the custom of your sex, doth rankly smell." . . .

Many English and American Puritans believed the virtuous woman should walk in the shadow of her male masters from the cradle to the grave. A daughter owed almost complete allegiance to her father's wishes. He was to supervise whom she might choose as friends, direct her to the service of others, and remind her to keep constant watch over the state of her soul. He was expected to reprimand her for tending to become a "Busie-Body" or "Pragmatical." Whatever he commanded (with exception of something sinful), she was to obey. His pleasure was her goal, and "her heart would melt/When she her Fathers looks not pleasant felt." The ideal daughter was like "a nun unprofest," a girl who never read lust-inducing plays and romances, who avoided the comb and the looking glass, and who relished serving her parents with a demeanor of "Virgin Modesty." When she reached a marriageable age, a daughter should "do nothing" without her father's approval; in marriage matters, she should be "very well contented . . . to submit to such condition[s]" as her parents "should see providence directing." In every familial relation the father, that "soul of the family," served as "governor of the governed." Apparently to emphasize the potency of such paternal overlordship, John Cotton in 1641 actually suggested hanging any maiden who allowed a lover to have sexual intercourse with her in her father's house.

In marriage the woman traded her father's surname for her husband's, in a symbolic transferral of the male right to "govern, direct, protect, and cherish" her. Her lack of an independent name accented the fact that she could not exist independent of men: as daughter she was to give "Reverence, subjection & Obedience" to her father, and as wife she was to give the same to her marital "master." Since he possessed more "quickness of witte . . . greater insight and forecast," that "Prince and chiefe Ruler" deserved her assistance, "reverand awe," and silent submission — if not outright fear. . . .

Theologians directed the "true wife" to be constantly concerned for her husband's welfare, even at the expense of her own. In Cotton Mather's words:

> When she Reads, That Prince Edward in his Wars against the Turks, being stabbed with a poisoned Knife, his Princess did suck the Poison out of his Wounds, with her own Royal Mouth, she finds in her own Heart a principle disposing her to shew her own Husband as great a Love. When she Reads of a woman called Herpine, who having her Husband Apoplex'd in all his Limbs, bore him on her Back a thousand and three Hundred English Miles to a Bath, for his Recovery, she minds herself not altogether unwilling to have done the Like.

Mather urged the wife to address her husband by the appropriate title of "My Lord." If she felt any "passion" against her mate, she left it unexpressed; but when he was in passion, she quickly strove to mollify it. The virtuous wife was to "carry her self so to her husband as not to disturb his love by her contention, nor to destroy his love by her alienation." She was to be at his beck and call, acting "as if there were but One Mind [His] in Two Bodies." . . .

A wife's major purpose in life, besides working on religious salvation, was to minister to her husband's needs. Her personal identity and social rank were derived through him. She was his appendage, as Cotton Mather explained in a letter to his sister-in-law, Hannah Mather. To be the "best of women in the American World," he urged Mistress Mather, "Go on to love him [her husband], and serve him, and felicitate him, and become accessary to all the Good which *he* may do in the world." . . .

. . . [It] was the Puritan contention that female activities ought to be largely limited to the home's safe environment, even though many non-Puritan women worked in various English agricultural pursuits. William Perkins wrote, "The woman is not to take libertie of wandring, and staying abroad from her owne house, without the man's knowledge and consent." Considering her an ineffective manager of "outward business and affairs," Puritan leaders urged the wife to busy herself with cooking, cleaning, spinning, child care, and other household tasks. Indeed, worldly concerns constituted a potential threat to her health in a way that monotonous household activities did not. A woman achieved respect largely by the extent to which "She looks well to the Wayes of her Household." . . .

In the final analysis, the spokesmen for the several Biblical Commonwealths posited an ideology of female weakness, deference, patience, and nurturance. Sex roles were sharply separated, with the male viewed as the stronger, ruling sex, one more protective than nurturant. As much as and perhaps more than their English contemporaries, the Puritan spokesmen of New England viewed male characteristics as expressions of their own "obvious" superiority. Michael Wigglesworth held that women's weakness made them "generally more ignorant, and Worthless." Nathaniel Ward found it hard to view women as anything other than "feather-headed" spendthrifts and "Squirrel-brained" friskers after the latest fashions, ladies "fitter to be kickt . . . then either honour'd or humour'd." He called "these nauseous shaped gentlewomen" no more than "gant-bar-geese, ill-shapenshotten-shell-fish, Egyptian Hyeroglyphics, or at the best . . . French flurts of the pastery." This acerbic minister maintained that "The world is full of care, much like unto a bubble/Woman and care, and care and Women, and Women and care and trouble." Another minister, William Hubbard, believed women to be little better than property; concerning a case wherein two men claimed the same woman as wife, he wrote that it took much time "to find who was the right *owner* of the *thing* in controversy."

Misogyny in New England had its limits, however. Although they affirmed the need for women to seek male theological advice, Puritans did allow women to work out their individual reckonings with God in the isolation of their closets. Some ministers attacked their male associates for refusing to recognize female worth. Cotton Mather wrote:

> Monopolizing HEE's, pretend no more
> Of Wit and Worth, to hoard up all the store.
> The Females too grow Wise & Good & Great.

This divine informed his readers, "It is a Common, but Causeless report that women's tongues [wag ceaselessly] and are frequently not governed by the fear of God." Similarly, John Cotton asserted that those men who viewed women as "a necessary Evil" were "Blasphemers." Yet another man, John Saffin, in a poem entitled "Cankers touch fairest fruites" directed his male readers away from the belief that women were "Woe to men." . . .

The reader may object that I have been painting too bleak a picture of the Puritans' ideas about the "weaker sex." After all, many scholars have pointed out that these religious reformers emphasized the importance of love — an attitude which theoretically facilitated the liberation of women from the shackles of male dominion. On the surface this argument seems plausible, as some Puritans indicated their approval of affection and the emotional closeness which sometimes develops with physical closeness. John Winthrop addressed his wife Margaret as "My Chiefe Ioye in this World" and, when away from her on business, wrote letters containing the following affectionate remarks:

[April 28, 1629] I kisse and loue thee with the kindest affection and rest Thy faithful husbande,

[May 8, 1629] the verye thought of thee affordes me many a kynde refreshinge, what will then the enjoyinge of thy sweet societye, which I prize aboue all worldly comforts,

[February 5, 1629/30] My sweet wife, Thy loue is such to me, and so great is the bonde between vs, that I should neglect all others to hold correspondencye of lettres with thee.

Edward Taylor viewed his relationship with his wife as "the True-Love Knot, more sweet than spice/ And set with all the flowre of Graces dress." To this divine, the wedding knot was the place "Where beautious leaves are laid with Honey Dew./ And Chanting Birds Cherp out sweet Musick true." Thomas Hooker described the ideal husband very romantically, as "The man whose heart is endeared to the woman he loves, he dreams of her in the night, hath her in his eye and apprehension when he awakes, museth on her as he sets at table, walks with her when he travels and parlies with her in each place where he comes." Such a husband cradled his wife's head on his bosom and "his heart trusts in her . . . the stream of his affection, like a mighty current, runs with ful Tide and strength." Thomas Thatcher wrote poetically to Margaret Sheafe, his betrothed, in the 1660s:

> Thy Joy I seek, thy comfort's my desire
> Whilst to enjoy thy bosom I aspire; . . . .

Puritans like Thatcher, Hooker, Taylor, and Winthrop certainly expressed loving sentiments, quite in accord with those English Puritan divines who described "setled affection," "companionship," and "tender loue" as the "glue" between marital "yoke-fellows." Many a divine directed the husband to support his wife, praise her virtues, honor her, and "bee not bitter, fearce, and cruell vnto her." Yet, when ministers celebrated the mutual delight and concord existing in "louing" union, they considered love "not so much the cause as . . . the product of marriage." A "duty" owed one's spouse and God, it became "nothing but Christian charity, and marriage supplied the chief form for the exercise of that charity." As one minister explained, love was "the Sugar to sweeten every addition to married life *but not an essential part of it*. Love was Condition in the married Relation." Since a couple need not love to marry, either sex could wed for less romantic considerations. A young man could legitimately search for a "goodly lass with aboundance of money" or a "very convenient" estate, as long as he had a desire to respect his wife-to-be and did not keep his motives from her. And a maiden could accept the hand of a suitor for equally mercenary motives, as long as she was honest about it. Such marriages had little to do with love; it magically appeared at some later date, if at all.

Nor did Puritans view love in egalitarian terms. Although a couple "are combined together as it were in one," Calvinists agreed that, even in the closest human relationship, "one is alwaies higher, and beareth rule, the other is lower, and yeeldeth subjection." . . . William Gouge pointed out that a couple "are yoak-fellows in mutuall familiaritie, not in equall authoritie. . . . If therefore he will one thing, and she another, she may not thinke to haue an equall right and power. She must giue place and yeeld," even if he be "a drunkard, a glutton, a profane swaggerer, an impious swearer, and blasphemer." Gouge and his contemporaries urged the wife, as a specific manifestation of her love, "to guid the house &c. not guid the Husband." The male-centered nature of such love becomes particularly clear in admonitions for her "wholly to depend on him, both in judgment and will." When the husband brought home unexpected dinner guests or failed to take her moods seriously enough, the enduring wife was to grin and bear it, for discontentment over such matters "argueth not a louing affection, nor a wiuelike subjection." Love meant that she empathized with his moods, in a nurturant manner, but that he did not need to reciprocate. In fact, even if she were "wiser, more discreete, and prouident then the Husband," those traits could not "overthrowe the superioritie of the man." The wise wife could advise him, but only with "humilitie and reuerence; shewing her selfe more willing to heare, then to speake."

. . . [T]he disobedient or contentious wife became one of the world's most despicable creatures — not only "an heart-sore to him that hath her," but no better than a wolf, a wart, a cancer, a gangrene, or even excrement. (By comparison, the harsh or churlish husband became only "a wild beast.") Quite revealingly, Puritan Alexander Niccoles explained the prevailing notion of male-centered love: a man "not only unitest unto thy selfe a friend," a "comfort for society" and "a companion for pleasure," but "in some sort a servant for profite too." Thomas Gataker went a step further, referring to the wife as a form of the husband's property. She "must resolue to giue herselfe wholly to him," Gataker wrote, "as her Owner, on whom God hath bestowed her." Still, in their effort to maintain security within the familial unit, as a counterpart to the insecurity occurring in the world outside, many Puritans disliked calling the wifely role "servitude" or "slavery." However, their overt endorsement of female subjection, coupled with affirmations of the husband's "superiority" and "authoritie" in "all things" at home, revealed that Puritans perceived marriage as servitude, although in a slightly different cast.

The Puritan notion of love served, then, not to liberate women; instead, it institutionalized sex-role oppression for both men and women. Whatever the realities of any particular interaction, as an idea it reinforced female submission and made it difficult for males to be anything other than controlling.

Such a concept of love fed male egocentricity. The Puritan male tended to emphasize what his wife could do for him, rather than what he could do for her. He loved her not for her uniqueness but for the extent to which she fulfilled the role expectations of the ideal female, including a self-sacrificing concern for his needs. Joseph Thompson cared for his wife because she studied how "to make my life Comfortable to me, as far as she could." Similarly, Richard Mather's wife was accounted "a Woman of singular Prudence" when she managed his secular affairs so well that he could devote himself totally to his own studying and "Sacred Imployments." Thomas Shepard applauded his mate for her "incomparable meekness of spirit, toward myselfe especially." Edward Taylor's wife, Elizabeth Fitch, was, in his opinion, "a Tender, Loving, Meet,/ Meecke, Patient, Humble, Modest, Faithful, Sweet/ Endearing Help," a woman "Whose Chiefest Treasure/ of Earthly things she held her Husbands pleasure." . . .

. . . Puritans could not agree with the Antinomian and Quaker belief that an intense feeling between husband and wife served as a reflection of, instead of a danger to, love for God. When Antinomian William Hutchinson said he thought more of his wife than of their church, the Puritans could only call him a man of "weak parts," one incapable of constraining his own affection or of regulating his wife's behavior.

Despite the Puritan desire to limit the genuine, earthly love that could develop between two people by subordinating it to the love of God and to demands arising out of sex role dominance and submission, some couples did marry for love and enter into very close relationships. That closeness developed not because of, but in spite of Puritanism. Ideologically, the egalitarian impulse of pure affection was undercut by the Puritan need to regard love first and foremost as duty — not as deep feeling brought to a marriage by the couple, but as a network of obligations imposed upon the couple by God. Such a notion of love, coupled with a belief system which accentuated male superiority, constituted an effort not only to be true to biblical prescriptions and to the sometimes conservative ethos of English culture, but also to countermand the Puritan male's peculiar feelings of impotence. . . .

An important issue arises at this point: Was Puritan sex-role ideology consistent with Puritan practice, or simply an unenforceable vision? Was it a purely intellectual identification with a glorified biblical past, or the genuinely descriptive adjunct of socially institutionalized sex roles? Such questions necessitate an examination of the extent to which the prevailing sex-role ideology was implemented.

Puritan society was organized in a way that explicitly affirmed the belief in sex segregation as a reminder of men's and women's different destinies. In church the men, women, maidens, and youths all sat separately, with the most prominent men sitting in the foremost, highest-status pews. Each sex also entered the meetinghouse by a separate door. . . . When the little girl attended a dame school to learn the rudiments of education, she studied at a curriculum somewhat different from that of the boys; while the latter grappled with Latin, penmanship, spelling, reading, and religion, the former learned cooking, weaving, and spinning, as well as reading, writing, and religion.

. . .[I]n other realms Puritans used institutional prohibitions to distinguish between the respective roles of men and women. Both spinsters and widows could own property, but neither could vote for public officials. Puritans considered the franchise an important means for protecting civil liberties, but for men only — as Nathaniel Ward wrote, without such protection, "men are *but* women." Nor could women vote in church affairs, prophesy, or even ask questions in church, for in all such cases "speaking argues power." A woman could speak only when singing hymns or, in a few churches, when she made a public request for the privilege of membership. Male members not only reserved full participation in church affairs for themselves, but also were reluctant to admit to membership women who were "full of sweet affection" but "a little too confident."

Puritan society provided virtually no avenues for women to seek fulfillment outside marriage. The school curriculum emphasized the importance of the woman staying in the home, and the apprenticeship system trained girls for no trade other than housewifery. There is no record of any New England mercantile establishment hiring a maiden to work outside the home until after King Philip's War, although in England a daughter could receive apprenticeship training as a shopkeeper. Maidens, wives, and widows could not hawk or peddle goods throughout the countryside, as was true in their Puritan homeland. An unwed woman could attempt to build some savings by working as a domestic servant, a doctor, or a schoolmistress; however, such occupations were very poorly paid. Without marriage, a woman could hardly expect to have any financial security.

Even if a woman did manage to accumulate a sizeable estate or income (through an inheritance, for example), she faced great social pressure to marry. If a lass remained single until age twenty-three, neighbors called her a "spinster." If she was still unwed at twenty-six, she received the more odious appellation of "thornback." Bookseller John Dunton remarked in 1686 that "an old (or Superannuated) Maid, in Boston, is thought such a curse as nothing can exceed it, and [look'd] on as a Dismal Spectacle." Some of Dunton's Puritan contemporaries believed that deceased old maids could do no better than to lead apes in Hell.

Men were expected to marry also, but community gossip did not focus on the bachelor as it did on the spinster. There was, in fact, no term of opprobrium comparable to "spinster," "thornback," or "old maid." The church members of at least one town, Salem, chose a thirty-six-year-old bachelor, Nicholas Noyes, as their minister (1683). Puritans did, however, establish vehicles for the regulation of bachelors' behavior, since Satan reportedly loved to provide erotic fantasies to tempt the minds of unwed males. Medfield, Massachusetts, set aside segregated housing, a special Bachelors' Row, to facilitate their supervision. The Middlesex County magistrates prosecuted many "singlemen" who failed to place themselves under family government between 1665 and 1679, while Plymouth, New Haven, and Connecticut colonies required bachelors to live with "licensed families." The Connecticut enactment actually specified that bachelors living alone pay a £1 fine each week — which undoubtedly helps to explain why Madame Knight wrote in 1704 that half of Connecticut's males were married by the time they reached twenty years of age.

Despite such pressures to marry, the prospective suitor could not simply court any girl he wished. He first had to secure the permission of the maiden's father, or face prosecution on a charge of "inveigling" the girl. All Puritan-controlled locales except Maine punished by a £5 fine or a whipping any man who "stole away" the affections of a maiden by "speech, writing, message, company-keeping, unnecessary familiarity, disorderly night-meetings, sinful dalliance, gifts. or in any other way." The severity of the punishment for inveigling suggests that Puritans took very seriously the father's right to convey his overlordship to another male, thereby depriving the daughter of any initial decision about whom she wished to woo her. A father could not "wilfullie and unreasonably deny any childe timely or convenient" marriage, but he could largely determine whom she married. The daughter could, of course, reject any suitor allowed to court her, but she then had to deal with the consequences of her decision. For example, when Lucy Downing refused to wed a candidate of whom her parents approved, her mother informed her that such behavior was unwise and disreputable. When a depressed Betty Sewall withdrew from Grove Hirst's suit, her father reminded her that such action would "tend to discourage persons of worth from making their Court" to her. A young woman capable of such independence could hardly be expected to transform herself into a submissive, obedient wife, a fact which further restricted her marital possibilities.

Young men had fewer limitations. Even though a father might attempt to "control" his sons by refusing to give them any of his property, they could hire themselves out to artisans, become fishermen, or enter a number of other occupations. Once a young man decided he wanted to marry, he could secure the appropriate paternal permission to court one or more lasses. His father did not need to approve of his choices, although certainly that was the preferred route.

Once a couple had wed, no law specified that the wife had to obey her husband's every wish. However, the law did give him great supervisory control over her property and behavior. At marriage, a wife had to relinquish control over whatever real estate she possessed or income she received. She could, through a prenuptial contract, attempt to retain some control over her own property, but the English Court of Chancery and the Massachusetts Assistants did not recognize the validity of such an agreement. Not until 1762 did the Bay Colony accept prenuptial contracts as binding, although Connecticut had done so as early as 1673. The authorities of New Haven, New Hampshire, and Plymouth never heard a case concerning the legitimacy of such a contract. Whatever their position on prenuptial agreements, all of the colonies respected the husband's "right" to regulate his wife's realty. Only some of her personal estate — her dresses, quilts, needles, and so on — remained in her hands after marriage.

Puritan legal practice reinforced the notion that a husband was his wife's overseer, and therefore held him accountable if she stepped out of line. When a woman committed a minor crime, the courts usually ordered her husband to pay for it, in a fit punishment for his indiscretion in allowing her to break the law. If a wife did not attend Sabbath services, for instance, her husband was held responsible for failing to bring her to the meetinghouse. If she sold alcoholic beverages without a license, he paid £5 to £10 for tolerating her behavior. With the husband lay the decision of whether to pay a fine assessed against his wife, or to subject her to a whipping instead. In one case the Plymouth General Court actually allowed the husband to punish his wife "att home" after she had beaten and reviled him (1655). The wife had almost no opportunity to discharge a fine by enlisting the aid of her family or a charitable neighbor. Of course, no woman received a trial by a jury of her female peers.

Although, as in English local and customary law, a wife could sue in court for wrongs done her (provided she had her husband's permission), usually her husband brought suit in her behalf. Whenever a wife hurled scurrilous remarks at a neighbor, both she and her husband automatically became parties to the suit. If the husband neglected to take civil action when his spouse was the injured party, her parents might bring suit on her behalf (in a slander suit, for example). Without husbandly or parental allowance, a wife could not seek damages for any injury, irrespective of its severity. Her honor belonged to her father or her husband, who protected it at his discretion. Under no circumstances could a woman sue her own husband for tortious acts (e.g., slander, assault) against her, although she could give evidence against him in a criminal case.

A wife's activity in "outward matters" was always contingent upon her husband's approval. She could contract for rents and wages, sell goods, and collect debts, but only if her husband had authorized her activity. Since Puritans believed the "weaker sex" had little ability in such dangerous matters, they wished to keep women within the home's protective confines. To prevent weak Puritan wives from unwarily responding to some sinner's solicitations, the Massachusetts General Court in 1674 barred any wife, in the absence of her husband, from entertaining any traveler without the allowance of the town selectmen, under the penalty of a £5 fine or ten lashes. She also had to busy herself with household tasks, in order to avoid prosecution on a charge of idleness. . . .

In Puritan ideology and practice, a wife could have few outright belongings. Neither her premarital possessions (with the exception of some personalty) nor her subsequent acquisitions, nor the use of her free time, nor even her criminal sentences were hers alone. Her status seemed quite like that of a servant, even though the latter's period of servitude was limited by contract.

. . . Still, despite such disadvantages, women were not completely under male control in Puritan New England. Single, widowed, or divorced women of means could open mercantile shops, own land, and maintain inns. These women could sue on their own behalf in court. Three extant petitions indicate that women attempted to have some political impact by petitioning the Massachusetts General Court or a Connecticut magistrate. In half of all cases where a deceased husband left a widow, she received the right to act as the executor of his estate — a position of some administrative importance.

Even though the husband could restrict his wife's activity in many ways, she retained certain legitimate claims on him (based not on her "rights" but on her supposed weakness, or need for protection). In Plymouth and New Haven, a wife's permission was necessary before a husband could sell their house or any of their land. In contrast, however, Connecticut and much of Massachusetts conceded that property transferral was the husband's prerogative. In his will the Connecticut husband usually referred to the couple's acquisitions as "my" lot or "my" dwelling house. When a husband made his will, he could not leave his wife penniless. In Massachusetts before 1649, Connecticut before 1696, Plymouth, and New Haven, the law reserved to the widow a dower right of one-third of the lands, houses, tenements, rents, and hereditaments her husband possessed. This widow's third was free from all debts, rents, judgments, and executions against her deceased mate's estate. Plymouth and New Hampshire also allowed the widow either all or part of her husband's personal estate, while in Massachusetts after 1649 the magistrates determined what portion she would receive. . . .

A husband could not beat his wife in order to reduce her to abject submission. As early as 1599 the English Puritan Henry Smith asserted, "If hee cannot reform his wife without beating, he is worthy to be beaten for choosing no better." Almost a century later Cotton Mather agreed that for "a man to Beat his Wife was as bad as any Sacriledge. And such a Rascal were better buried alive, than show his Head among his Neighbours any more." The Bay Colony's initial law code, the "Body of Liberties," in 1641 freed the wife from "bodily correction or stripes by her husband, unlesse it be [given] in his owne defence upon her assalt." Nine years later the Massachusetts General Court specified a fine of up to £10 or a whipping as punishment for any man who struck his wife, or for any woman who hit her husband. None of the other four Puritan colonies enacted such a law, although they did lightly penalize husbands who abused their wives too readily. . . .

We cannot know the extent to which wives possessed real "private power" or derived satisfaction from the marital power arrangement. . . . As a general rule, the specter of male overlordship is so apparent in institutional, intellectual, economic, and family life throughout the seventeenth century that it leaves little room to doubt women's difficulty in achieving, much less exerting, a sense of their own assertive independence. All of woman's protections and the few privileges she enjoyed as a widow did not, in the final analysis, facilitate her development beyond the limitations imposed by her sex-role conditioning.

STUDY GUIDE

1. Summarize the seventeenth-century Calvinist view of the nature of children and proper child-rearing. How do these views differ from the predominant attitudes of American society today, especially with regard to parental concerns about child development?

2. Describe the particular characteristics of the ideal wife in the seventeenth century as set forth in the sermons and laws. Develop an argument as to why such historical sources are or are not reliable guides to the actual relations of men and women in the day-to-day life of the family.

3. What limitations were there on women's equality in economic life, church, government, and social activities?

4. The changing status of women in our time has occurred as a result of a complex variety of factors. Which of the following do you believe to be most important: the decline of traditional religious views, industrialization, creation of new social agencies to handle needs that formerly rested upon the family, modern household technology, and women's suffrage?

BIBLIOGRAPHY

In this edition, Koehler's article replaces a selection from Edmund S. Morgan, *Virginians at Home* (1952), which gives a very different picture of courtship and marriage in a southern colony. A fuller study than Morgan's is Julia C. Spruill, *Women's Life and Work in the Southern Colonies* (1935). Morgan also wrote a work on family life in New England, presenting a somewhat different picture from the one in his study of Virginia: *The Puritan Family: Religion and Domestic Relations in Seventeenth-Century New England*, rev. ed. (1966); his chapter on husbands and wives is especially interesting. John Demos, *A Little Commonwealth: Family Life in Plymouth Colony* (1970) is a fascinating study of nearly all aspects of family life including husband–wife and parent–child relationships, housing, furnishings, and the psychology of life in the eighteenth century.

The women's liberation movement and the revived interest of historians in the history of minority groups have led to a virtual explosion in the study of women's history. Laurel T. Ulrich, *Good Wives: Image and Reality in the Lives of Women in Northern New England, 1650–1750* (1980) is an interesting study of three ideal types of women. Roger Thompson's *Women in Stuart England and America: A Comparative Study* (1974) indicates how colonial patterns differed from English conditions. Nancy F. Cott, *The Bonds of Womanhood: "Women's Sphere" in New England, 1780–1835* (1977) sheds some light on the late colonial period. Mary B. Norton, *Liberty's Daughters: The Revolutionary Experience of American Women, 1750–1800* (1980) and Linda G. DePauw, *Founding Mothers: Women in the Revolutionary Era* (1975) are concerned with the period indicated in the titles.

Ralph Eleazer Whiteside Earl (1785–1838), *Mr. and Mrs. Ephraim Hubbard Foster and Their Children*, c. 1825. Oil on Canvas (mattress ticking?), 53⅞ inches × 70⅛ inches. Courtesy of The Fine Arts Center, Cheekwood, Nashville, Tennessee. Gift of Mrs. Josephus Daniels, Jr., 1969.

This painting of Mr. and Mrs. Ephraim Foster and their children conveys the affectionate relationships that came to characterize the modern family.

4

DANIEL B. SMITH

Parents and Children

The preceding essay by Koehler describes marital relationships in seventeenth-century New England. By the late eighteenth century the modern family was beginning to emerge and was especially evident in wealthy, planter families of the Southern coastal region. Contrary to patterns of earlier centuries, children were seen as precious individuals, rather than as primarily economic assets to parents. Increasingly, love and affection were lavished upon children, and parents encouraged the development of their distinct personalities and of independence from parental control.

Perhaps in part because of the changed family environment, the America of the Revolutionary and Constitutional period was graced by the most extraordinary generation of public men and women in our history. No generation of American statesmen has equalled the achievements of that golden age, which included Washington, Jefferson, Franklin, Madison, Hamilton, Adams, Marshall, and dozens of others. Their achievements in law, political theory, diplomacy, invention, and other fields were remarkable; it is also remarkable at how young an age many of these men distinguished themselves. Jefferson drafted the Declaration of Independence at the age of 33. Washington was 21 years old when he was entrusted with a mission to warn the French out of the Ohio Valley, and he became commander of the Continental Army at 43. James Monroe entered the army at 16 and fought at New York, Trenton, Brandywine, Germantown, and Monmouth. At 25 years of age he was elected to the Continental Congress. His friend James Madison helped draft the Virginia Constitution at age 25, became a member of that state's Council of State at 27, and was the most influential person in drafting the U.S. Constitution at 36.

Hamilton wrote pamphlets at 19, became a lieutenant colonel and Washington's secretary at 22, and was elected to Congress at 27. Before reaching the age of 30, Franklin had become owner of *The Pennsylvania Gazette*, and had founded the Junto Club, a circulating library, and Philadelphia's first fire company.

Not all of these men were reared in the South or came from closely-knit, supportive families, but many Southern planters developed a warm regard for their sons and encouraged the development of strong character traits at an early age. Some historians have suggested that the Revolutionary War generation found the strength to revolt against the mother country because of the independence encouraged in them by the modern family. In the following essay, Daniel Blake Smith describes the pleasure that parents took in new infants, the encouragement they gave to autonomy in children, and the special relationship between fathers and sons in eighteenth-century Virginia.

Childbirth was an important event in the life of the family, but it was often marred by sickness and death. Medical knowledge about pregnancy, delivery, and infant care was slight, even by eighteenth-century standards. Until late in the century, obstetrics and pediatrics remained particularly weak and unexplored branches of medicine. Some planters followed the advice of "experts" in midwifery — usually English authors — but the information obtained from these sources often proved unreliable. Pregnancy, for example, was usually considered a sickness; thus expectant mothers were often bled near the end of their term, precisely when a reservoir of strength was most needed. Some believed that bleeding prevented miscarriage. But on the whole, planters depended more on past experience than on medical literature. Experienced midwives helped men decipher the mysteries of pregnancy and birth. Even someone as learned as William Byrd carefully took down a local midwife's theory that twenty weeks would elapse "from the time a woman is quick when she will seldom fail to be brought to bed."

Childbirth at home could be chaotic and full of danger for mother and child. When Becky Hansen of Maryland gave birth to a son in September of 1783, "confusion & distraction" reigned throughout the house. Another woman described the delivery of her sister-in-law as a "Scene of Sickness" with two children "dangerously ill" and the mother "so much complaining, and so low spirited in her lying-inn." Mrs. John Taylor's delivery of twins in 1771 ended in the death of one who "hanged himself in the navelstring." On July 7, 1766, Landon Carter was called back to his house when his daughter-in-law went into labor. He arrived to find the house in an uproar: "I found every body about her in a great fright and she almost in dispair. The child was dead and the womb was fallen down and what not." Eventually a "large dead child much squeezed and indeed putrified was delivered. . . ."

The world of family and kin that surrounded a newborn child usually offered a warm, affectionate environment for its development. Indeed an "increase in the family" brought considerable pride and elation to parents and kin. The paternal self-pride engendered at childbirth is suggested in the praise Thomas Davis gave St. George Tucker at the birth of Tucker's daughter in 1779. Davis was excited "at learning my much-esteemed, Thy amiable Fanny had escaped the Danger of Child-Birth & had presented to my Friend such a lovely Image of himself." John Galloway of Maryland was delighted when he saw his infant daughter in 1787. His wife's nurse commented on the "admiring Papa, and his graceful fondness. . . ."

A child's first important experience in the world comes in his relationship with his mother or nurse, especially in the feeding process. In this earliest stage of development, until about the age of two, a child is mainly concerned with the simple but essential task of "getting" and "taking," as Erik Erikson has suggested. His success in this incorporative mode of behavior depends in part on the willingness and ability of the parents to provide the nourishment a child needs and demands. And most important, the nursing bond significantly influences a child's earliest perceptions of the trustworthiness of the people around him.

Studies of childhood suggest that children in the preindustrial West often failed in their crucial efforts at "getting" and "taking." Many remained underfed and were left in the hands of mothers and nurses who distrusted their "primitive" demands for survival. Seventeenth-century European parents were ambivalent about children, whom they felt obligated to protect, but who were also, they sometimes believed, "demanding and dangerous little animals."

As a result of these tensions, the relationship between nurse or mother and child in early modern Europe resembled a struggle more than a cooperative effort. Mothers, especially after a difficult delivery, viewed breastfeeding as a debilitating experience, one in which an infant drained a mother of her vital substances. Some mothers feared that breastfed children might transmit to them some dread disease. Consequently, most women who could afford it put their children out to nurse, despite the advice of physicians that an infant would thrive best when nourished by its own mother. Moreover, poorly prepared solid food was often fed to children before they were fully able to digest it. High infant mortality rates of between 20 and 30 percent for seventeenth-century Europe reflect in part this low level of maternal care of children. It was not until the mid-eighteenth century that critics of child care in England and France became effective in encouraging maternal nursing.

In the colonial Chesapeake, maternal nursing was probably the most common form of infant feeding. Little is known about parent–child relations in Virginia and Maryland during the seventeenth century due to the scarcity of personal documents such as family papers and diaries. The fragmentary evidence that does exist, however, indicates that mothers probably breastfed their children. Nonetheless, infant and childhood mortality rates remained extremely high, perhaps as high as 40 percent, because of the endemic malarial environment that prevailed in the early Chesapeake. Infants frequently received from diseased mothers a short-term immunity to malaria which allowed many of them to survive infancy, only later to succumb to the disease as small children when their immunity had worn off.

In the eighteenth century, even though a larger number of families could afford to hire wet nurses, most women, except when ill, seem to have continued to nurse their own children. One woman in 1780, for example, was reported to be "too weakly to Suckel her little Girl & is Obliged to put it out to nurse." Another woman was seen "nursing her little girl, to whom she is quite devoted." In sharp contrast to parents in early modern Europe who feared that infants might communicate disease to those who nursed them, parents in the eighteenth-century Chesapeake worried more about children becoming ill from contact with sick mothers. For instance, Margaret Parker of Norfolk, Virginia, wrote to her husband in 1771 that their infant boy had "Sucked the fever from me I believe. I was obliged to get a woman to Suckle him a while till I get my milk again which the fever dryed up." Other women nursed their infants despite the pain and inconvenience. Breastfeeding, many women believed, ruined the shape of the breasts and doubtless some women hesitated to nurse their children for this reason. The experience of Mary Dulaney of Maryland, however, suggests that a mother's affection for a child could outweigh such concerns. A friend noted that Mary breastfed her infant boy despite her fear that "her good looks may be injured by nursing her fine son."

Maternal love, though, was not always the central motivation for mothers who decided to nurse their own children. Given the discomfort of frequent pregnancies and the danger and violent pain associated with childbirth in the eighteenth century, some mothers chose to nurse their offspring because the lactation period tended to delay conception. Landon Carter certainly felt that this was the strategy of his daugher-in-law in 1770 when, according to him, she continued to breastfeed her baby girl despite being sick herself. Carter complained that "the poor little baby Fanny is every time to share her Mamma's disorder by sucking her, and this because she should not breed too fast. Poor children! Are you to be sacrificed for a parent's pleasure?. . ."

Anyone who reads through the family letters and diaries from the eighteenth-century Chesapeake will discover an abundance of evidence of parental tenderness and affection toward young children. These sources clearly suggest that children were not treated as sinful beings whose willfulness and sense of autonomy had to be controlled, if not quashed, by age two or three — as children were apparently seen in much of Puritan New England. Rather, parents in Virginia and Maryland during the eighteenth century seemed to delight in the distinctively innocent and playful childhood years of their offspring. Parents and an assortment of kin — grandparents, uncles, aunts, and cousins — who frequently helped in child-rearing were usually quite fond of children and considered their activities pleasant diversions. Indeed, as we shall see, family and kin often indulged young children and granted them considerable freedom.

It is not likely that during the seventeenth century children had enjoyed such a prominent emotional place in Chesapeake households. Because of oppressive infant and child mortality rates and a short life expectancy in early Virginia and Maryland, parents may have invested less of their emotional life in their children than did eighteenth-century parents. When infants or children died, parents — especially fathers — showed little emotion or deep concern. Moreover, Protestant religious thought, which stressed the inherently sinful and inferior condition of children, shaped the character of family life in the seventeenth century. Fathers remained emotionally detached from infants and small children, insisting on the child's acceptance of self-control and obedience to paternal authority.

In eighteenth-century Virginia and Maryland, however, where the increasingly secular culture was committed to an expanding tobacco economy based largely on slave labor, religious values rarely intruded into family life and child-rearing, especially in Anglican households. Church-going became more of a social activity than a spiritual concern in gentry families; Sundays were occasions more for visiting and conviviality than for piety and prayer.

In the absence of overriding spiritual influences, Chesapeake parents tended to stress the positive, pleasurable capacities of children. Indeed, the personal documents of planter families, especially after mid-century, reveal a familial and social environment in which children were often the centerpiece of family affection. Mothers and fathers and kin, at least in well-to-do families, lavished attention on their children. One father from Queen Anne's County, Maryland, for example, was reported to be "Excessively fond of his Daughter a fine sprightly girl." Richard Tilghman confided to a friend in 1763 that his three-year-old daughter Anna Maria was "the plaything of the family." And Thomas Jefferson told his daughter Mary Jefferson Randolph that he hoped his granddaughter "will make us all, and long, happy as the center of our common love."

When away from their families, fathers who wrote home almost always asked to be remembered to their children. While staying in Williamsburg in the fall of 1755, George Braxton told his wife to "Give little Molly a thousand kisses for me." St. George Tucker was particularly fond of his children and stepchildren. His letters to his wife Frances ("Fanny") during his service in the Revolution suggest the pleasure he derived from parenthood. "Remember me with a Tenderness Truly Parental to my Boys," he wrote Fanny," and let Patty and Maria be assured I am neither unmindful nor indifferent in regard to them." Tucker, like many parents, used affectionate nicknames for his children. "My poor little Monkies are insensible to all that a parent can feel for them. . . ."

Despite the pleasure parents and kin clearly derived from young children, they approached child-rearing with serious purposefulness. They expected to develop in their offspring powers of self-discipline which, parents believed, would produce self-reliant, independent adults. And it was the warm, nurturant attitudes of Chesapeake parents that have been described above that allowed them to shape children into dutiful sons and daughters.

Parents were especially mindful of developing powers of self-sufficiency and strength in their children. They applauded but rarely demanded precocity in their children, unlike seventeenth-century Anglo-American parents, who sought to hurry children out of their childhood dependency. Still, initial signs of mobility and autonomy, suggested in early efforts at walking and talking, attracted close attention from observant parents. Lucy Terrell, according to her grandmother, Martha Jefferson Carr, "prattles everything she hears," and was "very spiritly." Years later, Mrs. Carr expressed the same interest in another granddaughter, one-year-old Martha Terrell. She was anxious to see "litte Martha's attempts to prattle & to see her shuffling across the room." Frances Randolph was equally proud of her daughter, "Mopsey," who "talks *prodigiously*. She will walk in a fortnight." In 1779 Charles Carroll of Annapolis reported to his son and daughter-in-law that their daughter Kitty, who was visiting Carroll, "has a language of her own and Endeavours to talk. . . ."

Chesapeake households were often complex units with servants and kin living on the plantation, making constant parental supervision of children unnecessary. Indeed, one senses from the letters and diaries of the period that children were allowed, and perhaps encouraged, to explore their immediate environment with little parental supervision. While visiting his friend Colonel Eppes in February of 1711, William Byrd was asked to help locate a small child who had just learned to walk and had wandered off from his little friends. "All the people on the plantation were looking for it," Byrd explained, "& I went likewise to look [for] it & at last found it, for which the women gave me abundance of blessings." Parents clearly admired rambunctious, energetic children, whom they seem to have given the run of the plantation. Margaret Parker reported to her husband that their young son was doing well, as he had been "employed all day making bonfirs." Landon Carter's grandson, despite being ill, was permitted to go hunting all day, and his younger brother George had to be "fetched" at the stables that evening "after candlelight." One woman who went to see her cousin noted that her cousin's two children, a two- and three-year-old, "were fighting on the carpet, during the whole visit. . . ."

The relatively permissive and nurturant environment that parents and kin seem to have provided infants and small children in the eighteenth-century Chesapeake shaped children's perceptions of parental authority and the larger society. The evidence from the personal documents of planter families, fragmentary as it is, suggests that fathers, far from remaining indifferent to young children, entered their affective world very early, perhaps as early as fathers do in modern families. Thus children, especially sons, may have absorbed paternal values and feelings of affection long before reaching the age when paternal guidance became more explicit — usually after six or so. Recent psychological studies of parent–child relationships demonstrate that children are more likely to adopt the behavior of nurturant models than those who are indifferent to them. The strong ties of affection and filial duty which bound many children to their parents in the eighteenth-century Chesapeake — often until the parents' deaths — were in part rooted in the close emotional regard that fathers, as well as mothers, displayed toward them during childhood. In short, many planters appear to have gained the lifelong gratitude and respect of their children more from fond paternal treatment than from assertions of authority or coerced obedience.

That fathers took such an early, affectionate interest in their offspring probably encouraged a strong sense of emotional security in their children. Parents seem to have offered themselves more as a collective unit for nurturance and discipline than as a sharply differentiated pair in which mothers provided the affection while fathers distanced themselves as stern disciplinarians. In the absence of clashing male and female child-rearing styles, children could form a clearer, more secure self-identity.

Boys matured into men in Chesapeake society under the powerful influence of their fathers. Indeed, the shaping force of paternal values was so strong that planters' sons often demonstrated and gave expression to a lifelong sense of duty and gratitude toward their fathers. It was not an authoritarian paternal presence, however, that commanded such obedience and respect. Instead, dutiful behavior emerged out of a relatively permissive mode of child-rearing which emphasized the development of self-confidence, autonomy, and the reciprocal obligations of fathers and sons.

In many respects boys grew up on their own in the eighteenth-century Chesapeake, with little parental intrusion into their early years. Religious instruction for children, though advocated by ministers and authors of child-rearing manuals, appears to have been largely non-existent in most Anglican planter families. Childhood autonomy was permitted in other ways as well. Except among the poorest families, especially those without any slave labor, there were few work responsibilities for sons under the age of twelve or thirteen. When labor became scarce, boys might help plant corn, sucker tobacco, or pick peaches in late summer and fall. In general, however, parents allowed their sons to run freely about the plantation with their sisters and "playfellows," composed usually of brothers and friends and relatives who lived nearby. Despite the distance between plantations, boys often visited their cousins, and frequent barbecues and balls, especially in the summer, gave them the opportunity to mix with children throughout the neighborhood. Planters' sons also made companions of slave children, though parents began to discourage this interracial contact when their sons reached puberty.

While parents did not control their sons' preadolescent years (roughly, the years between six and thirteen), fathers did begin to suggest, at least by example, what roles would be expected of their sons at maturity. From the time boys were first dressed like men in breeches and shirts — at around five or six — fathers gradually drew their sons away from home and began to show them a part of the adult male society in which they would participate. For example, planters carried their young sons with them on social visits to other men. Fathers seem to have considered these trips important in their sons' early understanding of a man's world beyond the family. Independence of movement by horse or boat to neighboring farms and taverns and to church and county court, where men gathered for business and conviviality, was an essential dimension of adult life. The close contact and emotional bond between a planter and his son helped to gradually dissolve the boy's ties to his mother and to give him an accurate idea of his physical skills, responsibilities, and values as a male in a plantation society.

When sons were old enough to handle a horse well — usually by their early teens — parents used them as messengers between plantations. As they matured, it was not uncommon for boys to take long trips alone to visit relatives or conduct business for their father. The experience of Henry Hollyday and his sons of the Eastern Shore of Maryland illustrates this point. Henry's eldest son, Jimmy, in his early teens, shuttled news between the home plantation and his uncle's farm in Talbot County. In September of 1781, Hollyday sent his nineteen-year-old son Thomas to a friend's home to exchange some paper money for specie. Frequently,

"Tommy" left home for weeks at a time to visit his uncle and friends in a neighboring county, while his father remained "uncertain when he will be at home again."

The freedom of movement that planters' sons enjoyed may have shortened the gap between childhood and adulthood. One traveler in late-eighteenth-century Virginia commented on this early mobility of sons: "A Virginia youth of 15 years is already such a man as he will be at twice that age. At 15, his father gives him a horse and a negro, with which he riots about the country, attends every fox-hunt, horse-race, and cock-fight, and does nothing else whatever." Nicholas Cresswell was even more forcefully struck by the independence of Virginia youth. "If they have any genius, it is not cramped in their infancy by being overawed by their parents. There is very little subordination observed in their youth. Implicit obedience to old age is not among their qualifications."

Undoubtedly a key dimension in the independence of planters' sons was the presence of black slaves on the plantation. Observing their fathers' daily disciplining of the slaves and exercising their own authority over house servants surely inured young men to the "command experience" and gave them a measure of autonomy and assertive power that sons elsewhere in early America did not possess. Jefferson worried about these lessons of dominance learned in planter households. "The parent storms, the child looks on, catches the lineaments of wrath, puts on the same airs in the circle of smaller slaves, gives a loose to his worst passions, and thus nursed, educated, and daily exercised in tyranny, cannot but be stamped by it with odious peculiarities." The strong-willed, self-confident character of the planter gentry derived in part from their almost lifelong experience as masters.

Despite the generally unrestricted plantation environment, which encouraged autonomy and self-reliance, most young men from planter families grew up profoundly dependent on their parents — especially their fathers — for their sense of identity and emotional security. Many sons seem to have been deeply attached to their fathers, finding in them strong male figures with whom they could easily identify. To a large extent, these deep emotional bonds had been nourished in infancy and early childhood when parents lavished attention and affection on their offspring. Respect and filial devotion came much easier to sons secure in the knowledge that their parents derived pleasure from their presence.

The origins of deference and duty of course can also be located in more practical matters. As boys matured into young men, they doubtless recognized that in an agrarian society their economic success depended largely on the generosity of their fathers. With little liquid capital available and few alternatives to farming, especially in the first half of the eighteenth century, most sons could begin careers and marry only with paternal consent and financial aid either by gift or inheritance. Many children were naturally disposed to try to please parents who had provided them with affection and considerable freedom since childhood. And fathers owned the family land and personal property, which in general they distributed evenly among dutiful sons.

Dutiful behavior required a strong dependence on parental values. The central message fathers tried to convey to their sons was the fundamental importance of achievement and self-government. Because they felt confident of their sons' continuing devotion to them, parents, particularly fathers, were able to encourage in their sons these seemingly conflicting values of autonomy and deference. And planters were careful to link all the achievements they expected — and sometimes demanded — of their sons to the essential requirement of filial duty.

We can see this paternal message at work most clearly in the early correspondence between young boys and their fathers. The St. George Tucker family of Virginia provides a vivid illustration of how father-son relationships revolved around the twin virtues of deference and self-improvement. During the Revolution, Tucker was separated from his family, but he often wrote to his stepsons offering them paternal advice on hard work and obedience. Receiving these letters from their soldier-father seemed to deeply affect the Randolph boys, strengthening their self-image as young men. Whenever the boys heard from him, Mrs. Tucker explained, "They fancy they are Men." The drive for self-improvement and to match paternal expectations grew strong in Tucker's children. Richard Randolph, St. George's stepson, expressed his commitment to paternal values: "I have been very negligent of my grammar, which I am very sorry to say, but be assured, I shall have my Syntax at my fingers end when you return. I know you give us good advice for our advantage, as no good can arise from it to you, but that you wish to see us all clever men, which I firmly believe." Paternal affection that flowed freely to infants and small children had to be earned by maturing sons through self-discipline and dutiful behavior. Tucker's stepsons appeared to grasp this lesson well. John Randolph seemed grateful for the paternal advice he had received, for, as he explained to his stepfather, "I will try all I can to be a good Boy & a favorite of Mamas & when you come home I hope shall be one of yours."

The central assumption governing parent–child relationships was that a child's ultimate happiness and self-worth depended on his knowledge of parental approbation. Fathers were occasionally explicit about this expectation. Thomas Jefferson, for example, insisted that his daughter use his letters to her so that "you may always have present in your mind those things which will endear you to me." Children recognized that parental love was now conditional, requiring evidence of self-improvement and achievement. As a result, sons quite literally performed for their fathers to demonstrate their worth to watchful parents. Some fathers regularly arranged to have their sons read aloud before them, after which the boys might learn if their father had been "highly pleased with their performance." Fathers also examined their sons' writing for signs of intellectual progress and expressions of filial duty. Consequently young boys penned their early letters with considerable apprehension. In 1782, Littleton Tazewell wrote to his father promising to obey him "in all things" and to "shew a good example to my dear sister and Aunt so as to merit your Praise." Ten-year-old Keith William Pratt presented himself in writing to his mother in November of 1731: "This is my first Performance, & I hope you will be so good as to Excuse my Imperfections, assureing you, I will Endeavor to Improve my Self, in everything which may make my Self Acceptable to you." To be sure, some boys employed such deferential language as much out of strategy as conviction in dealing with their parents, but Keith Pratt genuinely feared his mother's displeasure. The boy's tutor told Keith's mother that he "shed tears upon his being suspected of wanting Duty & Love for so good a Mother."

Paternal influence intensified when sons began to prepare for their careers. Schooling and apprenticeship experience, like marital decisions, strongly affected a young man's economic and political opportunities, and fathers guided their sons through these important decisions. Sons became in a very real sense "projects" of their fathers. Planters spent years trying to shape sons into adults who either reflected or surpassed paternal accomplishments and reputations. Much of this paternal shaping is a common dynamic in families at all times. What is striking about these eighteenth-century gentry households is the large measure of success fathers seemed to enjoy in creating sons in their own images. . . .

Because many young men depended so greatly on paternal approbation for their motivation and inner sense of worth, the withdrawal of such paternal support could release in them a flood of anxiety followed by effusive efforts to regain their parents' respect. Failure to live up to a father's expectations implied a lack of gratitude for the psychological and economic investments parents had presumably made in their children. Sons who had given evidence of "foolish dissipation" and "inconsistent" behavior while in school — usually associated with a love of "diversions" and ill-managed spending habits — worried incessantly about paternal rebukes. For example, William Quynn of Maryland, a medical student in Philadelphia, was apparently guilty of these youthful excesses, which, Quynn realized as he explained to his father, "incurred your displeasure." He reassured his father that these "follies of youth" would end and promised to "be useful to myself" and "a Pleasure to you."

When John Carter, who was apprenticed to a merchant in London, overspent the allowance his father provided him, he begged for paternal forgiveness of his "past extravagances." The extravagant use of time and money was particularly galling to parents, for it suggested a lack of the self-control necessary for a virtuous life. The behavior of John Carter angered his father precisely because it revealed in his son an inability to monitor his own impulses. Carter accepted his son's apologies for the moment, but warned him that if such overindulgence continued, "I must be so plain to tell you I shall have little dependence upon what you say hereafter in relation to the government of yourself. . . ."

Increasingly in the late eighteenth and early nineteenth centuries, sons came to decisions similar to those of William Quynn and Theodorick Bland, that in selecting a career their own innate talents, interests, and personal feelings could outweigh predetermined parental designs. Parental control diminished as well in marital decisions of the late eighteenth century, as sons and daughters began to choose marriage partners on the basis of companionship rather than accept matches arranged by parents. Part of this democratization of authority in the family grew naturally out of a relatively permissive child-rearing style that encouraged the development of self-confidence and assertiveness. Moreover, these new youthful sentiments reflected a shift from the rational, orderly world eighteenth-century planters had created to a growing eagerness to give expression to suppressed instincts and emotions. . . .

Despite the growing autonomy of young men in the last third of the eighteenth century, parents and children continued to feel a deep sense of duty to one another. In short, parental authority was reciprocal, not authoritarian in nature, for fathers and sons shared an obligation for care and respect throughout their lives. Above all, parental duty required fathers to teach their children the principles of self-reliant, virtuous conduct and to make financial provisions sufficient to insure their economic independence. These two obligations were interdependent, for men strongly believed that virtue and self-respect came only after the achievement of financial autonomy.

A few years after starting his own family, Richard Terrell bought some land along the Ohio River as "a fund" for his children. Terrell's brother-in-law, Peter Carr, praised him for the paternal decision for he recognized that this land "will make them independent, and you happy — for your happiness will certainly be increased by the reflection that they are independent. When this is attained, nothing is wanting to constitute earthly felicity but the steady and undeviating practice of virtue." Parents agonized over the possibility that they might fail in their responsibility to see their sons "well settled in the world." "My children are dear to me," James Mercer explained to his brother in 1783, "& it is so much *my Duty* to preserve them from the distresses of want, that I must stand *self-condemned* to risque it any longer." It was also a conspicuous sign of personal success and family honor for planters to have their sons well placed in the world.

Landon Carter, for example, was obviously proud of "the care I have taken of my family, the paying off children's fortunes, and putting out 3 sons with an Estate very well to pass in the world, still maintaining a large family at home, and all this without being in debt but a very trifle." Emphasizing the importance of a family's continued economic independence, Carter claimed that his central task as a parent had been "to leave those descended from me a reasonable subsistance to provide for those they shall be the instrument of birth to."

A son's duty to his parents involved more than just obedience and was often perceived as a lifelong obligation. Just as a father's principal responsibility was to guarantee the economic independence of his children, a son's essential task was to maintain that sense of self-reliance and financial autonomy. Despite the close kin networks that had grown up around most Chesapeake families by the mid-eighteenth century, an independently settled young man could rarely justify any sustained reliance on his parents or relatives for financial support. When he failed to make his own way or became heavily indebted, a son relinquished any claim to self-respect and confidence in his father's presence. The confrontation between Robert Bladen Carter and his father Robert Carter the Councillor in 1786 suggests how a misspent early career could reduce a young man to abject fear of his father. Having squandered the profits from an estate his father had given him, twenty-six-year-old Robert Bladen Carter approached his father asking for help: "This morning I waited on you in Your Library with an intention of asking you for some employment. It has and ever will be the case I am afraid, when before you; in any serious reflections, I have observed a stoppage in my throat and intellect vastly confused: What it proceeds from God only knows — It is my wish if you should choose to be imployed by you. Every exertion of body and mind will I exert in your behalf."

Becoming a burden on one's parents was an especially troubling familial sin, for it contradicted the proper expression of filial devotion: that sons were to provide comfort and aid — financial aid, if necessary — for their parents during their declining years. When a young man became dependent on his aging parents, it robbed them, as one son put it, of "those calm and peaceable enjoyments which old age and infirmity require." In the seventeenth and early eighteenth centuries when short life expectancies all but precluded the development of an elderly generation, few sons incurred this kind of family obligation. But clearly by the late eighteenth century caring for the aged — which by eighteenth-century standards meant those over fifty or fifty-five — became an increasingly common responsibility that sons were expected to accept.

In a society where protection against illness and financial loss was minimal, children were viewed in part as a form of economic and emotional security. As a result of the close bonds that developed between parents and children during the eighteenth century, parents came to expect that their children — especially their sons — would continue to provide pleasure and comfort to them in their "declining years." Aging fathers sometimes arranged for sons to manage the family estate. George Hume of Spotsylvania County, Virginia, at the age of fifty-three and with failing eyesight, grew especially dependent on his son for his economic well-being. "I thank God I have now a son (George) who does my business for me and when he leaves me I hope to have another (Francis) ready."

The strong paternal influence in planter families explored here was in part a consequence of demographic changes in the eighteenth-century Chesapeake. Short adult life expectancies — to about the mid-forties for adult men — created by the endemic malarial environment of early Virginia and Maryland compressed the life cycle and disrupted family life. Early parental death and consequent orphanhood were common experiences for many families, often confining the contact between fathers and sons to only a few years. Under these circumstances, many sons grew up with little sustained paternal guidance. As life expectancies rose in the eighteenth century — to about the mid-fifties for adult males — families grew in size and strength and parents established firmer control over their children. Increasingly, fathers and mothers could expect to see their children to maturity and to convey successfully to them important cultural and parental values. Perhaps for the first time in the Chesapeake, most fathers could gradually shape their sons in their own images.

But as we have seen, eighteenth-century planters did not try to crush the willful, autonomous tendencies in their sons. Indeed, rather like modern parents, Chesapeake fathers insisted that their sons become self-reliant, competitive, and economically independent. The modernization of the Chesapeake family, however, was far from complete, especially with respect to father–son relationships. However much planters encouraged autonomy in their sons, there was little interest in the "rugged individual" we associate with modern America, who made a total separation from his father, withdrawing psychologically as well as financially from paternal control. Individualism had limits in the farm families of the eighteenth-century Chesapeake, for land, transmitted through inheritance or parental gift, linked generations together in an expanding network of kin. And even the growing number of young men in the late eighteenth century who did not depend on family land and personal property for their economic security retained strong emotional commitments and obligations to their fathers and mothers.

STUDY GUIDE

1. Explain how attitudes toward children and child-rearing differed in seventeenth-century New England, as described by Koehler, and in

eighteenth-century Virginia. Would the difference in the two centuries or in the two different cultures seem to have played the most significant role?

2. Slave parents and children owned little or no property and were themselves owned by planters. How would this affect the slave family in such areas as parental authority and family stability?

3. In recent years, a good deal of writing has suggested that fathers in our time have not taken a very active role in raising children. Smith indicates that planter fathers displayed an early and affectionate involvement in their children's lives. What might have accounted for this in the rural, wealthy society of the Chesapeake area?

4. In our time, most men — and an increasingly large number of women — spend most of their day outside of the home, and children's time is occupied largely by involvement in school, athletic teams, and other activities external to the family. How has this affected parent–child relationships?

BIBLIOGRAPHY

Both the history of childhood and that of the condition of the aged are of considerable interest to those studying the family in America. Also, the history of women and of male–female relationships are inseparable from family history, so that the bibliography following the essay by Koehler (Reading No. 3) should be consulted. The books cited there by Morgan and Demos have chapters describing how children were viewed and reared in the colonial period. Later views are examined in Joseph F. Kett, *Rites of Passage: Adolescence in America, 1790 to the Present* (1977). Peter Slater, *Children in the New England Mind: In Death and Life* (1977) examines the attitudes of the Puritan world, while Jane T. Censer, *North Carolina Planters and Their Children, 1800–1860* (1984) extends the story of the Southern family to the Civil War. Both Smith's book and James Axtell, *The School upon a Hill: Education and Society in Colonial New England* (1974) have fascinating chapters on pregnancy, childbirth, and education. N. Ray Hiner and Joseph M. Hawes, *Growing up in America: Children in Historical Perspective* (1985) is a series of essays on childhood from colonial times to the present. One of the essays, by William G. McLoughlin, describes nineteenth-century evangelical attitudes towards child rearing, while another by David K. Wiggins is an interesting study of the play of slave children. Much less has been written about the aged in American society, but David H. Fischer has attempted a broad survey of social attitudes in his *Growing Old in America* (1977); Carole Haber, *Beyond Sixty-Five: The Dilemma of Old Age in America's Past* (1983) is also useful.

Jan Lewis, *The Pursuit of Happiness: Family and Values in Jefferson's Virginia*

(1983) complements the studies by Smith and Censer. Two broad works on the family are: John Demos and S. S. Boocock, eds., *Turning Points: Historical and Sociological Essays on the Family* (1978) and Melvin Yazawa, *From Colonies to Commonwealth: Familial Ideology and the Beginnings of the American Republic* (1985).

II THE NEW NATION

The quarter-century that followed the start of the War for Independence in 1775 is a remarkable period in American history. Seldom has there been a time in this country when the future seemed so promising and the problems so profound. Having broken from the mother country, Americans thought of themselves as in something of a state of nature, with a clean slate on which they could design new, republican institutions of government. By the end of the eighteenth century, every state except Connecticut and Rhode Island had written new constitutions. Together, the American people had adopted a federal constitution, established a government that was truly national in its operation, and enunciated political ideas that became so deeply embedded in the national consciousness that they are referred to as the "American Credo."

Besides the enduring monuments of American political and constitutional practice that were raised, these twenty-five years also witnessed remarkable achievements in other areas. The break from England did much to accelerate the development of American democratic thought and equalitarian social attitudes. It also encouraged a spirit of nationalism in literature, architecture, and other aspects of American cultural life. Basic directions in foreign policy were enunciated, and there were significant developments in American economic life.

Of course, our American ancestors could not foresee the extraordinary economic and political success of the United States. Indeed, between 1775 and 1800, it was questioned whether or not the republic would survive. The first essay in this section gives us a sense of the initial optimism and nationalism of the revolutionary forces as well as of the frightening prospect that Washington's army would not succeed. Many Americans questioned the wisdom of declaring independence, and the fifty thousand colonists who fought on the side of the British were but a small reflection of the deep division in American society. The treatment of the Loyalists is described in the second selection. The third and fourth essays discuss the beginnings of the Industrial Revolution and the movement toward egalitarianism during the late eighteenth and early nineteenth centuries. The third reading describes the emergence of broad-based national denominations of American Protestantism that appealed to common men and women. Growing out of the great religious revival that swept the country after 1800, these religious groups held forth to all people a promise of salvation that the closed sects of the seventeenth century had not. The final selection describes the several technological and industrial changes that were to make this country preeminent in industrialization.

"Valley Forge, 1777" by A. Gibert depicts the suffering of Washington's soldiers that made it difficult to enlist large numbers of volunteers.

5

CHARLES ROYSTER

Building an Army

During much of their history, Americans have considered themselves a special people, destined by God to serve as an example for the rest of humanity. The religious sects who settled here, including the Puritans, saw their colony as "a Citty upon a Hill, the eyes of all people uppon us." In the eighteenth century, many revolutionary leaders believed that there was a conspiracy in England aimed at suppressing colonial liberties and that they had a sacred duty to defend America as the last bastion of freedom. Americans, they felt, were a virtuous people who were destined by God to lead the world in establishing a free and noble republic that would abolish the kings, armies, and corrupt ministries that enslaved Europe. The defense of liberty would be made by untrained citizen–soldiers, moved to courageous deeds by their love of freedom and their faith in God. Their fear of regular, standing armies gave rise to a long tradition of anti-militarism, a commitment to civilian control of the military, and a belief that American wars could be fought by voluntary enlistment of average citizens. It also perpetuated a myth that the Revolutionary War was won by patriotic farmers who turned out in large numbers to promote the glorious cause.

During the first year of the war, a considerable amount of such enthusiasm was displayed in the patriotic songs and poetry, in the parades and celebrations, and even in the number of men who joined the ranks. By 1776, however, the enthusiasm had waned, and men deserted, went home on leave and never returned, or refused to enlist unless a bounty was paid for their doing so. Washington's army seldom exceeded 25,000 troops and was frequently much smaller. Increasingly Washington saw the need for a regular army of long-term enlistees, and increasingly the war was fought not by middle-class patriots, but by others who were hired to fight — the slave and servant who thus bought their freedom, or the young and the poor who saw so few opportunities in civilian life that even the meager pay in the Continental Army looked good. If the enthusiasm of the volunteer soldier soon flagged, so too did that of the civilian population, which complained about taxes and sometimes sold food and supplies to the British army rather than donating them to Washington's forces.

Charles Royster has written a book on the ideals of the American people during the Revolutionary War and how these ideals were eroded as the war progressed. The opening of the following selection from his volume describes the initial enthusiasm of the colonists as war broke out in 1775. Much of the remainder of the article discusses problems in maintaining this spirit, and the growing realization among Americans that, if the war was to be won, it would have to be by a regular army. The picture he paints is not very flattering, but as in every war, there were selfless men and women who persisted through thick and thin. The selection concludes with a vignette of a dashing, romantic hero whose life demonstrates that nearly every myth — including that of our patriotic ancestors — is based upon some kernel of truth.

From the Battle of Lexington to the Declaration of Independence, all kinds of military exercises, uniforms, and threats aimed at the British enjoyed a wide vogue among Americans. A letter from Philadelphia assured the British that "the Rage Militaire, as the French call a passion for arms, has taken possession of the whole Continent." Although commitment to American independence grew during the war, this popular *rage militaire* vanished by the end of 1776 and never returned. Even in 1776 it was a weak echo of its loudest moments in 1775. Months before the Lexington and Concord skirmishes, Americans had begun militia drills to prepare for armed resistance. As mobilization progressed, they enthusiastically celebrated the citizens' rapidly acquired skill in the manual of arms and in field maneuvers. An observer who believed what he heard would have concluded that the survival of liberty depended on widespread voluntary submission to military discipline.

From *A Revolutionary People at War: The Continental Army and American Character, 1775–1783* by Charles Royster. Copyright 1979 The University of North Carolina Press. Published for the Institute of Early American History and Culture. Reprinted by permission of the publisher.

After war began, the Continental Army, most of which besieged Boston until March 1776, became the focus of Americans' announced determination to surpass the British in military prowess as in virtue. Two strengths, they claimed, ensured this superiority: Americans used only the essentials of drill without an intricate, unnecessary dumb show; and Americans possessed "natural" or "native" or "innate" courage.

The printed manuals of arms and evolutions that Americans used — especially Lewis Nicola's *Treatise of Military Exercise* and Timothy Pickering's "easy" plan, adapted from an English model — emphasized simplicity, not show, by using the fewest possible movements to load, fire, and maneuver. General Charles Lee assured Americans that they could dispense with "the tinsel and show of war" and learn the essentials — to load and fire, to form, to retreat, to advance, to change front, to rally by the colors, to reduce from a line of fire (two deep) to a line of impression (four, six, or eight deep) — all in three months. The Massachusetts Council adopted Pickering's plan because it was not "clogged with many superfluous motions, which only serve to burthen the memory and perplex the Learner." . . .

The revolutionaries could not equal the complexity of British parade and decided they did not want to, but they greatly enjoyed what they had left. Judging from a few loyalist witnesses and from the long time it took the Continental Army to learn to drill, the countless town-square parades and maneuvers of 1775 must have looked pretty poor. In the *Virginia Gazette*, Robert Washington, who wanted a job training soldiers, acknowledged that Americans' early use of firearms, knowledge of the country, and "native Courage" made them superior in the woods. But he warned, "Let us not plume ourselves with this Conceit, that we shall always have the Bush to fight behind." He went to a muster to see "the *Prussian Exercise*, as they call it" but only saw men forming six deep, turning about-face, marching eighteen paces to the rear, opening ranks, and going through slow parade motions of prime and load — "you may call it *Prussian Exercise* if you please; but . . . to lead a Body of brave men, with such counterfeit Discipline, to face a disciplined Enemy, would, in my Opinion, be downright Murder." . . .

Reviews and drill attracted many spectators; Congress watched parade-ground evolutions on June 8, 1775. Companies drilled by moonlight. Boys between the ages of thirteen and sixteen volunteered. They were commended but turned away. Younger boys played soldier and organized their own companies for drill. One militiaman remembered 1775, the year of his thirteenth birthday: "I obtained a pamphlet in which this exercise was fully explained, according to the best system of the day, which was the Prussian. . . . I made myself so much a master, that I had the honour of standing before the company as *fugleman*." Everywhere revolutionaries reported rapid progress in discipline. . . . Some people who saw reviews wrote that Americans were or soon would be equal to any troops in the world.

People could believe this, despite the shortcomings in drill that they must have seen, because they thought that American soldiers were courageous by nature. The Americans' claim to have native courage later became grounds for questioning the importance of the Continental Army, but in 1775 it made the army, with its growing discipline, the main representative of American resistance. The revolutionaries' courage was bolstered by their conviction that God had given them the ability to choose and the zeal to defend liberty for themselves and for mankind. . . . Revolutionaries felt sure that against such strength the British could muster only the artificial courage of force, pay, and rote, while the loyalists had no courage at all. . . .

Early in the war, Americans, especially revolutionary leaders, talked freely about large numbers of casualties. The revolutionaries argued not only that death in a glorious cause was rewarding and that risking death was imperative, but also that they did not fear death. They would, according to the spirit of 1775, rush to the field of combat, eager to conquer or to die: "A spirit of enthusiasm for war is gone forth, that has driven away the fear of death." . . . Neither living nor dying in the cause of liberty proved so uncomplicated and easy as the ideals of 1775 announced. A revolutionary would need sources of strength besides native courage or would suffer for the lack of them.

Captain Joseph Jewett found it so as he took thirty-six hours to die of bayonet wounds in his chest and stomach after the Battle of Long Island. On the last morning, he "was sensible of being near his End, often Repeating that it was hard work to Die." In one of the battles of Saratoga, Captain John Henry, Patrick Henry's son, distinguished himself in combat. Afterward he walked among the American dead, pausing to recognize men he had known. Then he drew his sword, broke it, threw it on the ground, and raved, mad. Nine months later, his "ill state of Health," according to Washington, caused him to resign his commission. . . .

The army's experiences in 1775 and 1776 quickly revealed the contrasts between the ideals of 1775 and the conduct of the war. The first year of fighting the British and creating a regular army began the test of Americans' response to the problem of reconciling lapses in revolutionaries' conduct with the rigor of absolute ideals. Two kinds of failure threatened to undermine the cause: battlefield reverses, which called Americans' native courage into doubt, and the army's lack of discipline and decorum, which fell far short of the revolutionaries' hope for an army of Israel.

When Washington arrived at Cambridge in July 1775, the Massachusetts legislature apologized for the state of discipline in the army. The representatives told him that the men were "naturally brave, and of good understanding," but "the completion of so difficult and at the same time so necessary a task is reserved to your Excellency." Even before reaching camp, Washington could notice one of his difficulties: the sound of sporadic musket fire. The shots did not mean combat or even sniping at sentries. The firing was just what it sounded like — men shooting off muskets at random in camp. One of the revolutionaries' most often-repeated claims to superiority over the British army said that Americans learned the use of firearms from childhood. These claims exaggerated both American marksmanship and its usefulness in combat against a disciplined bayonet charge. Whatever the extent or the advantage of early familiarity with weapons, muskets in the hands of idle men proved very dangerous. Men used them to start fires; men discharged them to empty them; men fired at wild geese flying overhead. Some soldiers wounded or killed themselves by accident. Many men enjoyed snapping flintlocks for the fun of it; sometimes the musket was loaded and a nearby soldier was killed or wounded. In 1776 Washington was still saying in general orders, "Seldom a day passes but some persons are shot by their friends."

The Massachusetts legislature had warned Washington that the soldiers were "youth . . . used to a laborious life," who had not learned "the absolute necessity of cleanliness in their dress, and lodging, continual exercise, and strict temperance, to preserve them from diseases." Some soldiers felt that washing clothes was women's work; so they wore what they had until it crusted over and fell apart. Others sent their laundry home. Washington wanted the soldiers to bathe; those who would bathe wanted to swim all day and show off naked in front of "ladies of the first fashion" who happened to be crossing the bridge in Cambridge. Prolonged swimming threatened the men's health, as did refusing to bathe or to wash their clothes. . . . Throughout the war soldiers and officers suffered from "the Itch," a product of poor hygiene and sleeping on the ground. It could become so severe as to cover a man with scabs or strip off his skin. It left large numbers of men hardly fit for duty. Soldiers "Ointed for the Itch" with hog's lard or pine tar and brimstone — a process that made "the Devil of a Stink" and, in one case, "over came them so that we Thought they would a Died in the Night."

Every soldier's health was endangered by persistent problems with camp sanitation, which did most harm in the early years of the war. Open latrines for thousands of men were bad enough, but many soldiers would "Set Down and Ease themselves" wherever they felt like it. The remains of slaughtered cattle often rotted unburied. When the army stayed in one place for long, it sat amid a smoky miasma rising from green wood fires, gunpowder smoke, urine, feces, and animal offal. At first Washington thought that Massachusetts men were "an exceeding dirty and nasty people"; he later found that soldiers from all states would freely foul their own camp. The Continental Army became much cleaner in the years after

1777, but in 1781 Americans could still marvel at how clean their French allies managed to keep a camp.

Neglect of cleanliness, like carelessness with firearms, was a self-destructive response to the unforeseen hardships of life in camp. General Philip Schuyler put the soldiers' attitude in one word: "nonchalance." We might call it anxiety. Americans' inexperience in war caused many of their early problems, and the revolutionaries' respect for personal independence worked against quick, strict obedience to orders. Men who had shared the *rage militaire* of 1775 remained reluctant to master the soldierly skills that would help to keep them alive in the army. Even those soldiers who put self-preservation first by deserting a few weeks or months short of their discharge date risked, by their departure, the self-destruction of the army. Late in June 1775, eighteen men from Captain Winthrop Rowe's New Hampshire company deserted outside Boston, saying "that they didn't intend when they enlisted to join the Army, but to be station'd at Hampton" on the New Hampshire coast. . . .

Generals and doctors found that homesickness meant just that — sickness. The symptoms were loss of appetite, restlessness, and melancholy. Few of the New England soldiers had been far from their hometowns before; they would seldom have gone away for long; they would never have lived with thousands of others in new and uncomfortable constraint. The soldiers' strong local attachments came not only from their affection for family and friends but from lives wholly shaped by experience within a small area. Private Barber said of his company. "Most of us had not . . . been twenty miles from home." The ardor that had moved them to defend their beloved homes against the threat of invasion could not alone sustain all of them. They fell ill, yet recovered when discharged. No doubt some were malingering, but most who suffered from homesickness must have found it as real as smallpox or dysentery. Their longing was not just the disappointment or temporary low spirits we usually mean by the word "homesick." It was a lasting obsession. Repeatedly during 1776 and 1777 newspaper advertisements for deserters described soldiers as having a "dejected" look, a "down look," a "prodigious down look." One colonel reported from camp, "The Officers and Soldiers are possessed to get Home." . . .

The most notorious departers were the Connecticut soldiers who refused a request to stay beyond the end of their terms. The generals tried patriotic appeals, flattery, shame, drinks, and blows, but Colonel Jedidiah Huntington found that "we shall not with all our Rhetorick be able to retain many." When the soldiers marched, the generals encouraged the citizens and tavern keepers along the road to deny service to the soliders and to express contempt for their conduct. In Connecticut people were glad to see the soliders for a visit, but expected them to go back to camp. Many condemned the soldiers' departure from camp and shamed some men into reenlisting. . . .

Apart from the handling of army supplies, recruiting introduced more corruption into American society than any other activity associated with a standing army. But in this kind of corruption, we do not see a ruler taxing the people in order to employ favorites to support his rule. We see the people buying freedom from the demands of their own government. Everyone knew that this was happening, and even men who applauded the widespread suspicion of open-ended enlistments deplored the traffic in short-term recruits. They wanted men to enlist and reenlist for a fixed bounty. Some men did, but not enough. . . .

In 1776 the army again enlisted for one year. Against the wishes of the generals and the New England delegates, Congress resolved that "no bounty be allowed to the army on reinlistment." During the early months of 1776 the states tried to fill their regiments without a bounty. In January the Massachusetts legislature forswore both a bounty and a draft, while the *Connecticut Courant* addressed potential recruits, "Will it not be criminal, at a crisis like the present, to bury your martial talents because more of your money is not taxed from you and returned as a bounty. . . . The pay of the soldiery, though not equal to intentions of bribery, is equal to all the purposes of comfortable and manly subsistence." At first Virginia and North Carolina wanted to recruit even more battalions than Congress had asked them for. But the states failed to fill their regiments, and Congress acknowledged the failure on June 26, 1776, when it voted to grant ten dollars to men who enlisted for three years. . . .

An annual pattern of recruiting began in 1777. Congress assigned a quota to each state, which then assigned quotas to the towns. The commander in chief, the delegates in Congress, and Continental Army officers from the state wrote letters urging prompt compliance. The local militia commander held a muster and called for volunteers. A few men enlisted. Then weeks of dickering started. The state or the town or private individuals or all three sweetened the bounty. Meanwhile, citizens who did not want to turn out with the militia were looking for militia substitutes to hire. Continental Army officers were in the countryside trying to build their own company or regiment. As men held out for an offer they liked, Washington and the officers in camp wrote more letters urging the state to fill its quota promptly so that men could be trained before the fall campaign. By late spring or summer, all of the men who were going to enlist that year on any terms had done so, whereupon the state found that it had not filled its quota. Washington called for militia reinforcements. Drafting began in 1777 and sent men for terms ending in December, which ensured that the whole process would begin again next January. . . .

. . . Desertion . . . had many forms. Bounties inspired some soldiers to enlist several times with several units within a few days. Men bought or forged illegal discharges. Soldiers went to the enemy. More often, they went home. The army sent small detachments to catch them. Although the British and the loyalists encouraged men to desert and promised to reward or shelter them, deserters were most commonly helped by revolutionaries themselves, especially relatives. People not only refused to help army detachments apprehend deserters, but also helped the deserters escape arrest. In "many instances," according to Washington, "Deserters which have been apprehended by Officers, have been rescued by the People." Citizens also bought deserters' arms and clothing. States offered rewards for the arrest of deserters and threatened to draft, fine, and flog people who sheltered them. Trying another expedient, from time to time Washington offered amnesties. None of these measures, nor the whipping of captured men, nor the execution of some deserters, had any lasting effect. The most thorough study of the official returns estimates an average desertion rate of between 20 and 25 percent. The army's returns showed desertion to be declining in the later years of the war, as the army developed a core of long-term soldiers. . . .

The camps around Boston introduced both soldiers and civilians to a problem of discipline that followed the army throughout the war — the theft and destruction of property. The private homes and Harvard College buildings that were used for quarters inevitably got damaged. For a mile around Cambridge, soldiers pulled down every fence and cut down every tree for firewood. They threatened to start on houses until the legislature empowered the army to seize loyalists' woodlots. Soldiers also stole things on their own. Private Daniel Barber later said that "home and plenty are very different from the close quarters and deprivations to which a soldier is liable. The devil would now and then tell us, that it was no harm sometimes to pull a few potatoes and cabbages, and pluck, once in a while, an ear of corn, when we stood in need." . . .

Continental generals tried European discipline because they wanted to achieve their idea of a regular army and because they thought that the vulgar could best be restrained by force. Continental soldiers often were rough men, toward the enemy or toward civilians and each other. Throughout the war, people in the neighborhood of the army felt this harshness often. They withstood three kinds of plunder: official plunder, casual plunder, and private plunder. Official plunderers, following orders, took livestock and grain and left a paper certifying that they had done so; casual plunderers burned fence rails for firewood, turned horses loose in grain fields, and fouled buildings; private plunderers beat people up and robbed them.

Supply shortages and lack of pay encouraged men to take what they could find, as commanders and civil officials knew. However, some soldiers, abetted by junior officers, stole in order to turn a quick profit. They enjoyed threatening or using force against people who seldom could resist.

Soldiers argued that, since property would soon fall under British control, they might as well take it. To conceal theft from private homes, they set fire to the houses. "How disgraceful to the army is it," Washington said in one of his many futile orders against theft and destruction, "that the peaceable inhabitants, our countrymen and fellow citizens, dread our halting among them, even for a night and are happy when they get rid of us?" A few of the Continental Army's casualties occurred when citizens defended their property against looting soldiers, and soldiers who met resistance sometimes fired on citizens. . . .

[There were frequent quarrels and bloodshed within the army, as well as between soldiers and civilians.]

Much of the violence in camp took place when men were drunk. When Private James McCormick was tried for shooting and killing Private Reuben Bishop while drunk, his defense was that he had not intentionally murdered Bishop because he had meant to kill his company commander. Rum — West India for officers, New England for enlisted men — was the most common drink, but all ranks took stinking whiskey hot from the still, wring-jaw cider, or whatever they could get. A week before the Battle of Brandywine, General Peter Muhlenberg said that "many Soldiers [are] making a practice of getting drunk regularly once a Day and thereby render themselves unfit for duty." Men sometimes pleaded drunkenness, itself a crime in the army, as an excuse or extenuation for other crimes.

Alcohol in moderation, people then thought, promoted health. To treat "putrid fevers" army doctors prescribed, among other things, "wine (two or three bottles a day in many cases)." One gill, or four ounces of rum was part of the daily ration when available. At Valley Forge, Henry Knox urged the commissary to provide this ration: "We have found by experience that this would support the men through every difficulty." Sutlers who followed the camp sold more to those who had money; a man without cash could drink up his pay in advance. Washington tried twice to ban liquor dealers and then tried to license some, control their prices, and keep others away from the soldiers. None of these efforts succeeded for long. Men stole liquor, stole things to buy liquor, even sold their clothes to buy liquor. During the war, some of the biggest fortunes were made getting European manufactured goods for civilians, but some of the surest were made selling liquor to soldiers.

From the beginning the Continental Army disturbed many Christians because so many men swore. Today, the revolutionaries' admonitions against profanity may seem naive or futile. British soldiers had long been famous for their oaths. To Godfearing Americans, this was all the more reason for the Continental Army to reflect the righteousness of its cause by superior piety and self-restraint. Instead, all observers agreed, the Americans imitated the British more effectively on this score than on any other.

To judge by surviving examples, revolutionary profanity would sound mild to many people now. The same words were stronger then because they had not lost their religious meaning: profanity still permitted important theological distinctions. After Eli Showell was jailed for refusing to enlist, an officer came to him with a drawn sword and said, "Eli, now God damn your soul but . . . your life is your own, if you do not enlist I will run you through." Two sergeants worked the "son of a bitch" over, and Eli enlisted. Anthony Wayne may have been the greatest swearer among senior officers. Lieutenant Ebenezer Elmer got it this way: "Col. Wayne . . . finding no sentry, (as we have not kept one in the day time) he damned all our souls to hell, and immediately ordered two by night and one by day, which I immediately put in execution — but shall not forget his damns, which he is very apt to bestow upon people; but my great consolation is, that the power thereof is not in his hands, blessed be God for it." . . .

Against all these forms of disorder, officers relied mainly on one device: flogging. By British standards, which went up to 1,000 lashes, the Continental Army was lenient. Congress stuck to the Mosaic law of 39 lashes until 1776. For the rest of the war, the articles allowed 100. . . . For punishment of crimes such as plundering and firing guns in camp, Washington tried to make whipping more effective by authorizing lashes on the spot. He also kept asking Congress to raise the maximum to 500 because men could take 100 and remain defiant, leaving him no effective punishment short of death. The request, which had the support of James Madison, was never granted. Washington considered punishing men by confinement at hard labor, but this was not implemented, perhaps because it would have been hard to tell from routine service in the Continental Army.

Men were either whipped with a cat-o'-nine-tails or made to run the gauntlet. Since Washington believed that witnessing punishment deterred crime — a common assumption of the time — the soldiers were assembled and, after the adjutant read the sentence, either watched a drummer whip a guilty man tied to a post or whipped him themselves with sticks as he was marched between two lines of men. A bayonet in front of him kept him from going down the gauntlet too fast. One soldier, after undergoing the gauntlet, was "in a miserable situation . . . not able to move." The 100 lashes at the post might be spread over four days, with salt rubs between the four floggings. Before 50 lashes the back was "like a jelly," and the cat got clogged with blood. A dry one was substituted to cut more sharply. The soldiers had a name for the post to which they were tied: they called it "the Adjutant's Daughter." . . .

. . . One of Washington's arguments for raising the maximum number of lashes to 500 was that such authorized rigor would decrease the excesses of officers' arbitrary punishments. Most generals approved of calculated blows to correct stubborn men. However, some officers seemed to have succumbed simply to rage. At West Point one writer saw an officer and a subordinate beat a soldier bloody; "many officers gathering round, said *lay on*, and damning him that dare say otherways," until one officer stopped them. To this witness, beating a man who dared not resist was the sure sign of a coward. A few officers who inflicted especially cruel beatings were court-martialed. One who was found guilty of "a malevolence of temper scarcely to be equalled" got a severe reprimand. . . .

Courts-martial imposed many death sentences, but most condemned men were pardoned. Estimates of the number of executions in the Continental Army during the war range from forty to seventy-five. Mutiny, fighting for the enemy, and plundering were most likely to get a man hanged or shot. Washington and his generals used capital punishment as an example to discourage others from committing like crimes. Since Washington did not intend to execute all the men guilty of capital crimes, he tried to preserve the effect of the example. Soldiers were assembled for an execution; drummers marched the condemned man to the gallows or the firing squad; the adjutant read the sentence; the chaplain addressed the condemned man and the army; and when the blindfolded man was ready for execution, the general's pardon was read. In asking for a five-hundred-lash penalty, Washington complained that through overuse this charade had become ineffective. Hardly any evidence suggests that it ever had been effective, except to excite curiosity among most onlookers, sympathy among a few, and fainting or tears among the recipients of the commander's clemency. Several of the pardoned men were later hanged for new capital crimes. Executions followed some mutinies and, the generals believed, forestalled others by catching leaders, who were eliminated while the men returned to duty, glad to escape death. Hangings had little noticeable effect on desertion or plundering. Throughout the war, the Americans' use of capital punishment fluctuated between prolonged forbearance and abrupt severity. . . .

Neither corporal punishment nor capital punishment achieved the smooth system of interlocking wheels that Washington wanted for Continental Army discipline. Yet these punishments and the soldier's consent to serve were the main supports of the new Articles of War. The generals had complained to Congress that the first "Rules and Regulations" of 1775 were too weak, and Congress strengthened them in a new set of articles in August 1776. The new articles showed increased attention to the idiosyncrasies of American soldiers. The penalty clauses mentioned punishment by death more frequently than the old articles did, and increased the limit on flogging to one hundred lashes rather than thirty-nine. New sections tried to regulate sutlers, to stop fights, and to prevent or punish the new forms of graft that had appeared in the first year of war. Congress responded to the commanders' requests and tried to transform Americans into regular soldiers by bringing the government of the Continental Army closer to that of other armies. Congress was ready to experiment with firmer military law, but the "more severe and rigorous" articles that, according to President John Hancock, conveyed Congress's determination "to introduce obedience and regularity among the troops" could not change the independent minds of the soliders. . . .

By the end of the first year of hostilities, the Continental Army had begun to develop the character that it retained throughout the war. We see fewer signs of a whole populace marching against the invader and more calculated measures to raise a distinct body of soldiers; we hear less about ardent volunteers for regular army service and more about negotiations for pay, bounties, and conscription; we read less about young gentlemen who wanted to be privates and more about youths who wanted to become gentlemen; we find less hope for the soldiers' constant self-restraint and more fear of their casual violence. In the remaining years of the war, the army's survival, discipline, and patriotism helped to sustain the revolutionaries' perseverance. But in several troubling ways that army grew more like other armies than like the popular *rage militaire* of 1775. Some recurring elements of the soldiers' conduct violated the ideals that the Continental Army was supposed to promote. Before 1776 had ended, the war had permanently linked the achievement of American independence to this flawed military institution. Americans' reactions to both the victories and defeats of that year claimed to distinguish the revolutionary cause from the army on which it depended. At the same time, the public's response to battles and marches made that dependence ever clearer. Thus, the second year of war left the ideals of the revolution inextricably tied to the vicious as well as the virtuous elements of the Continental Army.

On July 15, 1779, Major John Stewart led an advance party following the forlorn hope in the assault on Stony Point. He often said that he did not want to live to be an old man, but Crazy Jack Stewart and Mad Anthony Wayne and the Light Infantry carried the fort and lived to hear their countrymen's praise. Congress voted Stewart a silver medal. It showed America, personified as an Indian queen, giving him a palm branch. In 1789 Thomas Jefferson brought the medal from France — too late for Stewart to receive it. In 1790 President Washington sent it to Stephen Stewart, saying that "it must afford some pleasing consolation when reflecting upon the loss of a worthy Son."

Two years before the action at Stony Point, Stewart had been taken prisoner by the enemy on August 22, 1777, while commanding a detachment covering the withdrawal from Staten Island following General John Sullivan's unsuccessful raid. Lieutenant William Wilmot said that Stewart "had never gave them an inch before he found that he had nothing left to keep them of[f] with." Placing a white handkerchief on the point of his sword, he walked forward to surrender, "as cool as if he had been going to shake hands with a friend." But Stewart did not long remain a prisoner. While confined aboard a prison ship, he "made his escape by descending silently to the water, and swimming to the New Jersey shore."

Already in 1776, when he was a lieutenant, Stewart had become known for "the most fashionably cut coat, the most *macaroni* cocked hat, and hottest blood in the union. . . ." He was six feet tall, well made, "handsome," and had "a fine presence for an Officer." Fifteen months after Stony Point, he almost got married. According to a friend, he "was damn'd nigh it. How he escaped I know not . . . her wedding Cloth[e]s are made, but . . . poor Kitty Crane, you must hug your sheets."

Stewart went south with the Maryland troops and made lieutenant colonel. He was well known and "much beloved" among officers of the southern army, who told "many extraordinary stories" of his bravado. Citizens who crossed him got arrested or beaten up or horse-whipped. He commanded the First Maryland Regiment at the liberation of Charleston in December 1782.

On Friday, March 21, 1783, a few weeks before the southern army was to disband, Stewart rode down a steep hill at a hard gallop in a stunt that looked certain to kill him and his horse. But he made it. Saturday evening, Colonel William Washington invited the officers to an entertainment near Sandy Hill, South Carolina. Stewart was riding there, on a level road, when his horse fell and threw him head first into a ditch, injuring his neck. Sunday morning Stewart died, at the age of twenty-five.

STUDY GUIDE

1. The conduct of war — like governmental institutions and class attitudes — may reflect the national characteristics of different societies. Some people, for example, believe there is a distinctive Prussian, English, or American way of making war. Do you see any peculiarly "American" traits in the attitudes of revolutionary soldiers?

2. The kinds of extraordinary disciplinary, recruiting, and desertion problems described by Royster are not usually associated with our army in World Wars I and II. Tell how the following factors might help to explain the apparent contrast: differences in governmental authority and organization, the backgrounds of the soldiers in the two periods, and developments in propaganda.

3. The Revolutionary War might also be compared to the Vietnam War. Some people today see the former as the embodiment of selfless sacrifice and patriotism, while viewing the widespread draft-dodging and dissent

during the Vietnam conflict as a national disgrace. How does Royster's article modify your view of these and other American wars?

4. What evidence do you see in modern America that our society has seriously modified its distrust of a standing army and militarism?

BIBLIOGRAPHY

Royster's book is a broad study of how the need to establish a regular army to fight the war conflicted with the revolutionary ideals of a citizen-soldiery and a virtuous republic. James K. Martin and Mark E. Lender, *A Respectable Army: The Military Origins of the Republic, 1763–1789* (1982) is one of several recent studies to argue that in this war, as in many later American wars, the fighting was done by the poor and unfortunate, rather than by the middle and upper classes. There are several books that give one an idea of the life of the average soldier, including C. K. Bolton, *The Common Soldier under Washington* (1902); Lynn Montross, *Rag, Tag, and Bobtail* (1952); Larry G. Bowman, *Captive Americans: Prisoners during the American Revolution* (1976); and Alfred H. Bill, *Valley Forge: The Making of an Army* (1952). E. Wayne Carp, *To Starve an Army at Pleasure: Continental Army Administration and American Political Culture, 1775–1783* (1984), complements some sections of Royster's book.

Military history used to be written as the story of battles and heroes. In recent years, historians have studied military history as it is related to the political, social, and economic life of a nation, and the way in which it may reflect the national character of a people. Walter Millis, *Arms and Men* (1956) covers most of American military history in this way, while Marcus Cunliffe, *Soldier and Civilians* (1968) deals with American thought from 1775 to 1865. Don Higginbotham, *The War of American Independence* (1971) is an excellent study of the Revolution that utilizes the perspective of the "new military history." If you enjoy studying history through biography, you might look at two books edited by George Billias that give sketches of the principal general officers in the Revolution: *George Washington's Generals* (1964) and *George Washington's Opponents* (1969). For some of the topics covered in your textbook and *The Social Fabric*, you should take a look at some primary sources, written by people who lived through the events of an earlier time. In *Private Yankee Doodle* (1962), George F. Scheer has edited the journal of Joseph Martin, a revolutionary soldier.

*"The Bostonians Paying the Excise-Man" by Philip Dawe, 1774,
shows the punishment of John Malcolm.*

6

WALLACE BROWN

Social War

One of the most elusive goals of the historian, and of the human mind in general, is objectivity. In our time, most historians recognize that, try as they may to avoid it, some prejudice and personal values are bound to creep into their thought and into the history they write. One illustration of this is in the difference in treatment that history accords to the winners and losers in any revolution. Rebels who fail don't get a very good press from historians, since their society is likely to denounce the revolutionary leaders as traitors or madmen. If the revolution succeeds, the same men may be celebrated as patriots and statesmen, while the ruling group that is overthrown is castigated as oppressive or corrupt.

Between 1765 and 1775, British colonial society developed some serious internal divisions and antagonisms. Upon the outbreak of war, provinces, towns, and families were split, and brother fought brother with all the hatred that civil war can engender. By 1783, as many as 80,000 people had been driven out of the colonies; farms and businesses of Loyalists were confiscated, and thousands of these British adherents were intimidated and mistreated. Many of them had been distinguished contributors to colonial society — governors, judges, ministers, farmers, craftsmen, and laborers. Had the British won the war, Thomas Hutchinson, Joseph Galloway, William Franklin, and Jonathan Boucher would today be as celebrated as are John Adams, Thomas Jefferson, Patrick Henry, and John Hancock.

One question worth pondering is what American society may have lost by the exile of the Loyalists and the victory of the Patriot cause. A substantial reservoir of political talent and experience certainly evaporated, but among the many who cast their lot for independence were an extraordinary number of men of talent to take the Loyalists' places. More difficult to judge is the loss to American thought and culture. A number of Loyalists were able or distinguished scientists, artists, writers, and religious leaders who made their contributions in Canada or Europe rather than here. More important than such individuals was the effect of the break upon American political and constitutional thought, which — it has been argued — suffered the loss of a valid conservative tradition with the exile of the Loyalists.

Another question that has interested historians since the Revolution began is just what a Tory or Loyalist was. The simplest definition is that he was one who remained loyal to England. This raises the question of why they were loyal, whereas immediate neighbors of similar background and position became revolutionary leaders. Many answers to this question have been offered — that it was one's religion that made the difference, or one's wealth, age, occupation, national origins, or temperament. Yet for all the Loyalists who were influenced by such factors, there were at least as many men of the same class who chose the Patriot side.

Wallace Brown, a contemporary student of these questions, has made use of statistical techniques to try to determine the percentage of Loyalists of different occupations, religions, and so forth. Since the statistical parts of his studies are based on fragmentary records, they have been criticized by some historians. However, his book *The Good Americans*, from which the following selection is taken, is a general study of Loyalism that is less dependent upon statistics than his earlier work. Chapter 5 of *The Good Americans* presents a vivid account of the suffering that Loyalists endured during the American War for Independence. If few groups have since been subjected to such direct violence, the persecution of the Loyalists nonetheless reminds one of the fate of many another unpopular minority in later American history. And it should make us cautious about accepting only a "winner's" view of historical losers.

In November, 1777, the Continental Congress recommended the confiscation of Loyalist estates, a suggestion already made by Thomas Paine, and in some places already acted upon. All states finally amerced, taxed, or confiscated much Loyalist property, and in addition New York and

Abridgement of pages 127–146 from *The Good Americans: Loyalists in the American Revolution* by Wallace Brown. Copyright 1969 by Wallace Brown. Reprinted by permission of the author.

South Carolina taxed Loyalist property in order to compensate robbery victims. Some towns simply raffled off Tory property. Patriot officers requisitioned horses and supplies from Loyalists rather than Whigs, and, of course, there was much old-fashioned looting, particularly of the property of exiles. . . .

Although the majority of active Loyalists suffered much loss of property, some attempted by various subterfuges to preserve their estates quite apart from having a wife or third party act as purchaser. One scheme was to make over one's property, or make a sham sale, to a sympathetic, moderate friend who had escaped suspicion.

Much commoner was the device used by exiles of leaving their wives or relatives behind in order to keep a foot in both camps. For example, Benjamin Pickman fled from Salem, Massachusetts, in 1775, but left his wife behind to look after their property, to which he returned ten years later. Some brothers may even have chosen opposite sides for such a reason. As the British claims commissioners commented on one split family, "it is possible that this may be a shabby family Compact . . . to preserve the property whether Great Britain or America prevailed."

The overall severity of the various laws against the Loyalists has been estimated as follows:

"Harshest" — New York, South Carolina.
"Harsh" — Massachusetts, New Jersey, Pennsylvania.
"Light" — Rhode Island, Connecticut, Virginia, North Carolina.
"Lightest" — New Hampshire, Delaware, Maryland, Georgia.

With some exceptions, notably Georgia, laws were harshest in states where Loyalists were most powerful, and as the war progressed, the purpose of the laws changed from conversion to "revenge and hate." Similarly, enforcement varied and was usually severest where danger was greatest and civil war bitterest.

A prominent Southern Tory reported that in Virginia, where the Loyalists were weak and little problem, the property of those who joined the British army went to their wives and children "on the Spot . . . as if the Father was dead," and he noted that his own wife "had never been molested but on the contrary treated with the utmost Kindness and Respect." Other Loyalists described being turned off their property with only the clothes on their backs.

But perhaps more typical was the fate of the Chandler family of Worcester, Massachusetts. Colonel John Chandler, a very prominent citizen of distinguished Massachusetts pedigree, dubbed "Tory John" and later in England the "Honest Refugee," fled from Boston with the British army to become a permanent, proscribed exile. For over two years his wife and family continued to enjoy their property undisturbed, until the Worcester Committee of Correspondence began a process that resulted in the confiscation of all but a third of their real and personal property, which third was reserved for Mrs. Chandler's use as long as she remained in the United States. Her husband did not return (he was forbidden to by an act of October, 1778), and on her death special legislation was needed to secure her property for her children.

A myriad of particularities could play a part in determining the extent of persecution. A well-liked or respected Tory (and there were a few such) might well escape, as might someone whose skills were especially valued, for example, a doctor. Influential but quiet Loyalists were more apt to avoid penalties than those of lower social standing or those more vociferous in their beliefs.

The zeal of the patriots could be extremely capricious and, as always with witch-hunts, frequently ridiculous and heavy-handed. One citizen was accosted for naming his dog "Tory," the implication being that a Tory was forced to lead a dog's life. In 1776 at Stratford, Connecticut, an Episcopal minister was brought before the local committee because he had officiated at a baptism where the child was named Thomas Gage. The committee viewed the action as a "designed insult" and censured the cleric. In the same state Zephaniah Beardslee reported that he was "very much abused" for naming his daughter Charlotte, after the queen. It may be noted that Beardslee, apparently a very serious Loyalist, had also been found drinking the king's health. The frequent persecution of Tories for this activity, however, is not as picayune as it seems, because toasts presuppose groups in taverns and the chance of Loyalist plots and associations. Thus, Abraham Cuyler held a gathering in Albany, New York, in June, 1776, that featured drinking and the singing of "God Save the King." At last the enraged Whig citizens crashed the party and carried the royal merrymakers off to jail. . . .

The results of Loyalism might simply be social ostracism — being sent to Coventry — as, for instance, happened to James Allen, who noted in his diary for February 17, 1777: "I never knew how painful it is to be secluded from the free conversation of one's friends"; and to George Watson, a mandamus councillor, when he entered a church at Plymouth, Massachusetts, and "a great number of the principal inhabitants left." Or it might mean serious loss of services, as when the blacksmiths of Worcester County, Massachusetts, refused to work for any Loyalists, their employees, or their dependents; or an economic boycott, as in Connecticut, where the local committee forbade "all Persons whatever viz. Merchants Mechanicks Millers and Butchers and Co. from supplying . . . John Sayre or Family with any manner of Thing whatever." Lawyers, teachers, doctors, apothecaries, and others often lost their customers and hence their livelihoods. Mathew Robinson, a Newport trader, from the first branded as "a Rank Torey," suffered several indignities, including the pulling down of his fences by a "multitude . . . under colour of laying out a Highway" and climaxing in 1781 when, after *"a New England Saint"* charged that Robinson "drank the King's Health, and damn'd the Congress and call'd them damn'd Rebels and Presbyterians," he was imprisoned by the rebels without examination, this being even "against their own Bill of Rights."

In many areas — for example, New York — the Loyalists were allowed to sell their property before departing, but such hurried, desperate sales were unlikely to net a fair price, and the result amounted to confiscation.

All wars and revolutions cause great mental strain and suffering, most of which goes unmeasured. The history of the Revolutionary era is liberally punctuated with stories of Loyalists who succumbed to melancholia, became mad, died, or committed suicide.

Alexander Harvey, a Charleston lawyer, wound up in a private English madhouse, having been "driven to Distraction" by his experiences as a Loyalist; George Miller, a North Carolina merchant whose fright had conquered his Loyalist principles, was thrown "into Convulsions" by the strain of serving in the American militia; Peter Harrison's death came after the shock of Lexington, and with it America lost its greatest colonial architect; several Loyalists, including the wife of William Franklin, simply died of "a Broken Heart"; the widow of Dr. Robert Gibbs of South Carolina recounted that the prospect of the loss of his property "so preyed upon his Spirits" that he died. Andrew Miller, of Halifax, North Carolina, was estranged from all his friends by his Loyalism, which literally killed him; others chose suicide — Millington Lockwood of Connecticut was wounded in the head, lost his reason, and drowned himself, while some years later, in London, after years of fruitless waiting for compensation, an unnamed, ruined Loyalist shot himself in despair, blaming an ungrateful country.

Although Americans at the time of the Revolution would clearly have found it odd, today one of the sharpest historical debates is over the question of how far the American Revolution was a *real* revolution. Even those historians who, noting the social dislocation, argue that the American Revolution was rather like the French Revolution stress the absence of the Terror. Mass executions there were not, a guillotine there was not, yet atrocities and terror there most certainly were. It is fitting that in the beginning the rebels "hoisted the Red Flag or Flag of Defence."

Leaving aside civil-war aspects such as the execution and maltreatment of prisoners and the burning of towns (by both sides: for example, the Americans fired Norfolk and Portsmouth; the British, Falmouth and Fairfield), we can cite a great range of fates that awaited the Loyalists; they were catalogued by "Papinian" as tarring and feathering, rail riding,

> . . . chaining men together by the dozens, and driving them, like herds of cattle, into distant provinces, flinging them into loathsome jails, confiscating their estates, shooting them in swamps and woods as suspected Tories,

hanging them after a mock trial; and all this because they would not abjure their rightful Sovereign, and bear arms against him.

Tarring and feathering (pine tar and goose feathers) became the classic Whig treatment of the Tories, and the British Government believed there was "no better proof of Loyalty" than suffering this punishment. A famous instance of it occurred in Boston on January 25, 1774, and is worth recounting in some detail.

At about eight o'clock in the evening a club-wielding mob milled along Cross Street. Their objective was John Malcolm, a distinguished but hot-tempered veteran of the French and Indian War, a native Bostonian, an ex-overseas merchant turned royal customs official, and a highly unpopular man for many reasons connected with both his personality (he was inordinately quarrelsome) and his job.

His recent arrival in Boston had been preceded by the unpopular news that in 1771 he had helped the governor of North Carolina against those reputedly Whiggish rebels known as the Regulators and that in October, 1773, he had officiously seized a brigantine at Falmouth (now Portland), Maine. Malcolm waited, ready and armed, behind barred doors. Undeterred, the mob raised ladders, broke an upstairs window, captured their prey, dragged him onto a sled, and pulled him along King Street to the Customs House, or Butcher's House, as it was popularly known, where the spectators gave three mighty cheers.

Although it was "one of the severest cold nights" of the winter, so cold that both Boston Harbor and even the very ink as it touched paper had frozen hard, the wretched man was put in a cart, stripped "to buff and breeches," and dealt the punishment of tarring and feathering, which American patriots were soon to convert into a major spectator sport. Malcolm, self-styled "Single Knight of the Tarr," as opposed to English Knights of the Garter, had already suffered the same indignity the year before for his conduct at Falmouth. He later claimed to be the first in America tarred for loyalty.

A contemporary description gives a good idea of how Malcolm and many others were treated:

> The following is the Recipe for an effectual Operation. "First strip a Person naked, then heat the Tar until it is thin, and pour it upon the naked Flesh, or rub it over with a Tar Brush, *quantum sufficit.* After which, sprinkle decently upon the Tar, whilst it is yet warm, as many Feathers as will stick to it. Then hold a lighted Candle to the Feathers, and try to set it all on Fire; if it will burn so much the better. But as the Experiment is often made in cold Weather; it will not then succeed — take also an Halter and put it round the Person's Neck, and then cart him the Rounds."

Malcolm, flogged and otherwise molested at intervals, was paraded around various crowded streets with his neck in a halter and was finally taken to the Liberty Tree, where he refused to resign his royal office or to curse Thomas Hutchinson, the hated governor of Massachusetts.

The crowd then set off for the gallows on Boston Neck. On the way Malcolm gasped an affirmative when one of his tormentors asked if he was thirsty and was given a bowl of strong tea and ordered to drink the king's health. Malcolm was next told to drink the queen's health; then two more quarts of tea were produced with the command to drink to the health of the Prince of Wales.

"Make haste, you have nine more healths to drink," shouted one of the mob.

"For God's sake, Gentlemen, be merciful, I'm ready to burst; if I drink a drop more, I shall die," Malcolm implored.

"Suppose you do, you die in a good cause, and it is as well to be drowned as hanged," was the reply.

The nine healths, beginning with the "Bishop of Osnabrug," were forced down the victim's throat. Malcolm "turned pale, shook his Head, and instantly filled the Bowl which he had just emptied."

"What, are you sick of the royal family?"

"No, my stomach nauseates the tea; it rises at it like poison."

"And yet you rascal, your whole fraternity at the Custom House would drench us with this poison, and we are to have our throats cut if it will not stay upon our stomachs."

At the gallows the noose was placed in position around Malcolm's neck and he was threatened with hanging, but he still refused to submit, whereupon he was "basted" with a rope for a while, and finally, on pain of losing his ears, he gave in and cursed the governor. The stubborn, brave man was further carted around the town, made to repeat various humiliating oaths, and finally deposited back at his home just before midnight, half frozen, an arm dislocated, and, as he said, "in a most mizerable setuation Deprived of his senses." Five days later, bedridden and "terribly bruised," he dictated a complaint to Governor Hutchinson, which his injuries obliged him to sign with an X.

The frost and tar caused an infection that made his skin peel extensively. However, he was careful to preserve a piece of skin with the tar and feathers still adhering (the stuff was the very devil to get off), which he carried to England as proof of his sufferings when, somewhat recovered, he set sail on May 2, 1774, to try to gain compensation for his loyalty.

Another Tory punishment that became traditional was the gruesome riding on a rail that sometimes followed tarring and feathering, but was severe enough in itself. It consisted of jogging the victim roughly along on "a sharp rail" between his legs. The painful effect of these "grand Toory Rides," as a contemporary called them, can readily be imagined. Seth Seely, a Connecticut farmer, was brought before the local committee in 1776 and for signing a declaration to support the king's laws was "put on a Rail carried on mens Shoulders thro the Streets, then put into the Stocks and besmeared with Eggs and was robbed of money for the Entertainment of the Company."

Persecution of the Loyalists came in many forms. In 1778 prisoners in Vermont were made to tread a road through the snow in the Green Mountains. The wife of Edward Brinley was pregnant and waiting out her confinement at Roxbury, Massachusetts, accompanied by "a guard of Rebels always in her room, who treated her with great rudeness and indecency, exposing her to the view of their banditti, as a sight 'See a tory woman' and striped her and her Children of all their Linens and Cloths." Peter Guire, of Connecticut, was branded on the forehead with the letters *G. R.* (George Rex). Samuel Jarvis, also of Connecticut, related that the following treatment made his whole family very ill:

> That your Memorialist for his Attachment to constitutional Government was taken with his Wife and Famely, consisting of three Daughters and one little Son by a Mob of daring and unfeeling Rebels from his Dwelling House in the dead of Night Striped of everything, put on board Whale Boats and Landed on Long Island in the Month of August last about 2 oClock in the Morning Oblieging them to wade almost to their Middles in the Water.

Probably the best-known mobbing in Philadelphia was that of Dr. John Kearsley, whose widow finally submitted a claim to the commissioners. Kearsley, a leading physician, pill manufacturer, and horse dealer, was a pugnacious American with strong Loyalist views. He was seized by a mob in September, 1775, and had his hand bayoneted; then he was carried through the streets to the tune of "Rogue's March." Sabine reports that he took off his wig with his injured hand and, "swinging it around his head, huzzaed louder and longer than his persecutors." This display of spirit notwithstanding, he nearly died following this treatment, according to his widow. His house was later ransacked, he was arrested, and he finally died in jail.

Atrocious punishments of Loyalists were sometimes carried out by local authorities in semilegal fashion — it was noted that the tarring and feathering of a New York victim in 1775 "was conducted with that regularity and decorum that ought to be observed in all publick punishments." But just as often mobs, drumhead courts, and all the horrors of vigilante policing were found. Indeed it is possible that the term "lynch law" derives from Charles Lynch, a Bedford County, Virginia, justice of the peace who became renowned for his drastic, cruel action against neighboring Tories.

The number of Loyalists subjected to cruel, often extra-legal, punishments can only be estimated, and likewise the number of those murdered or executed "legally" will never be known, but no one familiar with the sources — Whig newspapers are full of accounts of executions — can doubt that it is substantial, although the statement by a New York Loyalist that the rebels "made a practice of hanging people up on a slight pretence" is no doubt an exaggeration. Probably only fear of reprisals kept numbers from being much larger than they were. The carrying out of the supreme penalty was usually reserved for some overt aid to the British such as spying, piloting ships, guiding troops to the attack, recruiting, counterfeiting.

One of the most notorious executions of a Loyalist was that of John Roberts, a native-born Pennsylvania Quaker, who had aided the British occupying forces in Philadelphia and rather foolhardily had not departed with them. His trial was in 1778, and even many Whigs petitioned the authorities for a pardon, but in vain. A contemporary described the situation thus:

> Roberts' wife, with ten children, went to Congress, threw themselves on their knees and supplicated mercy, but in vain. His behaviour at the gallows did honor to human nature. He told his audience that his conscience acquitted him of guilt; that he suffered for doing his duty to his Sovereign; that his blood would one day be demanded at their hands; and then turning to his children, charged and exhorted them to remember his principles, for which he died, and to adhere to them while they had breath. This is the substance of his speech; after which he suffered with the resolution of a Roman.

In 1792 the state of Pennsylvania restored Roberts' confiscated estate to his widow, Jane, a belated act of justice, for it seems Roberts had been a scapegoat, only one among so very many who had cooperated with the British. Roberts' behavior would doubtless have made him a remembered hero had he suffered for the other side. Similarly, in Connecticut, Moses Dunbar was tried and hanged for accepting a British commission and recruiting troops at about the same time that Nathan Hale suffered the same penalty. Connecticut honors Hale but forgets Dunbar. One of the more bizarre executions was reported by the *Boston Gazette* for November 3, 1777, under the date line Fishkill: "Last Thursday, one Taylor, a spy was hanged at Hurley, who was detected with a letter to Burgoyne, which he had swallowed in a silver ball, but by the assistance of a tartar emetic he discharged the same."

But perhaps more moving across the years than accounts of atrocities are the more pedestrian misfortunes of war. Women in particular are always the great sufferers, being separated from their husbands and sons, living in constant dread of bereavement. In 1780 Mary Donnelly petitioned the British authorities in New York for relief. Her husband had been serving on board a privateer when "about seven months ago as my youngest Child lay expireing in my Arms an account came of the Vessil being lost in a Storm." Mrs. Donnelly was now destitute, "frequently being affraid to open my Eyes on the Daylight least I should hear my infant cry for Bread and not have it in my power to relieve him. The first meal I had eat for three days at one time was a morsel of dry bread and a lump of ice."

On June 6, 1783, Phebe Ward, of East Chester, wrote to her husband Edmund, a native of the province of New York:

Kind Husband   .

I am sorry to acquaint you that our farme is sold. . . .

thay said if I did not quitt posesion that thay had aright to take any thing on the farme or in the house to pay the Cost of a law sute and imprisen me I have sufered most Every thing but death it self in your long absens pray Grant me spedy Releaf or God only knows what will be com of me and my frendsles Children

thay say my posesion was nothing youre husband has forfeted his estate by Joining the British Enemy with a free and vollentary will and thereby was forfeted to the Stat and sold

All at present from your cind and Loveing Wife

phebe Ward
pray send me spedeay anser.

One of the most pathetic stories of all concerns Filer Dibblee, a native-born lawyer, and his family. In August, 1776, they fled from Stamford to Long Island, but a few months later the rebels turned Dibblee's wife and five children "naked into the Streets," having stolen the very clothes from their backs as well as having plundered the house. The family fled to New York City, where Dibblee obtained sufficient credit to settle at Oyster Bay, Long Island, but in 1778 the rebels plundered the family a second time and carried Dibblee as prisoner to Connecticut, where he remained imprisoned six months until exchanged. With further credit the family established themselves at Westhills, Long Island, where they were "plundered and stripped" a third time; then came a move to Hempstead, Long Island, and in 1780 a fourth ravaging. Dibblee now, for the first time, applied for relief from the commander in chief and received about one hundred dollars. In 1783 the whole family moved to St. John, New Brunswick, where they managed to survive a rough winter in a log cabin, but Dibblee's "fortitude gave way" at the prospect of imprisonment for his considerable indebtedness and the fate his family would suffer as a consequence. The result was that he "grew Melancholy, which soon deprived him of his Reason, and for months could not be left by himself," and finally in March, 1784, "whilst the Famely were at Tea, Mr. Dibblee walked back and forth in the Room, seemingly much composed: but unobserved he took a Razor from the Closet, threw himself on the bed, drew the Curtains, and cut his own throat."

Shortly afterward the Dibblee house was accidentally burned to the ground, was then rebuilt by the heroic widow, only to be accidentally razed again the same year by an Indian servant girl.

It is not surprising that imprisonment and escape loom large in Loyalist annals. The most celebrated prison was in Connecticut at the Simsbury (now East Granby) copper mines, where the ruins still afford a dramatic prospect. The isolated and strongly Whig back country of Connecticut was considered a good spot to incarcerate important Loyalists from all over the Northern colonies, and the mines, converted into a prison in 1773, were ideal. The "Catacomb of Loyalty," to quote Thomas Anburey, or the "woeful mansion," to quote an inmate, contained cells forty yards below the surface, into which "the prisoners are let down by a windlass into the dismal cavern, through a hole, which answers the purpose of conveying their food and air, as to light, it scarcely reaches them." The mere threat of the "Mines" could make a Loyalist conform. One prisoner regarded being sent there as a "Shocking Sentence (Worse than Death)." The mines received such celebrated Loyalists as Mayor Mathews of New York and William Franklin, who wrote of his "long and horrible confinement" and was described on his release as "considerably reduced in Flesh."

In May, 1781, there was a mass breakout. The leaders of the escape, Ebenezer Hathaway and Thomas Smith, arrived in New York some weeks later, and their alleged experiences were reported by Rivington's newspaper. Hathaway and Smith recalled that they had originally been captured on a privateer, sentenced, and marched the seventy-four miles from Hartford to Simsbury. The entrance to the dungeon was a heavily barred trap door that had to be raised

> by means of a tackle, whilst the hinges grated as they turned upon their hooks, and opened the jaws and mouths of what they call Hell, into which they descended by means of a ladder about six feet more, which led to a large iron grate or hatchway, locked down over a shaft about three feet diameter, sunk through the solid rock.... They bid adieu to this world,

and went down thirty-eight feet more by ladder "when they came to what is called the landing; then marching shelf by shelf, till descending about thirty or forty feet more they came to a platform of boards laid under foot, with a few more put over head to carry off the water, which keeps continually dropping." There they lived for twenty nights with the other prisoners, using "pots of charcoal to dispel the foul air" through a ventilation hole bored from the surface until the opportunity to escape came when they were allowed up into the kitchen to prepare food and rushed and captured the guards.

Some colorful Connecticut escapes in other places are also recorded. Nathan Barnum avoided appearing for trial in 1780 by inoculating himself with smallpox, whereupon he was "sent to the Hospital, where he was chained to the Floor to prevent his Escape, he found Means to bribe one of the Nurses, who not only brought him a File to cut off his Irons, but amused the Centinal, placed over him while he effected it. . . ."

Samuel Jarvis and his brother got out of prison "by the assistance of Friends who had privately procured some Women's apparel which they Dressed themselves in, and by that means made their escape through the Rebel Army." James Robertson asserted that while he was in jail at Albany, the British attacked and set the building on fire, whereupon, unable to walk, he managed to crawl into a bed of cabbages "and chewing them to prevent being suffocated" was found three days later badly burnt.

There was even a series of Tory hiding places between New York and Canada, rather in the fashion of the "Underground Railroad" of the pre–Civil War days.

The treatment of imprisoned Loyalists ranged over the widest possible spectrum. Simsbury was notoriously the worst prison, almost the Andersonville of the time. Many Loyalists suffered close confinement in much pleasanter conditions; others merely underwent houuse arrest; others were only prevented from traveling; some were on parole and, if banished to some remote part of America, were boarded with reluctant Whigs. Some worked in the normal way by day and simply spent the night in jail. In 1776 Thomas Vernon, a fanatically early riser, was removed, with three other prominent Rhode Island Loyalists, from Newport to Glocester, in the northern part of the state, because he had refused the test oath. The foursome's journey and their few months' stay in Glocester were pleasant and gentlemanly, almost Pickwickian. The friends walked and admired the countryside, ate, drank, and conversed well in the local inn where they lived; they planted beans, killed snakes, trapped squirrels, fished, played Quadrille (a card game); they were very well treated by the ladies of the house and by neighboring females. Their chief complaints were the lack of books, some local abhorrence of Tories, particularly by the men (their landlord said "the town was very uneasy" at their being there), a few fleas, tedium from the lack of friends and family, and some stealing of their food by their far from genial host. . . .

The Whigs suffered as the Tories did — legal persecution, mob action, imprisonment (the British prison ships were particularly horrible and gave rise to effective propagandist literature), and all the excesses of civil war. Adrian C. Leiby, the historian of the Hackensack Valley, for example, reports that there was barely a Whig family there that had not lost someone to a Tory raiding party. There is at least one recorded tarring and feathering of a Whig by British troops — of one Thomas Ditson, Jr., in Boston in March, 1775. In June, 1779, the *Virginia Gazette* reported the murder of a Whig captain by a party of Tories whom he had discovered robbing his house. A sentinel wounded him with a gunshot; then, after taking all the horses from the stables, the Tories pursued the captain into the house, where he was lying on a bed, and

> immediately thrust their bayonets into his body several times, continuing the barbarity while they heard a groan; and lest life might still be remaining in him, they cut both his arms with a knife in the most inhuman manner. The villain who shot him, had been his neighbour and companion from his youth.

The victim lived another two days.

STUDY GUIDE

1. Be prepared to discuss the following quotation from Sir John Harrington, who lived two centuries before the American Revolution:

   Treason doth never prosper; what's the reason?
   Why, if it prosper, none dare call it treason.

   Evaluate Harrington's epigram with respect to Loyalists and Patriots in the War for Independence; and second, explain why the favorable historical reputation of the losing Civil War general Robert E. Lee is an exception to Harrington's view.

2. Summarize the various devices used to punish the Loyalists — both in their persons and in their property. What was the relation between official policy by state governments and actual treatment of Loyalists by neighbors and townsfolk?

3. Does the picture presented in this chapter modify your view of the American Patriots? If so, how?

4. Is there any evidence here that would support the view that the Revolution was a civil war between different groups of colonials, as well as a war for independence from England?

BIBLIOGRAPHY

As suggested in the introduction to this selection, the Loyalists have not received very sympathetic treatment from American historians. Even more important than this is that they have generally been ignored. It was not until 1974, for example, that an extended biography of the distinguished Massachusetts Loyalist Thomas Hutchinson was finally published. Aside from the works of a few early scholars such as Claude Van Tyne, the serious study of Loyalism is a very recent phenomenon. A growing number of historians in the last two decades have devoted their attention to these forgotten Americans, most notably William H. Nelson, in *The American Tory* (1961); Wallace Brown, in *The King's Friends: The Composition and Motives of the American Loyalist Claimants* (1966); Paul H. Smith, who describes the military involvement of the Loyalists in *Loyalists and Redcoats: A Study in British Revolutionary Policy* (1964); and Mary B. Norton, in *The British-Americans: The Loyalist Exiles in England, 1774–1789* (1972). An earlier work that attempts to identify the character of the Tory mind and psychology is Leonard W. Labaree, *Conservatism in Early American History* (1948). This older work should be supplemented with Janice Potter, *The Liberty We Seek: Loyalist Ideology in Colonial New York and Massachusetts* (1983).

Anyone who is interested in the antagonisms in British colonial society can find a comprehensive survey in Elisha P. Douglass, *Rebels and Democrats: The Struggle for Equal Political Rights and Majority Rule during the American Revolution* (1955). Since 1950, however, many historians have argued that this was simply a war for independence, rather than an internal social revolution, and have suggested that eighteenth-century colonial society was characterized by broad consensus rather than conflict. This view has been argued in studies of individual colonies, in studies of revolutionary ideology, and in studies of the consequences of the Revolution. For some years the views of Edmund S. Morgan, Daniel Boorstin, Robert E. Brown, and other scholars were so widely accepted that a general consensus as to the conservative nature of the American Revolution seemed in the offing. More recently, this view has been challenged by a group of younger historians, frequently identified as the "New Left." In a series of articles, Jesse Lemisch and Staughton Lynd, among others, have argued that conflict did in fact exist in the revolutionary period, and that the laboring men of urban areas were as important as farmers in the uprising.

The views concerning the causes and character of the American Revolution are so varied and the important books so numerous that they cannot be mentioned here. The bibliographies of most textbooks will refer you to the more important studies, or you can find a good bibliography with selections from various historical writings, in George A. Billias, ed., *The American Revolution: How Revolutionary Was It?* (3rd ed., 1980).

"Sing-Sing Camp Meeting" by Joseph B. Smith, 1838 (Detail). One of the faithful is "treeing the devil."

7

EVERETT DICK

Religious Democracy

Religious organizations, like most institutions, reflect the social forces of their particular society and time. Even such a world-wide organization as the Roman Catholic Church has differed in doctrine and rites of worship in different countries, and most churches that survive a century or more undergo subtle changes. American Protestantism has been substantially transformed since it was first brought to these shores, and few of the changes have been so profound as those that came about in the first half of the nineteenth century.

Both New England Calvinism and the pietistic religions of Pennsylvania were brought to the colonies by small, tightly knit groups of devout believers. But the churches soon faced the question of whether or not to modify their doctrines and soften their requirements in order to retain the membership of later generations who held the beliefs less intensely and found the worship less satisfying. By the early 1700s, many people felt that the churches had compromised too much, and they responded enthusiastically to the first "Great Awakening," a religious revival movement that attracted many followers in the 1730s. The second major revival movement, which began about 1800, had its roots in a society that seemed to be increasingly secular and among a people who found a highly rational religion emotionally barren. Yet the remarkable religious awakening that swept across the country at the beginning of the nineteenth century was quite different from the earlier revival and had a much longer-range impact upon American Protestantism.

Theologically, one of the characteristics of the Second Great Awakening was the new emphasis upon Jesus, rather than upon God the Father or the remote Creator of the Deists, an emphasis that has dominated Protestant thought and worship ever since. Preaching the salvation of all men, Protestant churches in the early nineteenth century outgrew the boundaries of a single colony or state and developed broad, national denominations. Between 1800 and 1850, Protestantism also assumed a new sense of mission and destiny, as did the American secular philosophy of the period. Bible, tract, and missionary societies were formed to carry the Word to the unsettled West, and each denomination established a multitude of colleges to provide a Christian education for the young.

Many of these developments took place after the most emotional revivalism had subsided. Yet the whole first half of the century witnessed a strong element of religious emotionalism and democratization, as evidenced in the founding of several new faiths. Spiritualism, Mormonism, and Adventism all had distinctive appeals, but like the revival itself, they succeeded because they found a people who were receptive to an emotional religious experience. Evidence of the revival was seen in the eastern states even before 1800, but the frenzy took its most distinctive form in the frontier communities farther west. In the following selection, Everett Dick discusses religion on the American frontier.

Various causes operated to promote an unreligious atmosphere on the frontier. Often the less pious moved west. The lack of women had a tendency to remove the steadying influence normally present. Very rude surroundings, with an intense struggle for existence, tended to promote ungodliness.

Contemporary writers in early Kentucky noted with amazement the lack of piety in the country. A most liberal estimate of the number of church members in 1792 still left two thirds of the population outside the fold of the church.

In some instances in Alabama preachers were driven off. There is a tradition that at St. Stephens a Baptist minister was rowed across the river and told that if he ever returned he would be tarred and feathered. A minister by the name of Sturdevant labored a year without organizing a "society" or enrolling a member.

Timothy Flint complained that in Arkansas in 1819 part of the audience listened for a time to his sermon and then returned to the billiard room. . . .

From *The Dixie Frontier: A Social History of the Southern Frontier*, by Everett Dick. Copyright 1948 by Everett Dick. Reprinted by permission of Alfred A. Knopf, Inc.

The Baptists were the pioneers in religion in Kentucky and the most numerous body of Christians in the early settlement of the state. The first Methodist conference west of the Alleghenies was established by Bishop Asbury in the state of Franklin (now eastern Tennessee). He wrote of the work in Kentucky that "the Methodists do but little here, others lead the way." Despite slow growth in early years the Methodists became the leading denomination throughout the southern and southwestern frontiers. The Baptist church was next in size and influence.

. . . Under the leadership of Samuel Doak, the Presbyterians early possessed the field in eastern Tennessee. Educated at Princeton, he walked through Maryland and Virginia, driving before him a "flea-bitten gray horse loaded with a sack full of books." The Presbyterian belief was rigid, formal, and austere. The doctrine of predestination was not so popular on the frontier as the free-will doctrine of the Baptists and Methodists. As a result of the revival of 1800, however, a free-will branch of the Presbyterians, known as the New Lights, grew up.

When there were enough people in a neighborhood to support a church, all hands turned out and raised the walls for a meeting house. These churches were log cabins without floors and in the lower South were without any heating apparatus. Of these churches John Poage Campbell said:

> Numbers of them were open to everything and more like hog pens and stables, than places where men can worship God. . . . A pane of glass to let in the light and keep out the wind and rain is scarcely seen, a pew or decent seat about as rare. . . .

Preaching appointments were happy occasions. The people lived far apart, and there was preaching only as often as the itinerant came to the neighborhood, which usually was only once a month. It was a day of social communion as well as spiritual uplift. When the minister arrived he saw the fence and the yard around the building crowded with men, women, and children. Numerous guns leaned against the log cabin, with strings of squirrels, a few opossums, and numbers of partridges. In Indian days every man took his place on a bench wearing his shot-pouch, tomahawk, and scalping knife, and with his gun in his hand. Most of the congregation had on neither shoes nor stockings and were clad in apparel that was unlike that worn in more civilized areas. Every man brought his dogs. In that period an average congregation would consist of perhaps fifteen families. Each couple had an average of five children, two of whom were infants and a third was too small to keep quiet during services. It would be conservative to estimate five dogs to a family. As one minister facetiously remarked, there were in a congregation "forty-five babies and seventy-five dogs, with only sixty adults to police the mob." The preacher had his hands full to compete with quarreling dogs without and squalling children within.

There was much handshaking in the yard before meeting and much visiting there afterward. To smoke in church was not considered impious or out of order. On a hot summer day a new minister noticed a boy on his way to church swinging a firebrand to keep it burning. He was at a loss to know why fire was needed in summer. When he arrived in the yard after caring for his horses, he found the fire had been placed in a large stump and was burning freely. Old and young took out their pipes and, drawing from their roomy pockets home-cured tobacco, lighted their pipes at the stump and sat down to enjoy a smoke and visit before going in to the service. During the sermon he noticed a woman but a few feet in front of him nudge the one next to her, who nudged the one next to her, and the nudge was carried on down the bench. During this time every eye was fixed on the speaker. Soon the signal was repeated. Then all rose from the bench with almost military precision, quietly moved to the burning stump, lighted their pipes, and sat on the ground near by, smoking. During all this time they paid perfect attention, apparently never missing a word.

The people were fixed in their ideas of worship, anxious that the program be carried out in the old way, and informal and democratic enough to speak out if the minister forgot anything. When a new minister attempted to dismiss a service, a brother rose and in a loud voice drawled: "Ain't you goin' to give out no app'intment for the nixt round?" "Yes, brother," replied the preacher, "my colleague will be here in four weeks." Another brother called: "Give out the class meetin' for nixt Sunday." "At what hour?" "Three o'clock," was the reply. The minister then announced: "Let us be dismissed!" "Not yet! Not yet," implored a man with a red bandanna over his head. All was silence. "Ain't you goin' to give out prayer meetin' for next Thursday night?" "Yes; there will be prayer meeting in this house next Thursday evening." Someone offered: "Not in this house, brother; it will be at Brother M.'s, in the lower end of town." Finally the congregation was dismissed.

When the itinerant did not arrive at the announced time, the crowd would patiently await his coming for hours. John Mason Peck got lost while on his way to an appointment in 1818. He arrived at the clearing just at sunset and found more than twenty people who had waited since noon to hear the strange preacher. Often at church service business announcements, notices of lost stock, and other secular matters were "given out."

Although there were the beginnings of class distinction in social life, religion was one common plane upon which all classes met. The plantation-owners, their slaves, and "poor white trash" all worshipped together. The names of the slaves appear on the same church records as those of their masters and they were baptized together. As time passed, however, there was a tendency to hold a morning meeting for the whites and an afternoon session for the servants, although this was not a clear-cut rule. Negroes were often allowed to attend the morning sermon. In some instances a colored minister even preached to mixed congregations. Many Negro preachers could not read, of course, and it was necessary for them to get someone in the big house to read the Bible to them until a text was struck that suited them. Then they memorized it and other Scripture, and by means of homely but often apt illustrations they built up their sermon. . . .

At the conclusion of the service the Negroes could not separate without the breaking exercises, so called from breaking up the meeting. One who attended such an exercise said they sang the grandest, wildest, most beautiful African music he had ever heard. They began to sing and move in a procession by the pulpit, shaking hands with the minister as they passed. As the long column filed by, faces shone with delight as the music rose wilder and more exciting. Finally the handshaking ended, the meeting "broke," and the service was over.

The duties of church membership were taken seriously. If a man did not live up to his profession he was summoned to answer for his conduct. The Baptists held a monthly business meeting and the Methodists held one quarterly on Saturday. On these occasions the private lives of the members came up for review. Those whose conduct was deserving received a ticket admitting them to the communion the next day, and the black sheep were disciplined. These tickets were taken up by a sentinel at the door. . . .

The rules adopted by the Buffalo Lick Baptist Church of Kentucky provided for a moderator and efficient sensible rules of order covering all conceivable cases. Church trials were held regularly at these meetings. Witnesses were summoned and sworn in, they gave their testimony, and judgment was rendered by a vote of the church. Sometimes the offenses were church cases and warranted discipline by the church. Some, however, were of the nature of lawsuits or trials between individuals and were settled without cost or fees. Some of the cases that came before the Cooper Run Baptist Church in Bourbon County, Kentucky, for discipline were: neglecting to attend worship, chastising a slave too severely, playing the fiddle for dancing, horse-racing, telling a lie, committing adultery, forging the father-in-law's name on a marriage permit in order to get the girl, permitting gambling in one's house. The women were disciplined for slander, tale-bearing, whispering, and quarreling; one married woman was hailed before the brethren for "unjustifiable familiarity with a young man in permitting him to kiss her three times." At the Bent Creek Church, Lucy Clark was excluded for adulterating beeswax with tallow. James Carter was suspended for not settling a personal debt where he came from.

The churches apparently regarded dancing as a sin and sufficient cause for excommunication, while placing their endorsement on distilling whisky.

In 1795 a Kentucky church minute book recorded the fact that a certain woman was summoned to answer before the church for her disrespectful remarks about the distilling business. At the second meeting thereafter the same woman was excluded from membership for permitting dancing in her home.

Sectarianism arose after the Great Revival, and members were disciplined for hospitality to ministers of other churches. On a Mercer County, Kentucky, church minute book appear charges against a brother "for having Barton Stone preach his wife's funeral within the bounds of the church." His plea was that it was done at his wife's dying request, but would a like occasion arise again, he would be more circumspect.

Ministers, the Methodists in particular, were against the wearing of jewelry, ornaments, and fine apparel, which were considered an indication of pride. The Reverend Silas Drake pronounced earrings the devil's stirrups. One day at a meeting he saw a woman with large brown bows of ribbon on her hat and reproved her publicly, charging that her bows were of absolutely no use. She countered by charging that the buttons on his sleeves and the back of his coat were just as useless. He immediately pulled off his coat, cut off the buttons, and never wore them again.

The question whether a master could whip a black brother instead of taking the gospel steps was raised in one church and settled in favor of whipping. The marital status of slaves who had been married and separated from their spouses by sale and then married again came up at the Tick Creek Church in Kentucky. It was voted that the slave brethren were not guilty of adultery, but the masters were out of order in separating husbands and wives.

The Buffalo Lick Church, in Kentucky, voted to treat slaves the same as any other brother in the church in settling differences; that is, masters should settle a grievance with them as they would with a free brother.

Since drinking was almost as common as eating, it is not surprising that nearly all good church people drank. One never thought of entertaining without liquor in some form. A minister reported a conversation between two prominent church members who had been to market to lay in supplies for the annual revival. One asked the other: "How much 'sperits' did you git?" "Ten gallons," his brother replied. The other retorted: "Jest sech stinginess as that will spile the meetin' and kill the church. I got twenty gallons myself an' you are jest as able to support the gospil as I am, if you wuzn't so dog stingy." Ministers regularly took their morning eye-opener and their nightcap in the evening. Some even made whisky or trafficked in it.

By 1825 a consciousness of the evils of liquor began to arise. The Methodist church was the outstanding denomination in its advocacy of temperance and teetotal abstinence. In other churches the discussion over the use of liquor grew so heated that it was a red-hot issue for years, causing wrangling and ill feeling. St. Paul's admonition to Timothy to take a little wine for his stomach's sake was a tower of strength to those who liked their toddy. Disputes over one thing and another grew so spirited that churches were split. . . .

Worship was extremely informal. Loud shouts of "Hallelujah!" "Amen!" "Glory!" and other exclamations of praise and joy in Christ arose spontaneously. At a "love feast" of the Cumberland Presbyterians, a minister present said the procedure was for a man to rise, give his testimony, and then start out shaking hands with everyone in the church, continuing his remarks and ejaculations. A sister would rise, speak of the love of God, and then start out to embrace the other sisters. Before long almost the entire church was shaking hands and embracing, keeping time in their movements with a wild Western melody they were singing. Handshaking or kissing was very cordial when someone was converted, or "came through," as they called it.

. . . [A] "call to preach" was thought to exceed, by far, any preparation that might be made in the matter of education. There was a prejudice even against preparation for a particular sermon. A parishioner in visiting with a circuit rider remarked that since the minister had only one appointment a day and two on Sunday, he would have plenty of time to visit the homes of the people, and that if he did not "the sisters would be down on him." "But," replied the young minister, "I must have some time for rest and study." "As to study," replied the good brother, "I don't believe in it any way. It's no use; just get up, and look to God, and fire away."

A representative of the American Bible Society said that the deeper he got into the brush and the denser the ignorance of the people, the greater was the number of preachers. Some of them could not read at all and many mispronounced a large number of the longer words. An Indian man said that one of these inspired clergy, standing before the congregation, would recite this homiletic creed:

> Yes, bless the Lord, I am a poor, humble man — and I doesn't know a single letter in the A B C's, and couldn't read a chapter in the Bible no how you could fix it, bless the Lord! — I jist preach like old Peter and Poll, by the Sperit. Yes, we don't ax pay in cash nor trade nither for the Gospel, and arn't no hirelins like them high-flow'd college-larned sheepskins — but as the Lord freely give us, we freely give our fellow critturs. . . .

The mispronunciation of words and ignorance of their meaning often led the backwoods preacher into the most fantastic interpretations. One word, wrongly interpreted, often served as material for a whole sermon. One pious minister took for his text: "Wherefore, gird up the loins of your mind. . . ." He confused the word "loins" for "lines" and dwelt at length on the different kinds of lines: lines by which carpenters carried on their work, lines to divide land, stage lines for travelers, and lines with which to drive horses. In all these uses of the word he unfolded a deep mystery, to the delight of his hearers.

A preacher was explaining the reference in Ecclesiastes xii, 6: "Or ever the silver cord be loosed. . . ."

> "The doctors say that there is a cord that runs from the nape of the neck, down the backbone, through the small of the back, into the heart, right thar; and that when a man dies that cord always snaps: That is the silver cord loosed."
>
> "Ah," said a sister, her face radiant with delight, "Brother P —— has studied *that*."

The delivery of a written sermon was little short of a disgrace. Old Peter Cartwright said that "it made him think of a gosling that had got the straddles by wading in the dew." Some of the ministers of the Disciples of Christ were alarmed because they felt their brethren studied the Bible too much. One of these Bible students on his way to meeting was joined by one of the fearful, who told him he hated to see him take the Bible to church. When asked why, he said he was afraid someone would think he was going to preach from it.

Strong lungs, vigorous gestures, copious tears, a ready flow of language, and an ability to describe in picturesque language the horrors of a literal, eternal, burning hell and the joys and bliss of a home in the Heavenly Canaan were the chief stores of ordnance in the backwoods minister's arsenal. And yet his message was powerful. He spoke in the common language of the people and seasoned it with illustrations familiar to all. . . .

When Bishop Asbury traveled to Kentucky, the old general got a taste of the lot of the rank and file of his army. He wrote in his journal that among other trials he had "taken the itch; and considering the filthy houses and filthy beds . . . it is perhaps strange I have not caught it twenty times." Later he wrote: "Oh, the rocks, hills, ruts and stumps! My bones, my bones!"

The route of the itinerant was often through uninhabited country and he spread his blanket on the moss at the foot of a tree, arranged his saddle for a pillow, and slept beneath the stars. At four he was stirring. First he knelt in prayer, then rubbed down his horse. As soon as it was light enough, he took the Bible from his saddlebags and studied it before starting. By noon perhaps he reached his appointment.

Sometimes an Indian arrow or tomahawk laid low the man of God. In 1794 on the road from Kentucky to Tennessee two Baptist ministers were ambushed by the Indians and killed while traveling with a group.

Singular as were these "brush preachers," they did not quail at the duty of thundering out against sin in its various forms. They blasted dueling, drunkenness, dishonesty, immorality, and worldiness in general. Their lives of sacrifice bore fruit in the experiences of their congregations, who appreciated their labors.

The Great Revival of 1800 and its attendant institution, the camp-meeting, were pure products of the frontier of the Old Southwest. Although accounts vary, camp-meetings seem to have been started two or three years previously in various places in a small way. In the summer of 1800 in the Cumberland country of southwestern Kentucky they appeared in full bloom.

At the sacramental solemnities of a Presbyterian church on the circuit of the Reverend James M'Gready, two brothers named John and William McGee, one a Methodist and the other a Presbyterian minister, were in attendance. The two brothers preached, and such a stirring experience followed that when the time came for the next meeting the ministers appointed to preach were unable to do so. There were cries and sobs all over the house and excitement indescribable. The inhabitants round about, on hearing of the stirring times, flocked in in such numbers that the church house was unable to accommodate the crowd. The people were so anxious about their salvation that these woodsmen soon cleared out the underbrush, felled the pine trees for pews, improvised a platform of poles, and erected an altar in the forest. After enjoying the spiritual refreshing, the people did not want to go home, and while some went foraging for provisions, others began the erection of temporary abodes made of poles and boughs. Such bedding as had been brought was used to improvise tents. Near-by farms were visited to secure straw for beds. This gave the meeting a new impulse; others flocked in bringing camp equipage. People came fifty to one hundred miles in carriages and wagons and on horseback. The meeting lasted several days in spite of the fact that it was harvest time. The movement soon swept beyond the borders of Kentucky into the neighboring states. These camp-meetings during the Great Revival were interdenominational, with the Presbyterians, Methodists, and Baptists taking the lead. Sectarianism was wiped away. Later the Presbyterians dropped the camp-meeting plan, leaving it to the Methodists and Baptists.

For some years previous to this, certain strange religious phenomena had cropped out at times. Now, with the gathering of great crowds and a general revival sweeping the whole region, these spiritual "exercises" burst into full flower. The "falling exercise" appeared at the McGee meeting mentioned above. In this experience the individual felt the constriction of the large blood vessels, a shortness of breath, an acceleration of breathing, and dropped prostrate. The hands and feet were cold. He lay from one to twenty-four hours. Upon returning to normal he was sometimes in a state of despair and felt he was such a sinner he could never be saved. More often he rejoiced that his sins were forgiven and immediately began to exhort others to give their lives to Christ. Timid people without apparent talent often showed great ability in praying and exhorting at that time. Scoffers and unbelievers as well as those seeking salvation were "struck down." Whole families at home, individuals in bed asleep, on the road, or plowing in the field, were stricken. Children at school where there were no religious exercises were seized. John McGee in speaking of it said: "The people fall before the word like corn before a storm of wind; and many rose from the dust with Divine glory shining in their countenances. . . ."

The next most common phenomenon was known as "the jerks." It was similar to the falling exercise in affecting all kinds of people everywhere. Like the falling exercise, it frequently fell upon people at meetings, but those far from the meetings were stricken. Elder Jacob Young said he had often seen ladies take it at the breakfast table as they were pouring tea or coffee. They would throw the whole up toward the ceiling, sometimes breaking both cup and saucer. As they left the table their heads would be so violently jerked that their braided hair, hanging down their backs, would crack like a whip. Witnesses say that some were taken up in the air, whirled over on their heads, coiled up so as to spin about like a cartwheel. They endeavored to grasp trees or saplings, but were carried headlong and helplessly on. J. B. Finley said that as many as five hundred of these subjects might be seen in one congregation in west Tennessee, bending the whole body first backward and then forward, the head nearly touching the ground forward and back alternately.

The Reverend Samuel Doak, an educated conservative Presbyterian of east Tennessee, went north on a visit about 1804, and when he returned was welcomed by a large assemblage to hear him preach. In the midst of a moving sermon, he was seized with a strange convulsion that made his limbs jerk and twist. He soon began to jump and finally went jerking and rolling off the platform down the hill while his congregation stood awe-stricken. After a while he finished his sermon, but he continued to jerk more or less for some time.

Lorenzo Dow had heard of the strange doings in Tennessee and said that he, like the Queen of Sheba, went to see for himself and found it was the real thing. . . . As Elder Dow passed a camp-meeting site he noticed from fifty to one hundred saplings cut off about breast-high. This seemed a slovenly way to clear an area and he asked the cause. When informed that they were left for people to jerk on, he went to see and found the people had laid hold and jerked so powerfully that they had kicked up the earth like a horse stamping flies.

In the "barking exercise" the victim would bark like a dog as he chased the devil. One who saw this said the person affected jerked, foamed at the mouth, rolled into a hog wallow, and then rose and with arms uplifted began to bark as he took the trail through the woods. Half a mile off he found a creek and, still barking, stopped at a tree, placed his hands on it, and looking up exclaimed: "I have treed the devil."

Sometimes a whole congregation would be thrown into side-splitting convulsions of laughter. When it got started in an audience, everybody would be seized with hearty natural laughter. It would last for hours sometimes. This was known as the "holy laugh." The "holy dance" was probably a variation of "the jerks" and was ungovernable until it ran its course.

In some instances children ten years of age mounted a log and preached with eloquence and the wisdom of the learned.

Some, while lying on the ground as a result of the exercises, had visions and, on regaining their normal composure, told of having been taken to heaven, of the delightful scenes there and whom they saw. Others brought back reports of a trip to hell with its horrors. While in this supernatural state they were able to do astonishing feats. Many of these phenomena kept popping up on the frontier for the next third of a century and were carried into the new territories and states. The "holy dance" and other ecstasies appeared among both white and black worshippers in Alabama and Mississippi as late as 1835.

As a frontier institution the camp-meeting developed a standard pattern during the first few years of the nineteenth century. A forest area was selected near a sparkling stream with plenty of shade and grass for the hundreds of horses. A large square clearing was made and over this was constructed an immense brush arbor or, as a camp-ground became permanent, a long shed covered with clapboards. The logs were laid end to end in rows lengthwise, and rough slabs, split from other logs with wedges, were laid across these in tiers the full length of the arbor. At one end was a high platform, known as "the pulpit-stand," made of poles or poles and slabs. At the foot of the stand was a straw-floored enclosure about thirty feet square, known as "the altar" or "penitent's pen." A rail fence was built down the center of the arbor to separate the men from the women.

Forming a quadrangle or large ellipse of about two acres including the arbor, and some distance from it, were the dwelling-places of the worshippers. These were called "the tents," although in a permanent camp they were often pole pens covered with clapboards. Many, however, were tents made of tow, or improvised tents made by stretching quilts, sheets, and counterpanes around and over crude pole frames. On the fourth side of the quadrangle, behind the pulpit-stand, were the dwelling-places of the ministers. The women cooked with Dutch ovens, pots, and skillets around fires in the open air and served the meals on long clapboard scaffolds. At night the grounds were lighted by pine-knot fires built on wooden altars covered with dirt or flat rocks. As roads were improved enough to permit vehicles, many people came in covered wagons, which were their homes for the following few days. The underbrush was cleared for a great area around, permitting retirement for secret prayer. . . .

The day's program was regulated by the blowing of a cow's horn or tin trumpet. There were prayers at the general assembly before breakfast. After breakfast there ensued an hour of secret prayer in the woods. At ten and two were general meetings. At four came another hour of secret prayer in the woods. The big meeting of the day was at candle-lighting time in the arbor. It did not often adjourn until after midnight and during stirring times lasted until broad daylight.

The night meeting was picturesque, with the deep shadows of the primeval forest lighted up by lurid flames which cast a glare on the earnest ministers and their vast congregation. This scene, with its background of the majestic forest, presented an imposing effect. In this setting the great throng worshipped in a primitive way.

The meeting in the early evening proceeded with a good degree of decorum, but as the night progressed, wilder and wilder became the disorder. As the minister began to warm up to his subject, which itself was often a hot one — an eternal burning hell in which the wicked were suffering — people began to respond. So realistically was the destiny of sinners portrayed that the listeners could fairly feel its scorching breath and smell its brimstone.

. . . When the call for penitents was made, sinners pushed forward until the pen was filled with those seeking forgiveness. Then ensued in that enclosure the greatest confusion — shouting, screaming, leaping, jerking, clapping of hands, falling, and swooning away. Ministers and other workers stood by and urged those under conviction to "come through.". . . Thus the wild confusion continued, many times until daybreak. Between meetings in the large assembly the same sort of work for sinners and the same sort of exercises took place in the living-quarters.

So popular was the movement that everybody came. Although the primary objective was religious, the curious were there too. The ambitious and influential attended, for public opinion was all-powerful on the frontier and their presence was demanded in order for them to hold and extend their influence. Aspirants for office were there to gain popularity and electioneer in a quiet way. Young ladies were there to show themselves and their costumes. The young men went to see the girls and frolic in a quiet way. Couples promenaded about the camp-ground between meetings. It was an enjoyable social season as the long isolated frontiersmen met together for a time in the warmth of Christian fellowship.

Unfortunately some unconverted ones almost always caused trouble for the campers. These "rowdies," as they were termed, would fortify themselves with whisky illicitly obtained somewhere near by. They engaged in all sorts of devilment, from pranks down to riotous conduct and stealing horses and rigs. It was necessary to post a line of sentries around the quadrangle and sometimes the ministers slept on their arms, so to speak, by keeping clubs at hand in order to be able to rush out in the night as a sort of auxiliary police force to assist in clearing the grounds of evil-doers. Peter Cartwright had many an adventure with rowdies. Once he captured the whisky that they were drinking and thus dried up the mischief at its source. Another time he gained the victory by strategy. He appointed the leader of the rowdies captain of the camp guard. On still another occasion, when a timid officer feared to arrest a whisky-seller, Cartwright got the sheriff to appoint him and four other preachers as bold as himself a posse to arrest the trouble-makers. They took the culprit and never left him until he had paid a fine and costs. When the rowdies in retaliation attempted to rout the preachers from their quarters at night, he drove off one of their leaders by hitting him a violent blow with a "chunk of fire" and another a blow on the head that drove out his "dispensation of mischief." One rowdy leader was "struck down" by an unseen hand just as he came up quietly to hang a necklace of frogs around a preacher's neck, and he got up a converted man.

The Great Revival reached its crest with the tremendous camp-meeting at Cane Ridge in Bourbon County, Kentucky. A vast crowd variously estimated at from twelve to twenty-five thousand gathered. That vast sea of human beings seemed agitated as by a storm. The noise was like that of a giant waterfall. Hundreds were swept down in a moment as though batteries had swept the crowd with grapeshot, and then followed shrieks and shouts that fairly rent the very heavens. It was estimated that three thousand fell at that meeting. The congregation was so large that it had to be split up, and twenty-six ministers occupied various improvised pulpits such as stumps, fallen trees, and wagons as they each preached to good-sized groups.

The Cane Ridge meeting lasted seventeen days. Later camp-meetings usually lasted from four to ten days. At the close of the meeting it was customary to gather for a final blessing where so many had been enjoyed. Then with tears, benedictions, hearty handshakes, and fond embraces the worshippers took their way homeward.

There was a wide difference of opinion as to the Great Revival and camp-meetings that sprang from it. Many felt that the meetings and the exercises that accompanied them were of the devil. As an overview from the vantage point of several years' observation, perhaps the evaluation of Timothy Flint sums up the situation as well as any. Flint, a Harvard graduate, had little sympathy for camp-meetings on principle at first, but said of them:

> Notwithstanding all that has been said in derision of these spectacles so common in this region, it cannot be denied, that their influence, on the whole, is salutary, and the general bearing upon the great interests of the

community, good. . . . Whatever be the cause, the effect is certain, that . . . these excitements have produced a palpable change in the manners and habits of the people.

STUDY GUIDE

1. We often think of churches as performing basically a religious function. What functions, social and otherwise, did religion perform on the American frontier?

2. What evidence does Dick provide that religion on the frontier was equalitarian and democratic? How does frontier religion compare with that of such colonial groups as the Puritans and Quakers?

3. What types of misbehavior and moral transgressions did the frontier churches tend to condemn? Explain why they might disapprove of dancing, but tolerate liquor.

4. Different observers have given different explantations of religious exercises such as falling and barking. What arguments can you develop to support each of the following explanations: (a) the exercises represented a strong religious response by people who could not attend worship regularly; (b) the exercises provided people who lived in social isolation for an extended period with a means of "letting off steam"; (c) the exercises were a result of poor diet, poor health, and exhaustion produced by the camp-meeting environment?

5. Consider the reform movements of the 1830s, such as abolitionism and women's rights, and then think about the words of the Civil War song "Battle Hymn of the Republic." Is it legitimate to suggest that the sense of mission and the emotional urgency of Protestantism in this period shaped these other aspects of American life? Or was American religious life simply a reflection of the broader sense of missionary zeal and destiny among all of the American people in that period?

BIBLIOGRAPHY

There are a number of works on religion in the West and the great religious revival of the nineteenth century. One of the most prolific writers on American religious history was William W. Sweet, who wrote *Revivalism in America: Its Origin, Growth and Decline* (1944) and also edited four volumes of writings entitled *Religion on the American Frontier* (1931–1946). Among the most interesting books on the revival are Bernard A. Weisberger, *They Gathered at the River: The Story of the Great Revivalists and Their Impact upon Religion in America* (1958) and Charles A. Johnson, *The Frontier Camp Meeting* (1955). William G. McLoughlin, Jr., *Modern Revivalism: Charles Grandison Finney to Billy Graham* (1959) is a delightful series of sketches of revivalists from the early nineteenth to the mid-twentieth century. Among special studies on certain regions or aspects of revivalism, two of the best are Timothy L. Smith, *Revivalism and Social Reform in Mid-Nineteenth Century America* (1957) and Whitney R. Cross, *The Burned-Over District* (1950), which concerns the revival spirit in New York State.

Besides the studies of individual denominations, there are several general books on American Protestantism. Winthrop S. Hudson, *American Protestantism* (1961) is a general survey which provides an excellent introduction to the subject. Another book by Hudson, *Religion in America* (1965), is also worth reading, as are the works of two distinguished scholars — H. Richard Niebuhr, *The Kingdom of God in America* (1937) and Sidney E. Mead, *The Lively Experiment: The Shaping of Christianity in America* (1963).

There are two basic introductions to Catholicism and Judaism in the United States, the bibliographies of which contain references to many other works: John T. Ellis, *American Catholicism*, 2nd ed. (1969) and Nathan Glazer, *American Judaism* (1957). In *Freedom's Ferment: Phases of American Social History to 1860* (1944), Alice Felt Tyler describes some of the many smaller sects and new religions that arose in the early nineteenth century. Many of the special works on those subjects lack objectivity, but two good works on the Mormons are Thomas F. O'Dea, *The Mormons* (1957) and Fawn M. Brodie, *No Man Knows My History: The Life of Joseph Smith, the Mormon Prophet* (1945).

The most comprehensive book on the religious history of American blacks was published more than fifty years ago: Carter G. Woodson, *The History of the Negro Church* (1921). Shorter studies include E. Franklin Frazier, *The Negro Church in America* (1963) and Chapter 42 of the newest general survey of American religious history, Sydney E. Ahlstrom, *A Religious History of the American People* (1972).

For prospective buyers, Cyrus McCormick demonstrated his reaper, which led to a revolution in agriculture just as new methods and machines were revolutionizing manufacturing.

8

C. JOSEPH PUSATERI

Beginnings of Industrialism

When it was first used, the term "industrialism" had a very limited meaning, referring to certain changes in England between the mid-eighteenth century and 1830. It described the development of steam power and its application to coal mining and transportation, new inventions in the textile industry, the factory system of production, and the formation of new capital. Eventually, historians realized that those developments were only limited facets of much broader changes that are still taking place and that have spread to much of the world. The rudimentary development of the factory system and mass production that took place before 1830 has now progressed to completely automated production lines that produce, among other things, fast-food hamburgers with scarcely any human intervention. Today, the Industrial Revolution is seen as including new ways of organizing business and capital; new inventions and technology in office machinery as well as on the production line; new sources of power and raw materials, including man-made synthetics; a vastly expanded labor force; and new patterns of transportation and distribution. Many historians, in fact, consider the entire Industrial Revolution as only a part of a broad social, political, and economic development that they refer to as "modernization."

By any standard, the Industrial Revolution must rank with the invention of the wheel and the opening of the Western Hemisphere as one of the most influential changes in world history. Throughout most of history, only a very small elite had more than a bare subsistence level of living, while most of humanity was doomed to hereditary poverty. It is the wealth of modern industrialism that has enabled society, for the first time, to consider educating most people and to provide a nourishing diet, good medical care, and adequate housing. Every aspect of modern existence, from skyscrapers and jet planes to the possibility of nuclear war, reflects the influence of industrialization. Industrial changes of the past century have had so radical a social impact that the changes in this period might be greater than the accumulated changes of the previous nineteen centuries.

Though eighteenth-century England was the seedbed of industrialism, the American people since that time have embraced the movement with unparalleled enthusiasm. In the early nineteenth century, a whole host of American tinkerers invented or contributed to the development of steamboats, vulcanized rubber, the telegraph, and such farm machinery as the thresher. The following essay by C. Joseph Pusateri touches upon several key factors in industrialization: the development of the factory system in textiles; professional management divorced from personal ownership; interchangeable parts; the production line; steam power; and new methods of distributing and buying farm machinery by time payments.

"About 1760 a wave of gadgets swept over England." So began an anonymous English schoolboy's description of the transition from an agricultural to an industrialized economy. The term which describes this process — the "industrial revolution" — was coined by early nineteenth-century French observers, who were impressed by a succession of remarkable technological innovations and the rapid development of the factory system of production in England. They were convinced that the "changes brought about by the economic revolution were as fundamental in their effect on British life as were those wrought by the political revolution which had changed French life after 1789."

While this term has become a permanent part of the historical vocabulary, it remains somewhat misleading. Above all, historians reject the implication that the industrial revolution was a sudden, cataclysmic conversion which began about 1760. Rather, they view its onset as less a single event than a gradual process. Whatever its timing, it is clear that the nature of this economic transformation was revolutionary. As a historian of technology, Melvin Kranzberg, has observed: "In the sense that the process of industrialization thoroughly transformed every aspect of society, then it is proper to describe it as a revolution: it certainly revolutionized

From *A History of American Business* by C. Joseph Pusateri. Copyright © 1984 by Harlan Davidson, Inc. Reprinted by permission.

men's ways of living and working, and in the process gave birth to our contemporary civilization."

The industrial revolution began and progressed differently everywhere. Great Britain was the first nation in which the industrial sector of the economy outstripped the agricultural sector in terms of value of goods produced. For entrepreneurs, Britain had a large internal market which was free of the feudal restraints that hampered trade on the European continent. Moreover, a colonial empire supplemented the domestic market and provided both a source of valuable raw materials and, to a lesser extent, another market for finished goods.

Other factors in the early industrialization of Britain were important. Enough risk capital was available to finance investments in mechanization; and Britain had a sound monetary system, good land transportation, an impressive merchant marine, and favorable governmental policies. Moreover, public opinion was sympathetic to industrial development. Kranzberg has pointed out, "Not only the government but the entire society must develop values, attitudes and institutions favorable to industrialization. Specifically, these would include a desire for material progress, the approval of social mobility, a willingness to accept new ideas and techniques, and an appreciation of technological advance as leading to material betterment."

Americans shared similar values and attitudes. Yet the wonder of the advent of the industrial revolution in the new world is not that Great Britain preceded the United States, but that the United States was able to follow so closely behind. American industrial advances were as rapid as those of any other nation — with the exception of Great Britain — in spite of serious obstacles, including the difficulty of competing with England's well-established manufacturing sector.

There was little doubt that Britain was determined to keep its technological leadership. Parliament enacted laws which prohibited the export of any "textile, metal-working, clock-making, leather-working, paper-making or glass manufacturing equipment," and similar legislation prevented any skilled workmen from leaving the British Isles and entering "any foreign country outside the Crown's dominions for the purpose of carrying on his trade." In 1785, the Privy Council enforced this law by requiring that ships' captains submit, before sailing, a list of passengers by name, age, occupation, and nationality to port officials. Any British mechanics on board were arrested with penalties which were as high as a year's imprisonment and heavy fines. Despite such strict regulations, however, British authorities never successfully halted the emigration of skilled mechanics.

The sparse and scattered population of the United States, its high internal transport costs, and its shortage of investment capital also hindered the process of industrialization. Ironically, America's very abundance —

its immense store of cheap land and natural resources — posed another significant problem. Abundance made possible economic opportunities in farming and in extractive industries such as lumbering and the fur trade which attracted laborers away from factory jobs. Yet the United States could also rely on several material advantages. These included numerous waterpower sites, ample coal and iron deposits, and extensive forests to provide the charcoal used in iron production. Other advantages had to do with the American labor force. Thomas Cochran has described the presence of "exceptionally flexible workbench artisans — men who knew how to use tools and could improve on old processes." While skilled workmen in Europe tended to concentrate upon a single craft, American artisans "moved readily from making furniture or hoes to erecting textile machinery and ultimately to fashioning parts for steam engines; or from building houses to constructing paper mills; or from working for wages to becoming independent entrepreneurs."

Still another stimulus to investment in manufacturing was a favorable public policy on the part of state and federal government. States frequently granted subsidies, tax exemptions, loans, and even temporary monopolies to new manufacturing firms, and . . . state corporation laws were instrumental in large-scale enterprises. During the first twenty years of the nineteenth century, eight states chartered over five hundred manufacturing corporations, almost two-thirds of which were in Massachusetts and New York alone. The national government also contributed to the promotion of industrial development. Before the Civil War, its involvement was primarily confined to protective tariffs levied on imports, a form of assistance which most economic historians now agree had little effect in the growth of domestic manufactures. Another, more passive form of assistance was the absence of regulatory legislation which restricted the freedom of enterpreneurs.

A final important factor in industrialization was that entrepreneurs in the United States were, by the late eighteenth century, prepared to undertake the financing and management of manufacturing enterprises. They perceived their opportunities and willingly accepted the accompanying risks. In an age of mercantile capitalism, many members of America's first generation of industrialists, not surprisingly, were successful merchants who possessed the business acumen and the risk capital necessary to begin successful manufacturing firms. This mercantile influence, Victor Clark wrote, "pervaded all manufactures . . . and was so omnipresent that we might describe the antebellum period as a time when manufactures were integrating out of commerce."

The American industrial revolution began at the end of the eighteenth century. In 1790, the production of manufactured goods in this country was still in the handicraft stage, and it consisted of household manufacturing, small shops, and local mills. Along with handicraft was the "putting-out" system, which encompassed both household and shop production and was important in the making of clothing, hats, shoes, and textiles. In the case of shoes, merchant-capitalists of the early 1800s had leathers and linings first cut in a central shop in order to reduce wastage. These materials were next distributed to "outworkers" in homes or smaller shops, who finished the shoes by stitching, binding, lasting, and soling them. The merchant-capitalist then collected and marketed the completed product.

The putting-out system was, in essence, a handicraft form of production, and, with the introduction of machines, it gradually disappeared. For the merchant who depended on the system for his stock of merchandise, the system had disadvantages. There was a lack of quality control over a large number of scattered laborers; delivery dates for the finished goods were often uncertain. Nevertheless, for those industries in which manufacturing was not easily mechanized, the putting-out system persisted into the late nineteenth century.

Over time, factory-produced goods gradually displaced household manufactures and reduced small-shop output. Factory goods also eventually diminished the volume of imports flowing into the United States, a process which economists describe as "import substitution." From 1810 (the first year for which reasonably reliable data is available on manufacturing) to 1860, the value of American industrial output rose from approximately $200 million to about $1.9 billion. Seen from another standpoint, about 75,000 Americans worked in factories in 1820; forty years later, the number stood at 1.5 million. Although the majority of the population was still engaged in agricultural pursuits in 1860, the industrial revolution had clearly gathered great momentum.

A great deal of antebellum industrial growth occurred in consumer-goods industries. The federal census of 1860 revealed that, measured in terms of value added by manufacture, the cotton-goods industry ranked first. The emergence of cotton textiles as the nation's first "growth industry" was only logical. Cloth was a basic necessity for any family, and it provided a substantial market opportunity for would-be manufacturers. Furthermore, because the value of cloth per pound was high, it eased the disincentive of high transportation costs. The new technology for the factory production of cotton yarn and cloth which had already been introduced in England and Scotland by 1790 was susceptible to being "borrowed" by enterprising Americans. These factors were present even before Eli Whitney's invention of a cotton gin in 1793 and the emergence of the American South as the world's largest producer of raw cotton.

Hence, it was in cotton textiles that the factory system first developed in America. Although there is no universally accepted definition of a "factory," it possesses the following general characteristics: (1) it sells a substantial portion of its output in a regional or national, as opposed to strictly local, market; (2) its operations, carried on within one building or a group of adjacent buildings, involve a considerable capital investment in machinery and other equipment, which are usually power-driven; (3) its laborers work at the factory site rather than their homes or at other scattered locations, and they are subject to shop discipline. . . .

Before 1810, the limitations of the putting-out system had slowed any attempt on the part of American textile manufacturers to challenge Britain's textile supremacy. The step from yarn to cloth was a bottleneck which prevented American mills from introducing mass production. On the other hand, in England, the bottleneck had been eliminated by 1810. Beginning with the designs of Edmund Cartwright in the 1780s and continuing with the improvements of Thomas Johnson and William Horrocks, the British textile industry developed workable power looms by 1813, when some 2,400 were already operating in England and Scotland.

The man most instrumental in introducing the power loom to the United States was Francis Cabot Lowell. He was born in 1775, the son of a prominent Massachusetts attorney and judge, who had also been one of the organizers of the state's first bank in 1784. Because his father was married three times — to a Higginson, a Cabot, and a Russell — the son "grew up in an extended-kinship group second to none in Boston and its satellite towns on the North Shore, a family connection based upon several generations of merchant-shipowning." Young Lowell attended Harvard, where he excelled in mathematics, before joining a partnership in the import-export business with his uncle, William Cabot, in 1793. During the next two decades he was an all-purpose merchant and, in the process, entered into ventures with most, if not all, of Boston's business aristocracy, including Nathan Appleton and Lowell's brother-in-law, Patrick Tracy Jackson.

In 1810, Lowell decided to take his family to England for an extended stay because of his own and his wife's frail health. It seems likely, however, that business considerations were also paramount. . . .

During a two-year stay in the British Isles, Lowell traveled to manufacturing centers in England and Scotland. As a prominent American merchant, he was given the opportunity to observe closely textile factories in operation, including those which employed the new power looms. It took him little time to make up his mind. When Nathan Appleton visited him in Edinburgh in 1811, Lowell confided to him his determination to enter cotton manufacturing. . . .

In late 1812, Lowell began work on two fronts. In an attic room on Boston's Broad Street, he began constructing a power loom with the assistance of a British-born Yankee mechanic, Paul Moody, and, by 1814, they had assembled a working machine. Nathan Appleton later recalled "the state of admiration and satisfaction with which we sat by the hour, watching the beautiful movement of this new and wonderful machine, destined as it evidently was to change the character of all textile industry."

On a second front, Lowell sought out his friends in the mercantile community of Boston and won pledges of a substantial starting capital. Patrick Tracy Jackson also agreed to assist Lowell in the active management of the new enterprise, which, in February 1813, was incorporated as the Boston Manufacturing Company. The new corporation was one of the pivotal business firms in American economic history. As a historian of the industry, Caroline Ware, has written: "The most important thing which could have happened to the cotton industry was that, after twenty-five years of slow growth and small scale experimentation, it should have been taken up by men with the best business imagination in the land, unhampered by its traditions, concerned with making fortunes and building states, not with manufacturing cotton cloth." Although Ware probably does not give enough credit to the progress of the Slater mills, the Boston Associates undoubtedly brought the factory system to an entirely new level of organization.

The Boston Manufacturing Company was initially capitalized at $100,000, but, within a few years, this figure was increased to $400,000. These sums, unprecedented for the time, were necessary because of the greater investment in fixed assets which power-loom weaving required and because of the large scale of production. The new firm soon constructed a mill at Waltham on the Charles River, a short distance from Boston. It measured ninety feet by forty-five feet and was four stories high; its size was greater than anything ever seen in New England.

Production began in December 1814 at what some historians regard as the first modern factory in the United States. All within a single factory, the Waltham mill integrated and mechanized the manufacturing process from the raw material to the finished product, coarse cotton cloth. Within the mill, production flowed upward. On the ground floor, the carding machines combed, stretched, and prepared the raw cotton for the spinning frames on a middle floor and for the looms on the top floor.

The power loom and the integrated factory — because they enabled American manufacturers to compete with Britain after 1815 — have been called "virtually a life-saving innovation" for the textile industry. Under the putting-out system, mill owners paid hand-loom weavers three to seven cents per yard; the direct expense of power-loom weaving was, on the average, only one cent per yard. While many manufacturers who kept the putting-out system failed during the depression after 1815, the Boston Manufacturing Company prospered.

In 1817, just weeks after the premature death of Francis Cabot Lowell at the age of forty-two, the company distributed a 12.5 percent dividend to its shareholders. In the following years, dividends were even better, so much so that, by 1822, stockholders had received over a 100 percent return on their original investments. The substantial profits earned at Waltham spurred the Boston Associates to seek further expansion. But, by 1821, all available water-power sites near Waltham were in use, and so a search began for a new location.

Paul Moody discovered a promising site on the Merrimack River, about twenty-five miles north of Boston. When Moody reported his find, Patrick Tracy Jackson began to envision a manufacturing center — much larger than any single mill — which would include multiple factories operating on an unprecedented scale, and he had little trouble convincing the Associates to reinvest their Waltham earnings. Construction began in 1822. The stockholders organized a new corporation, the Merrimack Manufacturing Company, with a capitalization of $600,000. Since the site was isolated, workers were transplanted to it and housed in a new community for which Nathan Appleton suggested the name Lowell. By the fall of 1823 Lowell was in production.

In the following years, a succession of textile companies was established at Lowell — each growing out of the success of its predecessors, each controlled by the same small group of Boston entrepreneurs. By 1836 investment in the eight principal firms in the area was over $6 million, and Lowell mills employed over six thousand workers.

As important were the general management concepts which Lowell and his colleagues introduced. Collectively, these have become known as the "Waltham System." Its key features consisted of the following: the integration of all stages of production within a single plant; a substantial capitalization, which made possible larger-scale operations; the selection of mill managers for their overall administrative ability rather than their experience with textile manufacturing alone; the concentration upon only one standardized product in each factory, which facilitated high-volume production runs, low unit costs, and necessitated little skill on the part of workers; the marketing of the product through a single "selling house," instead of a large number of commission agents; and the employment of a unique labor force of young women who were housed in company-owned dormitories.

The most publicized feature of the Waltham System was its solution to the problem of securing factory labor — the dormitory or boardinghouse plan. This plan involved the active recruitment of young New England farm girls, who were housed in company-owned dormitories located near the mills. In order to break down the resistance of conservative Yankee families to sending their unmarried daughters to work and live in a distant factory town, the dormitories were under the charge of matrons of unquestioned character and under stringent rules designed to protect the virtue of their residents. . . .

Although the Waltham System established integrated factories in the United States, it made little attempt to integrate the administrative structure of the various companies. Decision-making authority was, in essence, triangular in the Lowell mills. The chief executive officer of each firm, who held the title of Treasurer, resided in Boston. He was selected for his administrative experience — invariably acquired in a mercantile background — rather than for any special expertise in textile production. The Treasurer's responsibilities were to purchase raw cotton for the mills, to maintain the accounts of the company, and to evaluate the efforts of the mill superintendent.

The mill superintendent or agent, the second leg of the administrative triangle, supervised the day-to-day operations of the mill. He was responsible for efficient production and for the management of the work force. Through detailed reports, the superintendent kept in constant contact with the Treasurer, his immediate superior.

The final leg of the triangle was the mill's selling house. Although, in theory, it was only responsible for marketing the final product, in reality it exercised internal decision-making power. Its knowledge of the market and its readiness to advance the textile firm further working capital against future shipments enabled the officers of the selling house to dictate the type and quantity of cloth each mill manufactured. Thus, even in the most advanced segment of antebellum American industry, little centralized managerial control existed. . . .

The textile industry played a decisive role in America's Industrial Revolution. In 1832, a survey of American manufacturing carried out under the direction of the Secretary of the Treasury found that 106 companies had assets of $100,000 or more. Of these, eighty-eight were textile firms.

A good deal of the technological progress associated with the industrial revolution in the United States stemmed from American adaptations of British innovations. Nevertheless, there were two important innovations which originated in the United States: continuous processing and the assembly of products using interchangeable parts.

Continuous processing — or, as it was later called, assembly line production — first occurred in the automated flour mill developed in the 1780s by Oliver Evans, a Delaware-born mechanical genius. In most mills, workers performed the back-breaking work of lifting grain to the top of a gravity system, which then fed it between millstones; they hoisted it up once more to store it in a silo. Evans sought a way of accomplishing these tasks with less human effort.

He designed and patented a system of interconnected machines which eliminated all hauling and heavy labor by means of buckets, hoppers, and conveyor belts. His invention performed every necessary mill operation without the aid of manual labor, and it required the services of just a single supervisor. The inherent advantages of Evans' automated mill were so plain that the techniques were widely adopted in the following years — often with complete disregard of the inventor's patent.

Immediately before the Civil War, the continuous-processing concept appeared again in the pork-packing houses of Cincinnati. At a "disassembly" line, a row of laborers at fixed stations butchered carcasses which hung from hooks and moved on overhead rails at a predetermined speed. Each worker carried out a single task such as splitting the animal or removing specific parts. The minute division of labor and the elimination of wasted motion resulted in a significant increase in productivity. The automobile assembly lines in Henry Ford's plants in Detroit several decades later had their roots in the early advances in continuous processing of the antebellum years.

The production of goods which use the principle of interchangeable parts necessitates that the parts be manufactured with such accuracy that any two pieces will be identical. The final product can then be assembled with little or no hand tooling of the components. The advantages of this method were threefold: (1) because the machines were driven by water or steam power, a saving in human labor was made possible; (2) the tending of the power-driven machinery required less skill than was necessary to tool parts by hand; (3) and, a broken component could be replaced from a standard stock of spares. The chief deterrent to the widespread use of the system was the expense of developing the necessary machine tools.

For many years, full credit for the innovation in the United States was given to Eli Whitney, the nation's most famous antebellum inventor. More recently, however, historians now describe Eli Whitney's part in interchangeable manufacture, at least in part, as a legend. Whitney first became interested in interchangeable parts during the unhappy aftermath of his invention of the sawtooth cotton gin. Whitney's brainchild had an enormous impact on the South. One Whitney biographer described it in this way: "His gin reduced labor fifty-fold without putting anyone out of work. Indeed, his invention would make employment for thousands — Negro slaves on the land, women and children in the factories, eager white men in the shops and the countinghouses. The United States would grow rich." The gin also firmly fastened the institution of slavery upon the South and, perhaps, in the long run made inevitable the Civil War.

Although Whitney's gin changed the course of southern agriculture and American history, it worked no magic on his own personal fortunes. In 1793, he had formed a partnership with Phineas Miller, a South Carolina plantation manager, to secure a patent from the federal government and to begin manufacturing gins. The partners foolishly expected that they could produce sufficient gins to clean all the South's cotton for a "commission" of one pound in every five, essentially the system which grist mills had long employed. But Whitney and Miller were never able to maintain exclusive control of their gin, its patent notwithstanding, because of production delays, the ease with which other manufacturers could duplicate the simple concept, the outrage of cotton planters at what they regarded as an exorbitant charge by would-be monopolists, and the importance of the gin for the South's economy.

Consequently, Whitney and Miller found themselves embroiled in an almost endless series of costly and time-consuming lawsuits to enforce their patent rights, while little revenue actually flowed into the firm's coffers. By 1798 Whitney was frustrated and disillusioned, and — more out of a sense of desperation than entrepreneurial enthusiasm — at this point he then chose to begin a new manufacturing venture.

A foreign-policy crisis offered an unexpected opportunity. In 1797, after the "XYZ Affair," diplomatic relations with the revolutionary government in France soured badly, and the United States soon found itself fighting an undeclared naval war in the Atlantic; rumors abounded of a French invasion force which threatened American shores. George Washington, then in retirement, was hastily called back from private life to command an expanded American army, and Congress rushed to provide the troops with adequate arms.

Whitney, perceiving an opening for himself, wrote to the Secretary of the Treasury on May 1, 1798. He proposed to supply the government with at least ten thousand muskets within a short time. The Treasury, eagerly accepting the offer without examining it too closely, contracted with Whitney for the delivery of four thousand muskets by the end of September 1799 and another six thousand a year later. The government promised to pay him regular cash advances with five thousand dollars immediately to assist in initial production. The price was set at $13.40 per musket.

No established arms manufacturer had ever turned out such a quantity of weapons in so little time, and, in Whitney's case, he needed to equip a factory, secure raw materials, and recruit workers. Not surprisingly, he failed badly in meeting his deadlines. He did not deliver even the first five hundred muskets until September 1801, and the full contract was not completed until 1809, long after the French crisis had passed.

When pressed about the protracted delay, Whitney responded in 1799 that he was producing his muskets by means of a new manufacturing principle. "One of my primary objects," he wrote, "is to form the tools so the tools themselves shall fashion the work and give to every part its just proportion — which when once accomplished, will give expedition, uniformity, and exactness to the whole." It was the first indication that he planned to make his muskets with interchangeable parts. Whitney's claims — and, in 1801, his demonstration in Washington (before an audience that included John Adams and Thomas Jefferson) of ten different lock mechanisms fitted into the same musket — were enough to sustain the patience of government officials, and they continued their cash advances.

Unfortunately for Whitney's reputation, recent scholarly research has cast serious doubt on his originality in arms production. His armory at Mill Rock, Connecticut, introduced little that was actually new, but instead heavily borrowed from other producers. Three sources played a larger role in bringing interchangeable parts to American manufacturing. One was the efforts of Simeon North, who produced various types of weapons for the government at his factory in Middletown, Connecticut, beginning in 1799. A second was the work at the federal government's own Springfield, Massachusetts, armory, especially under the direction of Roswell Lee (1815–1833). As significant was the progress made by John H. Hall at Harpers Ferry, Virginia (now West Virginia). In 1826, Hall, according to most historians, successfully produced the first fully interchangeable parts weapons ever manufactured in the United States, Whitney notwithstanding. Yet most modern writers do not simply dismiss Whitney's role in fostering what British observers later called "the American system of manufacturing." Until his death in 1825, he produced arms for both federal and state governments at his Mill Rock factory. Although more significant technical advances were probably made elsewhere, Whitney's prominence and his gift for publicity made him invaluable as a popularizer of the system.

The use of the principle of interchangeable parts was readily transferred from muskets to other products such as watches and clocks, sewing machines, locks, bicycles, typewriters, and agricultural implements. The common characteristic of its spread was the design and use of highly specialized machinery in production. Eventually, with the rise of an important group of machine-tool firms, the manufacture of this machinery became an industry in itself. As Nathan Rosenberg has written: "The machine-tool industry, then, came to constitute a pool or reservoir of the skills and technical knowledge essential to the generation of technical change throughout the machine-using sectors of the economy. Precisely because it came to deal with processes and problems which were common to an increasing number of industries, it played the role of a transmission center in the diffusion of the new technology." As a result, new, lower-priced manufactured goods were now available in a mass market. Where only the wealthy could purchase hand-tooled mechanical items, ordinary people could now buy items which previously they had either done without or accepted as hand-me-downs from affluent neighbors. And, the wider market encouraged even more innovations in succeeding years.

In large part, the availability of sufficient waterpower dictated the concentration of textile mills at sites such as Lowell, Massachusetts. Because of easy access to waterpower, manufacturers became interested only slowly in the use of steam engines in production. The indefatigable Oliver Evans experimented regularly with such engines, and, in 1802, he successfully installed one in a Philadelphia mill which he operated. Its success launched him in business as an engine builder, and he was probably the first person in the United States to specialize in that activity. It is estimated that, by his death in 1819, some fifty Evans engines were used along the Atlantic seaboard. Nevertheless, as late as 1850, the use of stationary steam engines in industry was not common. These engines were expensive in fuel, and mechanical breakdowns were frequent. Moreover, eastern manufacturers placed the annual expense of steam power at four times or more that of waterwheels or turbines. As the years passed, engines were improved, the cost of fuel (principally coal) became less, and new waterpower sites were more difficult to find. By 1870, therefore, steam had caught up with water as a means of driving industrial machinery, and it thereafter drew rapidly ahead.

The increased use of steam engines was linked to the development of the iron industry in the United States. Advances in iron manufacturing reduced the cost of engines and improved their efficiency and reliability. But the history of the iron industry before 1860 stands in sharp contrast to that of textiles. Both witnessed important British innovations during the last quarter of the eighteenth century, but, while American textile operators quickly adopted these breakthroughs, ironmasters in America abandoned their old-fashioned methods more slowly.

The British innovations included the use of coked coal to smelt iron ore into pig iron and the development of puddling and rolling techniques to refine the pig iron into usable wrought iron. The coke in England, which replaced charcoal in blast furnaces, turned England from a net importer of pig iron to a major world producer. And, while English forests were depleted, reducing the amount of charcoal that could be gleaned from timber, there was no lack of coal for coking. Puddling allowed pig iron to be heated and worked in a furnace which used mineral fuel rather than charcoal, and rolling eliminated the tedious pounding of pig iron on a forge with trip hammers.

American iron manufacturers were slow to employ these innovations. Timber was plentiful in the United States, while its supplies of soft bituminous coal (from which coke was produced) were located west of the Alleghenies, and facilities to transport it to seaboard manufacturers did not exist before the mid-nineteenth century.

On the eastern slopes of the Alleghenies in Pennsylvania, there were massive deposits of a different type of coal — anthracite. It was known as "stone coal," because of the difficulty [of] igniting it, and its development awaited technical solutions to this problem. By the 1830s, however, the mining of anthracite had become commercially feasible, and, for the first time, American ironmasters used a mineral fuel rather than charcoal in the smelting process. The production of pig iron rose — without an accompanying price increase — as anthracite became the most popular form of fuel. In 1830, nearly all American pig iron was produced with charcoal; by 1865 three-quarters of it was made with hard anthracite coal. But the importance of anthracite was short-lived, and, by 1875, coke began to surpass anthracite as a fuel for blast furnaces. . . .

One notable aspect of the antebellum iron industry's history was the appearance, for the first time, of integrated firms. Until the 1840s, firms limited their functions either to smelting iron ore or to refining pig iron. Smelting was carried out at rural "iron plantations," which encompassed as much as ten thousand acres or more of land. The extensive acreage was necessary because of the use of charcoal in blast furnaces, and the rural location of iron ore deposits also determined the country setting of these smelting operations. . . .

The transformation of the iron industry did not begin until the 1840s. The catalyst was the growth of railroads, which stimulated demand for metal rails. But the rail market was a fierce competitive arena; British mills offered a low-cost product which American refiners could not match. A few American manufacturers thus concluded that, only by reducing their costs substantially and by maintaining a steady production volume at high levels, could the British invasion be overcome.

A small number of producers began the integration of the smelting and refining phases of iron manufacture as a way to achieve these goals. For example, Benjamin Jones integrated his mill by buying blast furnaces, thanks to an infusion of outside capital provided by James Laughlin, a Pennsylvania commission merchant. As a result of this expansion of operations, the capitalization of the reorganized Jones and Laughlin firm rose from $20,000 to $175,000 by 1861, an increase which came from both Laughlin's financial support and reinvested earnings. In other instances, new integrated companies were founded on the initiative of commission merchants. They recognized the opportunities which the growth of the railroad network offered to firms efficient enough to compete with British suppliers. By 1860 the largest ironworks in the United States were all integrated rail mills, including Pennsylvania's Montour Iron, which employed some three thousand workers. Firms which were not integrated found themselves unable to keep even a modest portion of the rail market.

Integrated mills were, in fact, the future of the American iron industry. They produced their own pig iron — thus eliminating the need to purchase that supply from an iron broker — and they sold directly to the ultimate consumer, in this instance, a relatively limited number of railroads. In this fashion, the giant integrated steel enterprises of the post-Civil War era would operate successfully. . . .

A variety of new agricultural implements also widened the market for the products of the iron industry and extended further the dimensions of the American industrial revolution. Cast iron and steel plows, seed drills, rice threshers, mowers, and other devices fostered the development of the "farm-servicing" industry, which, by 1860, had become one of the ten most important in the American economy. But "the most continuous, concerted efforts by tinkers and inventors," as one historian writes, "to improve the methods of production and reduce labor costs" occurred in the cultivation of wheat.

Before 1830, the short harvest season was the main bottleneck to any major expansion in wheat output. Harvesting was still a manual process which involved the use of hand sickles or cradles — and which was not only arduous but also expensive. The average farm laborer could cut only about two and a half acres per day, and, during the short harvest period, larger farms relied upon outside labor, which they paid at the prevailing wage rates. A relatively high labor cost and the continued uncertainty of having an adequate number of workers were incentives for the wheat farmer to adopt labor-saving implements once they became available and mechanically and economically practicable.

The answer to the wheat farmer's problem appeared in the 1830s with the development of the first, still fairly primitive, reapers. The businessman thereafter most closely associated with them was Cyrus Hall McCormick. Along with McCormick, others — Obed Hussey, McCormick's own father, or perhaps another tinkerer of the period — also played a small role in the invention of the reaper. Cyrus McCormick's major contribution was, rather, his innovations in marketing and organization-building through which the reaper became widely popular. McCormick has also been credited with everything from a doubling of wheat acreage in the United States to the winning of the Civil War for the North. Perhaps equally important for our purposes, McCormick represents a transition figure who bridged the gap from the antebellum industrial revolution in the United States to the emergence of large-scale corporate enterprise.

Cyrus H. McCormick grew up on his father's farm in Virginia's Shenandoah Valley. Actually, Robert McCormick, the father, owned not a small farm, but an estate of twelve hundred acres, nine slaves, and eighteen horses. "He had," according to his son's biographer, "earned the right to indulge his passion for mechanical experiment without fear for the material comfort of his family, in case his inventions did not find a ready market." For years, Robert McCormick worked on a device to reap wheat. But it was his son Cyrus who, at the age of twenty-two, by modifying his father's design, produced a working model in 1831. Not until 1834 did the younger McCormick finally apply for a patent, apparently spurred on by reports that Obed Hussey, a brilliant but erratic inventor, had assembled his own reaper model and was already attempting to sell copies to farmers. Curiously, despite his patent, McCormick then put aside his reaper for the rest of the decade and devoted most of his time to a fruitless venture in iron manufacturing. As late as 1840, he still had not sold a reaper outside his own Virginia locale. But, after 1840, McCormick abandoned his debt-ridden iron business, made a series of needed improvements on his reaper, and began selling a modest number to eastern farmers. By the mid-1840s, however, he recognized that his real market lay in the prairies of the trans-Appalachian West, where wheat farming was rapidly finding a new locus and where a shortage of wage labor made the reaper especially valuable.

McCormick also saw that his Virginia workshop was too small and poorly situated to take adequate advantage of western demand. The addition of transportation costs to the selling price of the machine might either deter customers from a purchase or induce them to buy a lower-priced competitor's model. McCormick, it has been pointed out, "was one of the first American industrialists to face the necessity of making a major move in order to be closer to his markets."

In 1848, he closed his Virginia operation and moved westward to the growing city of Chicago. Previously, he had assembled reapers in his own shop and also licensed a few other manufacturers to produce them. Now, licensing agreements were terminated, and McCormick produced all reapers bearing his name from a single factory in Chicago.

In 1849, he envisioned selling as many as fifteen hundred reapers during that year's wheat-growing season. At the same time, he faced the challenge of marketing a complex and expensive product to interested but cautious customers. He pioneered a marketing strategy which, to an unprecedented degree, relied on heavy advertising and a network of salesmen who were responsible for demonstrating the ease of operation and the reliability under the pressures of a hectic harvest season of the McCormick reaper. Eventually, this sales force became more than just peddlers of machinery. A system of company agents was established, each, in effect, a franchised dealer for McCormick implements who was closely regulated by the central administration in Chicago.

The agents had multiple duties. They not only demonstrated and sold equipment, they also had to stand ready to service it when breakdowns occurred. Furthermore, since the reaper and similar McCormick products were expensive, a policy of selling on credit was introduced early. The price of the basic reaper in the 1850s, for example, was $115 cash, or $120 if purchased on credit. If a farmer bought on credit, he was expected to pay thirty dollars down and the balance after the next harvest, an arrangement which placed an additional burden on the company's agents, since they were required to evaluate the credit worthiness of buyers and collect past-due accounts from recalcitrant farmers.

No such elaborate marketing structure existed in any other field. As Harold Livesay has stated, "The success of this system of sales and service, the first of its kind, and not simply the productivity of his factory carried

McCormick to the top of the farm machinery industry and kept him there despite fierce competition and the expiration of his patents."

As the years passed, McCormick left more of the day-to-day management to his brothers William and Leander and later to salaried managers. Nevertheless, he remained unwilling to relinquish too much control, even as he dabbled in politics, religion, world travels, and other investments. As a result, by the time of his death in 1884, the firm remained ostensibly powerful, but was growing less and less efficient. In its prime, however, McCormick's organization was responsible for innovations which would serve equally well later manufacturers of other durable goods — notably, the twentieth century's most important consumer durable, the automobile.

It might be said that the American industrial revolution came of age in the eyes of those overseas in 1851. Prompted by a suggestion from Prince Albert, Great Britain issued an invitation to the world, proposing that all nations present their manufactures at a grand exhibition which was housed in a huge London hall later known as the Crystal Palace. Before it closed its doors, some six million people visited the Crystal Palace Exhibition, and American products unexpectedly were among the most popular and impressive attractions.

For the first time, the ingenuity and quality of manufactured goods from the United States won worldwide attention. Among American achievements, Charles Goodyear's India rubber articles, Gail Borden's food items, Samuel Colt's revolving pistols, and Cyrus McCormick's reaper all won medals and awards. With considerable pride, an American observer at the Crystal Palace reported: "The number of inventions exhibited . . . was in the highest degree creditable to us, and elicited from distinguished sources in Great Britain the admission that to 'the department of American notions' they owed the most important contributions to their industrial system." American industry had come of age and was prepared to eclipse the world's manufacturing leader, Great Britain.

STUDY GUIDE

1. Summarize the conditions and resources in the United States that were helpful in the "take-off" of industrialization in the early nineteenth century.

2. What were the basic characteristics of the "factory system," and how did it differ from the older, craft system of production?

3. Explain the role of each of the following in American industrial growth: continuous processing, interchangeable parts, steam power, the railroad, and purchasing on credit.

4. Some of the inventions of the early Industrial Revolution had been developed in England and France, but not much used there as compared to their rapid and wide acceptance in the United States. What factors can you think of in those countries — such as labor, tradition, markets, and the like — that might explain a somewhat more conservative attitude toward new inventions?

5. How do the life, the rewards, and the conditions of one's work differ for an inventor in today's corporate, industrialized world? What examples can you think of, in inventions or improvements of products, that are not used because they would affect a company's sales or profits? What problems does a single, independent inventor face today in developing such improvements?

BIBLIOGRAPHY

Pusateri's book is one of many surveys of American business history. The outstanding scholar of this field is Thomas C. Cochran. He has written a number of works, including *Frontiers of Change: Early Industrialism in America* (1981), *200 Years of American Business* (1977), and *The Age of Enterprise: A Social History of Industrial America* (1961), the last being co-authored with William Miller. Elisha P. Douglass, *The Coming of Age of American Business . . . , 1600– 1900* (1971) is superior to the brief survey by James O. Robertson, *America's Business* (1985) and a popular work by John Chamberlain, *The Enterprising Americans: A Business History of the United States* (1961).

A work used in earlier editions of *The Social Fabric — The Ingenious Yankees* (1975) by Joseph and Frances Gies — is a series of charming biographical sketches of American inventors. Technology in early America is discussed in Brook Hindle, ed., *America's Wooden Age: Aspects of Its Early Technology* (1975). Roger Burlingame's two earlier works are interesting reading, but somewhat outdated: *Engines of Democracy: Inventions and Society in Mature America* (1940), and *Machines That Built America* (1953). If you like a biographical approach to history, you might enjoy reading a full study of Oliver Evans, Samuel F. B. Morse, or some other American inventor. Jeannette Mirsky and Allan Nevins, *The World of Eli Whitney* (1952) is one of many.

As is made clear in the next selection by Barbara Tucker, the people who actually confronted the Industrial Revolution experienced considerable conflict and anxiety. Carefully acquired skills were outdated by the new machines, women and children competed with men for jobs, new and distant markets developed, and the industrial system seemed to be in conflict with some deeply held social and ethical beliefs. These sorts of concerns are studied in three volumes: Marvin Fisher, *Workshops in the Wilderness: The European Response to American Industrialization, 1830–1860* (1967); John F. Kasson, *Civilizing the Machine: Technology and Republican Values in America, 1776–1900* (1976); and Leo Marx, *The Machine in the Garden: Technology and the Pastoral Ideal in America* (1964). Your library might also have some of the works of Lewis Mumford, whose sweeping studies range over industrialization and urbanization, the social and psychological changes brought about by invention, and the European scene as well as nineteenth-century America. Two other works that relate aesthetics to industrialization are Siegfried Giedion, *Mechanization Takes Command: A Contribution to Anonymous History* (1948) and John A. Kouwenhoven, *Made in America: The Arts in Modern Civilization* (1962).

Some scholars have attempted to understand the impact of industrialism by cameo studies of individual towns or factories. Three exemplary works of this type are Alan Dawley, *Class and Community: The Industrial Revolution in Lynn* (1976); Stephan Thernstrom, *Poverty and Progress: Social Mobility in a Nineteenth-Century City* (1964); and Anthony F. C. Wallace, *Rockdale: The Growth of an American Village in the Early Industrial Revolution* (1978).

The literature on American economic development is too vast to be listed here. There are scores of fine studies of manufacturing, agriculture, railroads and canals, labor, the factory system, and finance. Gilbert C. Fite and Jim E. Reese, *An Economic History of the United States*, 3rd ed. (1973) has individual chapters on these subjects and an excellent bibliography. One classic work on the pre–Civil War period is George R. Taylor, *The Transportation Revolution, 1815–1860* (1951). Books on labor history are cited following Reading No. 9.

III THE AGE OF REFORM

One of the questions frequently asked of historians is how closely their reconstruction of the past approximates the past as it truly was. We seldom think of ourselves as being part of an "age," and we are scarcely aware of the patterns of development that later historians may detect. Fifty years from now, historians may look back on our times as a revolutionary period, an age of reform, a period of cultural decay, or a turning point in the disintegration of American society. Any such characterization of a period is somewhat artificial. It ignores many contradictory developments of the time and applies simple labels that are not always helpful to those trying to understand the period.

The last decade of the eighteenth century and the first quarter of the nineteenth century are generally regarded as a period of centralization and nationalism. Following the adoption of the Constitution in 1788, the Federalist period of Washington, Hamilton, and Adams was characterized by the strengthening of the national government in both domestic and foreign affairs and the development of national interests quite distinct from those of European powers. This nationalistic thrust was continued under the Virginia presidents from Jefferson to Monroe, though support for a domestic program along these lines was stronger in Congress than in the executive mansion.

The second quarter of the nineteenth century has proved to be more difficult to characterize. Though some historians emphasize the democratic features of the "Age of Jackson," others have suggested that it was basically an age of business entrepreneurs and social inequality. There is little doubt that the years from 1830 to 1850 were a time of great social ferment, and such a startling variety of reforms were undertaken that some historians call it "The Age of Reform."

The first reading concerns labor in the new factories discussed by Pusateri. Laborers faced the fundamental question of whether they might best improve their conditions through union organization or through politics. The second reading, discussing an area in which reform was needed but not attempted, traces the callous and sometimes brutal treatment accorded the American Indian in the nineteenth century. A host of other concerns, including pacifism, help for the handicapped, abolitionism, and the temperance crusade grew into national movements during this period. The temperance movement, which had one of the longest influences upon American thought, is discussed in the third reading. Many Americans believed that reform could best be achieved by creating local and state institutions to care for orphans, delinquents, the insane, and other unfortunates, while others attempted to form ideal, small communities to serve as a model for a perfect world. The last two readings discuss these two very different approaches to reform.

Though probably dating from a later time, this photograph of children working under adult, male foremen is representative of conditions in the huge New England cotton mills before the Civil War.

9

BARBARA M. TUCKER

The Industrial Worker

Many people equate the grand achievements of American business and industry with such remarkable men as Commodore Vanderbilt, Andrew Carnegie, and John D. Rockefeller. Important as leadership has been in American capitalism, one cannot understand the Industrial Revolution without an appreciation of the contribution of the millions of men, women, and children who made up the labor force in the new factory system. Besides its beneficial economic consequences, industrialization had some unfortunate social effects, and the history of labor was not necessarily characterized by steady improvement in either wages or conditions. Among the factors determining the condition of workers in a particular period were the available supply of labor, the skills necessary to a particular job, the type of industry in which one was employed, and the attitudes of courts and other governmental agencies toward labor and business. During much of our history, labor was considered a commodity whose value would fluctuate with supply and demand, just as the cost of raw materials or manufactured products might rise and fall.

The first half of the nineteenth century is an especially interesting period in American labor history. During these years, industrialization proceeded quite rapidly. Yet there was widespread ambivalence about the new machinery, the factory system, and the introduction of time clocks and factory whistles to regulate the cycle of one's life. There was also a well-established social philosophy as to the position of classes, the responsibilities of the employer, the relationship of work and leisure, and the roles of men and women in the labor force and in the home. Such deep social beliefs are not easily discarded; only grudgingly were they modified to meet the demands of the new industrialism. For a time, some of the new capitalists attempted to reconcile the old social philosophy of the paternalistic employer and his responsibility for the worker with the factory system of labor. Gradually management began breaking down older prerogatives of labor and insisting upon punctuality, obedience, and a pattern of discipline that might enhance efficiency on the shop floor.

Early labor historians — the so-called Wisconsin School — concentrated their study on the organized labor movement and labor-management confrontations. A newer group of scholars has developed the "New Labor History," investigating a much broader range of subjects. Domestic servants, unorganized office workers, slaves and others have been studied, with considerable attention devoted to workers' social and cultural values, rather than only their economic concerns. Barbara M. Tucker's book is a case study of the textile factories developed by Samuel Slater. But much of her attention is devoted to the relationship of family and religion to the development of the factory system.

To attract workers to his factories, Samuel Slater tried to construct a bridge to the past. The design of his factory colonies, the architecture of his company dwellings, and the institutions he established in the villages conformed in broad outline to those found throughout much of New England a century earlier. This link with tradition was not cosmetic, and it reached into the workplace. The occupations provided for men, women, and children, the conditions under which they labored, and the settlement of wages conformed to custom. Within the context of the new industrial order, familial values were preserved; alterations in the new economic orientation and structure of a society do not inevitably lead to major changes in its traditional units or beliefs.

In Slater's factory communities, a traditional division of labor based on age, gender, and the marital status of family members emerged. Married men performed customary tasks associated with a rural way of life, such as farming and casual labor, while their wives remained at home to care for the family. . . .

In the first decades of the nineteenth century, young children, adolescent boys and girls, and unmarried women comprised approximately three-fourths of the industrial labor force. From the outset few people opposed the employment of young people: quite the contrary, society condoned and encouraged it. H. Humphrey, noted author of child-training books, expressed the prevailing attitude toward the employment of children when he wrote:

> Our children must have employment — must be brought up in habits of industry. It is sinful, it is cruel to neglect this essential branch of their education. Make all the use you can of persuasion and example, and when these fail interpose your authority. . . . If he will not study, put him on to a farm, or send him into the shop, or in some other way provide regular employment for him.

. . . The young labor force of Union Mills in Webster was typical. In 1840 thirty children and adolescents worked in the carding department under the direction of an overseer and several second hands. Approximately two-thirds of the workers there were female; 52 percent were children from nine to twelve years of age, 31 percent were from thirteen to fifteen years, and the remainder were sixteen or older. In the spinning department, the gender ratio approximated that of the carding room. Children as young as eight were introduced to the factory system through employment in this department. Of the twenty-five laborers employed there, 32 percent were from eight to twelve years of age, 44 percent were from thirteen to fifteen, and the remainder were sixteen or older. An overseer and a second hand monitored the labor of the spinning-department employees.

One of the largest rooms in the factory was the weaving department, and there young women, not children, dominated the labor force. At Union Mills in 1840 sixty-nine women wove either full or part time. With the exception of two young sisters, Mary and Sophia Strether, aged eleven and twelve, all of the women employed in the weaving department were between the ages of fourteen and twenty-four. Although some hand-loom weavers remained on the payroll, most of the cloth produced by Samuel Slater and Sons in 1840 was woven by machine.

Most of the people employed at Union Mills belonged to kinship groups. During the eary years of industrialization family labor dominated the factory floors. Slater employed only a few people who had no kin working for a Slater enterprise or who did not live in the factory colonies; such employees were men who assumed skilled and supervisory positions and girls and unmarried women who tended power looms. . . .

Under the family system of labor, householders exercised considerable power within the factory, influencing the composition of the labor force, the allocation of jobs in the various departments, the supervision of hands, and the payment of wages. Bargaining between labor and management over the employment of children and labor conditions began before the youngsters entered the mills. On behalf of their children, householders negotiated a contract with Samuel Slater. Casual and verbal compacts at first, these agreements became more formal over time. Although written contracts certainly were initiated earlier, the first set of formal agreements found in the Slater company records are dated 1827; the last are dated 1840. Drawn up in February and March and effective from April 1, the annual contracts made between householders and Samuel Slater listed the names of kin employed, their rate of pay, and any special conditions pertaining to their employment. Typical of these agreements was one signed by John McCausland in 1828:

> Agreed with John McCausland for himself & family to work one year from Apr. 1st next as follows viz: —
> Self at watching ⅚ pr night = provided that any contract made with Saml. Slater for the year shall be binding in preference to this —
> Self to make sizing at 9/-pr. week
> Daughter Jane — 12 pr week —
> Son Alex.   —7/   "   "
> " James   —5/   "   "
> each of the children to have the privilege of 3 months Schooling and Alex to be let to the mule spinners if wished.

Education and training provisions were commonly included in the contracts. Parents sought release time from factory employment so that their children could attend school from two to four months annually, and permission was granted for both boys and girls to attend class. For their sons, householders sometimes sought further concessions. Like John McCausland, many parents wanted their sons to learn a skilled trade such as mule spinning, an occupation that commanded both prestige and high wages. . . .

While these contracts limited labor turnover and guaranteed Slater a steady supply of workers, they also ensured that parents would retain their position as head of the kinship unit and that children would not gain economic independence. Children looked to their parents to protect their interests. All children employed in the factory had to be sponsored by a householder; with few exceptions before 1830, Slater did not look beyond the kinship unit for labor.

Parents apparently also determined in which department their children would work and the conditions under which they would do so, although this is not stated specifically in the contracts. Family members often worked in the same department, attending machines side by side. Mule spinners hired and paid their sons, nephews, or close family friends to piece for them, and weavers hired kin to assist them at their machines. In 1840 Asa Day, a blacksmith employed by Union Mills, Webster, placed his daughters, Francis and Caroline, aged nine and thirteen, in the carding room. John Costis's six children, who ranged in age from nine to eighteen, also worked there, while the four Drake youngsters, aged ten to sixteen, worked together in the spinning department. In the weaving room, sisters often tended looms near one another. Mary Strether worked beside her older sister, Sophia; the Boster sisters, the three Faulkner girls, and the Foster and the Fitts sisters also worked there.

Parental concern did not end with the formal agreement. Although Samuel Slater established strict rules and regulations for the smooth, efficient operation of the factory, and although he demanded that workers be punctual, regular in attendance, industrious, and disciplined, he nevertheless bowed to parental pressures and allowed householders appreciable influence over the supervision of hands and the payment of wages.

The organization of the factory floor in the Slater mills was a reflection of the dominant position of the male householder. Within each department, the supervisory hierarchy came to reflect the hierarchy of the home. All positions of authority, from the second hand to the overseer, were filled by men. Although female labor was predominant in the industrial labor force, no woman filled a managerial position. Like children, women were the subordinates, not the supervisors. The prefactory family hierarchy, in which authority and power were vested in the husband, was transferred from the home to the new industrial order. The factory system did not challenge paternal authority; it perpetuated it. . . .

. . . In the organization and operation of his industrial communities, Slater respected the desires of householders and incorporated traditional values, practices, and customs within the new order. In return for his safeguarding of traditional prerogatives, householders provided Slater with a steady supply of tractable, industrious, reliable hands. The bargain that had been made between Samuel Slater and his workers in Pawtucket could be seen operating in Slatersville, Webster, Wilkinsonville, and the many other Slater-style communities throughout New England. As long as both labor and management adhered to its side of the agreement, harmonious relations between the two parties prevailed.

Industrial discipline posed some of the gravest problems faced by early factory masters, who had to devise various methods to teach people the so-called habits of industry: regularity, obedience, sobriety, steady intensity, and punctuality. Most manufacturers solved such problems in one of two ways: the stick-and-carrot approach as described by Sidney Pollard or the more subtle, internalized form of discipline as discussed by E. P. Thompson. Using the arguments of Max Weber and Erich Fromm, Thompson has maintained that rewards and punishments do not always succeed in creating a disciplined, tractable, steady, industrious laborer. Internal forces or "inner compulsion," he asserts, usually prove more effective in harnessing all energies to work than any other compulsion can ever be. For this method to be effective, each worker had to be made his or her own taskmaster, had to be made to feel guilty for "deviant" conduct, and had to develop an internal drive toward right and proper behavior. Among the British working class, Thompson ascribed that internal force to religion, especially Methodism. In Webster, Slatersville, and Wilkinsonville internal self-control also served to discipline the labor force. There the church and the family were the twin forces employed to exact compliance with factory rules and regulations. Discipline, however, did not begin and end at the factory door; beliefs taught in the church and the home circumscribed the behavior of the entire society. . . .

In Webster the Baptists, the Methodists, and the Congregationalists all received support from the Slater family, and although Samuel Slater and his sons belonged to the Congregational church, the Methodists in Webster received favored treatment. Samuel Slater encouraged the establishment of the Methodist church, and throughout the antebellum period his company continued to support it. Slater provided a plot of land for the church, laid its foundation, and bought sixteen of its forty pews for the exclusive use of his employees. Slater's company later built the parsonage and was responsible for the continued maintenance of church buildings. Whenever church officials required financial assistance, they turned first to the company and only later to the congregation. In effect the company became a church proprietor, exercising considerable influence over religious matters.

The Slater family encouraged its laborers to attend worship services and participate in other church activities. John Slater, Sr., expected all company employees to attend Sabbath services: "It has long been one of the established regulations of the mills, that the help are expected to attend public worship on the Sabbath. Also that no work will be done or repairs made by the company on that day." Manufacturers also allowed laborers leave to attend special church functions, often shutting down the mills and closing their shops so that all hands could attend revivals, camp meetings, and special quarterly sessions. During the summer revival of 1839, the mills were closed for several days to allow local Methodists to attend the meeting. "This being camp meeting with our Good Methodists," wrote factory agent Alexander Hodges, it "will be rather a broken one with the Mills." Clearly, Methodists formed such a large proportion of the labor force that their absence effectively curtailed operations.

By the late 1830s and early 1840s, Slater's labor force was predominantly Methodist. A comparison of employment ledgers and local church membership rolls reveals that prominent members of church boards, superintendents of Sunday schools, lay preachers, and stewards held important skilled and supervisory positions in local Slater factories. Charles Waite, resident manager of Slater's Phoenix Thread Mill, served variously as Sabbath school administrator, treasurer, and secretary-treasurer of the Methodist church. William Kimball, for ten years resident superintendent of the Slater and Kimball mill, served as the assistant secretary of the Methodist Sabbath school. At Union Mills, four of the six machinists, two of the four dressers, all of the bailers, and many of the mule spinners belonged to the church. Their sons and daughters filled the unskilled jobs in the carding, spinning, and weaving rooms. . . .

In part Samuel Slater and other manufacturers supported religion because they viewed it as a form of social control which facilitated the discipline of workers. The dictums and discipline advanced by the church became part of the foundation of a work ethic, and as such they served to train, discipline, and control workers. This was the case in Webster, where the Methodist church educated a whole generation in the dictates of their religion. The written tracts, hymns, sermons, and other literature used in the church all advanced the same messages: obedience, deference, industry, honesty, punctuality, and temperance. The lessons prepared the young operatives for ultimate salvation and also trained them to be good, obedient factory hands. In Webster the Methodist Sabbath school was the principal agency through which these values were taught.

The Webster Sabbath school flourished. In 1841 A. D. Merrill, minister of the local church, reported:

> The present state of the Sabbath School in the Webster Station of the M. E. Church must be viewed as in a state of more than ordinary prosperity. . . . It is the sentiment of the Superintendant that the school is more prosperous now than ever before at this season of the year since he resided in town. Such is the interest felt by the Superintendants and Teachers that they have during the last Quarter established a monthly Prayer meeting for the benefit and spiritual interest of the school.

This Sabbath school owed its origin to Samuel Slater. Like his mentor, Jedediah Strutt, Samuel Slater established Sabbath schools in each of his industrial villages. Based on the British system he had observed, these schools were to "condition the children for their primary duty in life as hewers of wood and drawers of water."

Through these Sunday schools, Samuel Slater sought to foster attitudes toward right and proper conduct that would make children good citizens and good workers. A hymn from Dr. Isaac Watts's songbooks sung by the children in Slatersville and Webster began:

> Why should I deprive my neighbor
> Of his goods against his will?
> Hands were made for honest labour,
> Not to plunder or to steal.

When churches became firmly established in Webster and Slatersville, Slater disbanded his Sunday school and relinquished moral education and industrial training to the churches.

In transferring moral education to religious bodies, Slater could be confident that the church would continue to inculcate virtues and beliefs sympathetic to the new industrial order. In Webster, for example, the men who ran the Sunday school were the same men who supervised local factory operations. For twelve to fourteen hours each day, six days each week, children worked under Charles Waite and William Kimball, and on the seventh day they listened while the same men interpreted the scriptures. . . .

Values taught in the Sunday schools proved favorable to factory discipline. One of the first lessons taught to children concerned obedience. This was the first law of childhood, the first rule of the church, and the regulation deemed indispensable for the smooth, efficient operation of the factory. Sabbath school teachers stressed this dictum and condemned all children who disobeyed those in authority, whether at home, at school, or in the factory. One lesson used to instill this particular value might have been introduced to children in the following way: "As you sit here now, listening to me," the Sabbath school teacher might begin,

> can you remember any disobedient habits of yours, that make the father and the Mother unhappy, when they look at you and see how fast you are growing, without growing better? Is it true that you have had a bad temper, and do not love to be controlled? . . . Is it true that you have grown, but have not grown out of any of these habits: just as bad as ever, just as disobedient, just as wicked with the tongue as ever?

Punctuality, a cornerstone of any work ethic, also received considerable attention from the Methodists. They were concerned about time. In an era when people were accustomed to family time and to task-oriented labor, Methodist children were being taught: "Be punctual. Do everything exactly at the time." In his reports to the company, factory agent and Sabbath school administrator Charles Waite often stressed the need for punctuality: "Punctuality is the life of business whether in the counting house or the factory." The severe style of life demanded of the faithful allowed no place for carefree play, laughter, or harmless pranks. "No room for mirth or trifling here," began a child's hymn on amusement titled "And Am I Only Born to Die?" Children were constantly warned that "life so soon is gone," that although

> We are but young — yet we must die,
> Perhaps our latter end is nigh.

All hymns carried a similar warning: children should "sport no more with idle toys, and seek far purer, richer joys," devote themselves totally to Christ, and obey the teachings of the church.

Many values, including punctuality, attention to duty, and seriousness of purpose, were neatly summarized in the Webster Sabbath school constitution, which was drawn up by local church officials. The constitution was in fact a code of conduct similar to that maintained in the factory. In part the constitution required all children "to be regular in attendance, and punctually present at the hour appointed to open school. To pay a strict and respectful attention to whatever the teacher or Superintendent shall say or request. To avoid whispering, laughing and any other improper conduct." Altogether these values became the moral foundation for a strict work ethic. But one element essential to the successful operation of this ethic was missing: internal self-discipline.

As a work ethic these dictums and values would have been much less effective had not the church also taught self-discipline, self-restraint, and self-regulation of behavior. All efforts were made to internalize values in order to create an inner discipline that would control and limit the child's behavior. Children were taught to "do good" instinctively and to develop an internal drive toward right and proper conduct. In effect, they became their own taskmasters; conscience rather than rewards and punishments directed their actions.

To achieve this end, Sunday school teachers linked proper conduct to grace or, to put it conversely, disobedience to damnation. An exchange used to close an infants' class made the connection explicit:

Teacher: Do you know who belong to Satan's army? Say after me — All who tell lies, all who swear and cheat; all who steal; all who are cruel.

In the child's mind, to cheat, to steal, to lie, or to misbehave in any way was to violate God's law, lose grace, and risk damnation. And such a risk was unthinkable. The songs published in *Hymns for Sunday Schools* describe hell in forceful and emotional terms:

> There is a dreadful hell,
>   And everlasting pains;
> There sinners must with devils dwell,
>   In darkness, fire, and chains.

Images of everlasting punishment and fears of eternal damnation worked to ensure a strict and steady compliance with the values advanced by the church.

The Sabbath school trained Webster's child workers well. In the factory, children quickly learned to obey all orders, for to disobey was to feel anxious and to risk censure or eternal damnation. Corporal punishment, fines, and the ultimate discipline — dismissal — were largely absent, and in fact were unnecessary when children readily and willingly, not to say cheerfully, obeyed the dictates of second hand and overseer. Operations almost always ran smoothly. Supervisors faced few disciplinary problems such as absence, theft, inattention to duties, or general mischievous behavior. The instructions children received in the Sabbath school were largely responsible for the exemplary behavior.

The tenets of the church were reinforced by lessons learned in the home. In the area of discipline the responsibility of parents was widely recognized. . . .

The values taught in the home were those required by industry: they served to make both dutiful, respectful children and submissive workers. Even the most liberal authorities on child-rearing practices, such as Lydia M. Child, cautioned parents that "implicit obedience is the first law of childhood," that "whatever a mother says always must be done." Other writers concurred. John Abbott, described by one historian as the Spock and Seuss to the people of the Civil War generation, went a step further and joined disobedience with wickedness. In *Child at Home* he wrote: "Think you, God can look upon the disobedience of a child as a trifling sin? . . . It is inexcusable ingratitude."

> The only path of safety and happiness is implicit obedience. If you, in the slightest particular, yield to temptation, and do that which you know to be wrong, you will not know when or where to stop. To hide one crime, you will be guilty of another; and thus you will draw upon yourself the frown of your maker, and expose yourself to sorrow for time and eternity.

All commands had to be immediately and cheerfully obeyed. Children were expected to respond to orders with glad and happy hearts. Again John Abbott: "Obedience requires of you, not only to do as you are bidden, but to do it with cheerfulness and alacrity"; and Theodore Dwight, Jr.: "Children should be obedient — must be obedient, habitually and cheerfully."

If obedience was the first law of childhood, then deference was the second. Children quickly realized their subordinate position within the patriarchal family. Mother taught that father was the head and ruler of the household, that he stood before them as God's representative on earth, and that, as supreme earthly legislator, he exercised complete control over their every action. According to Humphrey, "children must early be brought under absolute parental authority, and must submit to all the rules and regulations of the family during the whole period of their minority, and even longer, if they choose to remain at home." Once again religious injunctions were employed. Humphrey warned: "Now to disobey your parents, is to dishonor them. This you have done, and in doing it, you see you have broken God's holy law. We can forgive you, but that will not lessen your guilt, nor procure forgiveness from your heavenly Father. You must repent and do so no more."

Lessons taught in the home, reinforced by tenets learned from the scriptures, became the moral foundation for a disciplined labor force. Workers found little difference between disciplinary patterns in home and factory. Both home and factory were paternalistic, and both were controlled by men who expected unquestioning compliance with all commands. Children merely transferred their values and behavior patterns from the home and the church to the factory; old values were easily accommodated by the new institution.

Changes under way within the factory would have important consequences for the family system of labor. It was difficult for the Slater family to achieve a higher level of economic rationality while householders continued to influence factory operations. Disciplinary policies, placement procedures, and conditions of labor, customarily part of the domain of householders, were in conflict with the rational organization and operation of the factory floor. Authority could not remain divided between householder and factory master. By the 1830s management appeared to be ready to sacrifice the moral discipline associated with the family and the church in order to obtain more extensive control over the individual worker. Privileges once accorded the householder in the factory came under scrutiny and began to be dismantled as economic factors became the primary influence in the actions of management. . . .

Among the first issues addressed by the Slater family was the work schedule. The Slater family introduced Sunday and overtime work, and members of the same family began working different shifts. Some children worked extra hours on Tuesdays and Wednesdays, others on Thursdays and Saturdays; householders and older boys worked on Sundays. Mothers could not be certain when all members of the family or unit would be together. Sunday lost significance as the traditional day for family as well as for religious communion. Further inroads against tradition followed. Morning and afternoon breaks, which had long been periods for workers to meet and chat with kin, to exchange gossip with fellow workers, even to slip out of the mill and dash home or run errands, were abolished. Agents complained that workers took advantage of the breaks, that they stretched the allotted fifteen minutes into forty-five or sixty minutes. By eliminating rest periods, Slater forced more work from his laborers.

Parental supervisory prerogatives also came under attack. Samuel Slater and Sons assumed the power once vested in mule spinners to hire, pay, discipline, and dismiss piecers. A mule spinner no longer had the right to hire and supervise his sons or to teach them his trade. Parents were also forbidden to enter the mill and supervise their children while they were in the overseer's charge. Householders who objected to this regulation were fired. Peter Mayo's entire family, for example, was discharged because he attempted "to control his family whilst under charge of overseer and disorderly conduct generally." Economic incentives and penalties began to replace traditional forms of control within the factory. To encourage acceptable standards of work and behavior, the stick-and-carrot approach was introduced. Black marks were recorded against weavers for shoddy work and fines for tardiness, absence without leave, or disorderly conduct were deducted from their wages, while good work was rewarded by extra allowances.

A further assault against long-standing practices occurred when manufacturers abandoned the family wage system and began to pay wages directly to individual workers. Initiated in the mid-1830s, this method of payment was first introduced in the weaving department, but when parents complained, the former system was restored. In the early 1840s the firm tried once again, and this time it succeeded. By 1845 each worker received his or her wages. On settlement day in 1845 Daniel Wade, a watchman, and his two adolescent daughters, Laura and Elmira, both weavers, received separate pay slips. Children now could dispose of their own income. With the introduction of the new pay system, contracts were eliminated.

When the householder collected all wages, he controlled the available income and distributed it according to his priorities. With this new arrangement, however, economic power shifted in part to children and adolescent wage workers, and the householder's domination of the family was threatened. Parents had to negotiate with each child over the disposal of his or her wages. With economic independence, with jobs available to individuals in Webster and elsewhere, children, charges, and boarders could move out of the family home and take up residence in local boardinghouses or leave the community altogether. By this time the company operated two large factory boardinghouses, one that accommodated fifty-six men and women and another that housed twenty-eight people. Local residents also took in lodgers. . . .

While Slater checked the power of the householder, he also tried to introduce new policies that would increase the productivity of his labor force. The workday was stretched another fifteen, twenty, or thirty minutes, depending on the whim or the needs of the factory agent. It should be remembered that few workmen had clocks, and that a factory bell summoned hands to work, signaled breaks for lunch and dinner, and tolled again at quitting time. But factory time invariably fell behind true time, and agents exacted extra work from hands. This was the case not only in the Slater mills but throughout southern New England. At the Hope factory in Rhode Island, operatives started work approximately twenty-five minutes after daybreak and did not leave for home until the factory bell signaled the end of the day at 8:00 P.M. But as the *Free Inquirer* reported, 8:00 by factory time "is from twenty to twenty-five minutes behind the true time." Many manufacturers defended this practice, arguing that "the workmen and children being thus employed, have no time to spend in idleness or vicious amusements." Forced to maintain the production schedules set by the manufacturer and to cut costs where possible, supervisors lengthened the workday to obtain additional labor from hands.

To increase production further, the stretch-out and the speedup were intensified. Slater crowded more and more machines into already cramped spinning, carding, and weaving rooms and assigned additional machines to each worker. In the weaving department, for example, the number of looms attended by each weaver was increased steadily from two to three to four and then to six. Not only did the hands operate more machines, but the machines were run at higher speeds. Initially the speedup was management's response to the pressure of weavers who worked on a piece-rate basis (approximately 20 cents a cut for weaving 4-by-4 sheeting and shirting), who could increase their earnings only by producing more cloth. In 1837 Alexander Hodges complained to the head office: "The weavers are being uneasy about the speed being slow and some of the new ones will leave. I think we had better put on a little in order to keep the best of them nothing short of this will answer as the mills in this vicinity have advanced the prices." Soon, however, the speedup became a method to increase production. Writing to Union Mills in 1855, Fletcher confided, "As soon as the supply of good weavers can be obtained, . . . the increased speed of looms will show itself by increased quantity." Piece rates remained constant at the earlier level. The speedup and stretch-out were introduced into almost every room in the factory, without an appreciable increase in pay. . . .

Supply and demand factors, new technology, education laws, and factory acts worked together by the 1850s to transform the labor force employed at Samuel Slater and Sons. The route pursued by the firm led toward an autonomous worker, one who was cut off from his or her family and looked to the factory system for opportunity, support, and survival. The labor force had been streamlined; the family unit, tied to a firm social base, was replaced by an individual tied to the wage economy.

STUDY GUIDE

1. Older traditions emphasized the importance of the family, parental authority, and the differences between men's and women's work. How did the early industrialists such as Slater attempt to reconcile the new factory system with these preindustrial traditions?

2. Explain how the ethical and moral values of Protestant Christianity were related to the goals of industrial management.

3. How did the Slater Company break down traditional prerogatives of labor and older patterns of parental control?

4. In another country or another period, the expansion of the available

labor force by the introduction of women, children, and immigrants might not have resulted in a general degradation of the position of all labor. What, in the position of labor in the early nineteenth century or in the general state of the Industrial Revolution at that time, might account for the fact that such degradation did happen in the United States?

5. What similarities and differences are there in the lot of workers in the early nineteenth century and in the present with respect to: their ability to bargain to improve their positions; the training necessary for their jobs; their mobility; their relationship to their employers; their security?

BIBLIOGRAPHY

As was indicated in the Introduction to this reading, labor history has moved in new directions in recent years. Yet a good deal of very fine work was done in an earlier period that is both readable and illuminating. Norman Ware's *The Industrial Worker, 1840–1860* (1924) gives a graphic description of conditions in the factories, while Carl Bridenbaugh's *The Colonial Craftsman* (1950) studies labor in the preindustrial period. Two early works on the textile mills are: Caroline F. Ware, *The Early New England Cotton Manufacture: A Study in Industrial Beginnings* (1931), and Hannah Josephson, *The Golden Threads* (1940). The writings of factory women are published in Philip Foner, ed., *The Factory Girls* (1977), while Steven Dunwell, *The Run of the Mill* (1978) is a marvelous collection of photographs and illustrations of the factories, with an accompanying text.

A large number of works such as that by Tucker study industrialization in particular towns or industries. The following studies are representative: Paul G. Faler, *Mechanics and Manufacturers in . . . Lynn, Massachusetts, 1780–1860* (1981); Thomas Dublin, *Women at Work: The Transformation of Work and Community in Lowell, Massachusetts, 1826–1860* (1979); and a book by Anthony F. C. Wallace who turned from studying the Seneca Indians (Reading No. 1) to examining a factory town in his book *Rockdale: The Growth of an American Village in the Early Industrial Revolution* (1978). Michael Frisch and Daniel J. Walkowitz, eds., *Working Class America: Essays on Labor, Community, and American Society* (1983) is a collection of "new labor history" essays. Full-scale, individual studies include: Bruce Laurie, *Working People of Philadelphia, 1800–1850* (1980); Sean Wilentz, *Chants Democratic: New York City and the Rise of the American Working Class, 1788–1850* (1984); and Howard Rock, *Artisans of the New Republic: The Tradesmen of New York City in the Age of Jefferson* (1979). The bibliographies following readings Nos. 8 and 14 list other relevant works.

There are a number of one-volume surveys of American labor history that carry the story beyond the Civil War. Henry Pelling, *American Labor* (1960) is a very brief introduction. Joseph G. Rayback, *A History of American Labor* (1959), and Ronald Filippelli, *Labor in the U.S.A.: A History* (1984) are longer works.

Robert Lindneux's "The Trail of Tears" vividly depicts the suffering of the Cherokees during their removal from their ancient homeland.

10

DALE VAN EVERY

Trail of Tears

In the Declaration of Independence, Jefferson had written that "all men are created equal" and are divinely endowed with the rights of life, liberty, and the pursuit of happiness. The members of the Continental Congress who signed their names to that proclamation were concerned with the rights of the colonists in relation to the governing power of England. Few of them considered these ringing phrases as guaranteeing social or political rights to minorities within American society. Some few voices were raised to suggest that women, blacks, and Indians might have a greater cause to revolt than did the planters, lawyers, and merchants who led the revolution against the authority of King George III. Throughout much of American history, various national, racial, and religious groups were treated as less than equal and beyond the protection of the Bill of Rights.

The Age of Reform exhibited some striking contrasts in American sentiment. In many respects, it is a most revealing period for judging both the achievements and the failures of the American people in living up to the philosophy expressed in the Declaration. The 1830s witnessed the first great period of American social reform, with scores of organizations founded to assist the handicapped and the unfortunate. But it is also a decade that, one might say, lives in historical infamy, because American Indian tribes were removed from their ancient homelands, as whites coveted and took over their lands.

In the selection that follows, Dale Van Every suggests that this is the ultimate catastrophe that can befall a people. Being torn from the land of one's birth, losing most or all of one's belongings, being forced to find a livelihood as best one can in an unfamiliar country, and losing one's very sense of identity are experiences we can hardly comprehend. The story of the removal of the Civilized Tribes of the south-eastern United States — the Creeks, Chickasaws, Choctaws, Semi-noles, and Cherokees — to new territories beyond the Mississippi River, and the numerous casualties they suffered along the "Trail of Tears," is one of the most famous and tragic in American history. In the North, the same story was repeated with different characters on a somewhat smaller scale. Whatever the Declaration of Independence meant to white, male Americans in the early nineteenth century, it must have appeared to be a bitter mockery to the native Americans who were forced out of their homes by this cruel invasion.

History records the sufferings of innumerable peoples whose country was overrun and possessed by alien invaders. There have been relatively fewer recorded occasions, as in the instance of the Babylonian Captivity of the Jews, of an entire people being compelled to abandon their country. This has been universally regarded as the ultimate catastrophe that can befall a people inasmuch as it deprives them of the roots which sustain their identity. Upon the exiles has been pronounced a sentence that by its nature denies all hope of reprieve or relief. To Indians, with their inherited conception of the land of their birth as the repository of those spiritual links to their ancestors which were holy and therefore indissoluble, the prospect of expulsion was clothed with added dreads beyond human evaluation.

The threat was in all its aspects so monstrous that in the spring of 1838 the bewildered masses of the Cherokee people, homeless, hungry, desti-tute, still remained incredulous that so fearful a fate could actually impend. Outrageously as they had been harassed for the past ten years by Georgia and Alabama white men, they still clung to their trust that most white men wished them well. This was a confidence instilled in them by the reports of John Ross [a respected Cherokee chief] who had been made more conversant with the apparent truth by his wide travels across the immense white nation stretching beyond the Cherokee horizon. They had been further prepared to accept his judgment on the inherent goodness of the white race by their own experience with the many white men who had lived among them as teachers, missionaries and counselors, sharing their struggles and tribulations. Their more recent experience with [Gen-eral John] Wool and his officers and with [General R. G.] Dunlap and his

Adaptation of Chapter 18 from *Disinherited: The Lost Birthright of the American Indian* by Dale Van Every. Copyright © 1966 by Dale Van Every. By permission of William Morrow & Company, Inc.

Tennesseans had strengthened their impression that the white race could not be wholly committed to their destruction.

Ross was still in Washington engaged in a final frantic effort, with some dawning hope of success, to wring from the administration a temporary postponement of removal. His followers were continuing to obey his injunction that they persist in their nonviolent resistance. Most continued to refuse even to give their names or a list of their belongings to the agents commissioned to organize the details of the migration. May 23, two years from the date of the President's proclamation of the Senate's ratification of the treaty, was the day, as all had for months been warned, when their residence in the east would become illegal but they still could not believe that a development so frightful could be given reality by that day's sunrise. Even after five regiments of regulars and 4,000 militia and volunteers from adjacent states began pouring into their country they still could not believe.

Major General [Winfield] Scott arrived May 8 to take command of the military operation. His May 10, 1838 address to the Cherokee people proclaimed the terrible reality in terms no Cherokee could longer mistake:

Cherokees — The President of the United States has sent me with a powerful army, to cause you, in obedience to the treaty of 1835, to join that part of your people who are already established in prosperity on the other side of the Mississippi. Unhappily, the two years which were allowed for the purpose, you have suffered to pass away without following, and without making preparations to follow, and now, or by the time this solemn *address* shall reach your distant settlements, the emigration must be commenced in haste, but, I hope, without disorder. I have no power, by granting a farther delay, to correct the error that you have committed. The full moon of May is already on the wane, and before another shall have passed away, every Cherokee man, woman, and child . . . must be in motion to join their brethren in the far West. . . . My troops already occupy many positions in the country that you are to abandon, and thousands and thousands are approaching from every quarter, to tender resistance and escape alike hopeless. . . . Chiefs, head men, and warriors — Will you then, by resistance, compel us to resort to arms? God forbid. Or will you, by flight, seek to hide yourself in mountains and forests, and thus oblige us to hunt you down? Remember that, in pursuit, it may be impossible to avoid conflicts. The blood of the white man, or the blood of the red man, may be spilt, and if spilt, however accidentally, it may be impossible for the discreet and humane among you, or among us, to prevent a general war and carnage. Think of this, my Cherokee brethern. I am an old warrior, and have been present at many a scene of slaughter; but spare me, I beseech you, the horror of witnessing the destruction of the Cherokees.

Scott sincerely hoped that the enforced removal could be accomplished not only without bloodshed but without undue hardship inflicted upon the unfortunate thousands being ejected at bayonet's point from their homes. He had been impressed by Ross during conferences with him in Washington and like most professional soldiers of his time had developed a genuine regard for Indians. In his May 17 general orders to his troops he sternly admonished them to practice restraint:

> Considering the number and temper of the mass to be removed together with the extent and fastnesses of the country occupied, it will readily occur that simple indiscretions, acts of harshness, and cruelty on the part of our troops, may lead, step by step, to delays, to impatience, and exasperation, and, in the end, to a general war and carnage; a result, in the case of these particular Indians, utterly abhorrent to the generous sympathies of the whole American people. Every possible kindness, compatible with the necessity of removal, must, therefore, be shown by the troops; and if, in the ranks, a despicable individual should be found capable of inflicting a wanton injury or insult on any Cherokee man, woman, or child, it is hereby made the special duty of the nearest good officer or man instantly to interpose, and to seize and consign the guilty wretch to the severest penalty of the laws. The major-general is fully persuaded that this injunction will not be neglected by the brave men under his command, who cannot be otherwise than jealous of their honor and that of their country.

Scott's intentions were humane but the larger portion of his army were state levies unaccustomed to discipline and without his professional susceptibilities. The nature of the operation required the army's dispersion in scattered detachments over a wide area. Most of the Cherokee to be removed were inhabitants of Georgia and their apprehension was conducted by Georgia militia who had long as a matter of policy been habituated to dealing harshly with Indians. Prison stockades had been erected at assembly and embarkation points in which the Cherokee were to be herded and confined while awaiting transportation west. There was little or no likelihood of attempted resistance. Most had been disarmed during Wool's regime and the irresistible military power that had been brought to bear was self-evident. The classic account of what next transpired is that recorded by James Mooney. His contribution to the Bureau of American Ethnology, eventually published in the 19th Annual Report in 1900 under the title *Myths of the Cherokee*, included a history of the Cherokee based upon years of field work. His narrative of the 1838 expulsion was drawn from personal interviews with survivors, white officers as well as Cherokee victims, and had therefore much of the vitality of an eyewitness report:

> The history of this Cherokee removal of 1838, as gleaned by the author from the lips of actors in the tragedy, may well exceed in weight of grief and pathos any other passage in American history. Even the much-sung exile of the Acadians falls far behind it in its sum of death and misery. Under Scott's order the troops were disposed at various points throughout the Cherokee country, where stockade forts were erected for gathering in

and holding the Indians preparatory to removal. From these, squads of troops were sent to search out with rifle and bayonet every small cabin hidden away in the coves or by the sides of mountain streams, to seize and bring in as prisoners all the occupants, however or wherever they might be found. Families at dinner were startled by the sudden gleam of bayonets in the doorway and rose up to be driven with blows and oaths along the weary miles of trail that led to the stockade. Men were seized in their fields or going along the road, women were taken from their wheels and children from their play. In many cases, on turning for one last look as they crossed the ridge, they saw their homes in flames, fired by the lawless rabble that followed on the heels of the soldiers to loot and pillage. So keen were these outlaws on the scent that in some instances they were driving off the cattle and other stock of the Indians almost before the soldiers had fairly started their owners in the other direction. Systematic hunts were made by the same men for Indian graves, to rob them of the silver pendants and other valuables deposited with the dead. A Georgia volunteer, afterward a colonel in the confederate service, said: "I fought through the civil war and have seen men shot to pieces and slaughtered by thousands, but the Cherokee removal was the cruelest work I ever knew." To prevent escape the soldiers had been ordered to approach and surround each house, so far as possible, so as to come upon the occupants without warning. One old patriarch, when thus surprised, calmly called his children and grandchildren around him, and, kneeling down, bid them pray with him in their own language, while the astonished onlookers looked on in silence. Then rising he led the way into exile. A woman, on finding the house surrounded, went to the door and called up the chickens to be fed for the last time, after which, taking her infant on her back and her two other children by the hand, she followed her husband with the soldiers.

Within days nearly 17,000 Cherokee had been crowded into the stockades. Sanitation measures were inadequate in those makeshift concentration camps. Indian families, accustomed to a more spacious and isolated existence, were unable to adapt to the necessities of this mass imprisonment. Hundreds of the inmates sickened. The Indian was by his nature peculiarly susceptible to the depressions produced by confinement. Many lost any will to live and perceiving no glimmer of hope, resigned themselves to death. Those who had become converts found some comfort in the ministrations of their white and native pastors. In every stockade hymn singings and prayer meetings were almost continuous.

All physical preparations had been carefully planned in advance by the federal authorities in charge of the migration so that little time might be lost in getting the movement under way. In the first and second weeks of June two detachments of some 800 exiles were driven aboard the waiting fleets of steamboats, keelboats and flatboats for the descent of the Tennessee. They passed down the storied waterway by the same route taken by the first white settlers of middle Tennesse under John Donelson in 1780. In the shadow of Lookout Mountain they could survey the wilderness vastnesses from which for 20 years bands of their immediate forebears had sallied to devastate the white frontier, some of them commanded by war chiefs who had lived to be condemned to this exile. Then, at Muscle Shoals there came an ironic contrast between the past and the future as Indians being driven from their ancient homeland were committed to transportation by the white man's newest invention. They disembarked from their boats to clamber, momentarily diverted, aboard the cars drawn by the two puffing little locomotives of the railroad recently constructed to move freight and passengers around the rapids. Returning to other boats, they resumed their seemingly interminable journey in the debilitating heat of an increasingly oppressive summer. The attendant army officers, however sympathetic, were helpless against the waves of illnesses. Scott, moving new contingents toward embarkation, was appalled by the reports he received of the mounting death rate among those who had already been dispatched.

The troops assembled for Cherokee expulsion had been by considered governmental design so numerous as to present a show of military power so overwhelming as to provide no faintest invitation to Indian resistance. By the army's first pounce more than nine tenths of the population had been rounded up and driven into the stockades. There remained only a handful of the wilder and more primitive residents of the higher mountains still at large. This handful, however, represented a problem causing Scott serious concern. Were they provoked to resist they might among their remote and cloud-wreathed peaks prove as difficult to apprehend as were the Seminole in their swamps. From this tactical threat sprang the one heroic action to gleam across the otherwise unrelieved despondency of the removal scene.

Tsali was an hitherto undistinguished mountain Cherokee who suddenly soared to an eminence in Cherokee annals comparable to the homage accorded an Attakullaculla, an Old Tassel, a Sequoyah or a John Ross. The stories of his inspired exploit, drawn from eyewitnesses, survivors and references in contemporary official records, vary in detail and have become encrusted by legend but coincide in most essentials. According to the more generally accepted version, a young Cherokee woman upon being assaulted by two soldiers killed both with a hatchet. Tsali hid the weapon under his shirt and assumed responsibility for his kinswoman's act. Scott could not permit the death of his soldiers to remain unpunished and served notice on the band of mountain Cherokee of which Tsali was a member that a scapegoat must be produced. The band felt that it had a reasonable chance to elude pursuit indefinitely but its councils were impressed by the advice of a white trader, William Thomas, a friend of his native customers in the notable tradition of Ludovic Grant, Alexander Cameron and John McDonald. Thomas pointed out the advantage that could be taken of Scott's demand. Tsali was prepared to offer his life for his people. His fellow tribesmen thereupon notified Scott that he would be turned over to American justice in return for American permission to remain unmolested in their mountains. Scott, eager to escape the uncertainties of a guerrilla campaign in so difficult a terrain, agreed to recommend this course to Washington. Tsali was brought in, the voluntary prisoner of his compatriots. His Cherokee custodians were required to serve as the firing squad by which he, his brother and his eldest son were executed. The story became one of the few Indian stories with a happy ending. Thomas continued for years to interest himself in the prolonged negotiations with the governments of the United States and North Carolina which eventually resulted in federal and state recognition of Cherokee title to their mountain holdings. Tsali's sacrifice had permitted this fraction of the nation to become the remnant of the East Cherokee [and] to cling to their homeland where they still are colorful inhabitants of the North Carolina mountains.

Aside from the Tsali episode the roundup of the Cherokee proceeded without interruption. By June 18 General Charles Floyd, commanding the Georgia militia engaged in it, was able to report to his governor that no Cherokee remained on the soil of Gerogia except as a prisoner in a stockade. Scott was able to discharge his volunteers June 17 and two days later to dispatch three of his five regular regiments to sectors where military needs were more pressing, two to the Canadian border and one to Florida.

Meanwhile so many migrants were dying in the drought and heat to which the initial removal was subjected that Scott was constrained to lighten the inexorable pressures. The Cherokee Council, which though technically illegal still spoke for the Cherokee people, begged for a postponement to the more healthful weather of autumn. Scott agreed. In July Ross returned and in conferences with Scott worked out a further agreement under which the Cherokee would cease passive resistance and under his supervision undertake a voluntary migration as soon as weather permitted. Scott was glad to be relieved of further need to use military force. The administration was glad to be offered some defense against the storm of northern criticism. Even Georgia made no serious protest, inasmuch as the Cherokee had already been removed from their land to stockades and there remained no questioning of the state's sovereignty. The one remonstrance, aside from the complaints of contractors, was voiced by the aging [Andrew] Jackson from his retirement at The Hermitage in a letter of August 23, 1838 to Felix Grundy, Attorney General of the United States:

> . . . The contract with Ross must be arrested, or you may rely upon it, the expense and other evils will shake the popularity of the adminstration to its

center. What madness and folly to have anything to do with Ross, when the agent was proceeding well with the removal. . . . The time and circumstances under which Gen'l Scott made this contract shows that he is no economist, or is, *sub rosa*, in league with [Henry] Clay & Co. to bring disgrace on the administration. The evil is done. It behooves Mr. [President Martin] Van Buren to act with energy to throw it off his shoulders. I enclose a letter to you under cover, unsealed, which you may read, seal, and deliver to him, that you may aid him with your views in getting out of this real difficulty.

Your friend in haste,
Andrew Jackson

P.S. I am so feeble I can scarcely wield my pen, but friendship dictates it & the subject excites me. Why is it that the scamp Ross is not banished from the notice of the administration?

Ross, having at last recognized the inevitable, gave to his preparations for the voluntary removal the same driving energy and attention to detail he had until then devoted to resisting removal. All phases of the organization of the national effort were gathered into his hands. All financial arrangements were under his supervision, including the disbursement of the basic federal subsistence allowance of 16 cents a day for each person and 40 cents a day for each horse. For convenience in management en route the 13,000 Cherokee remaining in the stockades were divided into detachments of roughly a thousand to head each of which he appointed a Cherokee commander. At a final meeting of the Cherokee Council it was provided that the constitution and laws of the Nation should be considered equally valid in the west.

The first detachment set out October 1, 1838 on the dreaded journey over the route which in Cherokee memory became known as The Trail of Tears. The last started November 4. The improvement in weather awaited during the tedious summer months in the stockades did not materialize. The spring migration had been cursed by oppressive heat and drought. The fall migration encountered deluges of rain followed by excessive cold. To the hundreds of deaths from heat-induced diseases were now added new hundreds of deaths from prolonged exposure.

The most vivid general account of the 1838 migration is again that of James Mooney, assembled from the recollections of participants:

. . . in October, 1838, the long procession of exiles was set in motion. A very few went by the river route; the rest, nearly all of the 13,000, went overland. Crossing to the north side of the Hiwassee at a ferry above Gunstocker creek, they proceeded down along the river, the sick, the old people, and the smaller children, with the blankets, cooking pots, and other belongings in wagons, the rest on foot or on horses. The number of wagons was 645. It was like the march of an army, regiment after regiment, the wagons in the center, the officers along the line and the horsemen on the flanks and at the rear. Tennessee river was crossed at Tuckers (?) ferry, a short distance above Jollys island, at the mouth of the Hiwassee. Thence the route lay south of Pikeville, through McMinnville and on to Nashville, where the Cumberland was crossed. Then they went on to Hopkinsville, Kentucky, where the noted chief White-path, in charge of a detachment, sickened and died. His people buried him by the roadside, with a box over the grave and poles with streamers around it, that the others coming on behind might note the spot and remember him. Somewhere also along that march of death — for the exiles died by tens and twenties every day of the journey — the devoted wife of John Ross sank down, leaving him to go on with the bitter pain of bereavement added to heartbreak at the ruin of his nation. The Ohio was crossed at a ferry near the mouth of the Cumberland, and the army passed on through southern Illinois until the great Mississippi was reached opposite Cape Girardeau, Missouri. It was now the middle of winter, with the river running full of ice, so that several detachments were obliged to wait some time on the eastern bank for the channel to become clear. In talking with old men and women at Tahlequah the author found that the lapse of over half a century had not sufficed to wipe out the memory of the miseries of that halt beside the frozen river, with hundreds of sick and dying penned up in wagons or stretched upon the ground, with only a blanket overhead to keep out the January blast. The crossing was made at last in two divisions, at Cape Girardeau and at Green's Ferry, a short distance below, whence the march was made on through Missouri to Indian Territory, the later detachments making a northerly circuit by Springfield, because those who had gone before had killed off all the game along the direct route. At last their destination was reached. They had started in October, 1838, and it was now March, 1839, the journey having occupied barely six months of the hardest part of the year.

President Van Buren in his December 1838 message to Congress announced the administration's view of the event:

... It affords me sincere pleasure to apprise the Congress of the entire removal of the Cherokee Nation of Indians to their new homes west of the Mississippi. The measures authorized by Congress at its last session have had the happiest effects. By an agreement concluded with them by the commanding general in that country, their removal has been principally under the conduct of their own chiefs, and they have emigrated without any apparent reluctance.

A traveler who had encountered the Indians en route was moved by the President's words to write his own eyewitness report which was published in the January 26, 1839 *New York Observer* under the heading "A Native of Maine, traveling in the Western Country":

... On Tuesday evening we fell in with a detachment of the poor Cherokee Indians ... about eleven hundred Indians — sixty wagons — six hundred horses, and perhaps forty pairs of oxen. We found them in the forest camped for the night by the road side ... under a severe fall of rain accompanied by heavy wind. With their canvas for a shield from the inclemency of the weather, and the cold wet ground for a resting place, after the fatigue of the day, they spent the night . . . many of the aged Indians were suffering extremely from the fatigue of the journey, and the ill health consequent upon it . . . several were then quite ill, and one aged man we were informed was then in the last struggles of death. . . . The last detachment which we passed on the 7th embraced rising two thousand Indians with horses and mules in proportion. The forward part of the train we found just pitching their tents for the night, and notwithstanding some thirty or forty wagons were already stationed, we found the road literally filled with the procession for about three miles in length. The sick and feeble were carried in wagons — about as comfortable for traveling as a New England ox cart with a covering over it — a great many ride on horseback and multitudes go on foot — even aged females, apparently nearly ready to drop into the grave, were traveling with heavy burdens attached to the back — on the sometimes frozen ground, and sometimes muddy streets, with no covering for the feet except what nature had given them. . . . We learned from the inhabitants on the road where the Indians passed, that they buried fourteen or fifteen at every stopping place, and they make a journey of ten miles per day only on an average. One fact which to my own mind seemed a lesson indeed to the American nation is, that they will not travel on the Sabbath. . . . The Indians as a whole carry on their countenances every thing but the appearance of happiness. Some carry a downcast dejected look bordering upon the appearance of despair others a wild frantic appearance as if about to burst the chains of nature and pounce like a tiger upon their enemies. . . . When I past the last detachment of those suffering exiles and thought that my native countrymen had thus expelled them from their native soil and their much-loved homes, and that too in this inclement season of the year in all their suffering, I turned from the sight with feelings which language cannot express. . . . I felt that I would not encounter the secret silent prayer of one of these sufferers armed with the energy that faith and hope would give it (if there be a God who avenges the wrongs of the injured) for all the lands of Georgia. . . . When I read in the President's message that he was happy to inform the Senate that the Cherokees were peaceably and without reluctance removed — and remember that it was on the third day of December when not one of the detachments had reached their destination; and that a large majority had not made even half their journey when he made that declaration, I thought I wished the President could have been there that very day in Kentucky with myself, and have seen the comfort and the willingness with which the Cherokees were making their journey.

The first migrants reached their destination on the plains beyond the western border of Arkansas January 4, 1839. Other contingents continued to straggle in until late in March. Examination of all available records by Grant Foreman, outstanding authority on Indian removal, led him to conclude 4,000 Cherokee had died either during confinement in the stockades or on their 800-mile journey west.

While the Cherokee were traversing their Trail of Tears their fellow southern Indians were committed to afflictions as dismal. The processes of removal were grinding out the cumulative calamities that had been visited upon a race by governmental fiat.

The Chickasaw had at length embarked upon their self-governed migration. They were the aristocrats of the Indian world, long noted for the prowess of their warriors, the beauty of their women and the speed of their horses. They had bargained shrewdly until they had wrung every possible advantage from federal authorities, including uninterrupted control over their affairs and a good price for their lands in western Tennessee and northwestern Mississippi. When finally they started west it was a movement under their own leadership undertaken at a time of their own choosing after repeated inspections of their new territory and the route to it by their own representatives. They traveled in comfort, well supplied with equipment, food and money. It might have been expected that were removal ever to be conducted under acceptable conditions it might prove so in their case. But it did not. Their relative prosperity became one of the major causes of their undoing. Sensing unusual profits, contractors gathered stockpiles of supplies along the way in such quantities that the food spoiled before it could be eaten. The travelers were charged exorbitantly for transportation and their every other requirement. They picked up smallpox en route and the disease reached epidemic proportions after their arrival. Most had arrived too late to get in an 1838 crop and they were soon as hungry as their poorer fellow colonists. The move west had made plaintive beggars of the once proud and warlike Chickasaw.

Nearly 2,000 Seminole, rounded up by various devices, pseudo-agreements and military pressures, were also on the way west in 1838. Having suffered so much more than other migrants before their start, they continued to suffer more en route. Many had scarcely emerged from their swampland refuges before they were crowded, naked and undernourished, aboard ship. Others had already endured long periods of imprisonment by which they had been weakened. Most were detained for weeks and months en route in noisome concentration camps in Tampa, Mobile and New Orleans. In addition to all their other privations and afflictions they were continually harassed at every stop and in every new state jurisdiction by the claims of slave dealers to the ownership of Seminole prisoners who showed evidence of Negro blood. A considerable proportion of Seminole were Negroes who had for generations been considered members of the tribe and even though they were closely guarded prisoners each group of exiles fiercely resisted every atempt to single out any of their number for delivery into slavery. The problem of identification had been complicated by the flight to the Seminole of many actual slaves during the war. Some of the slave traders' claims were thus clothed with a species of legitimacy which made adjudication of every dispute more difficult. As one controversial example, among the Seminole prisoners of war taken by the Creek auxiliaries in 1837 had been 90 black Seminole whom they had sold to traders. In all these disputes federal and state authorities, except for the attendant army officers, in their anxiety to expedite the removal tended to support the traders' claims to an extent that provoked a congressional investigation. Meanwhile, in Florida the war went on, with American troops now under the command of Brigadier General Zachary Taylor, later President of the United States, continuing their attempts to run to earth the some 2,000 Seminole still in hiding.

The year 1838 also witnessed the initiation of a companion Indian removal in an adjoining country. Bowl's band of Cherokee, the first recorded migrants who had fled their homelands in 1794, had eventually settled on the Texas side of the Red River in what was then Mexican territory. Joined by other Cherokee and other Indians, the colony had increased to some 8,000. At the outbreak of the Texas revolution Sam Houston had negotiated a treaty of friendship with Bowl's Cherokee which saved the Americans in Texas from possible attack by Indians at the precarious moment they were being assaulted by Santa Anna in return for a Texan recognition of Cherokee title to the land on which they had settled. But in 1838 Mirabeau Lamar, upon succeeding Houston as President of Texas, immediately proclaimed his intention of expelling all Indians from the republic. In the ensuing 1839 campaign the aged Bowl was killed, still clutching the tin box containing the documents and deeds relating to the 1836 treaty of friendship with Texas. The Texas Cherokee were driven across the Red River to share the fortunes of the West and newly arrived East Cherokee on the upper Arkansas.

Indian removal had now been accomplished. Aside from a few scattered remnants, such as the Seminole fugitives in the Florida swamps, the few mountain Cherokee in North Carolina, the Choctaw residue in Mississippi and an occasional tiny enclave in the north, every Indian nation which had originally occupied the immense expanse of woodland extending across the eastern half of the United States had been compelled to seek new homes on the plains beyond that woodland's western margin. It had required a persisting effort over a period of 15 years, distinguished not only by the sufferings inflicted upon Indians but by the virulent disagreements excited among Americans, to give effect to the outwardly plausible policy announced by [James] Monroe and [John] Calhoun in 1825. Removal had been a contemporary success in the sense that the national government had proved able to impose its will and the states concerned had been rid of unwanted Indian inhabitants. But for the Indians and for the larger interests of the United States it had been a deplorable failure. The opportunity for Indians to become useful and valued members of American society, an achievement many had seemed on the verge of attaining in 1825, had been heedlessly postponed for more than a century.

Most informed Indians had long realized that such an assimilation represented the one lingering hope that Indians might ever regain comfort and security. The mass of Indians, less aware of the economic and political realities, had as long clung despairingly to the more appealing hope that they might yet contrive some escape from the white incubus. Removal dealt crushing blows to both hopes. In the west progressive Indians were compelled to begin again, under far greater handicaps, the painful climb toward citizenship and all Indians were subjected to white exactions more distracting than any they had known in the east. It was only after decades of miraculously patient struggle that Indians were finally to gain recognition of the principle that the rights of the conquered are even more precious than the prerogatives of their conquerors.

During the three centuries Indians had been retreating before the inexorable advance of alien invaders they had been bitterly conscious that they were suffering greater deprivations than the loss of their lands and lives. Their entire way of life, their whole world as they had known it, was in the course of obliteration. They understood, as could nobody else, by how wide a margin their post-invasion opportunities to pursue happiness failed to match the opportunities they had known before invasion. There was little enough comfort in the reflection that these opportunities were being denied them by a force physically too strong for them to resist.

In their despair Indians had sought consolation in resort to the supernatural. Native prophets, such as those who had inspired the followers of Pontiac and Tecumseh, had emerged again and again to preach the doctrine of original blessedness. They had exhorted Indians to eschew every compromise with white influence, especially by forswearing the use of white tools, weapons and alcohol, so that by a return to their ancient purity they might regain the strength to regain their former freedoms. These movements had been frustrated by their adherents' realization that obedience left Indians even more defenseless than before. By the time of the removal Indians were increasingly addicted to more extravagant religious phantasies. A favorite conceit, intermittently erupting for generation after generation until its final resurgence as the Ghost Dance excitement among the Plains Indians in the late 1880's, envisioned the evocation, by appropriate prayers, dances and rites, of the innumerable spirits of all Indian dead who would return to earth as a mighty host capable of expelling the white invaders and thus restoring the land of peace and plenty Indians had once enjoyed.

Even so superior an intellect as Sequoyah's was subject to wishful fancies. He had from his youth believed that the one Indian hope to retain their identity as a people was to withdraw from white contamination. He had himself moved west nearly 20 years before removal and all his life had sought by advice and example to persuade Indians to shun intercourse with whites. In his declining years he became obsessed with the possibility that the Lost Cherokee, reputed by tribal legend to have disappeared into the farthest west in the forgotten past, still lived in innocence, freedom and security in some distant land. In his frail old age, still in pursuit of this relic of the Indian golden age, he set out on a two-year journey in search of a remote Cherokee colony reported to have found sanctuary in the mountains of Mexico. His 1843 death in a Mexican desert was giving ultimate poignancy to the discovery all Indians were being required to make. For them there was no way back. There was only the way ahead.

STUDY GUIDE

1. Describe where each of the Indian tribes discussed in this essay — the Cherokee, Seminole, and Chickasaw — lived before removal and how each of these nations reacted to the forced removal.

2. What problems did the Indians face with respect to weather, supplies, health, and transportation on the trail west?

3. How did the sentiment of General Scott, who was directly responsible for supervising the Indian removal, differ from that of Andrew Jackson? How does a knowledge of the politics of the period help in understanding the views expressed in Jackson's letter?

4. Discuss the deeper, psychological impact of removal upon the Indian tribes. Explain what factors in the nineteenth century made it difficult for the Indian to resist removal.

5. What differences can you think of between the removal of the Indians in this period and the forced removal of Japanese-Americans from their homes on the Pacific coast to concentration centers during World War II?

BIBLIOGRAPHY

A great deal has been written about the removal of the eastern Indian tribes to lands beyond the Mississippi. As Van Every's selection indicates, it is a gripping story. Unfortunately, some of the books that are most reliable are not very interesting, and some of the most interesting are not very reliable. Grant Foreman has probably written more on this subject than anyone. The first of his titles cited here is on the removal of the tribes north of the Ohio River, and the second is on the situation of the Indians in their new homelands following removal: *The Last Trek of the Indians* (1946); *The Five Civilized Tribes* (1934); and *Indian Removal: The Emigration of the Five Civilized Tribes of Indians* (1932). R. S. Cotterill, *The Southern Indians* (1954) is one of the best general works on the Civilized Tribes of the Southeast. Three other works dealing directly with those tribes are Arthur H. De Rosier, Jr., *The Removal of the Choctaw Indians* (1970); Angie Debo, *The Rise and Fall of the*

Choctaw Republic, 2nd ed. (1967); and Gloria Jahoda, *The Trail of Tears* (1975). Alvin M. Josephy, Jr., *The Patriot Chiefs* (1961) is a series of nicely written sketches of Indian leaders from Hiawatha to Chief Joseph.

Much of the recent writing in the field of Indian history has tried to "get inside" Indian life and culture. Valuable as such works are, it is also necessary to study white attitudes and government policy. Several works examine these subjects, both in earlier American history and in the 1830s, when the eastern Indians were removed. Two of the best works on the earlier period are Reginald Horsman, *Expansion and American Indian Policy, 1783–1812* (1967) and Bernard Sheehan, *Seeds of Extinction: Jeffersonian Philanthropy and the American Indian* (1973). Two volumes on Indian policy during Jackson's administration are Ronald N. Satz, *American Indian Policy in the Jacksonian Era* (1975) and Michael P. Rogin, *Fathers and Children: Andrew Jackson and the Subjugation of the American Indian* (1975). Politics and government policy, even in the nineteenth century, frequently reflect the values and attitudes of the American people, or a substantial majority of them. The popular beliefs that made Andrew Jackson such a hero with the American people are set forth in John W. Ward, *Andrew Jackson: Symbol for an Age* (1962), a very readable volume that includes some suggestive passages on Jackson's personal attitude toward Indians. In recent years, legal suits by various Indian tribes in federal courts have raised the question of who actually owns parts of the United States. Wilcomb Washburn, *Red Man's Land, White Man's Law* (1971) is a study of land titles and Indian policy. Another work, not directly related to removal but containing information of considerable interest on Indian–white relations, is Wilbur R. Jacobs, *Dispossessing the American Indian* (1972).

The bibliography following the essay by Anthony F. C. Wallace, "Indian Life and Culture" (Reading No. 1), lists several general works on Indian history. Two other readable works of this sort are William Brandon, *The American Heritage Book of Indians* (1961), which includes many illustrations, and Angie Debo, *A History of the Indians of the United States* (1970).

This cartoon, "Drunkard's Progress," expresses the belief of prohibitionists that intemperance was the leading cause of personal tragedy and social ills.

11

MARK E. LENDER
JAMES K. MARTIN

America: Wet and Dry

In the last decade, the American people have become extraordinarily health conscious. Millions have kicked the smoking habit, and many more have modified their eating habits in order to lose weight and decrease their intake of sugar, salt, and fats. Fish and chicken have grown in popularity on restaurant menus, and even modest-sized towns may have one or more vegetarian restaurants. Vitamin and health food stores, once hard to find, are now a common fixture in shopping malls. The national craze for jogging and other ways of keeping fit has provided new stimulus to sporting goods manufacturers who once catered largely to team sports. Americans, it seems, are being converted from sports spectators to active participants. Whether these occurrences represent passing fads or long-range changes in American life-styles is still an open question: A skeptic might note that among the most avid handball players are a significant number who stop off for two martinis after work.

One person's reform may be considered radical nonsense or reactionary folderol by another. Thus, the Age of Reform was also an age of serious divisions in American society. Some people founded a peace society, and others went off to war against Mexico; some women struggled to expand their opportunities and assert their rights, and were taunted for their efforts; abolitionists preached in small towns and large cities, and found their lives in danger. One movement, the attempt to control alcoholic consumption, crossed many of these lines of division. Protestants and Catholics, abolitionists and their opponents, and Northerners and Southerners could be found in the ranks of the temperance crusade.

The following selection from the book *Drinking in America: A History*, by Mark E. Lender and James K. Martin, covers the history of the temperance movement from the late eighteenth century to the Civil War. The authors describe the easygoing attitude of most Americans toward the Devil's brew, which many people felt was actually beneficial, as well as the growing abuse of alcohol in the nineteenth century and the movement to dry up the country. Eventually, the prohibitionists achieved passage of an amendment to the United States Constitution to make America dry, but widespread violation of the Volstead Act during the 1920s suggested that many Americans were still wringing wet.

The bitterest denunciation of distilled spirits came in the immediate aftermath, and as part of the zeitgeist, of the Revolution. The Revolutionary period witnessed heightened concern that society's traditional values were being lost — that luxury and vice were threatening public virtue and liberty itself. A great many people traced these unwanted developments to American links with the British nation, which supposedly had grown increasingly decadent over the years, thus representing a corrupting influence on America. The result was what Revolutionary leaders often described as a rise in social dissipation and a decline in public spirit. . . . They hoped that the Revolution would represent a cleansing process for Americans and that it would fire a rebirth of individual and public virtue.

"Virtue" was the catchword of republicanism. It dictated that citizens act, vote, and think not out of hopes for personal gain but out of a sense of public duty and concern for the general good. A nation founded on this premise had to maintain traditional concerns about order and stability, and republicans believed that true liberty could exist only in a society composed of such a virtuous people. Providence, they held, would certainly shepherd the fortunes of such a republic as long as it adhered to these principles.

Yet victory in the War for Independence failed to allay many republican fears. . . . Society as the colonials had known it was hardly falling apart, but the old deferential patterns — and voluntary compliance with them — were clearly giving way to a more individualistic, pluralist set of values. The doctrine of liberty espoused during the Revolution went a long way toward weakening communal responsibility for individual behavior in many areas. But while republicans cherished the ideals of the Revolution, no one (who was willing to admit it) wanted these ideals to proceed to anarchy or to a decline in general morality or civil order. And in this concern for social stability and virtue, few things seemed to have more disruptive potential than the intemperance that apparently was accompanying the startling rise in the use of distilled spirits.

This unsteadying fear lay behind America's classic early stricture of drunkenness: *An Inquiry into the Effects of Ardent Spirits on the Human Mind and Body* (1784), by Dr. Benjamin Rush of Philadelphia. Rush commanded attention. An ardent republican, he had been active in Revolutionary politics, signed the Declaration of Independence as a Pennsylvania delegate, and served for a time as Continental army surgeon general. Rush enjoyed a reputation after the war as perhaps the new nation's foremost physician. His interests ranged widely — his writings on mental illness earned him the title "Father of Psychiatry" — but most Americans of his time came to know him for his work on behalf of temperance. Rush had spoken out publicly against the use of hard liquor since at least 1772, but his masterpiece was the *Inquiry*.

The tract represented a radical challenge to previous thinking; it assaulted the old dictum that alcohol was a positive good. Rush had no quarrel with beers and wines, which he believed healthful when consumed in moderate amounts, but he correctly pointed out that Americans were now drinking primarily "ardent spirits," and, he argued, these did more than cause drunkenness. Consumed in quantity over the years, they could destroy a person's health and even cause death. More important was how alcohol went about its lethal business: For Rush was the first American to call chronic drunkenness a distinct disease, which gradually, but through progressively more serious stages, led drinkers to physical doom. In fact, he described an addiction process and specifically identified alcohol as the addictive agent. As Rush claimed, once an "appetite," or "craving," for spirits had become fixed in an individual, the victim was helpless to resist. In these cases, drunkenness was no longer a vice or personal failing, for the imbiber had no more control over his drinking — the alcohol now controlled him. In Rush's view, the old colonial idea that drunkenness was the fault of the drinker was valid only in the early stages of the disease, when a tippler might still pull back; once addicted, even a saint would have a hard time controlling himself. . . .

As a good republican, he abhorred intemperance (and the strong drink that caused it). It was a personal and social vice, and it struck at the very heart of the Revolutionaries' vision of the good republican society. Allow drunkenness to flourish, Rush cautioned, with its attendant crime, degraded individuals, broken families, economic loss, and other disruptions, and the Revolution would have been fought in vain. "Our country," he warned, would soon "be governed by men chosen by intemperate and corrupted voters," rather than by citizens of virtue. "From such legislators the republic would soon be in danger," openly susceptible to demagoguery. Nor, of course, would the Almighty look favorably on a people who preferred to drink whiskey when they had the opportunity to build a golden edifice dedicated to liberty and a moral republican order. To avert such a calamity, Rush advocated not only personal abstinence from hard liquor but also a return to strict communal sanctions against drunkards. Drunkards, Rush pointed out, were the antithesis of virtuous citizens; they were incapable of managing their own affairs, could become mentally enfeebled, and certainly could not be responsible enough to vote. Better, Rush said, to lock them up in special asylums until they regained whatever faculties remained (he suggested the name "Sober House" for the asylum he envisioned for Philadelphia). He also urged that "good men of every class unite and besiege" their leaders with demands for fewer taverns and heavy taxes on "ardent spirits" as further means to stem the tide of intemperance. So while Rush was no prohibitionist, he saw considerably more at stake in American drinking practices than did the vast majority of his countrymen. . . .

As the nineteenth century dawned, the drinking habits that had so worried Dr. Rush continued unabated. Relatively heavy and frequent drinking, with the very American preference for hard liquor, had become common throughout the nation. In fact, the period from the 1790s to the early 1830s was probably the heaviest drinking era in the nation's history. Consumption estimates tell the story dramatically: From an annual average of 5.8 gallons of absolute alcohol per capita (for people aged fifteen or older) in 1790, mean absolute alcohol intake rose to 7.1 gallons a year by 1810 and, with minor fluctuations, remained at about that level until at least 1830. Of these amounts, as Samuel Dexter noted in 1814, "the quantity of ardent spirits . . . surpasses belief." And Dexter, who in 1814 was president of the Massachusetts Society for the Suppression of Intemperance — he had earlier served as treasury secretary and secretary of war — apparently knew what he was talking about, even if he was an interested source.

Dexter's data closely approximate modern consumption estimates . . . which suggest that by 1800 (and possibly earlier) about half the absolute alcohol consumed was in the form of distilled liquor; this proportion was well over half after 1810. In 1830, for example, when average annual consumption was about 7.1 gallons (absolute), some 4.3 gallons were in hard liquor, while only 2.8 came from beer, cider, or wine. Again, however, as in dealing with the colonial drinking figures, it must be kept in mind that these were national averages, based on the entire population over fifteen years old. So, if, as Dexter insisted was necessary, we adjust our figures by excluding slaves and "others who, through disrelish, delicacy, or principle, drink little or none," average consumption levels for actual drinkers would have been much higher.

These figures seem almost too high. To drink enough whiskey, beer, or whatever to reach seven gallons of absolute alcohol in a year would be, for most people, a genuine feat, and we cannot be sure how accurate the estimates of nineteenth-century consumption really are. But at the same time, an extensive body of evidence (in the form of local histories, diaries, and travel reports) suggests that our best estimates are not far off the mark and that drinking had reached unparalleled levels. It seems clear that most Americans of the early nineteenth century drank pretty much as their Revolutionary period brethren had. They simply drank at an accelerated rate.

The question becomes why? For one reason, the old notion that alcohol was necessary for health remained firmly fixed. It was common to down a glass of whiskey or other spirits before breakfast, "and so conducive to health was this nostrum esteemed," noted a journalist in 1830, "that no sex, and scarcely any age, were deemed exempt from its application." Instead of taking coffee or tea breaks, Americans customarily stopped every morning and afternoon for eleven o'clock ("eleveners,") and four o'clock drams. At the appointed hours, laborers in fields, offices, and shops halted and picked up the jug. Even school children took their sip of whiskey, the morning and afternoon glasses being considered "absolutely indispensable to man and boy."

Ardent spirits were a basic part of the diet — most people thought that whiskey was as essential as bread. In the evenings plenty of liquor was drunk during and after dinner to aid digestion and sleep; before retiring one took a "strengthening" nightcap, with one recipe calling for "whiskey, maple syrup, nutmeg, and boiling water, the whole dashed with rum." Taking a "healthful" dram, then, could have people drinking all day — a fact not unnoticed by many contemporary commentators. In "every corner," one Englishman recorded while traveling the Mississippi in the 1820s, "north or south, east or west, was the universal practice of sipping a little at a time, but frequently."

Social drinking, if anything, was even more prevalent in the nineteenth century than it had been in the colonial era. Even nondrinkers generally kept a supply of whiskey on hand for guests, and it was a rare occasion on which people got together without a bottle of spirits. "The friend who did not testify his welcome, and the employer who did not provide bountifully" in liquor "for his help, was held niggardly," one commentator noted. "The consequence was that, what the great majority indulged in without scruple, large numbers indulged in without restraint." According to a British observer, the Americans believed the British could settle nothing save over a good dinner; the Americans, he found, did nothing except over a drink. "If you meet you drink," he said, "if you part you drink; if you make an acquaintance you drink. They quarrel in their drink, and they make it up with a drink.". . . .

. . . [C]ontemporary sources also indicate that early in the nineteenth century not very many persons saw disgrace in a binge; few, unlike Dr. Rush, considered such behavior a real threat to the moral fabric of the republic. Behavioral norms had in fact evolved to the point that imbibing citizens could take in stride quite a bit of what we would today consider problem drinking. This phenomenon was partly a reflection of the newer noncommunal, individualistic orientation that was emerging with the Revolutionary era — an outlook that put greater emphasis on personal liberty, self-reliance, and equality of opportunity among free citizens unfettered by unreasonable social and governmental restraints. This more latitudinarian world view stood in stark contrast to the community centered ethos of the colonial period and to the republicanism of Benjamin Rush, which emphasized a society of moral-political harmony and common purpose. Politically, this credo became more apparent with the election of Thomas Jefferson in 1800 and perhaps reached its zenith with the presence of Andrew Jackson in the presidency after 1828. The new mood exalted the rights of the common person, fostered a diversity of ideas, and preached the hatred of any form of privilege; it encouraged people to employ their wits and seek their fortunes individually, restrained only by their natural abilities. . . .

In this age of nascent democracy, drinking and beverage choice served to enrich the egalitarian ethos. For some citizens, downing American whiskey took on connotations of national feeling. "Good rye whiskey," one patriotic toper advised in 1814, "or high-proof apple-brandy," rather than wines or imported spirits, were the drinks for loyal men and women of the republic. Corn whiskey, particularly bourbon, earned yet more honors as a national drink. Harrison Hall, one of the most prominent distillers of the early 1800s, never tired of singing the praises of corn spirits. The French sipped their brandy, he noted, "the Hollanders swallowed gin; the Irish glory in their whiskey"; the English had their beloved porter. So, Hall reasoned, "why should not our countrymen have a national beverage?" Hard cider had its partisans for the honor, especially in New England. Whether enjoying cider or bourbon, however, many drinkers consciously identified their preferred beverage with a keen sense of nationhood, and they thus saw their imbibing as a patriotic act. . . .

In the presidential race of 1840, the Jacksonian opponents of William Henry Harrison printed an article alleging that the old man would be better off in a log cabin with a jug. The insult was a monumental blunder. In the "log cabin campaign" that followed, Harrison's managers played up the imagery — it had a certain common touch that voters liked. Harrison's supporters even passed out thousands of small bottles of hard cider just to make sure the voters remembered who their best friend really was. Harrison won easily.

Even earlier, at rough-hewn Andrew Jackson's inauguration gala in 1829, the imbibing crowds in the White House had become so rowdy that officials feared the revelers would tear the place apart. The solution was masterful: The staff carried the liquor out to the lawn; the gathering followed (naturally); and the mansion's doors swung shut. Few doubted, then, that America was in good hands as long as its leaders were willing to have drinks with the populace. . . .

As acceptable as drinking was to most Americans, it nevertheless had its critics. . . . In Litchfield County, Connecticut, for instance, some two hundred of the "most respectable farmers," challenging the wisdom of the day, concluded that drinking on the job did more harm than good and, in 1789, discontinued the customary liquor rations for farm labor. In 1808, a small group in Moreau, New York, founded the nation's first temperance society, also citing the deleterious impact of liquor on farm productivity.

Indeed, as these first temperance groups were being born, the United States was getting ready to enter an era of intense social reform activity — activity that merged temperance with goals as diverse as school reform, abolition, and women's rights. This ferment, growing out of the times, left the young republic in turmoil over a host of new social forces — forces that moved the nation steadily toward its modern character as a pluralist democracy. Thousands streamed toward the frontiers and beyond the influence of Eastern institutions; the increasingly powerful Jeffersonians (followed by the Jacksonians of the 1820s and thirties) offered citizens a democratic ideology stressing unfettered individualism as the basis of freedom, as opposed to the communal ideals of traditional republicanism; the arrival of major immigrant populations, unfamiliar with American values and having their own creeds and customs, also seemed likely to affect the character of the young nation; and around the corner loomed the industrialization process, with unknown consequences for the largely agrarian order of the postrevolutionary generation. While no one could predict where these trends would eventually lead, many Americans rejoiced at the apparent evolution of old social relationships and values and saw in the dawning age new and greater political and economic opportunities for all citizens. On the other hand, the specter of change also left a great many people, especially older native American families, perplexed and apprehensive.

Those who questioned the wisdom of these potentially radical changes were the nineteenth-century heirs of the old republicans. . . . Like Benjamin Rush, former President John Adams, and others of the Revolutionary generation (many of whom were still alive in the early 1800s), they worshipped basic political liberty and the institutions of the republic, but only in the context of a stable social-moral order governed by men of sufficient character and virtue to appreciate what was needed for the welfare of all citizens. . . .

For many neorepublicans, safeguarding society depended, as they frankly admitted, upon social and governmental leadership by men such as themselves — men of proven distinction, who would set high examples of personal conduct and had the courage to act vigorously in defense of accepted standards. Historians have termed this strain of thought the "stewardship tradition"; that is, a moral elite would act as stewards for the rest of the nation, guiding and correcting their behavior. . . .

These moral stewards honestly thought that they knew best how to order the affairs of other men and women. And they were equally convinced that reform would be a vital step in fulfilling the old republican dream of establishing the United States as a beacon of promise for the rest of humanity. If they could see to it that Americans acted in a manner worthy of their destiny, Providence itself — working largely through the major Protestant denominations — would guide the fortunes of the nation. . . .

The reform impulse flowed into a number of channels and became a hallmark of the American experience before the Civil War. Any condition or situation labeled evil generated an effort — and frequently a formally organized national society — to set it right. Temperance was only one facet of this general phenomenon: Peace, abolition, the elimination of profanity and Sabbath-breaking, women's rights, mental health, the rekindling of orthodox Protestantism, concern over immigration (including, in its extreme forms, some of the anti-Catholicism noted earlier), education, and other causes all attracted champions. Temperance reform, however, as the period advanced, became one of the most popular causes. As drunkenness lay demonstrably at the root of other social ills, or at least symbolized such aspects of rampant pluralism as immigration and the roughhouse lifestyle of the American West, the attack on intemperance appeared particularly important. How, for example, could the nation logically promote better care for the mentally ill or the imprisoned if it allowed people to drink themselves to insanity or to a life of crime? Why reform public education when children returned each day from school to besotted parents, or end poverty when the poor squandered their pay on liquor? It seemed impossible to cure national ills without acknowledging the centrality of the liquor question, and legions of reformers quickly came to accept what Rush had pointed out long before: The elimination of drunkenness would prove crucial to avoiding internal civil disruption — thus literally preserving the republican experiment itself. . . .

A formal national temperance movement emerged in 1826: the American Society for the Promotion of Temperance (later known as the

American Temperance Society). Leadership rested firmly in the hands of socially prominent clergy and laymen, whose proclaimed purpose was the reformation of the nation under the guidance of "holy men" who would "induce all temperate people to continue temperate" through abstinence from ardent spirits. The early temperance movement, then, was *not* a prohibitionist crusade; in adopting this moderate approach, the new society had taken a page right out of Benjamin Rush. Rush, whose memory the society revered and whose writings became movement gospel (he would eventually be known as the "Father of Temperance" and the "True Instaurator"), had counseled precisely such a course. Permitting the measured use of nondistilled beverages would prevent the drinking excesses associated with hard liquor.

Armed with this moderate doctrine, the Society for the Promotion of Temperance performed admirably. It virtually assumed the national leadership of temperance activities. The society helped organize local units, sent lecturers into the field, distributed literature (including the *Inquiry*), and served as a clearinghouse for movement information. Within three years, in large measure inspired by society proselytizing, 222 state and local antiliquor groups were at work across the land. The crusade was by no means at peak strength numerically, nor did it have any appreciable political influence at this stage; yet temperance reform now constituted a burgeoning national movement. . . .

Fear of alcohol addiction, the enslavement to drink that Rush had described, was instrumental in bringing about a crucial change in the meaning of temperance — the shift from temperance as abstinence from distilled beverages to temperance as total abstinence. . . .

The most forceful statement of this position came in Lyman Beecher's *Six Sermons on Intemperance.* Beecher delivered them from the pulpit in Litchfield, Connecticut, in 1825. In 1826 he published them, and the *Six Sermons* took their place with Rush's *Inquiry* as temperance movement classics. Any drinking, he argued, was a step toward "irreclaimable" slavery to liquor; people simply could not tell when they crossed the line from moderate use to inebriety — could not tell, that is, until too late. Look out, he said, if you drank in secret, periodically felt compelled to drink, and found yourself with tremors, inflamed eyes, or a "disordered stomach." "You might as well cast loose in a frail boat before a hurricane, and expect safety," Beecher explained, and "you are gone, gone irretrievably, if you do not stop." But most could not stop; the power of alcohol was too strong. This fact, he noted, coupled with the abolition of the liquor traffic, would at least end the country's alcohol problem, as the "generation of drunkards" would "hasten out of time." Total abstinence, Beecher concluded, was the only sure means of personal salvation and societal stability.

The temperance movement controversy over total abstinence gave rise to one account of the origin of the term "teetotaler." In Hector, New

York, the local temperance society debated the matter in 1826. To compromise, it allowed members a choice of pledges, one foreswearing all liquor, the other just distilled spirits. However, those going completely dry received at T — for total abstinence — next to their names on the society rolls, thus becoming known locally as "T-totalers." The term spread generally as other societies introduced total abstinence pledges. . . .

. . . At a . . . national temperance convention in Saratoga, New York, in 1836, the delegates formally endorsed total abstinence as the movement's interpretation of temperance. There was still some resistance among the rank and file, but by the end of the decade the issue was virtually closed. Temperance reform, for the first time, had gone fully "dry."

More remarkable, however, was the extent to which the rest of the nation followed suit. In 1835 the national temperance society estimated that two million people had renounced the use of distilled liquor (causing some four thousand distilleries to close), while nearly a quarter of a million persons had become total abstainers. Membership in temperance organizations had climbed to about 1.5 million. Thousands of others, without any temperance affiliation or signing any pledge, also cut back on their drinking, even if they did not stop entirely. The cumulative effect sent national liquor consumption plummeting. From a high of just over seven gallons of absolute alcohol per capita annually in 1830, consumption estimates fell to slightly more than three gallons by 1840 — the largest ten-year drop in American history. . . .

While the temperance movement mulled over the question of prohibition, events transpired that temporarily took the antiliquor initiative away from the established reform societies. A dry revival, led by men with no prior temperance connections, swept the nation in the 1840s, catching reformers almost completely by surprise. This remarkable dry explosion was the "Washington movement," founded by six Baltimore topers in 1840. Sitting in Chase's Tavern one evening, or so tradition has it, these gentlemen turned to a discussion of their tippling ways, which they admitted were undermining their lives. As a consequence — and perhaps as a lark — one of the group, charged with reporting back to his companions, attended a nearby temperance lecture. The delegate emerged from the lecture a new man, not only taking the pledge himself but also persuading his friends to do the same. They decided to work for the reform of other drinkers, and calling themselves the Washington Temperance Society (in honor of the first president), they drew up a total abstinence pledge.

The group succeeded beyond its wildest expectations. Over a thousand men took the society's pledge by the end of the year, and "missionaries" then carried the Washingtonian theme to New York City, where they attracted thousands. After this, the Washingtonians came to represent a full-fledged revival. Societies patterned on the Washingtonian model sprang up everywhere; churches opened their sanctuaries for meetings; and Washingtonian lecturers, such as the spellbinding John B. Gough and John Hawkins, joined the ranks of the most sought-after speakers in the country. . . .

The Washingtonians were unlike other regiments in the antidrink army. Their emphasis was on saving individual alcoholics, not general social reform. To them, alcoholism was a problem of the isolated drinker, not part of a broader social malaise or a matter of ideological neorepublicanism. Helping the drunkard was the end in itself. At a time when the formal temperance movement was advocating prohibition, the Washingtonians remained cool toward legislatively oriented solutions to the problem. Indeed, to keep the focus on alcoholics and their problems, Washingtonians often closed their meetings to clergy and to members of other temperance organizations. . . .

Yet the meteoric rise of the Washingtonians held the seeds of their eventual decline. Like all other revival phenomena, the movement lost momentum, and by 1844 its activities were on the decline. By 1847 almost all the local societies had stopped meeting (although the Boston chapter continued to gather until 1860). More important than declining momentum was the loss of church and non-Washingtonian temperance support. The established churches, which had been allies, had come to resent Washingtonian opposition to their presumed leadership of the dry struggle, and they began to close their doors to movement activities. This prompted Washingtonian attacks on the church, which in turn exacerbated bad feelings. Some clergy envied the success of the lay movement, hurt that ex-alcoholics proved better reformers than learned ministers. "As [the clergy] were neither the originators nor the leaders in the movement," wrote one temperance man, "they felt themselves ignored, [and] therefore refused to have any affiliation for, or lend any assistance to it." At the same time, and for the same reasons, the older temperance societies also began to withdraw support. The societies worried further that the Washingtonians had drained off energies that might otherwise have flowed to them and that the revivalist-oriented group lacked the institutional structure and the wider reform vision necessary to preserve the republic. The neglect of legal authority in the fight against liquor was a mistake, they insisted. Even a generally sympathetic temperance observer felt compelled to note that the "triumph of moral suasion was short and doubtful." In that the emotional appeal of the Washingtonians had diverted attention from the societies working toward legal suasion, their activities were actually an "evil." It was true that the Washingtonians had neither long-range programs nor a central organization to sustain what they had won. To save drunkards and then to see thousands of them relapse because liquor was still freely available made less and less sense to the stewardship-oriented societies. In their eyes, the Washingtonian experience was proof that real progress could be attained only through legislation. . . .

. . . Thousands of people, who before had merely dreamed of a dry republic, now saw this goal as within the realm of possibility. They began to bombard state legislatures with demands for the abolition of demon rum. Among some politicians, support for prohibition was already there. As early as 1846, temperance forces in Maine, under the leadership of Neal Dow, had persuaded the legislature to outlaw the manufacture and sale of distilled liquors. Although the law lacked penalties harsh enough to compel full compliance, the response of the legislators was enough to make temperance advocates in other states optimistic. . . .

Enthusiasm and political pressure finally came to a head in 1851. Neal Dow's Maine Law of that year gave prohibition advocates their first great legislative breakthrough, and they moved quickly to follow up on their victory. In August 1851, another temperance convention met in Saratoga Springs and issued a battle cry for the passage of Maine Laws throughout the nation. Lobbying at the state level redoubled, and prohibition became the goal of what was now clearly one of the most comprehensive political efforts the nation had ever seen. After an enthusiastic campaign directed in part by old stalwart Lyman Beecher, Massachusetts went dry less than a year later. Maine Laws next carried the day in Vermont, Minnesota Territory, and Rhode Island (1852); Michigan (1853); Connecticut and Ohio (1854); and Indiana, New Hampshire, Delaware, Illinois, Iowa, and New York (1855). Similar measures almost won in Wisconsin (where prohibition twice cleared the legislature in 1855, only to meet a governor's veto), Pennsylvania, and New Jersey; across the border, the Canadian provinces of Nova Scotia and New Brunswick added their names to the dry column as well.

Politicized morality thus seemed well on its way to rolling back the tide of over two hundred years of American drinking habits. By the mid-1850s, many dry reformers were congratulating themselves on having destroyed the old consensus on drinking as a positive good, and they eagerly looked forward to national prohibition. Their confidence appeared fully justified. During the 1850s, enough Americans had stopped or moderated their drinking to drop national annual consumption levels well below three gallons of absolute alcohol per capita. These were the lowest rates in the nation's history. . . .

But those who prophesied a dry millennium were wrong. The Maine Laws in fact marked the high tide of temperance influence in the antebellum years — a tide that ebbed quickly with the approach of the Civil War. By the late 1850s, masses of people feared a violent confrontation over slavery and the preservation of the Union. Most Americans, including some important temperance leaders, increasingly gave the impending sectional struggle a higher priority than they did the battle against the traffic. Popular interest in the cause, so keen in the early fifties, was fading fast by the latter part of the decade as "Bleeding Kansas," the Dred Scott case, John Brown's Harper's Ferry raid, and Southern rumblings about secession began to dominate newspaper headlines. Also aiding the disenchantment with prohibition were a number of European medical reports that concluded that alcohol, while dangerous in excess, was not deleterious in moderation. All this caught the temperance movement off guard. Opponents of prohibition took heart. . . .

Events in Maine were typical of those in other locales. The original Maine Law lasted only a few years. It was replaced in 1858 by a measure that kept prohibition on the books in name alone. There was neither popular nor political support for a stiffer law, and even Dow admitted that any effort to achieve real prohibition would have to wait until the nation had sorted out its sectional differences. Indeed, by the time Confederate guns opened on Fort Sumter in April 1861, prohibition had all but collapsed as a major public issue.

Yet the legacy of the prohibition struggle remained. The movement had indelibly etched total abstinence on much of the popular mind. It had convinced many that the dry doctrine held the key to the stability and prosperity of the republic. And if its political manifestation, prohibition, had fallen on hard times, thousands remained loyal to the idea nonetheless. In fact, the antebellum movement set an important precedent: Few temperance advocates in subsequent years would seriously advance any other method than legal prohibition as a solution to the liquor question.

STUDY GUIDE

1. In this selection, the authors use a number of what may be unfamiliar terms, each of which has a broad and important concept behind it. Look back over the essay, and be prepared to explain the meaning of the following terms and what period or group each is associated with: republican ideology; noncommunal, individualistic orientation; egalitarian ethos; stewardship tradition.

2. In what ways did the arguments of Benjamin Rush and Lyman Beecher differ?

3. Contrast the early groups, such as the American Temperance Society, with the Washingtonians with respect to techniques, social backgrounds, and attitude toward religion.

4. The above selection (as well as Reading No. 12 on juvenile reform and Reading No. 19 on abolitionism) suggests that there was a very strong

element of Protestantism in the reform movements of this period. How can you explain this in terms of traditional Christian thought or in terms of the changes taking place in American society in the nineteenth century that threatened the position of Protestantism?

BIBLIOGRAPHY

The bibliographies following other readings in this section list some of the general works on reform, many of which have one or more chapters on the temperance crusade. Besides the book from which the above selection was taken, two other book-length studies of the pre–Civil War crusade have been published recently: Ian R. Tyrell, *Sobering Up: From Temperance to Prohibition in Antebellum America, 1800–1860* (1979) and W. J. Rorabaugh, *The Alcoholic Republic: An American Tradition* (1979). An older work that is fuller in some ways than the recent studies is John A. Krout, *The Origins of Prohibition* (1925). The concern of nineteenth-century Americans with other aspects of health is delightfully summarized in Chapter 9, "The Body and Beyond," of Ronald G. Walters, *American Reformers, 1815–1860* (1978), and is more fully detailed in Stephen Nissenbaum, *Sex, Diet, and Debility in Jacksonian America: Sylvester Graham and Health Reform* (1980).

It is not surprising that much more has been written about drinking and prohibition in the 1920s than in the nineteenth century. History is largely the study of changing developments over time, and studies that are limited to one chronological period can sometimes be misleading. Thus, on a topic such as prohibition, one should compared the pre–Civil War period with the twentieth century to understand the evolution of laws and attitudes. Many of the comical aspects of the 1920s are told in Henry Walsh Lee, *How Dry We Were: Prohibition Revisited* (1963). Andrew Sinclair's study, *Prohibition: The Era of Excess* (1962), published in paperback as *Era of Excess: A Social History of the Prohibition Movement*, emphasizes the nativistic and backward-looking tendencies of the movement. A similar point of view is taken by Joseph R. Gusfield in *Symbolic Crusade: Status Politics and the American Temperance Movement* (1963) and by Norman Clark in *The Dry Years: Prohibition and Social Change in Washington* (1965). James H. Timberlake, in *Prohibition and the Progressive Movement, 1900–1920* (1963), makes a case for prohibition as a facet of progressive reform. In "New Perspectives on the Prohibition 'Experiment' of the 1920s," *Journal of Social History* (Fall 1968), pp. 51–68, John C. Burnham disagrees with those who have labeled the prohibition movement a failure. Burnham offers a number of statistical studies to prove his contention that as a consequence of prohibition, the social and medical health of the nation — and particularly that of lower-income groups — improved markedly.

Photograph by Jacob A. Riis, The Jacob A. Riis
Collection/Museum of the City of New York

Though from a somewhat later period, this famous photograph by Jacob Riis depicts the grim reality of nineteenth-century street life for urban children.

12

CHRISTINE STANSELL

Juvenile Reform

Every society has to deal with social problems, which might range from controlling those who disobey its laws and mores to assisting the poor, aged, or orphaned, who cannot care for themselves. In the Seneca culture described by Anthony Wallace (Reading No. 1), ridicule, as when Red Jacket was nicknamed Cow-killer, was often sufficient to enforce tribal mores. The British colonists used religion and law as tools of social control, but the family was the single most important social agency. In the absence of the many institutions that now exist, the colonial family served as a hospital for the care of the sick, an orphanage and retirement home, a house of correction and reform, and a school and apprenticeship program. By the nineteenth century, various social changes, including the rise of cities, made it impossible for the family to handle all these services.

By 1830 the needs had become quite apparent, and a remarkable group of men and women undertook — in some cases singlehandedly — to do something about the growing social problems. In every major city, societies sprang up to reform conditions in jails and almshouses, to help the handicapped, to combat alcoholic intemperance, to fight for women's rights, and to abolish slavery. Thomas Gallaudet established a school to help the deaf and mute, while Samuel Gridley Howe developed methods to assist the sightless. Dorothea Dix was scandalized by the treatment of the mentally ill, who were frequently jailed, sometimes in shackles, rather than treated in hospitals. It is estimated that she traveled 40,000 miles and investigated more than eight hundred jails and almshouses. Her petitions to legislatures led twenty states to adopt her recommendations, and thirty-two new hospitals were established. Thousands of lesser-known women and men worked in the antislavery crusade, the peace movement, and other reform organizations of the Jacksonian era.

Whether a society tries simply to punish its deviant members or to reform and care for them can help us in understanding the values and the view of human nature in that society. Through much of Western history, the individual has been assumed to have free will to do good or evil. The possible influences of social and psychological factors upon behavior were not recognized, so criminals were considered entirely responsible for their crimes and punishments were often severe. Change began in the eighteenth century, on both sides of the Atlantic, with the development of a new feeling — a concern for other human beings that we call humanitarianism. The number of capital crimes was reduced, imprisonment rather than mutilation became more common, and mental institutions, reform schools, and houses of refuge were founded. Frequently, the philosophy of the reformers reflected their own values — that Christian education would reform the recalcitrant or that discipline and training in a craft would help the orphan to lead a worthy life.

In the following essay, Christine Stansell discusses a group of men and women of the new middle class who felt that home and family were the foundations of Christian civilization. They were appalled at the thousands of poor children who roamed the streets of New York, scavenging, peddling, stealing, and prostituting themselves. Hundreds were homeless, but most had families who did not view street life as particularly pernicious. Children of the poor learned to survive and to contribute to the family at an early age, and the poor did not regard it as unusual that people spent more time in the streets than at home. Unable to understand the different values and family life of the poor, the reformers tried to remove boys from their families and to make over the life-style of the poor to fit their own image of domestic bliss.

On a winter day in 1856, an agent for the Children's Aid Society (CAS) of New York encountered two children out on the street with market baskets. Like hundreds he might have seen, they were desperately poor — thinly dressed and barefoot in the cold — but their cheerful countenances struck the gentleman, and he stopped to inquire into their

This shortened version of the article "Women, Children, and the Uses of the Streets" is reprinted from *Feminist Studies*, Volume 8, No. 2 (Summer 1982): 309–335, by permission of the publisher, Feminist Studies, Inc., c/o Women's Studies Program, University of Maryland, College Park, MD 20742.

circumstances. They explained that they were out gathering bits of wood and coal their mother could burn for fuel and agreed to take him home to meet her. In a bare tenement room, bereft of heat, furniture, or any other comforts, he met a "stout, hearty woman" who, even more than her children, testified to the power of hardihood and motherly love in the most miserable circumstances. A widow, she supported her family as best she could by street peddling; their room was bare because she had been forced to sell her clothes, furniture, and bedding to supplement her earnings. As she spoke, she sat on a pallet on the floor and rubbed the hands of the two younger siblings of the pair from the street. "They were tidy, sweet children," noted the agent, "And it was very sad to see their chilled faces and tearful eyes." Here was a scene that would have touched the heart of Dickens, and seemingly many a chillier mid-Victorian soul. Yet in concluding his report, the agent's perceptions took a curiously harsh turn.

> Though for her pure young children too much could hardly be done, in such a woman there is little confidence to be put . . . it is probably, some cursed vice has thus reduced her, and that, if her children be not separated from her, she will drag them down, too.

Such expeditions of charity agents and reformers into the households of the poor were common in New York between 1850 and 1860. So were such harsh and unsupported judgments of working-class mothers, judgments which either implicitly or explicitly converged in the new category of the "dangerous classes." In this decade, philanthropists, municipal authorities, and a second generation of Christian evangelicals, male and female, came to see the presence of poor children in New York's streets as a central element of the problem of urban poverty. They initiated an ambitious campaign to clear the streets, to change the character of the laboring poor by altering their family lives, and, in the process, to eradicate poverty itself. They focused their efforts on transforming two elements of laboring-class family life, the place of children and the role of women.

There was, in fact, nothing new about the presence of poor children in the streets, nor was it new that women of the urban poor should countenance that presence. For centuries, poor people in Europe had freely used urban public areas — streets, squares, courts, and marketplaces — for their leisure and work. For the working poor, street life was bound up not only with economic exigency, but also with childrearing, family morality, sociability, and neighborhood ties. In the nineteenth century, the crowded conditions of the tenements and the poverty of great numbers of metropolitan laboring people made the streets as crucial an arena as ever for their social and economic lives. As one New York social investigator observed, "In the poorer portions of the city, people live much and sell mostly out of doors."

How, then, do we account for this sudden flurry of concern? For reformers like the agent from the CAS, street life was antagonistic to ardently held beliefs about childhood, womanhood and, ultimately, the nature of civilized urban society. The middle class of which the reformers were a part was only emerging, an economically ill-defined group, neither rich nor poor, just beginning in the antebellum years to assert a distinct cultural identity. Central to its self-conception was the ideology of domesticity, a set of sharp ideas and pronounced opinions about the nature of a moral family life. The sources of this ideology were historically complex and involved several decades of struggles by women of this group for social recognition, esteem, and power in the family. Nonetheless, by midcentury, ideas initially developed and promoted by women and their clerical allies had found general acceptance, and an ideology of gender had become firmly embedded in an ideology of class. Both women and men valued the home, an institution which they perceived as sacred, presided over by women, inhabited by children, frequented by men. The home preserved those social virtues endangered by the public world of trade, industry, and politics; a public world which they saw as even more corrupting and dangerous in a great city like New York.

Enclosed, protected, and privatized, the home and the patterns of family life on which it was based thus represented to middle-class women and men a crucial institution of civilization. From this perspective, a particular geography of social life — the engagement of the poor in street life rather than in the enclave of the home — became in itself evidence of parental neglect, family disintegration, and a pervasive urban social pathology. Thus in his condemnation of the impoverished widow, the CAS agent distilled an entire analysis of poverty and a critique of poor families: the presence of her children on the streets was synonymous with a corrupt family life, no matter how disguised it might be. In the crusade of such mid-Victorian reformers to save poor children from their parents and their class lie the roots of a long history of middle-class intervention in working-class families, a history which played a central part in the making of the female American working class.

Many historians have shown the importance of antebellum urban reform to the changing texture of class relations in America, its role in the cultural transformations of urbanization and industrialization. Confronted with overcrowding, unemployment, and poverty on a scale theretofore unknown in America, evangelical reformers forged programs to control and mitigate these pressing urban problems, programs which would shape municipal policies for years to come. . . . In their experience with the reformers, the laboring poor learned — and were forced — to accommodate themselves to an alien conception of family and city life. Through their work with the poor, the reformers discovered many of the elements from which they would forge their own class and sexual identity, still ill-defined and diffuse in 1850; women, particularly, strengthened their role as dictators of domestic and familial standards for all classes of Americans. The reformers' eventual triumph in New York brought no solutions to the problem of poverty, but it did bring about the evisceration of a way of urban life and the legitimation of their own cultural power as a class.

The conflict over the streets resonated on many levels. Ostensibly the reformers aimed to rescue children from the corruptions and dangers of the city streets; indeed the conscious motives of many, if not all, of these well-meaning altruists went no further. There were many unquestioned assumptions, however, on which their benevolent motives rested, and it is in examining these assumptions that we begin to see the challenge which these middle-class people unwittingly posed to common practices of the poor. In their cultural offensive, reformers sought to impose on the poor conceptions of childhood and motherhood drawn from their own ideas of domesticity. In effect, reformers tried to implement their domestic beliefs through reorganizing social space, through creating a new geography of the city. Women were especially active; while male reformers experimented, through a rural foster home program, with more dramatic means of clearing the streets, middle-class ladies worked to found new working-class homes, modeled on their own, which would establish a viable alternative to the thoroughly nondomesticated streets. . . .

Unlike today, the teeming milieu of the New York streets in the mid-nineteenth century was in large part a children's world. A complex web of economic imperatives and social mores accounted for their presence there, a presence which reformers so ardently decried. Public life, with its panoply of choices, its rich and varied texture, its motley society, played as central a role in the upbringing of poor children as did private, domestic life in that of their more affluent peers. While middle-class mothers spent a great deal of time with their children (albeit with the help of servants), women of the laboring classes condoned for their offspring an early independence — within bounds — on the streets. Through peddling, scavenging, and the shadier arts of theft and prostitution, the streets offered children a way to earn their keep, crucial to making ends meet in their households. Street life also provided a home for children without families — the orphaned and abandoned — and an alternative to living at home for the especially independent and those in strained family circumstances.

Such uses of the streets were dictated by exigency, but they were also intertwined with patterns of motherhood, parenthood, and childhood. In contrast to their middle- and upper-class contemporaries, the working poor did not think of childhood as a separate stage of life in which girls and boys were free from adult burdens, nor did poor women consider mothering to be a full-time task of supervision. They expected their children to work from an early age, to "earn their keep" or to "get a living," a view much closer to the early modern conceptions which Philippe Ariès describes in *Centuries of Childhood*. Children were little adults, unable as yet to take up all the duties of their elders, but nonetheless bound to do as much as they could. To put it another way, the lives of children, like those of adults, were circumscribed by economic and familial obligations. In this context, the poor expressed their care for children differently than did the propertied classes. Raising one's children properly did not mean protecting them from the world of work; on the contrary, it involved teaching them to shoulder those heavy burdens of labor which were the common lot of their class, to be hardworking and dutiful to kin and neighbors. By the same token, laboring children gained an early autonomy from their parents, an autonomy alien to the experience of more privileged children. But there were certainly generational tensions embedded in these practices: although children learned independence within the bounds of family obligation, their self-sufficiency also led them in directions that parents could not always control. When parents sent children out to the streets, they could only partially set the terms of what the young ones learned there.

Street selling, or huckstering, was one of the most common ways for children to turn the streets to good use. Through the nineteenth century, this ancient form of trade still flourished in New York alongside such new institutions of mass marketing as A. T. Stewart's department store. Hucksters, both adults and children, sold all manner of necessities and delicacies. In the downtown business and shopping district, passers-by could buy treats at every corner: hot sweet potatoes, bake-pears, teacakes, fruit, candy, and hot corn. In residential neighborhoods, hucksters sold household supplies door to door: fruits and vegetables in season, matchsticks, scrub brushes, sponges, strings, and pins. Children assisted adult hucksters, went peddling on their own, and worked in several low-paying trades which were their special province: crossing-sweeping for girls; errandrunning, bootblacking, horseholding and newspaperselling for boys. There were also the odd trades in which children were particularly adept, those unfamiliar and seemingly gratuitous forms of economic activity which abounded in nineteenth-century metropolises: one small boy whom a social investigator found in 1859 made his living in warm weather by catching butterflies and peddling them to canary owners.

Younger children, too, could earn part of their keep on the streets. Scavenging, the art of gathering useful and salable trash, was the customary chore for those too small to go out streetselling. Not all scavengers were children; there were also adults who engaged in scavenging full-time, ragpickers who made their entire livelihoods from "all the odds and ends of a great city." More generally, however, scavenging was children's work. Six- or seven-year-olds were not too young to set out with friends and siblings to gather fuel for their mothers. Small platoons of these children scoured neighborhood streets, ship and lumber yards, building lots, demolished houses, and the precincts of artisan shops and factories for chips, ashes, wood, and coal to take home or peddle to neighbors. "I saw some girls gathering cinders," noted Virginia Penny, New York's self-styled Mayhew. "They burn them at home, after washing them."

The economy of rubbish was intricate. As children grew more skilled, they learned how to turn up other serviceable cast-offs. "These gatherers of things lost on earth," a journal had called them in 1831. "These makers of something out of nothing." Besides taking trash home or selling it to neighbors, children could peddle it to junk dealers, who in turn vended it to manufacturers and artisans for use in industrial processes. Rags, old rope, metal, nails, bottles, paper, kitchen grease, bones, spoiled vegetables, and bad meat all had their place in this commercial network. The waterfront was especially fruitful territory: there, children foraged for loot which had washed up on the banks, snagged in piers, or spilled out on the docks. Loose cotton shredded off bales on the wharves where the southern packet ships docked, bits of canvas and rags ended up with paper- and shoddy-manufacturers (shoddy, the cheapest of textiles, made its way back to the poor in "shoddy" ready-made clothing). Old rope was shredded and sold as oakum, a fiber used to caulk ships. Whole pieces of hardware — nails, cogs, and screws — could be resold: broken bits went to iron- and brass-founders and coppersmiths to be melted down; bottles and bits of broken glass, to glassmakers. The medium for these exchanges were the second-hand shops strung along the harbor which carried on a bustling trade with children despite a city ordinance prohibiting their buying from minors. "On going down South Street I met a gang of small Dock Thieves . . . had a bag full of short pieces of old rope and iron," William Bell, police inspector of second-hand shops, reported on a typical day on the beat in 1850. The malefactors were headed for a shop like the one into which he slipped incognito, to witness the mundane but illegal transaction between the proprietor and a six-year-old boy, who sold him a glass bottle for a penny. The waterfront also yielded trash which could be used at home rather than vended: tea, coffee, sugar, and flour spilled from sacks and barrels, and from the wagons which carried cargo to nearby warehouses.

By the 1850s, huckstering and scavenging were the only means by which increasing numbers of children could earn their keep. A decline in boys' positions as artisans' apprentices and girls' positions as domestic servants meant that the streets became the most accessible employer of children. Through the 1840s, many artisan masters entirely rearranged work in their shops to take advantage of a labor market glutted with impoverished adults, and to survive within the increasingly cutthroat exigencies of New York commerce and manufacturing. As a result, apprenticeship in many trades had disappeared by 1850. Where it did survive, the old perquisites, steady work and room and board, were often gone: boys' work, like that of the adults they served, was irregular and intermittent.

There were analogous changes in domestic service. Until the 1840s, girls of the laboring classes had easily found work as servants, but in that decade, older female immigrants, whom employers preferred for their superior strength, crowded them out of those positions. By the early 1850s, domestic service was work for Irish and German teenagers and young women. In other industrial centers, towns like Manchester and Lowell, children moved from older employments into the factories; New York, however, because of high ground rents and the absence of sufficient water power, lacked the large establishments which gave work to the young in other cities. Consequently, children and adolescents, who two generations earlier would have worked in more constrained situations, now flooded the streets.

... When respectable parents sent their children out to scavenge and peddle, the consequences were not always what they intended: these trades were an avenue to theft and prostitution as well as to an honest living. Child peddlers habituated household entryways, with their hats and umbrellas and odd knickknacks, and roamed by shops where goods were often still, in the old fashion, displayed outside on the sidewalks. And scavenging was only one step removed from petty theft. The distinction between gathering spilled flour and spilling flour oneself was one which small scavengers did not always observe. Indeed, children skilled in detecting value in random objects strewn about the streets, the seemingly inconsequential, could as easily spot value in other people's property. As the superintendent of the juvenile asylum wrote of one malefactor, "He has very little sense of moral rectitude, and thinks it but little harm to take small articles." A visitor to the city in 1857 was struck by the swarms of children milling around the docks, "scuffling about, wherever there were bags of coffee and hogshead of sugar." Armed with sticks, "they 'hooked' what they could. . . ." Police Chief George Matsell reported that pipes, tin roofing, and brass doorknobs were similarly endangered. Thefts against persons, pickpocketing and mugging, belonged to another province, that of the professional child criminal. . . .

As scavenging shaded into theft, so it also edged into another street trade, prostitution. The same art of creating commodities underlay both. In the intricate economy of the streets, old rope, stray coal, rags, and sex all held the promise of cash, a promise apparent to children who from an early age learned to be "makers of something out of nothing." For girls who knew how to turn things with no value into things with exchange value, the prostitute's act of bartering sex into money would have perhaps seemed daunting, but nonetheless comprehensible. These were not professional child prostitutes; rather, they turned to the lively trade in casual prostitution on occasion or at intervals to supplement other earnings. One encounter with a gentleman, easy to come by in the hotel and business district, could bring the equivalent of a month's wages in domestic service, a week's wages seamstressing, or several weeks' earnings huckstering. Such windfalls went to pay a girl's way at home or, more typically, to purchase covertly some luxury — pastries, a bonnet, cheap jewelry, a fancy gown — otherwise out of her reach.

Prostitution was quite public in antebellum New York. It was not yet a statutory offense, and although the police harassed streetwalkers and arrested them for vagrancy, they had little effect on the trade. Consequently, offers from men and inducements from other girls were common on the streets, and often came a girl's way when she was out working. This is the reason a German father tried to prevent his fourteen-year-old daughter from going out scavenging when she lost her place in domestic service. "He said, 'I don't want you to be a rag-picker. You are not a child now — people will look at you — you will come to harm,'" as the girl recounted the tale. The "harm" he feared was the course taken by a teenage habitue of the waterfront in whom Inspector Bell took a special interest in 1851. After she rejected his offer of a place in service, he learned from a junk shop proprietor that, along with scavenging around the docks, she was "in the habit of going aboard the Coal Boats in that vicinity and prostituting herself." Charles Loring Brace, founder of the CAS, claimed that "the life of a swill-gatherer, or coal-picker, or chiffonier [ragpicker] in the streets soon wears off a girl's modesty and prepares her for worse occupation," while Police Chief Matsell accused huckster-girls of soliciting the clerks and employees they met on their rounds of counting houses.

While not all girls in the street trades were as open to advances as Brace and Matsell implied, their habituation to male advances must have contributed to the brazenness with which some of them could engage in sexual bartering. Groups of girls roamed about the city, sometimes on chores and errands, sometimes only with an eye for flirtations, or being "impudent and saucy to men," as the parents of one offender put it. In the early 1830s, John R. McDowall, leader of the militant Magdalene Society, had observed on fashionable Broadway "females of thirteen and fourteen walking the streets without a protector, until some pretended gentleman gives them a nod, and takes their arm and escorts them to houses of assignation." McDowall was sure to exaggerate, but later witnesses lent credence to his description. In 1854, a journalist saw nearly fifty girls soliciting one evening as he walked a mile up Broadway, while diarist George Templeton Strong referred to juvenile prostitution as a permanent feature of the promenade in the early 1850s: "no one can walk the length of Broadway without meeting some hideous troop of ragged girls." But despite the entrepreneurial attitude with which young girls ventured into prostitution, theirs was a grim choice, with hazards which, young as they were, they could not always foresee. Nowhere can we see more clearly the complexities of poor children's lives in the public city. The life of the streets taught them self-reliance and the arts of survival, but this education could also be a bitter one.

The autonomy and independence which the streets fostered through petty crime also extended to living arrangements. Abandoned children, orphans, runaways and particularly independent boys made the streets their home: sleeping out with companions in household areas, wagons, marketplace stalls, and saloons. In the summer of 1850, the *Tribune* noted that the police regularly scared up thirty or forty boys sleeping along Nassau and Ann streets; they included boys with homes as well as genuine vagabonds. Police Chief Matsell reported that in warm weather, crowds of roving boys, many of them sons of respectable parents, absented themselves from their families for weeks. Such was Thomas W., who came to the attention of the CAS; "sleeps in stable," the case record notes. "Goes home for clean clothes; and sometimes for his meals." Thomas's parents evidently tolerated the arrangement, but this was not always the case. Rebellious children, especially boys, evaded parental demands and discipline by living on the streets full-time. Thus John Lynch left home because of some difficulty with his father: he was sent on his parents' complaint to the juvenile house of correction on a vagrancy charge.

Reformers like Matsell and the members of the CAS tended to see such children as either orphaned or abandoned, symbols of the misery and depravity of the poor. Their perception, incarnated by writers like Horatio Alger in the fictional waifs of sentimental novels, gained wide credibility in nineteenth-century social theory and popular thought. Street children were essentially "friendless and homeless," declared Brace. "No one cares for them, and they care for no one." His judgment, if characteristically harsh, was not without truth. If children without parents had no kin or friendly neighbors to whom to turn, they were left to fend for themselves. Such was the story of the two small children of a deceased stonecutter, himself a widower. After he died, "they wandered around, begging cold victuals, and picking up, in any way they were able, their poor living. . . ."

Not surprisingly, orphange among the poor was a far more complex matter than reformers perceived. As Carol Groneman has shown, poor families did not disintegrate under the most severe difficulties of immigration and urbanization. In the worst New York slums, families managed to keep together and to take in those kin and friends who lacked households of their own. Orphaned children as well as those who were temporarily parentless — whose parents, for instance, had found employment elsewhere — typically found homes with older siblings, grandparents, and aunts. The solidarity of the laboring-class family, however, was not as idyllic as it might seem in retrospect. Interdependence also bred tensions which weighed heavily on children, and in response, the young sometimes chose — or were forced — to strike out on their own. Step-relations, so common in this period, were a particular source of bad feelings. Two brothers whom a charity visitor found sleeping in the streets explained that they had left their mother when she moved in with another man after their father deserted her. If natural parents died, step-parents might be particularly forceful about sending children "on their own hook." "We haven't got no father nor mother," testified a twelve-year-old wanderer of himself and his younger brother. Their father, a shoemaker, had remarried when their mother died; when he died, their stepmother moved away and left them, "and they could not find out anything more about her. . . ."

All these customs of childhood and work among the laboring poor were reasons for the presence of children, girls and boys, in the public life of the city, a presence which reformers passionately denounced. Children and parents alike had their uses for the streets. For adults, the streets allowed their dependents to contribute to their keep, crucial to making ends meet in the household economy. For girls and boys, street life provided a way to meet deeply ingrained family obligations. This is not to romanticize their lives. If the streets provided a way to meet responsibilities, it was a hard and bitter, even a cruel one. Still, children of the laboring classes lived and labored in a complex geography, which reformers of the poor perceived only as a stark tableau of pathology and vice. . . .

To what degree did their judgments of children redound on women? Although reformers included both sexes in their indictments, women were by implication more involved. First, poverty was especially likely to afflict women. To be the widow, deserted wife, or orphaned daughter of a laboring man, even a prosperous artisan, was to be poor; female self-support was synonymous with indigence. The number of self-supporting women, including those with children, was high in midcentury New York: in the 1855 census report for two neighborhoods, nearly 60 percent of six hundred working women sampled had no adult male in the household. New York's largest charity reported in 1858 that it aided 27 percent more women than men. For women in such straits, children's contributions to the family income were mandatory. As a New York magistrate had written in 1830: "of the children brought before me for pilfering, nine out of ten are those whose fathers are dead, and who live with their mothers." Second, women were more responsible than men for children, both from the perspective of reformers and within the reality of the laboring family. Mothering, as the middle class saw it, was an expression of female identity, rather than a construction derived from present and past social conditions. Thus the supposedly neglectful ways of laboring mothers reflected badly not only on their character as parents, but also on their very identity as women. When not depicted as timid or victimized, poor women appeared as unsavory characters in the annals of reformers: drunken, abusive, or, in one of the most memorable descriptions, "sickly-looking, deformed by over work . . . weak and sad-faced." Like prostitutes, mothers of street children became a kind of half-sex in the eyes of reformers, outside the bounds of humanity by virtue of their inability or unwillingness to replicate the innate abilities of true womanhood.

In the 1850s, the street activities of the poor, especially those of children, became the focus of a distinct reform politics in New York. The campaign against the streets, one element in a general cultural offensive against the laboring classes which evangelical groups had carried on since the 1830s, was opened in 1849 by Police Chief Matsell's report to the public on juvenile delinquency. In the most hyperbolic rhetoric, he described a "deplorable and growing evil" spreading through the streets. "I allude to the constantly increasing number of vagrants, idle and vicious children of both sexes, who infest our public thoroughfares." Besides alerting New York's already existing charities to the presence of the dangerous classes, Matsell's expose affected a young Yale seminarian, Charles Loring Brace, just returned from a European tour and immersed in his new vocation of city missionary. Matsell's alarmed observation coalesced with what Brace had learned from his own experiences working with boys in the city mission. Moved to act, Brace in 1853 founded the CAS, a charity which concerned itself with all poor children, but especially with street "orphans." Throughout the 1850s, the CAS carried on the work Matsell had begun, documenting and publicizing the plight of street children. In large measure because of its efforts, the "evil" of the streets became a central element in the reform analysis of poverty and a focus of broad concern in New York.

Matsell, Brace, and the New York philanthropists with whom they associated formed — like their peers in other Northeastern cities — a closely connected network of secular and moral reformers. By and large, these women and men were not born into New York's elite, as were those of the generation who founded the city's philanthropic movement in the first decades of the century. Rather, they were part of an emerging middle class, typically outsiders to the ruling class, either by birthplace or social status. Although much of the ideology which influenced reformers' dealings with the poor is well known, scholars have generally not explored the extent to which their interactions with the laboring classes were shaped by developing ideas of gentility: ideas, in turn, based upon conceptions of domestic life. Through their attempts to recast working-class life within these conceptions, this still-inchoate class sharpened its own vision of urban culture and its ideology of class relations. Unlike philanthropists in the early nineteenth century, who partook of an older attitude of tolerance to the poor and of the providential inevitability of poverty, mid-Victorians were optimistic that poverty could be abolished by altering the character of their almoners as workers, citizens, and family members. The reformers of the streets were directly concerned with the latter. In their efforts to teach the working poor the virtues of the middle-class home as a means of self-help, they laid the ideological and programmatic groundwork for a sustained intervention in working-class family life. . . .

There were, then, greater numbers of children in the New York streets after 1845, and their activities were publicized as never before. Faced with an unprecedented crisis of poverty in the city, reformers fastened on their presence as a cause rather than a symptom of impoverishment. The reformers' idea that the curse of poor children lay in the childrearing methods of their parents moved toward the center of their analysis of the etiology of poverty, replacing older notions of divine will. In the web of images of blight and disease which not only reflected but also shaped the midcentury understanding of poverty, the tenement house was the "parent of constant disorders, and the nursery of increasing vices," but real parents were the actual agents of crime. In opposition to the ever more articulate and pressing claims of New York's organized working men, this first generation of "experts" on urban poverty averred that familial relations rather than industrial capitalism were responsible for the misery which any clear-headed New Yorker could see was no transient state of affairs. One of the principal pieces of evidence of "the ungoverned appetites, bad habits, and vices" of laboring-class parents was the fact that they sent their offspring out to the streets to earn their keep.

The importance of domesticity to the reformers' own class identity fostered this shift of attention from individual moral shortcomings to the family structure of a class. For these middle-class city dwellers, the home was not simply a place of residence; it was a focus of social life and a central element of class-consciousness, based on specific conceptions of femininity and childrearing. There, secluded from the stress of public life, women could devote themselves to directing the moral and ethical development of their families. There, protected from the evils of the outside world, the young could live out their childhoods in innocence, freed from the necessity of labor, cultivating their moral and intellectual faculties.

From this vantage point, the laboring classes appeared gravely deficient. When charity visitors, often ladies themselves, entered the households of working people, they saw a domestic sparseness which contradicted their deepest beliefs about what constituted a morally sustaining family life. "[Their] ideas of domestic comfort and standard of morals, are far below our own," wrote the Association for Improving the Condition of the Poor (AICP). The urban poor had intricately interwoven family lives, but they had no *homes*. Middle-class people valued family privacy and intimacy: among the poor, they saw a promiscuous sociability, an "almost fabulous gregariousness." They believed that the moral training of children depended on protecting them within the home; in poor neighborhoods, they saw children encouraged to labor in the streets. The harshness and intolerance with which midcentury reformers viewed the laboring classes can be partly explained by the disparity between these two ways of family life. "Homes — in the better sense — they never know," declared one investigating committee; the children "graduate in every kind of vice known in that curious school which trains them — the public street." The AICP scoffed at even using the word: "Homes . . . if it is not a mockery to give that hallowed name to the dark, filthy hovels where many of them dwell." To these middle-class women and men, the absence of home life was not simply due to the uncongenial physical circumstances of the tenements, nor did it indicate the poor depended upon another way of organizing their family lives. Rather, the homelessness of this "multitude of half-naked, dirty, and leering children" signified an absence of parental love, a neglect of proper childrearing which was entwined in the habits and values of the laboring classes. . . .

It was through the famed placing-out system that the CAS . . . sent poor city children to foster homes in rural areas where labor was scarce. With the wages-fund theory, a common Anglo-American liberal reform scheme of midcentury which proposed to solve the problem of metropolitan unemployment by dispersing the surplus of labor, the society defended itself against critics' charges that "foster parents" were simply farmers in need of cheap help, and placing-out, a cover for the exploitation of child labor. At first, children went to farms in the nearby countryside, as did those the city bound out from the Almshouse, but in 1854 the society conceived the more ambitious scheme of sending parties of children by railroads to the far Midwest: Illinois, Michigan, and Iowa. By 1860, 5,074 children had been placed out.

At its most extreme, the CAS only parenthetically recognized the social and legal claims of working-class parenthood. The organization considered the separation of parents and children a positive good, the liberation of innocent, if tarnished, children from the tyranny of unredeemable adults. . . . Since the CAS viewed children as innocents to be rescued and parents as corrupters to be displaced, its methods depended in large measure on convincing children themselves to leave New York, with or without parental knowledge or acquiescence. Street children were malleable innocents in the eyes of the charity, but they were also little consenting adults, capable of breaking all ties to their class milieu and families. To be sure, many parents did bring their children to be placed-out, but nonetheless, the society also seems to have worked directly through the children. In 1843, the moral reformer and abolitionist Lydia Maria Child had mused that the greatest misfortune of "the squalid little wretches" she saw in the New York streets was that they were not orphans. The charity visitors of the CAS tackled this problem directly: where orphans were lacking, they manufactured them.

Placing-out was based on the thoroughly middle-class idea of the redeeming influence of the Protestant home in the countryside. There, the morally strengthening effects of labor, mixed with the salutary influences of domesticity and female supervision, could remold the child's character. Thus domestic ideology gave liberals like Brace the theoretical basis for constructing a program to resocialize the poor in which force was unnecessary. Standards of desirable behavior could be internalized by children rather than beaten into them, as had been the eighteenth-century practice. With home influence, not only childrearing but the resocialization of a class could take the form of subliminal persuasion rather than conscious coercion.

Earlier New York reformers had taken a different tack with troublesome children. In 1824, the Society for the Reformation of Juvenile Delinquents had established an asylum, the House of Refuge, to deal with juvenile offenders. As in all the new institutions for deviants, solitary confinement and corporal punishment were used to force the recalcitrant into compliance with the forces of reason. But Brace thought the asylum, so prized by his predecessors, was impractical and ineffectual. Asylums could not possibly hold enough children to remedy the problem of the New York streets in the 1850s; moreover, the crowding together of the children who were incarcerated only reinforced the habits of their class. The foster home, however, with its all-encompassing moral influence, could be a more effective house of refuge. . . .

This is an overview of the work of the CAS, but on closer examination, there was also a division by sex in the organization, and domesticity played different roles in the girls' and boys' programs. The emigrants to the West seem to have been mostly boys: they seem to have been more allured by emigration than were girls, and parents were less resistant to placing out sons than daughters. "Even as a beggar or pilferer, a little girl is of vastly more use to a wretched mother than her son," the society commented. "The wages of a young girl are much more sure to go to the pockets of the family than those of a boy." Brace's own imagination was more caught up with boys than girls; his most inventive efforts were directed at them. Unlike most of his contemporaries, he appreciated the vitality and tenacity of the street boys; his fascination with the Western scheme came partly from the hope that emigration would redirect their toughness and resourcefulness, "their sturdy independence," into hearty frontier individualism. Similarly, the agents overseeing the foster home program were men, as were the staff members of the society's much-touted Newsboys' Lodging-House, a boardinghouse where, for a few pennies, news boys could sleep and eat. The Lodging-House, was, in fact, a kind of early boys' camp, where athletics and physical fitness, lessons in entrepreneurship (one of its salient features was a savings bank), and moral education knit poor boys and gentlemen into a high-spirited but respectable masculine camaraderie.

Women were less visible in the society's literature, their work less well-advertised, since it was separate from Brace's most innovative programs. The women of the CAS were not paid agents like the men, but volunteers who staffed the girls' programs: a Lodging-House and several industrial schools. The work of the women reformers was, moreover, less novel than that of the men. Rather than encouraging girls to break away from their families, the ladies sought the opposite: to create among the urban laboring classes a domestic life of their own. They aimed to mold future wives and mothers of a reformed working class: women who would be imbued with a belief in the importance of domesticity and capable of patterning their homes and family lives on middle-class standards.

Yet it was this strategy of change, rather than Brace's policy of fragmentation, which would eventually dominate attempts to reform working-class children. The ladies envisioned homes which would reorganize the promiscuously sociable lives of the poor under the aegis of a new, "womanly" working-class woman. In the CAS industrial schools and Lodging-House, girls recruited off the streets learned the arts of plain sewing, cooking, and housecleaning, guided by the precept celebrated by champions of women's domestic mission that "nothing was so honorable as industrious *house-work*." These were skills which both prepared them for waged employment in seamstressing and domestic service and outfitted them for homes of their own: as the ladies proudly attested after several years of work, their students entered respectable married life as well as honest employment. "Living in homes reformed through their influence," the married women carried on their female mission, reformers by proxy.

Similarly, the women reformers instituted meetings to convert the mothers of their students to a new relationship to household and children. Classes taught the importance of sobriety, neat appearance, and sanitary housekeeping: the material basis for virtuous motherhood and a proper home. Most important, the ladies stressed the importance of keeping children off the streets and sending them to school. Here, they found their pupils particularly recalcitrant. Mothers persisted in keeping children home to work and cited economic reasons when their benefactresses upbraided them. The CAS women, however, considered the economic rationale a pretense for the exploitation of children and the neglect of their moral character. "The larger ones were needed to 'mind' the baby," lady volunteers sardonically reported, "or go out begging for clothes . . . and the little ones, scarcely bigger than the baskets on their arms, must be sent out for food, or chips, or cinders." The Mothers's Meetings tried, however unsuccessfully, to wean away laboring women from such customary practices to what the ladies believed to be a more nurturant and moral mode of family life: men at work, women at home, children inside.

In contrast to the male reformers, the women of the society tried to create an intensified private life within New York itself, to enclose children within tenements and schools rather than to send them away or incarcerate them in asylums. There is a new, optimistic vision of city life implied in their work. With the establishment of the home across class lines, a renewed city could emerge, its streets free for trade and respectable promenades, and emancipated from the inconveniences of pickpockets and thieves, the affronts of prostitutes and hucksters, the myriad offenses of working-class mores and poverty. The "respectable" would control and dominate public space as they had never before. The city would itself become an asylum on a grand scale, an environment which embodied the eighteenth-century virtues of reason and progress, the nineteenth-century virtues of industry and domesticity. And as would befit a city for the middle class, boundaries between public and private life would be clear: the public space of the metropolis would be the precinct of men, the private space of the home, that of women and children. . . .

Neither the clearing of the streets nor the making of the working-class home were accomplished at any one point in time. Indeed, these conflicts still break out in Manhattan's poor and working-class neighborhoods. Today, in the Hispanic *barrios* of the Upper West and Lower East sides and in black Harlem, scavenging and street huckstering still flourish. In prosperous quarters as well, where affluent customers are there for the shrewd, the battle continues between police on the one hand, hucksters and prostitutes on the other. Indeed, the struggle over the streets has been so ubiquitous in New York and other cities in the last 150 years that we can see it as a structural element of urban life in industrial capitalist societies. As high unemployment and casualized work have persisted in the great cities, the streets have continued to contain some of the few resources for the poor to make ends meet. At the same time, the social imagination of the poor, intensified by urban life, has worked to increase those resources. All the quick scams — the skills of the con men, street musicians, beggars, prostitutes, peddlers, drug dealers, and pickpockets — are arts of the urban working poor, bred from ethnic and class traditions and the necessities of poverty.

Neither is the conflict today, however, identical to the one which emerged in the 1850s. The struggle over the streets in modern New York takes place in a far different context, one defined by past victories of reformers and municipal authorities. Vagrancy counts against children are now strengthened by compulsory school legislation; child labor laws prohibit most kinds of child huckstering; anti-peddling laws threaten heavy fines for the unwary. Most important, perhaps, the mechanisms for "placing out" wandering children away from "negligent" mothers are all in place (although the wholesale breakdown of social services in New York has made these provisions increasingly ineffectual, creating a new problem in its wake). The street life of the working poor survives in pockets, but immeasurably weakened, continually under duress.

In more and more New York neighborhoods, the rich and the middle-class can walk untroubled by importunate prostitutes, beggars, and hucksters. The women gossiping on front stoops, the mothers shouting orders from upstairs windows, and the housewife habituees of neighborhood taverns have similarly disappeared, shut away behind heavily locked doors with their children and television sets. New York increasingly becomes a city where a variant of the nineteenth-century bourgeois vision of respectable urban life is realized. "NO LOITERING/PLAYING BALL/SITTING/PLAYING MUSIC ON SIDEWALKS IN FRONT OF BUILDINGS," placards on the great middle-class apartment houses warn potential lingerers. The sidewalks are, indeed, often free of people, except for passers by and the doormen paid to guard them. But as Jane Jacobs predicted so forcefully two decades ago, streets cleared for the respectable have become free fields for predators. The inhabitants of modern-day New York, particularly women and children, live in a climate of urban violence and fear historically unprecedented save in wartime. In the destruction of the street life of the laboring poor, a critical means of creating urban communities and organizing urban space has disappeared. As the streets are emptied of laboring women and children, as the working-class home has become an ideal, if not a reality, for ever-widening sectors of the population, the city of middle-class hopes becomes ever more bereft of those ways of public life which once mitigated the effects of urban capitalism.

STUDY GUIDE

1. A good many children and young people became the object of reformers' concern, and many were placed in reform schools, not because they had committed a crime, but because of something in their character, circumstances, or behavior. Describe some of these factors.

2. What do you see as the views of the reformers with respect to (a) the causes of street children's behavior; (b) the relationship of economic class to good citizenship and virtue; and (c) the different goals of the male and female reformers.

3. Stansell remarks that the reformers were "part of an emerging middle class, typically outsiders to the ruling class, either by birthplace or social status" who were unconsciously motivated by "developing ideas of gentility." Explain what she means by this. Do you find this explanation convincing?

4. Many of the reforms of the Jacksonian period were undertaken by private

societies with private funds. What factors in our time have caused most social welfare work to be carried out by government agencies with public funds? What private agencies still operate in such fields?

5. Cities like New York have very high welfare costs because so many people migrate there from other states, which are thus relieved of such a burden. What would be the advantages and disadvantages of having all social problems handled by the federal government, since such problems cross state lines?

BIBLIOGRAPHY

The subject of the treatment of juvenile delinquents and orphans is but a part of such broader topics as the society's view of deviance, the development of state institutions in the modern world, and the spirit of reform in Jacksonian America. Three studies that deal very broadly with change in nineteenth-century America are Robert E. Riegel, *Young America, 1830–1840* (1949); Alice F. Tyler, *Freedom's Ferment: Phases of American Social History to 1860* (1944); and Glyndon G. Van Deusen, *The Jacksonian Era, 1828–1848* (1959). The following three books on pre–Civil War reform are of special interest here: David B. Davis, ed., *Ante-Bellum Reform* (1967); Clifford S. Griffin, *Their Brother's Keeper: Moral Stewardship in the United States, 1800–1865* (1960); and Ronald G. Walters, *American Reformers, 1815–1860* (1978).

The bibliography following the reading by Daniel B. Smith (Reading No. 4) has a section concerning the history of childhood. Two works especially pertinent to the early nineteenth century are Bernard Wishy, *The Child and the Republic: The Dawn of Modern American Child Nurture* (1968) and Robert M. Mennel, *Thorns and Thistles: Juvenile Delinquency in the U.S., 1825–1940* (1973). Anyone interested either in social welfare as a profession or in American social values would do well to read some of the histories of American treatment of the criminal, the mentally ill, and the poor. Myra C. Glenn, *Campaigns Against Corporal Punishment: Prisoners, Sailors, Women and Children in Antebellum America* (1984) studies the movement to modify harsh punishments. Blake McKelvey, *American Prisons: A Study in Social History Prior to 1915* (1936) is an older study, while W. David Lewis, *From Newgate to Dannemora: The Rise of the Penitentiary in New York, 1796–1848* (1965) is more modern. Albert Deutsch, *The Mentally Ill in America: A History of Their Care and Treatment from Colonial Times,* 2nd ed. (1949) is a good survey. Two other books go into greater depth on mental institutions and views of insanity: Norman Dain, *Concepts of Insanity in the United States, 1789–1865* (1964) and Gerald N. Grob, *Mental Institutions in America: Social Policy to 1875* (1973). David J. Rothman, *The Discovery of the Asylum: Social Order and Disorder in the New Republic* (1971) deals with nearly all of the social institutions, including orphanages and houses of refuge, in the period. Two works dealing with incarceration of the young are: Robert S. Pickett, *House of Refuge: Origins of Juvenile Reform in New York State, 1815–1857* (1969), and Joseph M. Hawes,

Children in Urban Society: Juvenile Delinquency in Nineteenth-Century America (1971). Raymond A. Mohl, *Poverty in New York, 1783–1825* (1971) and Paul S. Boyer, *Urban Masses and Moral Order in America, 1820–1920* (1978) are other books for somewhat advanced students, while Robert H. Bremner, *American Philanthropy* (1960) is a brief introduction of general interest.

Shaker Village, Inc., Canterbury, N.H.

These New Hampshire women (c. 1914) reflect the continuity of nineteenth-century Shaker values of simple dress and segregation of the sexes.

13

EDWARD D. ANDREWS

Utopian Communes

One of the most unusual developments of the counterculture of the 1960s was the establishment of hundreds of communes across the United States. Ranging from a few people buying a farm they planned to work together to much larger groups with a distinctive philosophy of life, these experiments in living revealed a disenchantment with the larger, competitive society and emphasized the sharing of an "extended family."

This was by no means the first movement of this sort in American history. The first settlers of several of the colonies had been members of small, tightly knit groups that stressed a strong sense of mutual responsibility among the members. The same spirit had sometimes characterized new communities on the frontier as Americans moved west. Such religious sects as the Mormons and Moravians had displayed a similar unity of spirit and purpose. The clearest parallel to the communes of the 1960s can be found in the many groups in the 1830s that established small settlements in the Northeast and Midwest in an attempt to create a perfect community as an example for society as a whole.

Some of the communities were formed by European immigrants, such as the Rappites of western Pennsylvania, and some were based on social philosophies of European origin. Others were natively American, such as the Brook Farm community in Massachusetts. Some were religiously oriented; others were socialistic. They embodied a wide range of beliefs including vegetarianism, free love, celibacy, and the abolition of money. So varied were they that there was no such thing as a typical community that would give one an idea of life in any of the others.

Yet there were common impulses and common beliefs behind the founding of most of them. One, of course, was a dissatisfaction with the state of society. There was also a widespread belief that it was possible to establish a perfect social order among a small group of people. Ideas about what constituted perfection differed from one group to another; some thought it was to be found in the common ownership of property, while others believed it would only be achieved by coming into a perfect kingdom ordained by Christ. Finally, most of these groups believed that if a perfect community could be created on a small scale, with thirty or one hundred people, it would serve as a model that could be extended to the entire society.

The Shakers, founded by Mother Ann Lee, were one of several religious groups that adhered to the rule of celibacy in their communities and thus died out for lack of new recruits. Like many of the religious minorities of the early nineteenth century, the Shakers were millennialists, who believed in the second coming of Christ as the answer to the world's problems. In their case, they felt that Mother Ann was the female embodiment of the second coming, and that the millennium was already here — in the small Shaker communities in which they lived. In his book *The People Called Shakers: A Search for the Perfect Society*, Edward D. Andrews explains the theology and worship of the Shakers and also describes the daily life and human relations in a celibate, religious community that hoped to create a perfect order for American society.

Chief among the factors affecting all Shaker life was the unique relationship existing between brethren and sisters. The application, under the same roof, of the seemingly irreconcilable theories of equality and separation set the movement apart from other communal-religious institutions and aroused, more than any other characteristic of the church, skeptical comment and barbed abuse. Every reliable source, however, indicates that the dividing line was held. One sex was always conscious of the presence and support of the other. But to pass that invisible boundary was to invite both bondage of soul and communal disfavor.

Convictions concerning a fundamental tenet of the order, of course, aided the adjustment: for the rule of celibacy was a selective agent, attracting not only those who believed in the principle on doctrinal grounds, but those others, chiefly women, who were drawn in because of their desire to escape from marital difficulties and broken homes. For persons oppressed by poverty and economic ills the Shaker community, like the cloister, offered the opportunity for a renewal of life in useful service, in which case the rule was accepted as a condition of security. Once the rule was accepted, the Shakers underwent a thorough course of instruction. The work of God, they were told, proceeded by a spiritual union and relation between male and female. If, in the course of the period of probation, the cross seemed repellent, they were free to withdraw or remain in an "out family." On the other hand, should they wish to travel on to the junior and senior order, they did so in full realization of what it entailed. If husband and wife entered together, they were usually assigned to separate families. . . .

. . . [Joseph] Meacham's basic law — that "no male or female shall support, or have a private union or correspondence together, neither shall they touch each other unnecessarily" — was also supported, in time, by detailed "separation acts" and ordinances for the "purity of the mind." It was "contrary to the gift," for instance, for a brother to pass a sister on the stairs, for a brother to go into a sister's room without knocking, for a sister to go to a brother's shop alone, for brethren to shake hands with the sisters and give them presents, and so on.

Surveillance was facilitated by the smallness of the family and the lack of privacy. From two to six individuals shared each sleeping or retiring room, the day's routine was organized, and most of the work was done in groups. In meeting, . . . the ministry could supervise proceedings through shuttered apertures; and at Pleasant Hill, two watchtowers on the roof of the dwelling served a similar purpose during the day. The Millennial Laws stated that if anyone knew of any transgression, he or she was morally obligated to reveal it to the elders, "otherwise they participate in the guilt." Under such conditions an atmosphere of mutual suspicion was almost inevitable; the feeling that one was being spied upon during every hour of the day and night was bound to deprive the individual of dignity and self-respect.

The most noteworthy device for regulating sex relations, however, was a constructive one. As the church was being organized, Meacham realized that "correspondence" was unavoidable, that brethren and sisters must consult on temporalities, that social solidarity could not rest on negative grounds. Since they "*would* have a union together," he testified, "if they had not a spiritual union, they would have a carnal." His corrective was the "union meeting," which for over seventy years, from 1793 on, played an important role in Shaker domestic life. These gatherings usually took place two evenings a week and twice on Sundays. A group of four to ten members of each sex met in a brethren's retiring room, where they sat facing each other in rows about five feet apart. (If girls and boys were present, they were placed beside their elders or by themselves in ranks in the rear.) Then, for a stated period, one hour on week nights and one or two on the Sabbath, each member of the group conversed freely and openly with the person opposite him on some familiar or suitable subject; or the occasion might be turned into a singing meeting. The pairs had been carefully matched, on the basis of age and "condition of travel," by the elders. No one was worthy to attend if he or she harbored any ill-feeling toward another.

The conversation — "simple, sometimes facetious, rarely profound" — was limited, for sacred, literary, and certain secular topics were all prohibited. Some visitors, like [A. J.] Macdonald, found the meetings dull. Nevertheless the time seemed to have been agreeably passed; the company had their own world to talk about, with zest and unrestraint if they wished; "gentle laughter and mild amusement" were not unknown; and in the early years smoking was customary. The union meetings, in fact, belied the common assumption that the Shakers were an austere folk, though discipline varied with the family or community and was likely to be more strict in the Church Order. Self-restraint and sobriety, however, never excluded simple joys. One observer comments on "the amenity of their intercourse [which was] much less restricted than is generally supposed." Another noticed that they were "disposed to be merry and enjoy a joke." Mary Dyer attended meetings at Enfield (N.H.) where there were pipes to smoke, cider to drink, and melons, apples, and nuts to eat; and where the participants sang such "merry love songs" as

> I love the brethren the brethren love me
> Oh! how happy, how happy I be,
> I love the sisters, the sisters love me,
> Oh! how happy, how happy I be.
> How pretty they look, how clever they feel,
> And this we will sing when we love a good deal.

A former member of a Niskeyuna family recalled that two aged brethren, one a Whig and the other a Democrat before they joined the order, used to argue their political principles in these meetings; and that a young sister, on one occasion, raised the issue whether members would not be better Shakers if they were allowed to study instrumental music, languages, and fine literature. The aristocratic Mrs. Hall found the Believers at this community "a very conversible set of people" — a verdict later shared by Howells, who felt that the renunciation of marriage was "the sum of Shaker asceticism."

These social gatherings were nevertheless misinterpreted by the world: as Isaac Youngs put it, "advantage was taken by some apostates and evil minded persons . . . to construe this sacred order of union, [especially the placing of certain brethren with certain sisters] into a particular union or connection, as savoring of husband and wife." Eunice Chapman, for one, testified to seeing "the spiritual husbands, each with their spiritual wife," withdraw after meeting to their different apartments — observing to one of the sisters that there must be "general courtship throughout the house." Furnishing further grounds for detraction was a custom connected with the meeting, namely, that of assigning to each sister general "oversight over the habits and temporal needs" of the brother sitting opposite her — taking care of his clothes, looking after his washing and mending, providing new garments when they were needed, and so forth — in return for which the brethren "did needful favors for the sisters." Visitors sometimes noticed the tender solicitude of a brother toward a certain sister, or vice versa. Though such attention was a violation of the letter of the Separation Acts, it seems to have been accepted, quite naturally, as a justifiable expression of spiritual union.

A combination of factors — the system of orders and surveillance, communal opinion, the rites of confession and atonement, the force of principle, the union meeting, the freedom to withdraw from the society — fostered and enforced a relationship between the two sexes which one enthusiast called "more harmonic than anyone seriously believes attainable for the human race." As to its effectiveness, we have the empirical judgment of the student Macdonald:

> I have always found that those who spoke ill of the Shakers on this subject, to be ignorant, and low minded persons, who probably judged others by themselves, and who founded their opinion upon mere supposition. Those who have been most among them, and consequently the best Judges, have been compelled to believe, that the Shakers are generally speaking, sincere, both in the Belief and practice of abstinence from sexual coition. I have heard Individuals who have lived with them, for periods varying from thirty years, to a few months, all declare, that there was no such immorality among the Shakers, as had been attributed to them. In the vicinity of Union Village, O. I heard suspicions and suppositions, in abundance, and have no doubt the same surmises may be heard in the vicinity of any of their settlements. But I have never met with one individual who was a Witness to or could prove a Case of immoral conduct between the Sexes in any of the Shaker Communities. . . .
>
> It is quite true that sometimes, young Shakers in whom the tender passion is not entirely subdued, fall in love with each other, but these generally contrive to leave the Sect, and go to the "World" to get married and reside.

The "order of the day" left little room, indeed, for vain or idle thoughts. At the sounding of the bell or "shell," the Shakers arose early in the morning, between four o'clock and five in summer, between five and five-thirty in the winter. After kneeling together for a moment of quiet prayer, the occupants of each retiring room stripped the sheets and blankets from their narrow cots, laying them neatly over two chairs at the foot, on which the pillows had previously been placed. Fifteen minutes after rising, the rooms had been vacated, the brethren had gone to their morning chores, and the sisters were entering to close the windows, make the beds, and put the room in order. At breakfast time, six, six-thirty, or seven, the chamber work was finished, fires had been started in the dwelling rooms and shops, the cattle fed, the cows milked, and arrangements for the day's industry were all complete.

Before all meals — the early breakfast, the noon dinner, the six o'clock supper — brethren and sisters would assemble, each group by themselves, in appointed rooms, where for a ten or fifteen minute pause which was a kind of "broad grace," they quietly awaited the bell. Then, in two columns led by the elders and eldresses, respectively, and in the order in which they were to be seated, they proceeded to the dining hall. Taking their places behind their chairs or benches, the sexes at separate tables, they knelt in prayer at a sign from the lead, and after a meal eaten in monastic silence, knelt again before departing directly to their labors. . . .

A series of table monitors, emphasizing economy and good manners at meals, testifies to the concern with standards of behavior. An early monitor (undated manuscript) illustrates how detailed was the instruction:

First, All should sit upright at the table.

2d The Elder should begin first, after which all may take hold regularly.

3d When you take a piece of bread, take a whole piece (if not too large) and when you cut meat, cut it square & equal, fat & lean, & take an equal proportion of bones — take it on your plate together with the sauce, whether it be cabbage, herbs, potatoes or turnips; and not be cutting small pieces in the platter and putting directly into your mouth.

4th When you have tea or coffee, and any kind of minced victuals or meat cut into mouthfuls, it may be proper with a knife or fork to eat it directly from the platter. . . .

8th Eat what you need before you rise from table, and not be picking & eating afterwards.

9th When you have done eating, clean your plate, knife & fork — lay your bones in a sung heap by the side of your plate — scrape up your crumbs — cross your knife & fork on your plate with the edge towards you.

10th When you reach a mug or pitcher to a person give the handle; and when you take hold of bread, biscuit, pies, etc. to cut or break, take hold of that part which you intend to eat yourself, and cut it square & equal — then you will not leave the print of your fingers for others to eat. . . .

12th If you are obliged to sneeze or cough, don't bespatter the victuals, make use of your handkerchief.

13th Clean your knife on your bread before you cut butter, & after cutting butter before you put it into apple sauce, etc. but never clean it on the edge of the platter etc.

14th Scratching the head, picking the nose or ears, belching, snifing the nose, drinking with the mouth full of victuals, or picking the teeth, are accounted ill manners at a table & must be left off.

15th And lastly, when you drink, never extend your under lip so far down that one would think the cup was agoing to be swallowed whole. Always wipe your mouth before & after you drink your bear (beer) or water at the table.

Note — Children under the age of 12 or 14 years must have their pie cut for them & laid by their dishes — Also, when they have bread & butter, suitable pieces must be properly spread & laid by their dishes. . . .

After the evening chores were done, at seven-thirty in summer and eight o'clock in winter, all repaired to their apartments for half an hour, known as "retiring-time," when, on the evenings devoted to family worship, the Shakers disposed themselves in ranks, sitting erect with hands folded "to labor for a true sense of their privilege in the Zion of God." If perchance one should drowse, it was the order to rise and bow four times, or shake, and then resume one's seat. At the end of the period, announced by the ringing of a small bell, brethren and sisters formed separate columns in the corridors, marched two abreast to the meeting-room, and, after bowing as they entered, formed ranks for worship.

Assemblies varied with the time and place. In the early years of the order, and often during revivals, "labouring" meetings were held nightly, and sometimes during the day. As the society expanded, however, evenings not devoted to union meetings or the regular religious service were given over to the practice of songs and exercises. Thus, at New Lebanon in the 'seventies, singing meetings were held on Tuesday and Friday, union meetings on Sunday and Wednesday, and "labouring" meetings on Thursday and Saturday. On Mondays, during this more liberal period, there was a general assembly in the dining hall, where the elder read letters from other communities, selections from the news of the week, or some appropriate book. At the conclusion of such gatherings, to which strangers were admitted on occasion, the family retired quietly to rest. The occupants of each room, after kneeling again in silent prayer, went to bed at a uniform hour — nine o'clock in winter and ten in summer.

Anyone watching such temperate people in the intervals between work and worship would have been impressed, above all else, by the tranquillity of their movements and behavior, as though the daily round was itself a service. No sign of tension or aggressiveness was apparent; speech was subdued; doors were opened and closed with care; all "walked softly." The dwelling, whose orderly, neatly furnished rooms were seldom occupied during the day, was also, in a true sense, a sanctuary. Many a visitor, like Hester Pool, was sensitive to that "indescribable air of purity" which pervaded everything, feeling with her "that this purity is a portion of the mental and moral as well as the physical atmosphere of the Shakerian home." Though all comings and goings followed the pattern of plainness, in the simplicity of domestic life there was an element of freedom, grace, and the contentment, or perhaps resignation, of those who had made peace with themselves and with the world.

The Children's Order was also carefully regulated. Boys and girls lived apart from each other and the rest of the family under "caretakers" responsible to the elders or eldresses. In the indenture agreements the trustees bound the society to provide them with "comfortable food and clothing," the common branches of learning, and training in such manual occupation or branch of business as shall be found best adapted to the "minor's genius and capacity." In return, the parent or guardian relinquished all rights over the child's upbringing. At maturity the youth was free to leave or remain.

In education emphasis was placed on character building and the useful arts. Though the early Believers, "being chiefly of the laboring classes and generally in low circumstances of life," were not in a condition to pay much attention to letter learning, Mother Ann strongly recommended religious and "literary" studies. Meacham advocated the kind of learning that would lead to order, union, peace, and good work — "works that are truly virtuous and useful to man, in this life." The idea that instruction should concentrate on developing good habits and useful talents was subsequently expanded by Seth Wells, the superintendent of the Shaker schools. Self-government, Wells believed, was the prerequisite of both moral and literary education. "When a man is able to govern himself, and subdue his evil propensities . . . he is then in a fair way to be benefitted by moral and religious instructions. . . ."

Nor was innocent recreation considered superfluous. The girls at Canterbury had gymnastic exercises and a flower garden; the boys played ball and marbles, went fishing, and had a small farm of their own. Picnics, sleigh rides, and nutting and berrying parties lent diversion to the ordinary routine. Elkins' frank account of his boyhood at Enfield is the record of a not uncolorful life, with interesting companions, mild paternal control, and normal healthful experiences in a beautiful countryside. Elder Briggs recalls that wood-chopping and maple-sugaring were gala times, like picnics, and mentions the diversions of fishing, swimming, and playing ball, the half-holidays once a week during warm weather, the refreshments during haying, which consisted of sweet buttermilk; lemon, peppermint, checkerberry, raspberry, and currant shrub; cake, cheese, and smoked herring. One who had been a young Shakeress at Niskeyuna remembers many happy days in the Children's Order there:

> Hiding beneath an arcade of the bridge which spanned the dear old creek, we would pull off shoes and stockings, and wade knee-deep in the cool, bright water. Then, loading our long palm-leaf Shaker bonnets with dandelions, which, grown to seed, looked like little white-capped Shakeresses, we would float them down the stream in a race, the boat which won being

decorated with buttercups and violets. What mud-pies we made and baked in the sun! What fun we had secreting golden kernels of corn in clam-shells, and peeping from our hiding-place to see the chickens find them and peck them up, firmly believing that they "gave thanks" when they turned their bills up to heaven after sipping water. . . . We had no world's toys, but were just as contented with our corn-cob dolls, clam-shell plates, acorn-top cups, and chicken-coops for baby houses.

From sources such as the above we suspect that Shaker life was not always as austere as its principles would have had it be; that the Believers, in their effort to extinguish natural affections, tried to do the impossible — particularly where children were concerned. We read of candy-making parties, culinary favors tendered by the "kitchen-sisters," humorous tolerance when children behaved "contrary to order," the attachments for favorite children, close friendships within the Children's Order. Human nature was constantly breaking up the artificial restrictions designed to subdue "carnal desire." It seems that the lot of Shaker youth compared favorably with that of the sons and daughters of farmers in the rural America of the period. . . .

The belief in progress, or "travel," found expression in the field of medicine as in education. Ann Lee's bias against physicians was shared by Joseph Meacham, who assured a doubter that "they that have my spirit have no occasion to go to world's doctors." In the early years Shakers were healed by faith or the laying on of hands. The "gift" against professionals was still held in 1813, when Mother Lucy's attitude to that effect was recorded; but Father Job Bishop, speaking "beautifully" on the same subject, qualified his stand by asserting that a surgeon might be called "in case of a broken bone or any very bad wound." About this time greater reliance was placed on regimen and simple medicines, with resort to shocking, bleeding, sweating, poulticing, and blistering. With the development of the herb industry in the 1820s, the Thomsonian medical practice, which relied on steam baths and herbal remedies and required little academic knowledge, came into increasing favor. Another step was taken in 1840, when messages prohibiting the use of strong drink, swine's flesh, and tobacco ushered in a reform which was more than temporary. In mid-century, largely through the influence of Elder Frederick Evans of New Lebanon, Grahamism and vegetarianism won converts in certain families. Proper diet, supplemented by the water treatment, simple massage, and hot herbal drinks in case of sickness, was the prevalent prescription late in the century. Faith in the "healing gift," however, persisted all this time, with many a cure allegedly effected by spirit touch and mental control.

As interpreted by Elder Evans, the science of health had a theological basis. To provide better food, clothing, and housing, a better distribution of heat, improved lighting, ventilation, and sanitation was the proper field of science. In the "new earth" the human body should be "the central object of influence and attraction," whose "salvation" was no less important than the "health" of the soul. Evans suggested eight main principles of dietetics:

1. Supply the family with at least one kind of course grain flour. Avoid cathartics.
2. Have the "sickly and weakly" cease using animal food, especially fats.
3. Keep the skin clean by regular bathing, with the water at such a temperature as to cause a warm, glowing reaction.
4. Keep room at a temperature not exceeding 60°.
5. Clothing — "regulated on the same principles as water and fire" — should be light, "a little less than you could possibly bear." The young should dispense with underclothes. "Sleep under as little clothing as possible."
6. Breathe pure air. Every room of the home should be of equal temperature. Ventilation of bedrooms important.
7. Thorough ventilation of beds and bedding.
8. "Be comfortable in mind and body."

While these views were the opinion of one person, a natural reformer, they were not unrepresentative of Shaker practice. The vent pipes over the lamps, the slots placed between the two sashes of every window, and the holes in the baseboards in the halls and under the radiators in the gathering rooms were additional evidences of a concern for fresh air. Baths, sinks, and water closets were well ventilated. Pure spring water was ingeniously piped for refrigeration. Temperate outdoor labor, regular hours, wholesome food, good clothing, comfort of mind, and the utmost cleanliness everywhere combined to promote the health of all. On the latter characteristic in particular, often contrasting favorably with conditions elsewhere, strangers were wont to remark from the earliest times. "Great importance is attached to cleanliness," *Blackwood's* correspondent reported in 1823; "this luxury they appear to enjoy in a truly enviable degree." "Visit them upon any day in the week," the historian of the town of Shirley wrote, "at any hour of the day, and when they are engaged in almost any employment, and you will scarcely ever find them in dirty dishabille. The shirts and pants and frocks of the men are rarely soiled, and the plain linen caps and kerchiefs of the women never." "Everything is . . . kept so delicately clean," remarked an English visitor in 1884, "that an air of refinement, not to say luxury, seems to pervade [the] bedchambers, in spite of their absolute simplicity."

Testimonies on the health of the Shakers are nevertheless conflicting. . . . With allowances made for prejudice, it is a matter of wonder, from the phrases used about the sisters, whether they were in health or out. They were called "a wretched-looking lot of creatures" (Fountain); "their pale faces . . . and flabby condition indicated . . . a low state of health" (George Combe); "the females and sedentary people . . . were occasionally indisposed" (*Blackwood's* correspondent); "the females . . . look remarkably pale and sallow" (Silliman); the woman were "pallid, thin and withered" (Martineau); the sisters, with few exceptions, were "old, wizened, ascetic — perfect specimens of old maids" (Colonel A. M. Maxwell). The difference in the physical appearance of males and females was due, according to one mid-century author, to the "unaspiring, earthly" quality of the former, and the effect on such natures of a comfortable life, outdoor work, plenty of food, and an absence of anxieties. "The Shaker woman, by contrast, has a more melancholy lot. Love — 'the first necessity of woman's nature' — is dwarfed, in her case, to most unnatural ugliness. She must renounce the natural affections." On the other hand, Finch was struck with "the cheerfulness and contented looks" of the people in all the communities; Dixon remarked on "the rosy flesh" of the people of New Lebanon — "a tint but rarely seen in the United States"; and the usually reliable Nordhoff spoke of the "fresh fine complexion [which] most of the Shaker men and women have — particularly the latter."

If the Shaker way of life was detrimental in any way to physical well-being, certainly life was not shortened. The longevity of members of the sect has often been reported. In 1875 Nordhoff, making the first fact-finding tour of the communities, was impressed by the low rate of mortality: at Harvard, where the average age at death for a number of years was 60 to 68; at Union Village, where a large proportion of the members were over 70, and many over 90; at North Union, where many were past 80; at Pleasant Hill, where a considerable number lived past 90; and at Enfield (N.H.), Watervliet (N.Y.), and South Union, where the brethren and sisters often lived well over 75 years. . . .

When death occurred, complete simplicity marked the funeral. The coffin was pine, plainly lined, unpainted and unadorned. In the mind of the Believer, the life of the spirit was so real that death was but a way-mark in "travel," and the "trappings of grief" superfluous. Following the Quaker custom, the Shakers, led by the elders and eldresses of the family, devoted the main part of the service to personal tributes and memories. Songs were sung, and during one period of Shaker history, messages from the spirit were communicated by the instruments. The procession to the grave was not unlike the heavenly march of worship. Throughout the ritual the tone was one of reverence, strength, and inspiration.

Since followers of Mother Ann did not believe in physical resurrection, they thought of the living soul and not of the dead body. "He is not here," they testified at the burial service. Appropriate, therefore, were the simple slabs of stone, all alike and engraved only with initials, age, and date, which marked the resting place. Many advocated that even these be replaced by a mound of earth, or perhaps a shrub or tree, not as a memorial but rather as a contribution to earth's fertility and beauty.

Comparison of the living conditions of the early Shaker colonists with those prevailing a century or so later furnishes an index to the temporal progress of the society. In 1780 its possessions were limited to a few unpromising acres, a single cabin, the slim resources of John Hocknell. Eight years later the Believers at Niskeyuna were still poor. Money was scarce, and the community was not allowed to run into debt. According to the account of Jonathan Clark of Hancock:

> Our principle food was rice and milk, sometimes we went to the river to procure fish. . . . We had little, and sometimes no bread, butter or cheese, but upon this simple fare, we all subsisted during the Spring and Summer. . . . All our work was very laborious, and at the end, we looked more like skeletons, than working men. . . . Our breakfast consisted of a small bowl of porridge. Supper the same. Dinner, a small bit of cake about 2½ inches square which Aaron Wood cut up, and gave to us. One day Joseph Preston and another brother went to the River to catch Herring; and Joseph stated that he was so hungry, that he ate two *raw*, as soon as they came out of the water. . . . We had but little house room, and of course were obliged to lie upon the floor. . . . Fifteen of us lay upon the floor in one room; some had one blanket to cover them, while others had none. . . .

The "manner of dress and building" was in the same inferior state. "Those who first believed, in America," Youngs wrote, "adopted such dress as seemed the most suitable, of the common plain forms that prevailed among people at the time they lived in England"; and the form, fashion, and quality of garments were "extremely various." In form and manner of construction, buildings also were of poor quality and ill-adapted to the purpose for which they were needed.

In all departments, however, the Shakers, by the will to make everything uniform with the best, steadily raised their standard of living. During the nineteenth century the preparation of wholesome food was considered more and more important, and as a result the Shakers achieved a considerable reputation for their recipes and public meals. As for clothing, painstaking care came to be paid to the needs of age groups and occasions, to uniformity of color and material, to the marking and laundering of garments. Buildings, too, were constantly improved and their numbers increased to meet the expanding needs of the colony. In New Lebanon, for instance, from the few small farmhouses which the Shakers took over in the 1780s, the community grew until it had 125 buildings in 1839, and property, including 2,292 acres of land, valued at $68,225. Within the same period the original colony at Watervliet had grown to a community of over 2,500 acres, valued, with buildings, at $46,900. When Nordhoff made his survey in 1875, the home farms of the eighteen societies, taken by themselves, amounted to nearly 50,000 acres, to which figure must be added extensive outside holdings in mills, wood lots, and "outfarms" — one in Kentucky, owned by the Watervliet (N.Y.) society, as large as 30,000 acres — which were often operated by tenants.

Following the eight immigrants from England some seventeen thousand persons, at one time or another, were gathered into the society. To the Shakers this was a "great harvest" — the "blessed binders" had followed closely on the reapers, "severing all the worthless cockle till the work was done complete."

STUDY GUIDE

1. Explain the techniques the Shakers used in order to maintain celibacy. What explanation can you give for the skepticism about celibacy and the rumors of sexual excesses that often develop in the outside world with respect to convents, monasteries, and other celibate communities?

2. Describe the "order of the day" in a Shaker community and the religious life of the Shakers. Aside from separation of the sexes and the religious doctrines, what values and attitudes do you see among the Shakers that were not substantially different from those of many other farm folks in the period?

3. Though some might consider the Shaker life as barren and harsh, Andrews suggests that most of the Shakers felt a sense of freedom, contentment, and peace. What evidence is there in the selection that Shakers really felt this way, and how can one explain such a disciplined, plain, celibate life bringing happiness? What parallels are there between the Shaker philosophy and other experiments in alternative lifestyles that you know of (such as Henry Thoreau's experiment at Walden Pond)?

4. In terms of permanence and long-range influence upon American society, none of the other communitarian groups were any more successful than were the Shakers. What forces in American life and in the development of the American nation made it unlikely that these small-group experiments could successfully serve as a pattern for all of American society?

5. What do you see as the explanation for the development of so many communal groups in our own time? What evidence is there that such groups continue to have — on a reduced scale — the same problems that exist in the larger society?

BIBLIOGRAPHY

The historical literature on the Shakers and on other communitarian groups that flourished in the pre–Civil War years is both ample and interesting. A number of volumes can serve to introduce you to the entire range of communitarianism. You might begin with Arthur Bestor, Jr.'s prize-winning work, *Backwoods Utopias: The Sectarian and the Owenite Phases of Communitarian Socialism in America: 1663–1829* (1950), or with the same author's essay on "Patent-Office Models of the Good Society: Some Relationships Between Social Reform and Westward Expansion," *American Historical Review*, Vol. LVIII (1953), pp. 505–526. Additional surveys of the topic will be found in the following: Alice Felt Tyler, *Freedom's Ferment: Phases of American Social History to 1860* (1944), a description of almost all of the reform movements, communitarian and otherwise, of the period; Charles Nordhoff's older but still valuable volume, *The Communistic Societies of the United States* (1875; reprinted 1960); Mark Holloway, *Heavens on Earth: Utopian Communities in America, 1680–1880* (1951); and Everett Webber, *Escape to Utopia: The Communal Movement in America* (1959). More specific in focus is the volume from which the preceding selection was taken, Edward D. Andrews, *The People Called Shakers: A Search for the Perfect Society* (1953). Andrews also wrote volumes on Shaker furniture and on their music and dance. Other works on the Shakers have been written by Marguerite Melcher, Francis D. Nichol, and Clara E. Sears. In 1981 two books were published on the sexual practices — celibacy, polygamy, and complex marriage — of the Shakers, Mormons, and Oneidans: Lawrence Foster, *Religion and Sexuality: Three American Communal Experiments*, and Louis J. Kern, *An Ordered Love: Sex Roles and Sexuality in Victorian Utopias*.

There are biographies of Owen, Fourier, and many other communitarian leaders, and studies of most of the communities of the pre–Civil War period. Jane and William Pease describe communities founded to aid recently freed Negroes in their book *Black Utopia: Negro Communal Experiments in America* (1963). Other works of merit include Herbert W. Schneider and George Lawton, *A Prophet and a Pilgrim* (1942); Maren L. Carden, *Oneida: Utopian Community to Modern Corporation* (1969); and Lindsay Swift, *Brook Farm: Its Members, Scholars, and Visitors* (1961). It is not possible here to list the many works dealing with the post–Civil War period of utopianism or the broader aspects of utopian thought in American life. Three works that are essential in understanding these subjects are Donald Egbert and Stow Persons, eds., *Socialism and American Life*, 2 vols. (1952); H. Richard Niebuhr, *The Kingdom of God in America* (1937); and Robert S. Fogarty, *American Utopianism* (1972). The last of these is a collection of source material on utopian communities.

IV INDUSTRIAL NORTH AND PLANTER SOUTH

In our time, more than in any earlier period, the American people are a single people. They drive the same cars, use the same products, eat much the same food, and dress alike — whether they live in California or New England. With slight differences, their values and their popular culture — on the screen, on the airwaves, and in national magazines — are identical in Atlanta, Georgia, and Minneapolis, Minnesota. The homogeneity of modern American society tends to obscure the fact that differences among classes, nationalities, and sections played a prominent role in earlier American history. The strong nationalistic sentiments of the first three decades of the nineteenth century faded rapidly after 1830. Always somewhat distinct in language, politics, and social life, North and South saw their respective economic interests as being in conflict. Both hoped for the support of what was rapidly emerging as a third distinct section, the trans-Appalachian West. Industrialization and urbanization were making the Northeast a region of constant change. In mining fields and factory towns, on canal and railroad projects, the strange tongues of several European nationalities could be heard. In contrast, the South was largely untouched by industrialism and the urban growth that would eventually characterize the entire country. Few immigrants went South, and slavery, with all its social as well as economic implications, swept westward from the South Atlantic states into Mississippi, Alabama, and other newly opened cotton lands.

The West was less clearly defined than the North or South; indeed, what was West was ever-changing as the line of settlement passed from western New York to Ohio, Iowa, and beyond. What we now call the Midwest was a region of non-slave-holding farmers, many of them Scandinavians and Germans who had come directly west from the port of entry; others had moved west from the old northeastern states. Though the family farm was the ideal, midwestern agriculture was increasingly being drawn into the country's commercial and industrial growth.

The first reading in this section describes midwestern agriculture, with special attention to the lives of farm women whose contributions were essential to family survival. The second selection provides a graphic picture of slavery, the institution that was more important than any other in setting the South apart. Though the vast majority of Americans lived in rural areas, many of the immigrants settled in eastern cities such as New York, whose population numbered 813,000 by 1860. The third reading describes the conditions at home that led so many emigrants to leave Europe and the conditions they encountered here. The rapid urban growth and dislocation of so many people led to social conflict. The last reading describes the repeated riots and violence that occurred as different ethnic, religious, and racial groups confronted each other.

While middle-class urban women were idealized and placed on a pedestal by the "cult of domesticity," farm women worked as hard and unceasingly as men to ensure the survival of rural families.

14

JOHN M. FARAGHER

Farm Women

In 1790, shortly after Washington assumed the presidency, the United States census recorded a national population of 3,929,214, of whom only 51,000 people lived in the North Central part of the country. By 1820, the country's population had nearly tripled to 9,638,453, but the North Central region had grown even more dramatically to 859,000 persons. Thirty years later, the respective figures were 23,191,876 for the country as a whole and 5,404,000 in the North Central states. By 1850, the United States was becoming a major manufacturing and commercial center with a growing urban population that had to be fed. The internal migration of people that had been a trickle at the end of the Revolutionary War assumed the dimensions of a flood tide between 1820 and 1860. The New South supplied cotton, sugar, and cattle, while the Midwest became the nation's wheat and corn belt.

In the eighteenth century, the small, self-sufficient farm of 40 to 200 acres had been typical of northern agriculture. Worked entirely by family labor, there was a limit to the number of acres that could be cultivated because of the primitive farming methods of the time. In the nineteenth century, farm families were drawn increasingly into commercial agriculture. A reliable market for basic crops could be found in the East, and new transportation developments and the invention of threshers and other machines enabled midwestern farmers to meet the demand of the growing population.

Successful farming depended upon the contributions of men, women, and children. The following essay by John M. Faragher indicates how varied and crucial the work was of farm women. In towns and cities, the lives of men and women were played out in separate spheres. Men spent much of their time outside of the home, in offices and factories, to provide family needs. A "cult of domesticity" suggested that women's proper place was in the home, providing a civilized refuge for men and rearing children. Increasingly, women became consumers, patronizing the glowing department store palaces, rather than producers who grew the family's food, made its candles, and wove its clothing. Farm women could not afford the luxury of such leisure. Faragher provides a view of the isolation and work of men and women on midwestern farms and an understanding of how family farms were changed by America's commercial and industrial growth.

Farming in the antebellum Midwest was part of a way of life that stretched back through the centuries, a way of life on the verge of a fundamental reordering. Families were at the center of this rural political economy; working lives were regulated principally through families. Work was organized by a domestic division of labor, roles and routines were set by family patterns, production decisions determined by a calculus of family needs. This traditional way of life was very different from our own, and we would do well to base our understanding of men and women emigrants on a detailed look at their lives on the farm. . . .

. . . As the eastern seaboard became more a part of the Atlantic market, a new regional division of labor occurred, and commercial centers provided lucrative markets for farm products. Seventeenth-century opinion had stressed and valued self-sufficient farming and the closed circle of family labor. Farmers clung to these old attitudes tenaciously, but commercial values stressing economic rationality in market terms were more salient under the changed circumstances. Farming moved increasingly toward commercialization and specialization to meet the market demands of nascent urban communities. The view of farming as a business rather than a way of life was ascendant, if not dominant, in the Northeast by the first years of the nineteenth century.

Those who emigrated to the geographic and social periphery of the nation, on the other hand, met a different set of conditions. The move itself usually required some years of rather primitive living, but even after the early hunting-farming stage of pioneering had passed, the dominant fact of life in the Midwest was the isolation of farmers from the commerce of the East. Full entry of midwestern agriculture into the growing urban-industrial economy required effective transportation links with urban

From John M. Faragher, *Women and Men on the Overland Trail.* Copyright © 1979 by Yale University. Reprinted by permission of Yale University Press.

markets. The absence of transportation and market demands, R. Carlyle Buley notes in his seminal history of the early Midwest, "contributed to the practice of a self-sufficient domestic economy which in many regions by 1840 reached a high degree of development. . . ."

During the second quarter of the century the hopes and expectations of midwestern farmers paved the way for the changes introduced by the railroads; these finally solved the transportation problem and brought the Midwest fully into the market. The decisive moment of change came in the mid-1850s. As far as future developments were concerned, the nascent commercial trends and structures were unquestionably the most important aspects of the years before 1850, and historians emphasize them most. But we are concerned here with the actual way of life of the majority of farm families in the Midwest. Until the Civil War (and the period of overland emigration to the Pacific Coast was mostly antebellum), most midwesterners lived by the traditional means of family self-sufficiency, whatever their aspirations. Before the Civil War, as Paul Gates observes, most midwestern farmers were isolated from commercial opportunities and practiced diversified, home-consumption farming. With some exceptions the overland emigrants were coming from an essentially self-sufficient agricultural system.

The general shift to commercialism that began in the Midwest during the 1850s was accompanied by a revolution in farm technology. The steel plow, drill, reaper, mower, and thresher, although inventions of the 1830s, became commonly available during the fifties and were only fully utilized in response to the huge market demands, labor shortages, and high prices of the Civil War. This technology facilitated commercial production by cutting labor costs and shifting farming to a capital-intensive basis, allowing for specialization in highly marketable grain crops, and incidentally facilitating agriculture's entry into the credit market, since most farmers were forced to borrow heavily to finance their investments in machinery. The interdependence of commercial production and improved technology reminds us that until the Civil War the self-sufficiency of midwestern farmers was in large measure a feature of the means of production: hand power did not provide the average midwestern farm family with enough productivity to turn to strict commercialism.

The technology of most midwestern farms, then, was a traditional force, tying men and women to the hand-power heritage. The essential tools of the farm — the ones the overland emigrants carried in their wagons — were the chopping ax, broadax, frow, auger, and plane. Farmers used these tools to manufacture their own farm implements — hoes, rakes, sickles, scythes, cradles, flails, and plows — resorting to the blacksmith for ironwork. Except for the cradle, which came into wise use west of the

Alleghenies during the mid-1830s, the home production of these same hand implements had been a constant of farm life for centuries.

Hand technology set upper limits on the number of acres that a family could cultivate in a season; the only way productivity could be increased beyond that limit was by adding field hands. Working at maximum output, a farm family with two economically active males could utilize perhaps fifty acres of growing land with the traditional technology. Of these, perhaps one acre was devoted to the home garden, a score to small grain crops, the remainder to corn. In order simply to survive, a family required at least half an acre for the garden, the same for grain, and some ten acres in corn. Corn was the most essential; according to one observer, "it affords the means of subsistence to every living thing about his place." Before the 1850s the majority of midwestern families fell between these limits: most families lived on farms with forty to fifty improved acres.

As to livestock, an ox, or preferably a yoke of oxen, was essential, although when first starting out some families made do working a cow. Cows were necessary for milk and its products, however, and working them as draught animals negatively affected dairy production. A few sheep of mongrel breeds were necessary for wool, but mutton was almost never eaten. Geese and ducks were sometimes butchered, but they were valued most for their down. A family's meat supply was provided by the ever-present brood of chickens and the herd of swine, a dozen or more being necessary for a medium-sized family. These animals were frequently unsheltered, although on the better farms cattle might have a lean-to shelter for winter. As late as 1850 farmers throughout the Midwest were reportedly in the habit of letting cattle and hogs forage on available grass and mast. When butchering time came hogs were rounded up for the kill.

A farm family could gradually increase its level of consumption by clearing, draining, and preparing more land, and by increasing the size and improving the breed of its livestock. Then there came a limit, when the level of technology was a fetter on further expansion without resort to hired labor. The limit came, however, after the level of consumption had been raised to the level of contemporary comfort. "A backwoods farm," wrote an English observer, "produces everything wanted for the table, except coffee and rice and salt and spices." To the list of supplementals could be added occasional dry goods, shoes, and metal for farm implements. A self-sufficient family could produce enough for its annual table, along with a small trading surplus, but the task required the close attention of men and women to the needs of the land and the demands of the seasons.

The dominant paradigm of farm life was the cycle: the recurrence of the days and seasons, the process of growth and reproduction. Hand-power technology did not deceive men into thinking they could overcome nature; their goal was to harmonize man's needs with natural forces as best they could. The length of the working day, for example, was largely determined by the hours of sunlight. Candles and grease lamps were common but expensive, and the hearth's flickering light was too dim for more than a little work after dark. So most work was largely confined to daylight: up and at work by dawn, nights for sleeping. And in keeping with this daily round, midwesterners told time by the movements of the sun, not the clock. There was a variety of time phrases so rich they nearly matched the clock in refinement; the hours before sunrise, for example, were distinguished thus: long before day, just before day, just comin' day, just about daylight, good light, before sunup, about sunup, and, finally, sunup. Each period of the day was similarly divided. . . .

The cycle of the seasons encouraged a traditional view of work as well. Work was the expenditure of human energy to meet given tasks. When wheat was ready for harvesting, for example, men would readily work fifteen-hour days to bring it in before the precious grain was shed on the ground. On the other hand, when seasonal demands slackened, as in winter, a man might quit early without qualms, and few worried when a winter storm closed in the family for a few days. The persistent pace of modern labor, measured not by natural cycles but by the clock, was almost unknown to midwesterners. By the same token, work was understood not as the opposite of leisure but as life's requirement for all creatures, regardless of sex or age. Men, women, and children would share life's burdens. "The rule was," William Howells remembered of his farm life, "that whoever had the strength to work, took hold and helped."

The common work of the farm was, then, divided among family members, but the principal division of work was by sex. Men and women worked in different areas, skilled at different tasks, prepared and trained for their work in different ways. In an economy based on the family unit, women and men in midwestern society achieved common goals by doing different jobs. . . .

The functional principles of the general divisions of work by sex on the midwestern farm were quite clear and quite strict in application. In only a few areas did the work of men and women overlap. Most clearly, men were occupied with the heaviest work. First, they had responsibility for work with the broadax. If the family was taking up new wooded ground — as many Oregon emigrants would be doing, for example — the land had to be cleared. Frequently a farmer would gird the trees with his ax the first season to kill foliage, felling trees and removing stumps in the following winters. Logrolling, when the men of the neighborhood joined together to clear a field belonging to one of them, was a common late-winter social event for men. Construction, including making fences, was also a male job, as was the ongoing work in the family woodlot. Wood was chopped, hauled and stacked, or dumped near the house.

Men also controlled work with the plow. For new land a breaking plow, drawn by several yoke of oxen, was often needed, especially in prairie sod. Working improved acres was easier, but still hard, heavy work. And within the limitations of available labor and marketability, men were usually itching to put new land to the plow, so the plow was associated with work of the heaviest sort and understood to be male. Work in the cleared and plowed fields, where grain or corn grew, also fell to male control and supervision. Men plowed in spring or winter, sowed their wheat broadcast (until the 1850s), and planted their corn in hills. Men and boys harrowed and weeded until harvest, when they picked the corn together and cooperated in bringing in the wheat, men cradling and boys binding. Fieldwork kept men extremely busy. Two mature men on fifty acres of corn and wheat land spent three-quarters of the whole growing season plowing, planting, and harvesting, exclusive of any other work.

There was plenty of other work to do. Men were responsible for upkeep and repair of tools, implements, and wagons and care of the draft animals, the oxen, mules, or horses. Hogs and sheep, both pretty much allowed to roam, were herded, fed, and tended by men and boys. Finally, men were responsible for cleanup and maintenance of the barn, barnyard, fields, and woodlot. This meant ditching and trenching, innumerable repairs on all the things that could — and did — break, laying down straw and hay, and hauling manure.

Less important in fact, but work which nonetheless played an important role in male thinking, was hunting. For the early pioneers game provided most of the protein in the family diet. By mid-century those pioneer days had passed in the Midwest. But the rifle remained in its central place over the door or mantle long after the emergencies that might call it out had gone the way of the forests. Hunting remained, if only as an autumn sport or shooting match, a central aspect of male identity. "Even farmers," says Buley, "at certain seasons felt a peculiar restlessness." The hunting legacy had one practical consequence for male work loads: men had primary responsibility for slaughtering and butchering large farm animals. Indeed, when hogs ran wild, they were sometimes picked off by rifle shot. Hunting was the male activity that most embodied men's self-conceived role — keystone of the hearth, defender of the household, and main provider.

In fact, women were more centrally involved in providing subsistence for the farm family than men. Nearly all the kinds of food consumed by farm families were direct products of women's work in growing, collecting, and butchering. An acre or so of improved land near the house was set aside for the domestic garden. After husbands had plowed the plot, farm women planted their gardens. Housewives began by setting out onions and potatoes in early April, following up later that month by planting lettuce, beets, parsnips, turnips, and carrots in the garden, tomatoes and cabbages in window boxes indoors. When danger of late frosts had passed, the seedlings were moved outside and set out along with May plantings of cucumbers, melons, pumpkins, and beans. Women also frequently laid down a patch of buckwheat and a garden of kitchen and medicinal herbs — sage, peppers, thyme, mint, mustard, horseradish, tansy, and others.

The garden required daily attention. At first the seedlings needed hand watering. Then crops required cultivation, and the everlasting battle against weeds began. Garden harvesting could commence in late April and was a daily chore throughout the summer, supplying fresh vegetables for the family table.

Wives and daughters were also traditionally responsible for the care of henhouse and dairy. After a dormant winter poultry came alive in the spring. The farm-wise woman carefully kept enough chickens to produce both eggs for the kitchen and to set hens for a new flock of spring roasters. From late spring to late fall the family feasted regularly on fresh-killed rooster, selected and usually butchered by the housewife. Daughters and young boys gathered the eggs that were another mainstay of the summer diet. Women's responsibility for the henhouse extended even to cleaning out the manure by the bucket load.

Cows were sheltered in whatever served as a barn, and men's general supervision there relieved women of having to shovel the stalls. But women milked, tended, and fed the animals. The milking and the manufacture of butter and cheese was one of their central tasks. Cows were milked first thing in the morning and the last thing at night; housewives supervised the milking but parceled the job out to children as soon as they were able. Boys, however, with their father's sanction would rebel from milking; "the western people of the early days entertained a supreme contempt for a man who attended to the milking." Making good butter was a matter of pride among farm women. The churn had to be operated with patience and persistence if the butter was to come.

> Come butter, come;
> Come butter, come;
> Little Johnny's at the gate,
> Waiting for his buttered cake.
> Come butter, come.

The meter marked the up and down of the churn. When it had come, the butter was packed into homemade, hand-decorated molds, and pounds of it consumed each week. Cheesemaking was less general; ripened cheeses were the product of a minority. Nearly all women, however, were trained in the manufacture of cottage cheese and farmer's cheese. Dairy production was especially important to the household and central to the definition of women's work. In 1839 a Springfield, Illinois, newspaper reprinted with horror a report that New England women were pressuring their husbands to take over the milking.

There were some areas of food production where women's and men's operations overlapped, but these were the exceptions. When hogs were butchered in fall, men from several farms might work together; it was mainly when it became necessary to supplement the meat supply that women helped men to slaughter and dress the animal. In any event, women were always a part of the butchering, there to chop the scraps and odd pieces into sausage, prepare the hams for curing, and cook the ribs immediately. At other social and almost ritual occasions of food preparation — making cider or apple butter, rendering maple sugar — men and women regularly worked side by side. All of the work of the orchard was often a joint project.

The sexes also sometimes combined their energies during planting. If not preoccupied with field planting, men might help to set out garden seed. More likely, however, field planting would fall behind the schedule set by zodiac or moon, and men called their womenfolk out to help. Women most often assisted in the cornfield. "Tarpley made a furrow with a single-shovel plow drawn by one horse," Iowa farm woman Elmira Taylor remembered of the 1860s. "I followed with a bag of seed corn and dropped two grains of seed each step forward." A farmer with no sons worked his daughters in the fields at planting time without a second thought.

Food preparation was, of course, women's work, and by all reports midwestern men kept women busy by consuming great quantities at mealtime. Wives were responsible for preparing three heavy meals a day; most farm wives spent their entire mornings cooking and tried to save afternoons for other work. Included in the daily midwestern diet were two kinds of meat, eggs, cheese, butter, cream (especially in gravies), corn in one or more forms, two kinds of bread, three or four different vegetables from the garden or from storage, several kinds of jellies, preserves, and relishes, cake or pie, and milk, coffee, and tea. Making butter and cheese were only two of the innumerable feminine skills needed to set the farm table. . . .

Women cooked on the open hearth, directly over the coals; it was low, back-breaking work that went on forever; a pot of corn mush took from two to six hours with nearly constant stirring. Cast-iron, wood-burning cook stoves were available in Illinois in the mid-1840s, and by 1860 most midwestern women had been given the opportunity to stand and cook. The next great improvement in domestic technology was the general introduction of running water in close proximity to the kitchen. But throughout the antebellum Midwest, water had to be carried to the house, sometimes from quite a distance, and that invariably was women's work. Domestic work — housecleaning, care of the bedding, all the kitchen work, in addition to responsibility for decorating and adding a "woman's touch" — was a demanding task under the best of circumstances, and farms offered far from the best. The yard between the kitchen and barn was always covered with enough dung to attract hordes of summer houseflies. In those days before screen doors kitchens were infested; men and women alike ignored the pests. In wet months the yard was a mess of mud, dung, and cast-off water, constantly tracked into the house. A cleanly wife had to be a constant worker.

A farmer was said to be a jack-of-all-trades. But women's work outdistanced men's in the sheer variety of tasks performed. In addition to their production of food, women had complete responsibility for all manufacture, care, and repair of family clothing. During the first half of the nineteenth century, domestic manufacture gave way to industrial production of thread and cloth, but in the Midwest, from 1840 to 1860, while home manufactures declined, they remained an important activity for women. On the Taylor homestead in southeastern Iowa, for example, the assessed valuation of household manufactures declined from $73 in 1850 to $50 in 1860, but this marked a decline, not an end to the use of the wheel and loom: in 1861 Elmira Taylor spun her own wool, took it to a mill to be carded, and wove it into cloth throughout the winter on her mother-in-law's loom.

. . . Wool had first to be carded into lean bunches, then spun on the great wheel; the spinner paced back and forth, whirling the wheel with her right hand, manipulating the wool and guiding the yarn on the spindle with her left. Two miles of yarn, enough for two to four yards of woven wool, required pacing over four miles, a full day's work. An excellent spinner, sitting at the smaller flax wheel, could spin a mile of linen thread in a day.

The yarn was woven into wool and linen cloth or more commonly combined into durable linsey-woolsey on homemade looms. If cotton was available it was woven with wool warp to make jean. The giant loom dominated cramped living quarters when in use; it was knocked down and put away when weaving was completed. The cloth still had to be shrunk and sized (fulled) — a job usually put out to the fulling mill if one were nearby — and dyed, sometimes from home dyes, but increasingly with commercial dyes bought at local stores. Nearly all farm clothing was cut from this cloth. Coarser tow cloth, made from the short-fiber, darker parts of the flax, was used for toweling, bandage, menstrual cloth, rags, or rough field clothing. Pillows and mattresses were made of tow and stuffed with the down women collected from the geese and ducks in their charge. The finest homespun, the pure linen bleached scores of times till it reached its characteristic color, was reserved for coverlets, tablecloths, appliqué, and stitchery. For their annual clothing a family of four would require a minimum of forty yards of cloth, or at least two full weeks at the wheel and loom for an experienced housewife. This work was, of course, spread throughout the available time, and one could expect to find women spinning or weaving at almost any time of the day, at every season of the year. . . .

Every wife was a tailor, fitting and cutting cloth for her own slip-on dresses and those of her daughter, her son's and husband's blouses and pantaloons, and the tow shirts of the younger ones. If there was "boughten" cloth available — cotton or woolen broadcloth, gingham or calico — it was used for dress-up clothing, home-tailored of course. Socks, mittens, and caps were knit for winter wear, but every adult went sockless and children barefoot in summer. Underclothes were not manufactured or worn, for they were considered an unnecessary extravagance. . . .

On a more mundane level, clothes had to be washed, and women made their own soap for both the clothes and the family who wore them. Women loaded hardwood ashes into the ash hopper, poured water over, and collected the lye in the trough below. They boiled kitchen fats and grease, added the lye, and if everything was going well the soap would "come" after long, hot hours of stirring. They poured the hot soap into molds or tubs and stored it. Soapmaking was a big, all-day job, done only two or three times a year. Monday, by all accounts, was the universal washday. Rainwater was used for washing, or alternately a little lye was added to soften well water. The water was heated in the washtub over hearth or stove, soap added, and clothes were pounded against a washboard, then rinsed, wrung out by hand, and hung. The lye, harsh soap, and hot water chapped and cracked the skin; women's hands would often break open and bleed into the tub. In the winter, the clothes were hung outside where sore, wet hands would freeze painfully, or inside, draped over chairs or lines, steaming up the windows and turning the whole place clammy. Ironing and mending were also allocated one day each week.

To women fell a final task. Women bore the children and nursed them for at least the first few months, and in this they worked completely alone. Even after weaning, farm women remained solely responsible for the supervision of young children; both boys and girls were under their mother's supervision until the boys were old enough to help with the fieldwork, at about ten years, at which time they came under their father's guidance. Girls, of course, remained apprenticed to the housewife's craft. Farm mothers put their charges to work "almost as soon as they could walk," and although they could not contribute materially until they were five or six, the correct work attitude had by then been instilled. There was plenty that children could do around the garden, dairy, and henhouse; they watered, fed the animals, collected eggs, milked, hauled water, weeded, and performed innumerable other chores that housewives could never have finished but for the work of their children. . . .

Let us translate abstract fertility into the real terms of farm women's lives: childbearing had to be a dominant fact. Over half the emigrant women gave birth to their first child within their first year of marriage, another quarter the second year, and fully 98 percent by the end of the third. Thereafter a mean of 29.0 months intervened between births throughout a woman's twenties and thirties. For their most vital years farm women lived under the dictatorial rule of yet another cycle, a two-and-a-half-year cycle of childbirth, of which nineteen or twenty months were spent in advanced pregnancy, infant care, and nursing. Until her late thirties, a woman could expect little respite from the physical and emotional wear and tear of nearly constant pregnancy or suckling.

Given the already burdensome tasks of women's work, the additional responsibilities of the children were next to intolerable. Women must have searched for some way of limiting the burden. It is possible that mothers introduced their babies to supplemental feeding quite early and encouraged children's independence in order to free themselves from the restrictions of nursing, which had to seriously limit their capacity to work. There is almost no mention of child-feeding practices in the literature, but there are some indirect indications that babies were soon consuming "bread, corn, biscuits and pot-likker" right along with their parents. On the other hand, there was a prevalent old wives' notion that prolonged nursing was a protection against conception. To achieve a twenty-nine-month cycle without practicing some form of self-conscious family limitation, women would have had to nurse for at least a year.

Short of family planning, there was no easy choice for women in the attempt to reduce the burden of child care. Other groups had practiced family limitation before this time, but the need for labor may have been a mitigating factor here. It comes as no surprise, then, that as soon as it was possible, children were pretty much allowed and encouraged to shift for themselves, to grow as they might, with relatively little parental or maternal involvement in the process. We will find children little mentioned in overland diaries and reminiscences.

By no means were men the "breadwinners" of this economy. Both women and men actively participated in the production of family subsistence. Indeed, women were engaged in from one-third to one-half of all the food production of the farm, the proportions varying with regional and individual differences. Of the farm staples — meat, milk, corn, pumpkins, beans, and potatoes — women produced the greater number as a product of their portion of the division of labor. Women were also likely to be found helping men with their portion at peak planting time. To this must be added the extremely important work of clothing manufacture, all the household work, and the care of the children. To be sure, men and women alike worked hard to make their farms produce. But one cannot avoid being struck by the enormousness of women's work load. . . .

. . . The true inequity in the division of labor was clearly expressed in the aphorism, "A man may work from sun to sun, but a woman's work is never done." The phrase has a hollow ring to us today, but it was no joke to farm women, who by all accounts worked two or three hours more each day than the men, often spinning, weaving, or knitting late into the dark evening hours.

There are some areas of women's participation in farm life that suggest a higher status. Cross-cultural studies indicate that the responsibility for exchanging goods and services with persons outside the family tends to confer family power and prestige. "The relative power of women is increased if women both contribute to subsistence *and also* have opportunities for extra domestic distribution and exchange of valued goods and services." In the Midwest, the products of dairy, henhouse, garden, and loom were often the only commodities successfully exchanged for other family necessities. Powder, glass, dyes, crockery, coffee, tea, store cloth, metal utensils, and sugar were bought on credit from the local merchant; butter, cheese, eggs, vegetables, homespun, and whiskey were the main items offered in trade to pay the tab.

However, while it was true that women traded, the proceeds were not credited to them individually, but to the family in general. Commodity exchange in corn and grain surpluses, on the other hand, was most frequently used for male economic pursuits: paying off the farm mortgage, speculating in new lands, and as innovations in technology became available, experimenting with new farm equipment. Men's product was for male use; women's product was for the family. It has been claimed that "there was no doubt of her equality in those days because she showed herself equally capable in all the tasks of their life together, and she was proud to know that this was true. Her position and dignity and age-old strength was that of the real help-mate in everything that touched the welfare of the family and the home." From a modern perspective equal work may seem a first step toward sexual equality, but the question of power is not only a question of what people do but also of the recognition they are granted for what they do and the authority that recognition confers. There is little evidence to suggest that men, for their part, gave women's work a second thought. That it was a woman's lot to work that hard was simply taken for granted. . . .

STUDY GUIDE

1. Explain how the Industrial Revolution and commercial growth affected midwestern farming.

2. In our time, distinctions have been softened between what is properly men's and women's work. What made such gender distinctions much more important in the nineteenth century, and what in our times have been the forces that have modified them? Are there gender differences between men and women, other than biological, that apply to all time periods or are most of them culturally induced?

3. Some writers have suggested that women should be paid a fair wage for housework and the other contributions described by Faragher. What arguments might be advanced for and against such a proposition?

4. How does the life and work of a woman today differ from that of the women described in the essay? In what ways are they similar?

BIBLIOGRAPHY

Very few historical fields have developed so rapidly and resulted in the publication of as fine a body of scholarship as has women's history in the last ten years. One of the early limitations of women's history was its extreme emphasis upon middle- and upper-class women. Faragher's book is one of many that deals with more average women. Other works dealing with the life of women moving west are: Sandra L. Myres, *Westering Women and the Frontier Experience, 1800–1915* (1982); Glenda Riley, *Frontierswomen: The Iowa Experience* (1981); and Walter O'Meara, *Daughters of the Country: The Women of Fur Traders and Mountain Men* (1968). Wealthier women in nineteenth-century America increasingly hired "help" or domestic servants, both native women and thousands of immigrant women. Their story is told in Faye E. Dudden, *Serving Women: Household Service in Nineteenth-Century America* (1983), and Daniel Sutherland, *Americans and Their Servants: Domestic Service in the United States from 1800 to 1920* (1981). A number of the books listed in the bibliography following the reading by Tucker (Reading No. 9) discuss the laboring force in factories. Barbara M. Wertheimer, *We Were There: The Story of Working Women in America* (1977) is a broader work treating women in a variety of areas. Although the history of black women has been given less attention than that of white women, Gerda Lerner does discuss it in her short work, *The Woman in American History* (1971).

The position of wealthier women and the roles they were expected to play has been the subject of a great many books. Barbara Welter wrote influential essays on the "cult of true womanhood" and other topics which are collected in her book *Dimity Convictions: The American Woman in the Nineteenth Century* (1976). There are studies of women in different regions, such as Anne F. Scott, *The Southern Lady: From Pedestal to Politics, 1830–1930* (1970), Catherine Clinton, *The Plantation Mistress: Woman's World in the Old South* (1982), and Marilyn F. Motz, *True Sisterhood: Michigan Women and Their Kin, 1820–1920* (1983). For a variety of reasons, many women chose to remain single; their lives are studied in Lee V. Chambers-Schiller, *Liberty a Better Husband: Single Women in America. . . , 1780–1840* (1984). Other works studying professional women include: Barbara J. Harris, *Beyond Her Sphere: Women and the Professions in American History* (1978); Barbara J. Berg, *The Remembered Gate: Origins of American Feminism. . .* , *1800–1860* (1978); and Susan Conrad, *Perish the Thought: Intellectual Women in Romantic America, 1830–1860* (1976). Nancy Woloch, *Women and the American Experience* (1984), and Catherine Clinton, *The Other Civil War: American Women in the Nineteenth Century* (1984) are two of many broad surveys of women's history.

Compared to the thousands of sources and secondary works on the South and the Far Western migration, rural life in the Midwest has been relatively slighted. Everett N. Dick, *The Sod House Frontier, 1854–1859* (1937) describes the primitive life and isolation of farm families on the northern plains. Allan G. Bogue studies a more limited area in *From Prairies to Corn Belt: Farming on the Illinois and Iowa Prairies in the Nineteenth Century* (1963). Howard S. Russell describes three centuries of New England agriculture in *A Long, Deep Furrow* (1976), while Hal S. Barron considers those who did not migrate in *Those Who Stayed Behind: Rural Society in Nineteenth-Century New England* (1984). Paul W. Gates, *The Farmer's Age: Agriculture, 1815–1860* (1960) is one of the best general studies of the period.

The Granger Collection, New York

The opening of new cotton lands in the West made the slave auction a
striking feature of southern life.

15

LESLIE H. OWENS

The Black Family

By 1800 slavery had been eliminated in the North, and in 1808 Congress banned the further importation of slaves from Africa. Although some illegal importation continued, other factors primarily accounted for the extraordinary elaboration and expansion of slavery in the nineteenth century. One such factor was the invention of the cotton gin, described in the essay by Pusateri (Reading No. 8), which allowed the quick cleaning of as much cotton as slaves could pick. A second contributing cause was the opening of rich new lands beyond the Appalachians, which created a market for slaves and gave rise to the domestic slave trade within the United States. Between 1820 and 1860, the slave population of the state of Mississippi alone increased from fewer than 35,000 to more than 435,000. In short, southern planters found slavery economically profitable. There was also a high birth rate among American blacks, and by the eve of the Civil War nearly four million black people lived as permanent, hereditary slaves. Forming the chief labor force from the tobacco fields of Virginia to the cotton fields of Alabama, blacks were crucial to southern agriculture and the southern economy. These chattels, bought and sold like livestock, were an easily marketable property that could bring ready cash to the slaveowner.

But slavery was more than a key feature of southern economic life. Its influence was all-pervasive, affecting law, education, social class, sexual mores, and other aspects of life. No one in the South escaped the influence of slavery and racism, neither slave nor slave-owner, free Negro or non-slave-holding white. Wilbur J. Cash has written, "Negro entered into white man as profoundly as white man entered into Negro — subtly influencing every gesture, every word, every emotion and idea, every attitude."

Few things were influenced more radically than the black family. Today, much is made of the growing instability or breakdown of the American family. The daily press has become a record of divorce, juvenile delinquency, alcohol and drug abuse, wife-beating, and parent–child hostilities so extreme that murder is sometimes the outcome. Imagine, then, what might happen to a family under these conditions: a mother and her children might have to watch the father being whipped; a mother-wife might be forced to have sexual relations with a stranger who invades the family cabin; the children might be sold at the age of ten or twelve to a distant owner, never to see their parents again. Such were the possibilities for the black family under slavery, and some people have suggested that such experiences scarred the black family to the present day.

A full understanding of the black, or any other, family can be gained only by comparisons with families in other periods and societies. Recently, historians have devoted considerable energy to studying the family as a social institution in periods ranging from ancient China to medieval France to contemporary America. They have come to new conclusions as to the role of the Industrial Revolution in affecting the family, how pervasive single-parent households were in earlier periods, and whether or not the "nuclear" family — consisting of parents and children only, rather than broadly extended kin relationships — is a typically modern form. Leslie H. Owens's book *This Species of Property* is an excellent study of slave life and culture, and his chapter on the black family is especially poignant. Despite their enslavement and the breakup of families owing to the slave trade, blacks had a strong sense of family ties and family affection. Many slaves who attempted to escape seem to have been trying to get back to their families, and after the Civil War, thousands of ex-slaves solidified their informal alliances with marriage licenses and wedding ceremonies.

Few aspects of the slave's bondage have come in for as much speculative writing as the impact of slavery upon the slave family. Researchers in many disciplines have argued that bondage rent asunder this most basic of American institutions, injured black identity, and left scars to haunt black Americans down to our day. But all this needs further examination.

Planters usually evidenced concern and not a little ambivalence, as several historians have preferred to put it, when reaching the decision to split up a black household. The practice was in sharp contrast to what many felt to be right, though planters consistently overcame nagging doubts. An agent representing John McDonogh of Louisiana complained to him that a slave trader "refused to give me a little negro boy and girl belonging to the Mulattresses, claiming that he could not separate the families." He added bluntly, "It was a poor reason." It cannot be denied that the slave family took a tremendous beating; its members were sold to satisfy creditors and purchased to increase personal wealth. . . .

To avoid the public disapproval that increasingly attached to putting slaves on the auction block, some masters sold their bondsmen privately. For the slave, however, the impact remained the same, and scenes of mothers crying because they would never see their children again are more than products of historical imagination. George Tucker, a nineteenth-century Virginia novelist, offended many of his southern readers by writing, "One not accustomed to this spectacle [an auction] is extremely shocked to see beings, of the same species with himself, set up for sale to the highest bidder, like horses or cattle; and even to those who have become accustomed to it, it is disagreeable."

Historically, the auction block has both real and symbolic importance. The lyrics from a slave melody, "No more auction block! No more, no more," capture both meanings. For slaves it meant a parting — often final — from relatives and friends. Unable to face such doubtful futures some ran off or mutilated or killed themselves. To curb such occurrences planters sometimes gave only a day's or even just a few hours' notice to bondsmen selected for selling and then guarded them closely or locked them up. One master, no doubt guilty of understatement, conceded that his "Negroes will probably be somewhat distressed at being sold." He therefore advised his son, "You must say what you can to reconcile them."

Slave traders held auctions, advertised well in advance, several times during each year in local towns and cities. A great throng of slaveholders or potential slaveholders attended each session, accompanied sometimes by their wives, who might be clad in stylish dresses. It was, at the larger slave auctions, a time of gala social functions running through the day into late evening. The traders sponsored most of these events and invited planters up to their hotel rooms for pre-auction drinks and casual conversation. There was much imbibing and not a little carousing. Gangs of youths roamed the streets shouting names at free blacks, perhaps indicating a desire to see them returned to bondage. All had a good time except members of the black community — slave and free.

Of course the bondsman's participation in the auction began much earlier than these social functions. His psychological preparation started at the moment his master told him that he was to be put on the market. Parents gathered children too young to understand their fate around them and told stories of going on a long trip and not seeing one another for a great while. It could easily be the infants and adolescents who were being put up for sale, for nearly "all traders dealt in those from 10 to 12 years of age and many advertised for those from 6, 7, 8, and 9." A Virginia agent wrote to a prospective buyer in 1850, "Boys and Girls are selling *best.*" For this reason Harriet Tubman, the underground railroad heroine, recalled that while she was in bondage, "every time I saw a white man I was afraid of being carried away." The domestic trade, few would deny, was a basic reason for some bondsmen having only faint memories of their parents and of children growing up under the adoptive care of childless slaves and other foster parents. Frederick Douglass's well-known confession is emblematic: "I never saw my mother to know her as such, more than four or five times in my life. . . . I received the tidings of her death with much the same emotions I should have probably felt at the death of a stranger." . . .

To soothe those slaves intended for auction planters sometimes explained their reasons for selling them, hoping to win their confidence. Dr. James Marion Sims of Alabama wrote to his wife about an impending sale: "Let them understand that it is impossible for us to keep them . . . already are there mortgages on some of them and there is no telling when they may be foreclosed. . . . Let them know too that it lacerates our hearts as much as it does theirs to be compelled to the course we suggest." Masters also promised not to allow reputedly cruel planters to purchase aggrieved bondsmen. Was this merely deception? In many cases it undoubtedly was. Yet there was not always cause to view a master's promises suspiciously, for some tried to keep their word. . . .

The time finally came for slaves to travel to the auction. In preparation, masters plucked out some of the older slaves' gray hairs or painted them over with a blacking brush. This was an illegal practice, but nonetheless widely engaged in, and traders delighted in outsmarting one another and uncovering the hucksters' deceptions. Masters also had some slaves grease their bodies to make their muscles or a smiling face shine, but also to cover up recent or old marks of abuse. At the larger slave markets such as Richmond, Natchez, New Orleans, and Wilmington, North Carolina, bondsmen were placed in slave pens to await the arrival of auction day. The abolitionist James Redpath visited the one in Wilmington in the 1850's and reported it filled with slaves of both sexes. . . .

The sale began as the auctioneer's voice boomed out over the crowd's noise: "Now gentlemen, who bids for Tom? . . . His only fault is that he has a great idea of his own reserved rights, to the neglect of those of his master." Several slaves were on the platform. The auctioneer commented on each one's relative value and merits, "and when the hammer at length falls, protests, in the usual phrase, that poor Sambo has been absolutely thrown away."

An historian has written that many slaves were apparently unaffected by the auction experience "and were proud of the high prices that they brought." This would seem to be an oversimplification of how slaves actually felt. Many, though colorfully dressed, wore somber expressions on their faces. At the Charleston market Captain Basil Hall noted a puzzling air of indifference in the slaves' manner. And another observer, on a different occasion, remarked that "the poor victims did not seem to think hard of this matter, but regarded it as a matter of course." In reality, some slaves had simply resigned themselves to being sold, and saw little need for a display of emotion that might later bring them punishment.

But it seems that many slaves determined ahead of time to take an active part in the direction of the bargaining. They looked over the buyers, as the buyers did them, and selected several preferable ones. Often their decision hinged upon a knowledge of the planter's wealth and the living conditions and work load he would subject them to. They learned the needed information by keeping alert, quizzing other slaves, and sometimes confronting purchasers directly with rather blunt questions. Some were deliberately offensive to small planters, believing that slaves owned by them lacked social status and also life's necessities. The slave John Parker explained: "I made up my mind I was going to select my owner so when any one came to inspect me I did not like, I answered all questions with a 'yes' and made myself disagreeable. So far as I was concerned the game was on, and I began to play it." William Hayden claimed that because of his "utter indifference and apparent independence" to the events around him when he was on sale at an auction in Natchez, Mississippi, many prospective "purchasers were at a loss to know if, in reality, I were a slave, and subject to the hammer." Slaves not as well attuned as Parker or Hayden to fine points of bargaining were less subtle. They might even kick or spit on buyers they did not like, and, according to the traveler E. S. Abdy, even shouted, "You may buy me . . . but I will never work for you." Such threats turned many buyers away, but others were willing to accept the risk, confident in their ability to handle any bondsman.

Another method employed by slaves was simply to complain of imaginary ailments to every buyer except the desired one. Prospective purchasers often believed these stories because of those real instances of doctored-up slaves whose masters sought to dupe the unsuspecting buyer. Female slaves acted the coquette, offending planters and the sensibilities of accompanying wives. They bickered and nagged at masters, convincing many that they would be a disruptive force in any work gang. They also made threats not to bear any children while owned by an undesirable master, and even to put infants that might be born to death. Only planters somewhat unfamiliar with slave management took these warnings lightly. For most, there was always a faint memory of a time on one's plantation or on a neighbor's when a slave had carried out an unheeded threat. . . .

But before a buyer sealed his purchase of a slave, he usually wanted to examine him physically. He looked at his teeth, limbs, and back, felt and poked muscles. Often buyers touched female slaves in most familiar ways, and the auctioneer and members of the crowd told obscene jokes. An English observer at Richmond noted, "I beheld with my own eyes a man . . . go and examine a poor African girl . . . grasping her arms and placing his course [sic] hand on her bosom!" Many domestic slaves were unprepared emotionally for such examinations, and when they occurred many broke into tears, almost as if for the first time the full weight of their bondage pressed down upon them.

For more intimate examinations, a small yard was set aside. Slaves carried back there, according to the ex-slave Solomon Northup, were "stripped and inspected more minutely." Buyers looked for scars or signs of syphilitic ailments, for example, and examined the pelvic areas of females for purposes of speculation on their future as childbearers. The ordeal was especially difficult for husbands who were powerless to assist weeping wives. Yet bondsmen submitted reluctantly to such examinations if they provided the chance of being purchased by a preferred owner. Prospective buyers also compelled slaves to jump and dance as further proof that their limbs were operative. . . .

Because of the frequency of auction block scenes, the composition and stability of the slave family has been the subject of much confusion. Was the family in a state of constant disruption? And if this was commonly so, what impact did such disruption have upon the development of its members' identities and general mode of being?

The primacy of one's family relationships in shaping one's character is axiomatic among today's social theorists. Family members gain personal strength from being loved and trusted by one another, and the family unit serves as a shield against outside attacks and the feeling of emptiness that often comes from being alone. The principles are easy to understand, but the elusive nature of the slave family makes them difficult to apply. Even the concept "family" as it applies to slaves needs reconsideration. With regard to them we might view it as several overlapping concepts. Slavery made it essential that the slave family be a great deal more inclusive than its white counterpart. Its ranks included not only blood relatives but also "adopted" relatives. Few slaves seemed lacking in aunts or uncles, real or otherwise.

The odds against survival of the slave family intact were formidable. To begin with, marriage was not legally binding between slaves in any of the southern states. As late as 1855 there was a petition before the North Carolina Legislature requesting "that the parental relation . . . be acknowledged and protected by law; and that the separation of parents from their young children, say of twelve years and under, he strictly forbidden, under heavy pains and penalties." Though such memorials were frequent, legislators never heeded them, for their implementation would merely have served to increase the moral questions that bothered many slave-holders, as well as greatly restrict the domestic slave trade. In the main, masters dictated the rules governing slave unions. What they were not able to dictate, however, was the seriousness with which bondsmen took their vows. These a sizable majority stood by steadfastly. . . .

Once married, separations were usually not a matter of impulse on the slave's part. The domestic trade annulled an inestimable number of unions, but in the instance of voluntary separations some planters wanted to know the causes for the disunion and, in the case of James Henry Hammond of South Carolina, believed in disciplining the offenders. Slaves, never-theless, have gained a reputation for licentiousness and immorality that is out of proportion, considering the circumstances under which they lived. There were, of course, slaves who had several wives or husbands. But ulterior motives of both slave and master often spawned these arrange-ments. One planter thus discouraged his slave Peter from marrying a woman on another plantation because of "temptations to get into the rascality or meanness." He perhaps suspected that such a marriage would lead to eventual disobedience by Peter should their judgments differ on when Peter might visit his proposed wife. And he probably feared Peter's performing some unauthorized errands. Yet other slaveholders sometimes reasoned that preventing a slave from taking a wife of his choice could lead to serious managerial problems with him. At any rate, slaves whose spouses died often remarried as soon as they could. The practice was not uncommon among planters and overseers as well. It was "very common among slaves themselves to talk of" marriage, wrote ex-slave William Wells Brown. What bothered him was that after marriage, "some masters, when they have sold the husband from the wife, compel her to take another" almost immediately, ignoring her personal feelings. . . .

Many past and present researchers have assumed that the slave family was a very loosely organized group whose primary cohesion was provided by women. The black sociologist E. Franklin Frazier capsulized this interpretation in his 1939 study when he characterized the slave mother "as the mistress of the cabin and as the head of the family." Frazier also mentioned that the mother had a "more fundamental interest in her children" and was able to develop "a spirit of independence and a keen sense of her personal rights." His canonization of slave women catapulted them to the forefront of modern discussions about the slave family. Was he correct in his conclusion about the matriarchal structure of the family? His picture seems somehow too inflexible, for the slave family developed in ways which Frazier seems not to have imagined.

Under some conditions — when slave children were infants — southern laws provided that masters could not divide slave families. What these laws sought primarily to prevent was the separation of child from mother; the father might still be sold. Indeed, when planters spoke of slave families they often referred to husbandless women and their children. The logic rings familiar even today, in that when a husband and wife legally separate the wife normally obtains custody of the children. We seldom assume, however, that the husband has been a passive agent in the family. Why then should we assume this to be so in the case of the slave, when there is no significant precedent for such an assumption in the slave's African past or in many of his American associations? Of course, this is not to deny that a slave father was a great deal more helpless than a free father today.

A variety of circumstances determined the position of the slave mother as well as the father. If women were the heads of the households, they rarely gained that dominant status among slaves at large. Women worked side by side with men at nearly every task on the plantation, but there were certain duties considered women's work that men declined to do. Some male slaves refused to do washing for this reason. Cooking was usually the task of women, as was sewing and some forms of child care. Sometimes masters punished males by forcing them to work with women labor gangs in the fields or compelling them to wash the family's clothes and attend to housecleaning. So great was their shame before their fellows that many ran off and suffered the lash on their backs rather than submit to the discipline. Men clearly viewed certain chores as women's tasks, and female slaves largely respected the distinction. . . .

The often peculiar marriage and dating relations of bondsmen have caused many scholars to doubt their morality. Females have borne the brunt of unfavorable conjectures. Scores of mulatto children fathered by masters have been used to support arguments that bondswomen were indiscriminate in their selection of male sex partners. Added to this was the fact that in the "southern states the prostitutes of the communities are usually slaves, unless they are imported from the free states."

Motherhood in bondage provided extremely difficult tests of a slave's energies and identity. The slave had to play the role of wife and mother under circumstances that marred her effectiveness at each. Her plantation duties eroded the time she had to spend with husband and children. Distractions were infinite. This was akin to the condition that some planters' wives found themselves in, trapped in a continuous cycle of chores.

Slavery struck most directly at bonds of affection joining husband and wife. The slave trade occasionally separated slaves married only a few weeks. We may suppose that some slaves were reluctant to love anyone deeply under these circumstances. Yet most spent several years with one owner and one husband or wife, and came to know their fellow bondsmen well. Thus when slaves married it was often the consequence of courtship extending over some time. The resultant marriage was steeped in emotional attachment. "Our affection for each other was strong," wrote a slave of his marriage, "and this made us always apprehensive of a cruel parting." The slave Sam, like so many others, ran away from his Virginia master because he thought "it a hard case to be separated from his wife."

Planters understood such affections. "You have a woman hired in the neighborhood whose husband we own," began a letter to Colonel Barksdale of Virginia. His "name is Israel, he is our Blacksmith, and he seems to be so much attached to her we [would] like very much for her to be hired near him . . . would you sell the woman?" A sound marriage meant a better worker for the planter and often a sense of purpose for the slave.

But slavery compelled an uneven husband-wife relationship. A master could physically discipline either while the other stood by helpless, at least for the moment. Slaveowners worked both hard, and they often had little time left to enjoy each other's company in the evening. The relationship nonetheless had many interesting potentials. "A slave possessing nothing . . . except a wife and children, has all his affections concentrated upon them," wrote Francis Fedric. Occasionally, the marriage partners focused so much attention on each other that the slightest change in the routine of one tended to disrupt the other's habits. Sickness is a good example. Wives and husbands often insisted that they nurse each other back to health, fighting bitterly against efforts to force them into the fields when the possibility of a loved one dying existed. Slaveholders severely punished many and accused them of merely trying to escape duties — but discipline was seldom an effective deterrent. A planter could, of course, make arrangements for such times; expecting that wives and husbands might be off work briefly or difficult to manage during days when important personal matters came up. Sometimes a sick husband would prolong his sickness by refusing to take medicine from any but the hands of his wife, whom he could also trust to find out if someone had "hexed" him. . . .

The arrival of children served in large measure to solidify the slave marriage. Yet some parents feared that slaveholders would mistreat offspring or sell them away. A few adults also refused to assume parental responsibilities. They married and had children, but declined or allowed others to take care of them, and were occasionally abusive parents. Still, most assumed parental ties eagerly and were, according to a Mississippi mistress, "all so proud of showing their children." While discussing the possible sale of a slave to an Annapolis slaveholder, Charles Ridgely wrote that she "is married in the neighborhood and has a family of young children, and would I think now be extremely unwilling to be separated from them."

In Africa "tribal customs and taboos tended to fix the mother's attitude toward her child before it was born," making children greatly appreciated, and such tendencies were not absent in American slaves. Few women probably did not want children, though they were aware they might not be able to devote the attention to them that would be required. The emotional outbursts of mothers following the deaths of infants, and their resistance to being parted from offspring, indicate that female slave attitudes in this regard were not markedly distinct from those of mothers worldwide.

In fact, many disruptions of the workday stemmed from slave parents' requests to tend their children. Masters set aside a period during the day for the nursing of babies, but there was also frequent disciplining of bondswomen when they failed to return to their duties on schedule. Yet mothers repeatedly risked the lash in order to allow their body temperatures to cool down enough for effective milk nourishment. Still, Moses Grandy observed that overseers forced many to work in the field carrying full breasts of milk. "They therefore could not keep up with the other hands," and when this happened overseers whipped them "so that blood and milk flew mingled from their breasts." It does not appear that he was merely trying to achieve literary effect with this dramatic statement. But often mothers got their way, for it was difficult for a master to justify, either to his conscience or his hands, children found dead from want of care. The slave's human increase was also an owner's most valuable form of property. On many plantations masters periodically assigned one or two slaves to furnish the nursing needs of all infants. They also hired slaves to nurse their own offspring. . . .

In bondage, the varieties of adult family behavior served as the most significant models after which slave children patterned their own actions. We know that "where a variety of behavior or models is available, selection can be influenced either by affection and rewards, by punishment, or by awareness of what is appropriate." All these factors operated with peculiar force within and upon the slave family. J. W. C. Pennington, the fugitive blacksmith, experienced what he called a "want of parental care and attention." By way of explanation he added, "My parents were not able to give any attention to their children during the day." While this was not unusual, many parents did devote their evenings and weekends to family affairs — a first duty of which was to teach children the limits placed on their conduct. This was no simple task. . . .

For the young slave, family life was vastly important. His early years somehow slipped past with the idea probably seldom if ever occurring to him that he was but a piece of property. His main worries related to minor chores assigned to him at about age five or six by parents and master; and adult slaves at times bore much of the burden of these. Children also escaped much of the stigma of racial inferiority that whites attached to the personalities of their mothers and fathers. Concerning his childhood one slave reminisced, "let me say to you that my case were different from a great many of my colore so I never knew what the yoke of oppression was in the early part of my life." He was relatively carefree and innocent, he explained, until "the white boy . . . began to Raise his feathers and boast of the superiority which he had over me." . . .

It was not true that when black children learned to walk and then play with the master's children their "first lesson is to obey everything that has a white skin," as one bondsman claimed. Some masters' children learned this lesson the hard way when they tried to boss the little "niggers" about: "Every time they crossed me I jumped them," recalled one ex-slave about his white playmates.

Frequently the tendency among black and white children was towards a general equality. They played marbles together, and the slave children themselves spent many hours at this game: "My favorite game was marbles." They also played sheepmeat, a game of tag played with a ball of yarn that was thrown by one child at others running about the grounds. They enjoyed a great variety of childhood sports. Sir Charles Lyell, the English geologist, witnessed slave and white children playing, "evidently all associating on terms of equality." One slave narrator remembered too that he was very close to a son of his Virginia master: "I was his playmate and constant associate in childhood." He learned the alphabet and some of the elements of reading from him. "We were very fond of each other, and frequently slept together."

On large plantations communities of children were largely autonomous. Slave narratives relate that often one of the bondsman's earliest recollections of slavery was the sight of his mother or father being whipped or his brothers and sisters standing on the auction block. But this side of childhood can be overplayed. Fear did not perpetually pervade the environment. There are accounts of seeming childhood contentment which, though occasionally overdrawn by some interpreters, are to some measure accurate. The slaveholder did not constantly try to shape the character of slave children. There was little time for that. "The master, I think, does not often trouble himself with the government of these juvenile communities," observed a doctor from Kentucky. "He is not, therefore, an object of dread among them."

To a great extent, children learned to shape their behavior to the expectations of other slaves. A beginning lesson was to respect slave elders, particularly the aged. Tradition shaped this differential treatment. The child was, moreover, at the bottom of the hierarchy of both blacks and whites, while old slaves were in a manner the domestics of the slave quarters. Their functions were not unlike those of the slaves who ordered the master's children about and instructed them in etiquette. . . .

Some parents also saw initial work responsibilities, if properly performed, as an opportunity for their sons and daughters to escape the rigors of field labor. They encouraged their children to learn a trade if possible. A skill meant an opportunity to obtain preferred duties in later life. Masters wanted at least a few trained hands, chiefly as carpenters, for they increased the efficiency of the plantation as well as their own monetary value. John McDonogh of New Orleans hired a slave brickmason and later recommended him to a neighbor, suggesting that he might teach bricklaying to "two or three of your black boys" and "with two boys of 10 or 12 years of age to work with him in laying brick he will do all your buildings."

Occasionally, children's jobs required that they go through a prolonged or permanent separation from their families; but a determined parent was willing to accept this if it promised ultimately to provide an easier life for a son or daughter. The slave Julianna, age twelve, was the subject of a contract that engaged her services for six years. Her contractual master guaranteed "to teach her to sew, & bring her up to be a good seamstress, and a useful servant." The arrangement continued on a partially personal note: "In addition to the above I agree to allow the said girl Julianna to go to Shirley [Plantation] . . . once each year to see her relations, & remain with them one week each year."

Bondsman Henry Bibb was especially aware of the shortened childhood of the slave. "I was taken away from my mother," he wrote, "and hired out to labor for various persons, eight or ten years in succession." Other hired-out children were more fortunate than Bibb. Employed as families, as were "Great Jenny & her 3 youngest children," they partially escaped the emotional turmoil that accompanied separations. . . .

When the terms of bondage necessitated the division of families, parents often sought the aid of masters to reunite them. Lucinda, who served as a washwoman for a planter "nearly twelve years," asked him to hire her daughter Mary Jane from a nearby planter. "To oblige her," wrote her owner to Mary Jane's master, "I will become responsible for the amount, if you will let her have her daughter for the sum of Thirty dollars," which Lucinda was apparently willing to repay by her earnings during the remainder of the year. In another case, the slave George approached his master R. Carter about his daughter Betty — "7 years old, motherless, now at Colespoint-plantation — ." In a letter to his overseer, Carter noted that "George wishes Betty live at Aires, with his Wife who lives there." As if not to appear overly accommodating to George's wishes, Carter continued, "If Betty is not useful where She now lives — I desire to indulge George . . . you will accordingly permit him to take his daughter." At other times, slaves acted on their own to reunite themselves with loved ones. One runaway was persistent in this way: "She has a husband, I think, at his [a neighbor's] house & tho' taken up by him the first time came straight back to his house."

When a master abused or humiliated one member of a family, the rebuff reverberated throughout the slave household and beyond. An example appears in the opening pages of the fugitive blacksmith's narrative. Following the whipping of his father, J. W. C. Pennington remembered, "an open rupture" developed in his family [against their master]. Each member felt deeply offended by the deed, for they had always believed their conduct and faithfulness was exemplary. They talked of their humiliation in the "nightly gatherings, and showed it in . . . daily melancholy aspect."

Planters' ill-handling of slaves was only one of many factors that brought out family consciousness. Bondsmen's misdeeds against other bondsmen sometimes marked families for harassment and shame. A serious offense, such as stealing another's hunting catches, might lead to brief periods of social isolation, with members of the offending family finding themselves excluded from slave gatherings or nightly ramblings. Bondsmen saw themselves as having their primary identification with a distinct family unit to which they had responsibility and which had responsibility to them.

However, the slave family was a unit with extensions. Quite frequently it seems to have consisted of more than just parents and their natural children. It could include a number of blood or adopted relations — uncles, aunts, and cousins — who lived on the same plantation or on nearby estates. Adults "claimed" parentless children, and the slave community seldom neglected old slaves. Local bondsmen usually absorbed new arrivals on a plantation into a family setting and expected them to make a full contribution immediately. But can such a group really be called a family? Slaves considered it as such and treated adopted relatives with real affection.

The extended slave family frequently arose to augment or replace the regular family unit split up by slavery's misfortunes. There were deaths resulting from disease, accidents, and natural causes that left wives husbandless and children without parents. Then there were the family breakups caused by the slave trade. In an important, though not typical, exception, however, Robert Carter of Virginia agreed to sell his slaves to the Baltimore Company only "if the Company will purchase men their wives & children [ten families]." . . .

In slave families wives seldom possessed greater financial stability than husbands, a circumstance that often gives rise to psychological problems in men of minority households in our day. Both worked at tasks that the slave culture did not stigmatize as menial, so there was no need for the male to feel a lack of importance in his family on that score. The power of masters to disrupt families at any time weakened male slaves' sense of responsibility and dignity, but they did not invariably see this as a slight to their manhood. Yet for the slave who experienced the breakup of his household there remained that indelible hurt, as perhaps exemplified by Charles Ball's father, who "never recovered from the effects of the shock" of losing a portion of his family and became "gloomy and morose." Whenever the slave family — natural or extended — was intact, however, and slave males were reliably performing their duties, they most likely did symbolize authority within the family structure.

Except for sales of its members, much of the time slaveholders left the slave family to its own devices. And though the slave trade drove blood relatives apart, bondsmen's common persecution brought many of them back together in extended family groupings which provided for many of the emotional needs whose satisfaction the regular family, had it remained untouched, might have rendered less vexatious. Under these conditions the personalities of bondsmen were certain to gain much strength.

STUDY GUIDE

1. How would the following factors affect a slave's price on the auction block: age, sex, health, and attitude? What techniques were used by sellers to try to make a slave appear more valuable?

2. Summarize Owens's view of the role and attitudes of male and female parents in the black family under slavery. What kind of evidence does he use to argue that slaves made clear distinctions in the roles of men and women, though both did the same kind of field labor?

3. What generalizations can be made about the attitudes of masters toward selling slaves, toward slave marriages, and toward breaking up families?

4. Many European and American white families were "nuclear" — consisting only of parents and children without grandparents or uncles and aunts living in the same household. Owens suggests that the black family was more "extended," with considerable respect for age and the care of parentless children by others. Why would you expect such features to have developed in southern slavery?

5. What factors in modern society have somewhat modified the differences among families with varied backgrounds? Think, for example, of a southern rural and a northern urban black family; a second-generation Slavic family; a Chinese-American family; an Italian Catholic family. Compare the differences you see today in such groups with those that existed several decades ago.

BIBLIOGRAPHY

The book by Leslie H. Owens from which the preceding selection is taken is a fine study of life and culture under slavery. While it reveals much about slave conditions and the slaves' reactions to their enslavement, there are many other studies of slavery in the period just before the American Civil War. An older southern historian, who had a patronizing view of the Negro and a rather rosy view of slavery, was Ulrich B. Phillips. Despite the limitations of his work, he was one of the first scholars to study slavery as a total system, rather than as only an economic or a racial system. The most important of his works are *American Negro Slavery* (1918) and *Life and Labor in the Old South* (1929). The most interesting works of a general nature written since Phillips' books are Kenneth Stampp, *The Peculiar Institution: Slavery in the Ante-Bellum South* (1956) and John W. Blassingame, *The Slave Community: Plantation Life in the Ante-Bellum South* (1972). Virtually every major conclusion of earlier historians on the social and economic aspects of American slavery has been challenged in the highly controversial study by Robert William Fogel and Stanley L. Engerman, *Time on the Cross*, 2 vols. (1974).

An issue of great interest is the influence of slavery upon the personality of American blacks and their reactions to slavery. In his work *Slavery: A Problem in American Institutional and Intellectual Life*, 3rd ed. (1976), Stanley M. Elkins compares the American slavery system with the Nazi concentration camp. Elkins believes that the slaves identified with their oppressors, and he emphasizes the "Sambo" personality of the American black in studying the effects of slavery upon the black's psychology. Other scholars have argued that the Sambo role was merely a survival technique in a white world, and Gerald Mullin and John Blassingame suggest that there were different personality types.

Equally interesting is the question of the influence of slavery upon the black family. A number of writers, including Daniel Patrick Moynihan in a very controversial book, have suggested that the black family was characterized by strong mothers, irresponsible fathers, sexual promiscuity, and a general lack of stability. In an important book entitled *The Black Family in Slavery and Freedom, 1750–1925* (1975), Herbert Gutman disputed such conclusions, argued that there was a strong sense of family and kin among blacks, and provided the best study to date of the black family over an extended period. On this and other subjects, one can get the slave's own perspective from the collection of reminiscences of ex-slaves edited by Benjamin A. Botkin, *Lay My Burden Down: A Folk History of Slavery* (1945). Eugene Genovese, who previously had written about southern slaveholders, used such reminiscences as well as other sources to get at the daily life of southern slaves in *Roll, Jordan, Roll: The World the Slaves Made* (1974). Frank Owsley, *Plain Folk of the Old South* (1949) gives a fair picture of the life of poor whites, but the studies of slave life are generally better. Richard C. Wade, *Slavery in the Cities: The South, 1820–1860* (1964) is a study of the sizeable number of slaves who do not fit the plantation stereotype. John Hope Franklin, *From Slavery to Freedom: A History of American Negroes*, 3rd ed. (1967) is a general history of black Americans.

*An immigrant transfer barge docked at Castle Garden offers
transportation to the Erie Railroad, 1874.*

16

MARK WYMAN

Nation of Immigrants

The extraordinary flow of people from Europe, Asia, and Africa to the New World for more than three centuries constitutes the largest human migration ever experienced on this planet. All of us here are descendants of immigrants — of Indians who crossed the Bering land bridge from Asia, of early black and white migrants who settled the British colonies, of German, French, Italian, Russian, Hungarian, Chinese, or other immigrant ancestors who poured into the United States in the nineteenth century. By 1930 the tide had waned, but by then the country's history could not be understood without taking into account the impact upon American civilization of the many races and nationalities that had immigrated to the United States.

The most obvious question involved in the study of immigration history is why particular groups left their homelands to come to a strange country. Some factors were common to most groups of Europeans, but in each country special influences promoted emigration at a particular time. In the following selection, Mark Wyman gives a graphic description of the political, economic, and religious conditions that led hundreds of thousands of Irish to emigrate. A second question is why certain nationalities settled in the areas they did and tended to enter particular trades and occupations. Some remained largely in eastern cities as unskilled manual laborers, while others went on to Minnesota or Wisconsin to enter farming. One striking characteristic of early nineteenth-century population movements was the extensive immigration to the North and the relatively small number of immigrants who were attracted to southern states. This pattern was determined by a number of factors, including the greater industrialization taking place in the North, the slave labor system in the Old South, and the different social attitudes in the two regions.

Many immigrant groups, even in the colonial period, faced considerable hardship and animosity in establishing their roots in this land. In many ways, the difficulties increased during the nineteenth century, and even English-speaking groups such as the Irish found that adapting to the new culture posed serious problems. Most nationalities developed some sort of agency to assist them in preserving their heritage while adjusting to their new society; churches, schools, recreational associations, and other institutions served such purposes. Wyman describes the special problems faced by one such group, the Irish, a group that one might expect to have had fewer difficulties than some others.

Attitudes of immigrants toward their heritage have varied, as have attitudes of older Americans toward immigration policy and assimilation of new nationalities. For many years, much of our thought was dominated by the "melting pot" metaphor, which implied that the distinctive characteristics of each group should disappear into a new American nationality. In our time, there has been a resurgent interest in preserving the cultural heritage of various nationalities, and a suggestion that the melting pot theory be replaced by a cultural pluralism recognizing the integrity and contribution of different ethnic groups.

The British connection was an overbearing fact of life to the Irish. The English, rulers over most of the island since the twelfth century, treated nineteenth-century Ireland as a colony, seeking to snuff out local opposition and to mold the people to English ways. "In those days we were forbidden to *speak our native language in school*," an immigrant recalled of his childhood near Ballygar after 1810. "Our teacher would put a stone in our coats as a telltale to report if we spoke Irish." More than merely discouraging use of the native language — a campaign that some Irish groups supported because they regarded use of the Irish (Gaelic) as representing backwardness — the United Kingdom continued to enforce portions of the Penal Laws, anti-Catholic statutes dating back to 1695. These laws sought to reduce Catholicism to "helpless impotence" by prohibiting Catholics from holding important positions in law, commerce, or the military. In the eighteenth century the laws were the vehicle for breaking up Catholic estates, and widespread ruin accompanied their use. But the major long-term result was the degradation of the Irish peasantry. . . .

From Mark Wyman, *Immigrants in the Valley* (Chicago, 1983), pp. 10–25, 31–35, 39–48, 178–181, by permission of Nelson-Hall Inc., Publishers.

. . . British control had placed British landlords on most Irish land in preceding centuries, and Protestant Irish controlled much of the rest. By the early nineteenth century, the masses of Irishmen worked either as small farmers known as cotters, renting tiny plots of less than five acres, or as farm laborers. (Years later and a world away in Wisconsin an Irish immigrant farmer complained of crop prices in a letter home, then added the telling comment, "But we own the land." It was the crucial difference.)

These were a preindustrial people whose lives flowed with the rhythm of the seasons — of potato planting and harvesting, of digging turf (peat) — rather than the demands of a timekeeper. To many prefamine visitors, the Irish seemed indolent and lazy, although hospitable and much given to music and dance. A lady told of seeing County Kerry men who would walk ten miles into town for a penny-worth of tobacco or twopence worth of fish and thought their day was well spent. Light in their one-room hovels came from peeled rushes dipped in grease, and furniture was rare. An 1837 survey in Tullahobagly, County Donegal, found only 10 beds, 93 chairs, and 243 stools for a population of 9,000. Two touring Welsh clergymen reported that Irish girls "sit on their heels on the ground. . . . Seldom does one see either a chair or stool in the whole land." Pigs had the run of the house. Cotters were forced to work without pay for their landlords, planting and digging potatoes, reaping, haymaking, digging turf. No wonder Kerry folk "become prematurely old," the lady visitor remarked; "they lead a dreary life of hard work and privations, yet cheered by the blessed consciousness of fulfilling their duty. . . ."

Overdependence on the potato must be placed high among the factors creating the famine. In the eighteenth century, when Ireland shifted from pastoral to tillage farming and land division increased, the population adopted the potato as its basic food. It was nourishing, it was economical. An acre and a half would supply a six-member family's wants for most of the year. And it freed land for cash crops such as wheat, which required four to six times as much land as the potato for equal production of food. . . .

Hopes were high for the potato crop of 1846. When a priest traveled from Cork to Dublin at the end of July, he saw potatoes blooming "in all the luxuriance of an abundant harvest." But when he returned a week later, he wrote, "I beheld with sorrow one wide waste of putrefying vegetation." Others told similar stories of the entire green countryside suddenly turning scorched, as if a fire had passed over. Leaves withered, tubers decomposed. A people who had never known such all-encompassing disaster before searched desperately for expedients. They covered parts of the fields with cloth, they cut up the blighted potatoes and soaked them in water, they dried them in ovens, and they persisted in trying to eat them. One report from Clare told of people dining on food from which "so putrid and offensive an effluvia issued that in consuming it they were obliged to leave the doors and windows of their cabins open."

In this condition, where starvation already seemed possible, Ireland entered the winter of 1846–47. It was the worst in many years: gales swept fiercely over the island, snow lay deep everywhere, and typhus, dysentery (the "bloody flux"), and "famine dropsy" or hunger edema were widespread. Ireland's travail did not subside until 1851, despite a better crop in 1847.

People begged along the roadways and in the towns, searching for food — any food — and stealing when they could. Cork reported five thousand beggars in its streets, and a visitor said "every corner of the streets is filled with pale, careworn creatures, the weak leading and supporting the weaker," while women "assail you at every turn with famished babes, imploring alms."

In early 1847, the streets of Westport in County Mayo were filled with "gaunt wanderers," while at Bundorragha across the harbor the population "were like walking skeletons, the men stamped with the livid mark of hunger, the children crying with pain, the women, in some of the cabins, too weak to stand." All animals were gone from the farms except one pig, a visitor noted. . . .

It was increasingly evident that there were too many persons on the land. The bulge in Irish population in the early nineteenth century contributed to the severity of the famine, both in the starvation which followed when blight killed the potato crop and in stimulating counter-measures by landowners to save their estates. When Parliament in June 1847 put the responsibility for Irish relief on landlords, taxes quickly rose as workhouse populations mushroomed. The law divided Ireland into 130 "unions," averaging 62,884 each in population. Each union was to have a workhouse under control of some elected guardians and some ex officio guardians subject to Dublin. The 1847 amendments created outdoor relief — principally road repairs — while blocking any relief for those owning more than a quarter of an acre. . . .

Workhouses were quickly overcrowded with refugees from the famine and land clearances. A landowner visiting his estate in August 1848 admitted to being "utterly dismayed and appalled" after talking with the poor-law agent. There were 22,000 paupers on outdoor relief, out of a population of less than 78,000, and the union was £40,000 in debt because of it. Nearly an eighth of Tralee's population was in that union's work-houses in January 1851. Parliament had discovered the previous summer that some 336,000 persons were on some form of relief in Ireland. Many of these workhouse residents were helped to emigrate, and in Connaught it was reported that employed laborers subscribed sixpence each toward a fund which was then used to pay the lottery winner's passage to America.

With taxes for poor relief climbing, landowners sought ways to cut expenses. Emigration of tenants proved an efficient answer, removing the cotters, leveling their mud-walled cottages, buying them tickets for "Amerikay." Sir Benn-Walsh told of a Clare landowner who had emigrated fourteen hundred persons, and Benn-Walsh's own journal shows frequent use of this solution. At Forhane "the worst tenants have been got rid of at the expence of emigrating them. . . ."

Forced removals of Irish people from land they considered their own, carried out by officials who were to them an occupying power, brought a wave of violence across Ireland that has been somewhat downplayed in history because of the enormity of the era's prominent feature, the famine. Newspapers of the period provide some evidence of the resistance: "Mr. Ralph Smith, of Tullamore, is so obnoxious to his Carlow tenantry, because he served ejectments for non payment of rent, that they will not suffer him to cut down and save his crops, which are rotting in the fields. The ears were cut off the horses of three persons who volunteered their assistance, and the horse of another was shot." These were the "midnight legislators," the "rockites," who fought ejectment and, when that failed, fought the new occupants. When a "respectable farmer" in 1850 took over land in Clare from which tenants had been removed for nonpayment, all houses on the property were burned down the night before he was to take possession, and he refused to remain. That example kept another would-be local tenant from taking possession of his land. Bailiffs attempting to evict tenants at Ballykilcline were attacked, but a local jury acquitted the attackers. The evictions were finally carried out, but only with the aid of sixty policemen, twenty-five cavalry, thirty infantry, and a magistrate. Twelve policemen remained behind as guards.

The travail of Robert Pike of King's County shows the degree to which anti-eviction violence was upheld — or at least acquiesced in — by the tenantry. Pike's job was evicting tenants from his employer's land, tenants who had not paid rent for up to two years. He was almost killed when shots were fired at him as he drank tea in his home. Because of such incidents he went armed with a brace of pistols and a cane sword. But when going to evict seven families in Killyon in August 1850, Pike was attacked as he walked with a local farmer. The assailants ordered the farmer to leave, then beat Pike with his own sword. Pike suffered gunshot wounds in the back, chest, and abdomen and a skull fracture. No one but his walking companion could be found to testify on the incident although it occurred "in broad day light, upon an open public road . . . numbers of the peasantry going to market — several inhabited houses within a short distance of the spot, and nearly fifty people working in the bog. . . ."

Most of the other major traditions coming to play upon the famine era struggles involved religion — Catholic versus Protestant; Presbyterian versus Anglican versus Catholic; the pope versus the proselytizers; "faith" versus "fanaticism." Ireland was little affected by the Protestant Reformation, but English conquerors such as Oliver Cromwell attempted to fasten their brand of anti-Catholicism upon the Irish people, with only scattered success. It was people moving in from the east, such as the Lowland Scots brought to Ulster in the seventeenth century, who carried Protestantism with them. Thereafter, although Catholics formed more than three-fourths of the population, there were also Protestants in most areas. By the 1840s it was still true that most leadership positions were held by Protestants, however, and each town had its Protestant inn and its Catholic inn, Protestant stagecoaches and Catholic lines, and a host of other divisions along the Protestant-Catholic cleavage.

Presbyterians, who in the late eighteenth century seemed ready to join Catholics in battle against the Anglicans, increasingly backed off from joint activities. During the early nineteenth century the British government increased the Presbyterian endowment considerably, and the Catholic priests' growing power in antigovernment activities repelled many Presbyterians.

Protestant privilege was lessened by the struggle for Catholic emancipation, especially in its success in 1829. Compulsory taxes to support the Anglican church could not be collected in many areas, and the development of Catholic political consciousness and political skills during Daniel O'Connell's period of leadership threw further fears into Irish Protestants.

The famine, then, became a cauldron in which these religious animosities boiled. For example, Irish Catholics had traditionally held charity to be a duty for the donor. Poverty, they felt, carried not shame but even some merit. Emerging from a past where communal ownership was widespread, the Irish peasantry accepted begging as part of the yearly cycle; the community helped its less fortunate members without question. Prefamine estimates put the Irish farmers' annual donations of potatoes to the poor at a value approximating a million pounds. Long before the famine, priests had moved into leadership in organizing relief, and if unable to feed the beggar, the priest at least could locate sources for aid, even to the point of soliciting it. But this philosophy was rejected by many Protestants, in pulpit and press. Poverty held little merit for them, and they insisted that charity be handled so that it did not create a new class of beggars or endanger the economy. The fact that priests held important positions in dispensing local relief caused some Protestant agencies to refuse to donate famine help except through Protestants. Catholics, in turn, referred to those Catholics receiving help in Protestant soup kitchens as "soupers. . . ."

News from across the ocean told of a different way of life. Emigrant letters sent back to Ireland were usually optimistic. People leaving their homes looked ahead, not back, as the ship crossed the Atlantic. And the tales that reached County Cork and elsewhere contrasted sharply with experiences of the famine-beset, landlord-ruled land at home.

"I think on the hole you would better your self mutch by coming to this country," Henry Hutchinson wrote from Detroit to his brother in Caran in 1845. "Here every man is Lord of the soil he owns, there is no rent yearly. It is his and hairs for ever." An Irish travel book written in the form of letters sent home from America emphasized this point also: "The American farmer, Patrick, never pays any *rent*. When he takes a farm he buys it for ever." William Porter, a Chicago carpenter in 1851, admitted in a letter to his parents in County Down that "my heart wanders back to my native soil," but he stated, "You have a chance of rising in the world here which you have not there and the fear of want is not always staring you in the face." Wealth was not obtained "for the lifting" in America, but "what I mean is that people enjoys the fruits of their labour here."

Advertisements and letters in Irish newspapers gave the impression of abundant jobs in the United States and Canada. A British government emigration agent at Quebec sent a printed notice in 1851: "1,000 labourers wanted immediately, on the line of the St. Lawrence and Atlantic Railway"; spinners, rope-makers, tailors, smiths, male and female servants, and farm laborers were also called for. Similar reports reached Ireland in family letters.

A railroad worker in Vermont wrote a scornful letter back to the Galway Collector of Excise in 1848, announcing that "instead of being chained with poverty in Boughill I am crowned in glory." He wrote that he was "better pleased to come to this country than if you bestowed me five acres of land in Boughill."

Such stories were repeated often in the grapevine running between North America and Ireland. There was work, there was land, there was opportunity. Few negative reports made it back to Ireland, although as New York filled with immigrants some new arrivals sent word for their friends and relatives to head inland. "The seaports are filled to capacity with emigrants so that no chance can be had in them," one immigrant lamented in the prefamine era. By 1850, when the flood was great, an Irish girl similarly wrote home to Kingwilliamstown that "the emigrants has not money enough to take them to the interior of the country which obliges them to remain here in New York and the like places," bringing on a labor surplus and wage cuts. This was echoed by the Wisconsin emigration commissioner, who reported in 1853 that few Irish applied for information from his office, because most arrived "with but limited means," requiring them to "seize upon the first work offered them for subsistence."

Sometimes stronger warnings were sent home, including tales of signs proclaiming "No Irish Need Apply" and of the lengthy hours of labor in America. "If men and women worked at home as they work here they would have America in Ireland, but God help any one who has to work for his living in America," wrote one expatriate whose letter was printed in Irish newspapers. The writer urged Irishmen not to believe "half the favourable letters you see from America," for in reality people were fired from work one day to the next and had trouble locating another job.

More prestigious was the letter from Thomas D'Arcy McGee, the radical leader who had crossed to America in 1842, and as editor of the *Boston Pilot*, served as spokesman for his emigrating countrymen. In an open letter to Irish editors in 1850, McGee urged his compatriots to stay at home for the present because of a surplus of both educated job seekers and the unskilled. The big construction projects were finished, he contended. "There is, the coming year, no prospect of a large public work being organized," he warned, adding that New York was overstocked with 100,000 Irishmen "and how one-half of them live in honesty is a mystery to the other half." Another report in Irish newspapers at the same time said Irishmen were "begging in droves" in the streets of New York.

But McGee's prose barricade left one opening. "To such as can go direct from New York to Illinois or Ohio, this warning, though not needless, is yet inapplicable," he wrote. This became the goal for many: the new lands to the west. A magistrate for counties Clare and Galway told a parliamentary committee in 1849 that a former tenant of his had just returned from a visit to the United States: he "assured me that for 600 miles along the banks of the Mississippi (and he is a very respectable man) he had traversed the vast tracts of land, the worst acre of which was better than the best acre that I have in the world, and I have some of the very best in Ireland." The West lured others as well, such as William Williamson of County Armagh, who wrote to his brother that after arriving in New York "the rest of us put for the Good land of Illinois," where they eventually landed at Belvidere and promptly encountered an Irishman with "fifty acres of as good land as is in the state of Illinois. It is what is called here prairie, no trees or any [amount] of timber on it. . . ."

Lured by this vision of the West, thousands of Irish immigrants came by ship, canalboat, wagon, and foot to the Upper Mississippi Valley. Illinois had 27,786 of them by 1850 and 87,573 just a decade later. Missouri's Irish total rose from 14,734 in 1850 to 43,464 in 1860. Wisconsin went from 21,043 to 49,961 in the same ten-year span, while Iowa's Irish total was rising from 4,885 in 1850 (mainly in Dubuque County in the lead district) to 28,072 in 1860. This meant that the number of Irish in the region tripled during the decade before the Civil War, from 68,448 to 209,070. . . .

Mainly the better-off Irishmen left in the early years, but increasingly, poor peasants went as well. While "the better class of farmers in the county of Wexford" were reported in the exodus in the summer of 1850, an account from County Kerry the following summer also noted that "a very large proportion of those who are now leaving the county are poor persons." The reason: they "have had the means of emigration supplied to them by friends already in America." This observation impressed a Quaker leader testifying before a parliamentary committee on his relief work. A "very remarkable feature" of this exodus, he stated, was that relatives emigrating have "to an extent almost incredible, remitted money to their kindred at home."

It impressed Americans, too, when they saw poor Irish immigrants sending one pound a week home to help others in their families to cross over. Buried in the reports of individual American agents transferring $50,000 to Ireland over a twelve-month period were tales of individual heroism and sacrifice: the Irish immigrant woman toiling for two years to raise money to bring her six children to Chicago; the newcomer working to pay for his aged mother's trip. The process was eased when steamship lines began permitting Irish people in America to purchase fares for their families' journeys "from any port in Ireland, thro' to Milwaukee or Chicago. . . ."

. . . During the years following the famine, shipboard conditions deteriorated rapidly, and although by 1850 travel time had improved to under forty days to cross to Quebec and Montreal, this was still long enough to allow serious shipboard problems to develop. Passengers found that supplies promised by shipping agents were inadequate, although back in port they had sounded satisfactory enough. "Provisions at the rate of 2½ lbs. biscuit, 1 lb. flour, 5 lbs. oatmeal, 2 lbs. rice, 2 ozs. tea, 1 lb. sugar and molasses, and 21 quarts water, will be issued to each passenger weekly, with abundance of fuel and medicine," claimed a ship running from Cork to New York. A literate and articulate traveler in 1847 reported to Parliament that "the meat was of the worst quality" and, although enough water was taken on board, it was not distributed in adequate amounts, so that salt and rice had to be thrown overboard. He wrote that some passengers stayed for days "in their dark close berths, because they thus suffered less from hunger." But to this complaining passenger, disease and death did not form the only outcome of such a trip. A worse result, he said, was "the utter demoralisation of the passengers, both male and female, by the filth, debasement, and disease of two or three months so passed."

Other problems appeared as the vessels crossed the Atlantic. An Englishman traveling on a ship filled with Irish emigrants noted horrible conditions but blamed it on the Irish: "They where durty beyond all reason, did nothing but sleep all day, and prowl about at knight." Fighting placed someone in irons most days, he added, but he admitted that some of the trouble could be blamed on the ship's accommodations: "one stove for 300 passengers to cook by," resulting in many getting scalded, while "fighting for there crock of scilley called so by Irish." Anything laid down was lost if not guarded; "turn your head to one side it vanished to be found no more."

A new British passenger act in the spring of 1850 brought improvements, and complaints from immigrants began to decline. As a result, tales of shipboard life were varied among the 1.7 million Irish emigrating to "Amerikay" during the first decade after the famine began in 1845.

Many new arrivals in America searched to find other Irishmen, not a difficult task by mid-century. Daniel Guiny wrote from Buffalo that higher wages were possible if his group split up, "but we would sooner be all together." Soon after William Porter reached Chicago, he left his boardinghouse and "went to board with people from Ireland and I feel quite as well as if I was at home."

Many others also found their way inland quickly, directed both by advertisements and by reports of earlier travelers. An immigrant in Washington County, Iowa, told his friends in Ireland to "get a passage to Phildalfe than tak the rail roads fur Pitsburg . . . then over the Ohio river to the mouth ove the Mississippi river, thens to St. Luis, thens to Burlington in Iowa." Advertisements in Irish newspapers told of ships going directly to New Orleans, "the highway to the far west of America," where passengers could connect with steamboats up the Mississippi and Missouri rivers "to the rich districts of Illinois and Missouri and other western states." Soon reports told of vast numbers of immigrants on the Ohio and Mississippi riverboats, the greater number of them as deck passengers, where they were thrown in with the heterogeneous frontier population described by a traveling Irish priest: "Cards gentlemen and ladies all the way — such folks as met on Mississippi never met before — pick rascals of the United States."

To many, however, arrival in the New World brought no immediate relief from their suffering, but only prolonged it. When the ship *Waterford* landed at St. John's, Newfoundland in 1848, the British emigration officer there reported that he "observed some very miserable and emaciated persons"; all were able to walk to the reception buildings "although afflicted with fever and dysentery to a certain extent." He concluded he had rarely seen "a more dirty, reckless, and apparently lawless set of people" than the majority of those passengers. Long suffering, he added, "seems to have deprived them of all moral sense." Soon the arrivals of immigrants coming up the Mississippi to St. Louis brought such scenes to that city, and a special hospital was built near the docks for ailing or dying immigrants.

This portion of the emigration was ready prey for the hordes of sharpers in the ports. William Lalor admitted that his early troubles in America came mainly from his "total ignorance of the ways, manners, customs, prices . . . of the country by which I got fooled out of all my money within three weeks after landing." After that he became ill for some time. Many other immigrants lost out to the "runners" who soon surrounded them as they left the boat or inland stagecoach. "They thrust themselves upon [the immigrant] — they pull him this way and that — they stick their noses quite into his face — each claiming him as his own exclusive property." These runners fought for his trunk, demanding to take him to a hotel, which often was "a dirty, seven-by-nine barroom filled with loafers," in which he was forced to pay a dollar to escape. Some runners boarded trains, pretended to be railroad officials, and told immigrants their tickets were inaccurate but that properly made tickets could be bought from the runner. One report claimed that runners on trains coming westward to Chicago were changing thirty to forty tickets a day in this manner.

America was not turning out to be the paradise many had expected. One Irishman making his way west was greeted with help-wanted signs in Pennsylvania that read: "Niggers or Irish need not apply." A touring Irish priest was similarly dismayed by his irreverent traveling companions on a stagecoach crossing southern Wisconsin: "1 fellow ridiculed me hard and blasphemed at me three several times — others said nothing to him. . . . Today all rascals in stage — oh, oh!! obscenity oaths blasphemies. . . . Oh, what I suffered."

This was the New World: opportunity, but hard work; jobs, but insecurity of tenure; freedom of religion, but a surrounding population of critics, ridiculers, and proselytizers. The shock must have been great for many who had expected to find streets paved with gold. Irish immigrants landing at Boston's Deer Island reception station in 1850, accompanied by their priests, were taken first to a bathhouse, stripped of their clothes (which were burned), scrubbed with soap and water, given a haircut, and then required to attend Sabbath services. The priests' attempts to interfere with these arrangements were firmly rebuffed.

It would be no easy journey, this new life in America.

Immigrants learned early in the canal era that one of their principal barriers to an adequate existence was the uncertainty of wage payments. This problem would occur over and over for workmen as industrialism moved into the American frontier, where cash was in short supply and employers were often hundreds or thousands of miles away. The problem first hit the La Salle area during the 1830s, when canal laborers were repeatedly left unpaid for months while contractors scurried about the landscape rounding up cash. As the fifties dawned, the same phenomenon plagued railroad workmen, and their situation was worsened by the fact that thousands of them had been lured to the Upper Mississippi by the promise of high wages.

"WANTED! THREE THOUSAND LABORERS" the Illinois Central advertisements proclaimed in New York. One Irish carpenter reported in 1852 that after reading such handbills he had gone to the company's New York office, where agent Phelps had "positively asserted that I would have $2 per day, and that boarding could be had from $1.25 to $1.50." When this

Irishman arrived in Illinois, however, he found that "no carpenters were wanted" by the line. Other Irishmen told of large numbers of their countrymen hired with similar inducements, $1 a day promised, spending $5 apiece for passage to Chicago, and then beginning to work only to discover that wages were being cut without notice. When this occurred at Dixon, Illinois, and a group of railroad laborers demanded to be paid, they were told to come back in another month. Desperate for his wages and unable to wait a month, one of the Irishmen pressed forward, complaining vociferously, but he was suddenly confronted by the contractor's revolver aimed at his head. The worker was informed that "if he uttered another word" the contractor "would blow his brains out."

With top-level decisions and lower-level practices all geared to producing an abundant supply of labor, immigrants continued to be victimized by false promises. The Illinois Central's construction chief received a frantic note in late September of 1852 that some six hundred destitute Irishmen had arrived at Chicago to begin work: "What shall be done? They say Phelps promised employment on arriving in Chicago."

Soon the *Western Tablet,* the Irish Catholic newspaper published in Chicago, was reporting numerous cases of "scoundralism" against Irish workmen. The incidents followed the same pattern, although sometimes recruitment had occurred in Chicago rather than New York. Two Irishmen wrote that they had responded to handbills seeking three hundred men to work on the Wisconsin and Chicago railroad line, some thirty miles north of Chicago, with wages of one dollar a day promised and "every necessary comfort would be provided for our accommodation at the work." Once employed, the pair found that the foreman's "brutality and tyranny would eclipse that of any Negro driver," while bed and board were "of the most filthy and abominable kind." The two described what happened next: "Having been employed for about two days and a half, the boss informed us that he considered he had already sufficient men in the two gangs — there were in all about forty-five, and yet he had advertised for three hundred — so he would dispense with our services. On going to the office for settlement, instead of allowing us for the full time employed, we were curtailed about half a day, and ordered to take our wages out in goods from the store."

There were many more of these incidents — workmen counting railroad ties walked away unpaid, immigrants wondering why they had left their homes across the sea for this. Resentment and cynicism followed. "The 'poor exiles of Erin' are gulled and fleeced enough by the vultures and harpies of New York," one infuriated Irishman wrote after learning of a company's false recruitment claims, "without being cozened by cheating advertisements of 'three thousand men wanted on the railroad.'" These developments formed a large part of the backdrop for the drama that unfolded in La Salle and Peru in December 1853.

The facts, as sifted from a variety of often contradictory records, appear to be as follows: the predominantly Irish crew of some 450 men, working on excavations and the embankment for the Illinois Central bridge over the Illinois River, were informed in early December that their $1.25 daily wage had been retroactively cut to $1. Those dissatisfied would be paid off and dropped December 15, announced contractor Albert Story. Many of the men then went on strike, seeking to block others from working, hoping to force the contractor to pay them the promised wage.

On the fifteenth, as wages were being given out, an error was found in payroll records, and payments were suddenly stopped. The angered employees rushed to the contractor's office the next day and demanded their pay; in the scuffle the contractor, Story, was struck. He drew his pistol, fired, and fatally wounded one of his attackers. Story then hurried home, unaware that a railroad superintendent had already rescued Mrs. Story and the children. When he found his family gone, Story ran to the stable to get his horse, but the mob caught him and pummeled him to death with picks, shovels, and stones. That evening the sheriff and a posse began arresting Irishmen in their shanties and on neighboring hills.

Coming at a time of increasing tensions between native-born Americans and immigrants and between industrial workers and employers, the La Salle killings provoked a storm of indignation. The reform journal *Free West* stated that Story was killed while "defending his property" and claimed that the mob also tried to kill his wife and children; the journal conceded, however, that the workmen attacked "in consequence of a reduction in wages." From the German community of Belleville, the *Belleviller Zeitung* reported simply that it was a riot of Irish workers, with no mention of the wage cut. Reporting the militia's roundup of Irishmen, the *Chicago Tribune* proclaimed: "Had the whole thirty-two prisoners that were taken been marched out and shot on the spot, . . . the public judgment would have sanctioned it at once." The *North-Western Christian Advocate* provided its analysis: "Probable cause — rum."

Closer examination reveals a more complex situation. One major point was that the contractor had advertised widely for workmen at the $1.25-per-day wage and hundreds had arrived by November as winter began. Then came Story's blunt announcement of the wage reduction. To Irish workmen in America in 1853, a notice of wage reduction and a delay in payment were simply repetitions of an old theme; all events conformed to the pattern. Because the Irish felt themselves surrounded by a hostile community that regarded them as intruders and derelicts, their vigorous reaction is perhaps more understandable. (As Albert Story ran to his stable he yelled back that he was "man enough for a hundred Irishmen.") In contrast to the implications of the newspaper reports, the *Western Tablet* described the slain Irishman, Ryan, as a father of two children, who "had the name of being an honest and peaceable man."

The Illinois Central quickly decided to "clear the bluff of any vestige" of the former crew and began the bridge project anew with different contractors as well as new employees, guarded by soldiers. Although it was reported in the aftermath of the riot that "the ringleaders have all fled," twelve men were indicted and four were convicted of murder, but Governor Joel A. Matteson pardoned them after a circuit judge noted that none of the four was ever shown to have been a leader or participant in the murder. The governor, perhaps with an eye to the enormous immigrant vote, but certainly aware as well of La Salle's social and political environment, justified mercy toward the four Irishmen by noting that Story "shot one of their countrymen at a time when the Irish felt they had not been very well used, and when a good deal of excitement had prevailed upon the work. . . . A large number were present, and on the shooting of the man by Story there seemed to be created a general panic among the men and great excitement prevailed."

Reports in the Irish *Western Tablet* also went beyond the bare events, contending that "so long as railroad companies and contractors persist in holding out false promises to laborers, in order to allure them to leave comfortable employment and good homes, to live in rotten shanties and dismal swamps, we have no hope that this will be the last outrage of this kind."

The La Salle murders had a strong impact on the immediate area. Governor Matteson was hung in effigy when he visited La Salle, and the local native-born element grew bitter over the lack of a crackdown against the Irish. The following summer twenty-six community leaders informed the editor of a La Salle newspaper that they were withdrawing their patronage because, since Story's murder, he had "both truckled and bowed to Irish arrogance and outrage," and he had supported the governor's pardons for those convicted.

STUDY GUIDE

1. Irish emigration has sometimes been explained only in terms of the famine. Explain the role in emigration of religion, government, and the relation of population to available land.

2. How do you explain the poor economic and social conditions of the Irish once they arrived in America? Why was there less animosity towards some other groups, such as the Germans, though they were less likely to speak English?

3. The selection is concerned only with pre–Civil War migration, which was mostly from northern and western Europe. Based on your knowledge, indicate in what areas each of the following settled and what occupations

they tended to enter: Germans, Scandinavians, Hungarians, Jews, Poles, Italians.

4. There is not necessarily a positive relationship between attitudes of tolerance toward other groups and a history of having been persecuted or discriminated against oneself. How can you explain this irony, which we know to be characteristic of many minority groups?

5. What factors in modern American economic life and in new social attitudes might make a cultural pluralism, in which various nationalities and races live in mutual respect and appreciation of their differences, more feasible in the United States today than in the early nineteenth century?

BIBLIOGRAPHY

The study of immigration as a significant theme in the American experience is a relatively recent phenomenon. Two older studies by Marcus Lee Hansen are well worth reading: *The Immigrant in American History* (edited with a foreword by Arthur Schlesinger, Sr., 1940), and *The Atlantic Migration 1607–1860* (edited with a foreword by Arthur Schlesinger, Sr., 1945). Carl Wittke, *We Who Built America* (1964) is an especially well written account. More recent publications on this theme include a number of volumes by Oscar Handlin: his Pulitzer Prize-winning book, *The Uprooted: The Epic Story of the Great Migrations That Made the American People* (1951, revised 1973); *Race and Nationality in American Life* (1957), a series of essays on immigration; and *Immigration as a Factor in American History* (1969), a collection of documents relating to immigration with an introduction by Handlin.

A good, short survey of immigration as an aspect of American life is Maldwyn Jones, *American Immigration* (1960). Another general work by Jones is *Destination America* (1976), which has a great many illustrations of the immigrant experience. Thomas J. Archdeacon, *Becoming American: An Ethnic History* (1983) treats broad developments in ethnicity throughout American history, while John Bodnar, *The Transplanted: A History of Immigrants in Urban America* (1985) describes the impact of American capitalism on the immigrants and their institutions. Several of the major immigrant groups have been the subject of studies; others have not yet been seriously studied by professional historians. Four very good studies of different groups that migrated to the United States are Rowland T. Berthoff, *British Immigrants in Industrial America, 1790–1950* (1953); Theodore Saloutos, *The Greeks in the United States* (1964); Terry Coleman, *Passage to America: A History of Emigrants from Great Britain and Ireland to America in the Mid-Nineteenth Century* (1972); and Andrew Rolle, *The Italian Americans: Troubled Roots* (1980). Other specialized works treat the adjustment of different nationalities in America and the role of such traditional institutions as the church in the lives of the immigrants. Three works of this sort are Oscar Handlin, *Boston's Immigrants, 1790–1880: A Study in Acculturation* (1941, revised 1959); Louis Wirth, *The Ghetto* (1928), a classic study of Eastern European Jewish response to Chicago; and a more recent study by Jay P. Dolan, *The Immigrant Church: New York's Irish and German Catholics, 1815–1865* (1975). Lawrence J. McCaffrey, *The Irish Diaspora in America* (1984) deals with the spread of the Irish in this country, and Hasia R. Diner writes of Irish immigrant women in *Erin's Daughters in America* (1983). Ray A. Billington, *The Protestant Crusade, 1800–1860* (1938) is a study of nativism. An article on religious prejudice and anti-immigrant feeling is David B. Davis, "Some Themes of Counter-Subversion: An Analysis of Anti-Masonic, Anti-Catholic, and Anti-Mormon Literature," *Mississippi Valley Historical Review*, Vol. XLVII (1960), pp. 205–224.

Philadelphia's 1844 anti-Catholic riot, which required calling in the state militia, suggests the crime and violence that plagued early nineteenth-century cities.

17

MICHAEL FELDBERG

Urban Problems

Today a vast majority of the United States population lives in sizeable towns and large cities. Along the Atlantic seaboard, farmlands near the great urban centers have been turned into housing developments at such a rate that the hundreds of miles between Washington, D.C., and Boston are becoming one great urban corridor. The American people have become so thoroughly an urban people that few are left who know the difference between timothy and alfalfa or who have any idea of what the farm machine known as a harrow does. In recent years, an increasing number of farm museums have developed, where city folks can go on a Sunday afternoon to look at weathered farm equipment and see live sheep and cattle. There is a considerable irony in all this, since during much of American history the country was predominantly rural and the American dream was the acquisition of one or two hundred acres one could farm for oneself.

In the eighteenth century, most centers of settlement were nothing more than tiny farming villages. Boston, the largest city in 1730, had 13,000 people, while Philadelphia was second with 11,500 and New York third with 8,500. As late as 1790, the population of the largest American city, Philadelphia, numbered only 30,000. By 1860, it had risen to an incredible 565,000; New York was home to more than 800,000; and the relatively new, western metropolis of Cincinnati had 160,000 people. The extraordinary growth of cities in the nineteenth century brought new problems and required new policies and institutions for the solving of some of the older problems.

Epidemics of cholera and yellow fever swept American cities in the early nineteenth century, taking as many as 3,500 lives in a single year in New York. In the same city, hundreds of homeless poor, including orphaned children, roamed the streets begging, and tens of thousands of people lived in dark cellar holes and tenement buildings. Crime and gang violence became critical problems in the larger cities, as did the problem of supplying water, fire protection, and other services to these vast metropolitan areas. Singing the old refrain that the city is "a great place to visit, but I wouldn't want to live there," a visitor to New York in 1828 said that something about it made it "more a gratification to visit, than to abide."

Some of the urban problems were solved by private efforts, some by the development of professional government service departments to replace the earlier private fire-protection clubs. In 1860, for example, 79 private companies and 57 public works supplied water to the cities. Protection against crime and the devastating riots that swept American cities led to the creation of modern, trained police forces. The riots involved many different groups and issues, ranging from religious and ethnic hostilities to political warfare, economic competition for jobs, and abolitionist activity. The following essay by Michael Feldberg depicts crowd violence in Philadelphia in the 1840s.

Americans who remember the urban unrest of the 1960s can readily identify with the crisis of violence that gripped Jacksonian American cities. The 1830s, 1840s, and 1850s produced a constant stream of riots reminiscent of the "long hot summers" of the not-too-distant past. Jacksonian cities were torn by fighting between immigrants and native-born Americans, abolitionists and anti-abolitionists, free blacks and racist whites, volunteer firefighters and street gangs, Mormons and "Gentiles," even rival factions of Whigs and Democrats. And, like the 1960s, Jacksonian collective violence resulted in greatly enlarged and strengthened police forces better able to repress riots and disorders — either with or without death or injury to the rioters.

Yet there are some notable differences between the upheavals of the pre–Civil War decades and those of the 1960s. Compared with the death and devastation in Watts, Newark, or Detroit, Jacksonian rioting seems rather tame. Whereas a few major confrontations in the 1840s and 1850s took the lives of at least a dozen persons, deaths in Jacksonian rioting were a relatively rare occurrence. Certainly the property damage to Washington, D.C., after the assassination of Martin Luther King, Jr., or to Harlem during the New York Blackout of 1977, was unequaled by even the most destructive pre–Civil War violence.

From *The Turbulent Era: Riot and Disorder in Jacksonian America* by Michael Feldberg. Copyright © 1980 by Oxford University Press, Inc. Reprinted by permission.

In its own way, however, urban rioting posed for Jacksonian society a social and political crisis seemingly equal to that of the 1960s era of protest. To some contemporaries, violence in the 1830s and 1840s portended the possible destruction of American civilization. . . . As sober an analyst as Abraham Lincoln warned in 1837 that

> . . . there is even now something of an ill omen amongst us. . . . Accounts of outrages committed by mobs form the every-day news of the times. They have pervaded the country from New England to Louisiana; they are neither peculiar to the eternal snows of the former nor the burning suns of the latter; they are not the creatures of climate, neither are they confined to the slaveholding or the non-slaveholding states. Alike they spring up among the pleasure-hunting master of Southern slaves, and the order-loving citizens of the land of steady habits. Whatever their causes be, it is common to the whole country.

Lincoln was not exaggerating the dimensions of the crisis. Historian Richard Maxwell Brown has counted thirty-five major riots in Baltimore, Philadelphia, New York, and Boston during the three decades from 1830 to 1860. Historian John C. Schneider found that "at least seventy percent of American cities with a population of twenty thousand or more by 1850 experienced some degree of major disorder in the 1830–1865 period." The abolitionist movement, which kept its own count of anti-abolition and racially motivated mobs, reported no less than 209 such incidents for the 1830s and 1840s alone. . . .

The historical significance of rioting in a given period should not be measured solely by its frequency or intensity. Collective violence should be judged in its broader social and political contexts as well; it must be seen as one of several forms of interaction that can occur among groups, or between groups and their government. We must look at the functions Jacksonian rioting served, the kinds of groups that employed it, and the success of those groups in using violence to attain their goals. In the Jacksonian context, collective violence was one means by which various groups attempted to control competition among themselves, or by which they responded to changes in their relative status, power, wealth, or political influence.

. . . Jacksonian collective violence stemmed from a number of sources: the racial and ethnic tensions of the period; the era's ideological climate; the inability of political systems and legal institutions to resolve group conflict by peaceable means; rapid urbanization and population changes; and economic and technological innovation. What distinguishes Jacksonian rioting from collective violence in other periods of American history is not its sources, however, but the frequency of its occurrence, its effectiveness, and the relative inability of public authorities to control or suppress it. Yet the very success achieved by private groups through rioting called forth forces that, by the 1850s, would change the balance of power between rioters and local peacekeeping officials and impose professional police systems on American cities. The epidemic of collective violence in Jacksonian cities ultimately undermined the American public's traditional resistance to the creation of effective urban police forces. By the time of the Civil War, most of the nation's important cities had established recognizably modern police departments. . . . The creation of urban police departments became the most enduring legacy of Jacksonian collective violence.

The great Philadelphia Native American Riots of 1844 were certainly among the most dramatic and violent episodes in pre–Civil War American history. In both their Kensington and Southwark phases, they present a capsule portrait of the sources, uses, and consequences of Jacksonian collective violence. Although they grew out of cultural and religious conflict between Philadelphia's Protestant nativists and Irish Catholic immigrants, the riots were the immediate result of a political controversy over the use of the Bible in the Philadelphia public schools. The fighting also reflected the social and political disorganization of Philadelphia and the weakness of its peacekeeping system. . . . Above all, the two phases of the Philadelphia Native American Riots of 1844 illustrate the ease with which private groups in Jacksonian America employed collective violence as a tool for conducting social conflict and expressing political protest. The riots also reveal the difficulties public authorities faced when they tried to control group violence in the nation's rapidly changing cities.

By February 1844, Louisa Bedford had finally run out of patience. She was having a difficult enough time teaching elementary school in Kensington, a working-class suburb just north of Philadelphia. Now her job was made even more trying because of hard feelings between the parents of both her immigrant Irish Catholic students and her native-born Protestant students. . . . Two years earlier, in 1842, the Philadelphia County Board of School Controllers had ordered that the King James, or Protestant, version of Holy Scripture be used as a basic reading text in all Philadelphia public school classes. Upon hearing this, the Catholic Bishop of Philadelphia, the Reverend Francis Patrick Kenrick, asked that Catholic children be allowed to read the Douay, or authorized Catholic, version of Scripture, and that Catholic teachers not be compelled to read from the King James during reading exercises. The controllers denied Kenrick's request.

During the 1840s many American Protestants feared Catholicism because it seemed alien and anti-democratic. . . . Because of this widely held prejudice, the Philadelphia School Controllers were afraid to grant equal status to the Douay Bible by allowing it in the schools. . . . Yet to ease

Bishop Kenrick's objections to an obvious injustice, the Board of School Controllers saw fit to offer a compromise solution: Catholic children could leave their classrooms while Bible-reading exercises were conducted, but the Douay version was still not to be admitted into the schools.

This compromise pleased almost no one. Catholics believed that the plan ignored their bishop's plea for justice and equality; evangelical Protestants felt that Catholic children should be compelled to read the King James version as an antidote to their "priestly dictated" and "popish" beliefs. The solution also failed to please teachers like Louisa Bedford, who could not tolerate the disruption caused by her Catholic students waiting noisily outside her door until the Bible-reading session was over. To remedy this situation, Bedford took actions which, in a short time, led to the great Philadelphia riots of 1844.

Louisa Bedford was a Protestant, although not a militant evangelical. Seriously committed to teaching the working-class children of Kensington to read and write, she resented the chaos caused by the controllers' policy. Thus when School Controller and Irish Catholic politician Hugh Clark was making his weekly tour of Kensington's public schools, Bedford asked Clark if she could have a word with him. She explained her unhappiness to the politically astute Clark who, one suspects, was waiting for just such a moment. Clark then sympathetically offered an alternative to sending Catholic students out of her room: She could suspend *all* Bible reading in her class until such time as the School Controllers devised a better method for excusing Catholic students from the exercise. Clark volunteered to assume responsibility should she decide to follow this course. Bedford chose to accept Clark's offer and told her students that, for the time being, they would not have to do their Bible reading. Much to her relief, she turned to teaching other subjects.

. . . Word of Clark's decision to "kick the Bible out of the schools," as his enemies inaccurately described it, spread like wildfire throughout the city. Evangelical Protestants, most of them native-born Americans and the remainder immigrant Irish Protestants, had been organizing in Philadelphia for nearly a decade. The evangelicals were alarmed by what they believed to be the growing political and religious influence of Catholics, particularly Irish Catholic immigrants. Nativists, a name given to those who openly opposed all "alien" elements such as Catholics, immigrants, Mormons, and others who did not conform to the dominant white Protestant religious and cultural values of the era, had especially feared the political activism of the Irish Catholic clergy. . . . Protestants concerned with the increasing influence of Catholics and immigrants in American life joined a new political movement known as the American Republican party, which had branches in Philadelphia, New York, Boston, Baltimore, and New Orleans. The American Republicans held rallies and ran candidates to oppose the influence of immigrants in local politics. . . .

For the most part, American Republican leadership in Philadelphia was composed of "middling" and "respectable" men: lawyers, doctors, clergy-men, newspaper editors, shopkeepers, craftsmen, printers, barbers, den-tists, and teachers. These individuals were neither numbered in the ranks of the city's traditional upper classes — wealthy merchants, bankers, manufacturers, and gentlemen farmers — nor drawn from the ranks of the struggling poor. Rather, these American Republicans had formerly provided the bulk of middle-class voters for the Whig and Democratic parties. With their wives they filled the pews of Philadelphia's Methodist, Baptist, and Presbyterian churches. By their own description they saw themselves as the "bone and sinew" of society, the hard-working silent majority who, while never independently wealthy and secure like the upper classes, would never allow themselves to fall to the level of the impoverished or degenerate immigrants.

Because they saw themselves as the nation's only "real" Americans, nativists could not stand to see their public schools, or the political system in general, "captured" by persons who spoke with a foreign accent — especially an Irish brogue. The social isolation of America's Irish immi-grants and their continued loyalty to their native land particularly worried American nativists. They believed that the typical Irish immigrant would never become a loyal American citizen, freed of his allegiance to Ireland or to the Roman Catholic Church. They did not realize that the experiences of Irish Catholic immigrants with English-speaking Protestants had con-vinced the Irish to cling to their religion and to their nationalism. . . .

To maintain their solidarity, to resist integration into a Protestant-dominated society such as the one they had fled, the American Irish tended to cluster in self-imposed ghettos, to socialize in their own taverns, to attend mass in their own parish churches, and to meet in their own political and nationalist clubs. Such self-inflicted isolation upset Protestant American nativists, but the apparent political control that the Irish-born Catholic clergy seemed to exercise over their immigrant followers appeared to bother them even more. Nativists convinced one another that the American Irish voted overwhelmingly for the Democratic party, not because the Jacksonian political platform or personal style appealed to the newcomers, but because corrupt Roman Catholic priests "dictated" voting orders from Rome to their sheeplike parishioners. . . .

Philadelphia American Republicanism was closely allied with the most popular reform movement of the era, the temperance crusade. At its inception in the early 1800s, the American temperance movement was dedicated to persuading individuals to consume only moderate amounts of alcoholic beverages. In the 1840s, its national membership may have numbered over 100,000, and most of these members believed that all sales of drinking alcohol should be outlawed. Alcoholism had become closely associated with poverty, unemployment, crime, ill health, and broken families. Somewhat unfairly, it was also closely associated with urban immigrant communities: gin and rum with the Irish, beer with the Germans, and wine with the French and Italians. Since nativists considered immigrant groups, and especially the Irish, responsible for most of the nation's poverty, crime, and prostitution, their interest in temperance reflected their critical attitudes toward the life-styles of America's urban immigrant populations.

It was unfair of nativists and temperance advocates to equate alcohol consumption primarily with immigrants. The nation's upper classes were the chief consumers of good French wines, port, sherry, and Madeira. Many native Protestant workingmen were paid a portion of their wages in a daily allowance of rum, and nearly every workshop and factory employed young boys to run out frequently for buckets of beer. Drinking to excess was a universal problem that crossed ethnic and class boundaries. The vast quantities of alcohol consumed in Jacksonian America convinced many temperance advocates, nativist and non-nativist alike, that an individual's mere verbal pledge to drink moderately was not enough to keep him from abusing alcohol, and temperance crusaders increasingly switched from a voluntarist to a prohibitionist position. They argued that only by outlawing the sale of liquor could its evil effects be controlled.

The conversion of Philadelphia's temperance movement to a prohibitionist stance was tied in important ways to the American Republican and evangelical Protestant movements of the era. Closing bars and rum shops could have important social and political implications for immigrant communities. Taverns were one of the focal points in working-class Irish and German neighborhoods, and they often served as social and political centers. Their patrons did not usually welcome native Protestant — or even other ethnic — outsiders, and many a Philadelphia brawl was started when an unwitting stranger of the wrong ethnic background violated the sanctity of a German or Irish saloon. Particularly in Irish neighborhoods, taverns became symbols of Irish-Catholic separatism and Irish immigrant rejection of integration into wider American culture.

But nativists had political as well as cultural objections to the immigrants' fondness for alcoholic beverages. They argued that just as priests could control the consciences of immigrant Catholics through the religious doctrine of papal infallibility, so could tavern owners manipulate the political loyalties of immigrants by trading liquor for votes. Nativist temperance advocates feared an unholy alliance between Catholic priests and ambitious tavern-owning politicians that would maintain the immigrants' dependence on the Church and the bottle. The battle against liquor, then, was in part a battle to preserve American political freedom from Catholic-sponsored conspiracies.

One person's reform, though, is another person's oppression, especially when the targets of the reform movement saw nothing wrong in their style of life or religious values. Catholic and Irish community leaders believed strongly that the Constitution entitled community members to liberty of conscience in their religion, freedom of association in their social contacts, freedom of thought in their political beliefs, and freedom of choice in their use of alcohol. The Catholic Archdiocese of Philadelphia organized its own voluntary temperance societies, but it strongly opposed any attempt to legislate away the individual's right to indulge in alcohol. And while it urged its parishioners to attend mass on Sunday, the Archdiocese resisted efforts to suppress popular amusements on the Sabbath. Most important, Bishop Kenrick personally resented the efforts of Protestant activists to "save" Catholic children by forcing them to read the King James Bible in the public schools.

Unfortunately for Bishop Kenrick and the rest of Philadelphia's Catholics, the school Bible issue stirred intense hatred in the "City of Brotherly Love." The city's nativists chose (deliberately or otherwise) to interpret Kenrick's request to grant equality to the Douay Bible as a demand that the King James Bible be *removed* from the public schools. . . .

Thus it is clear why Hugh Clark's suggestion to Louisa Bedford that she suspend Bible reading in her Kensington classroom caused such upheaval throughout Philadelphia. It was as if the bishop's alleged conspiracy had finally come out in the open. The first word of Clark's actions was carried by Henry Moore, a Methodist minister who burst into a prayer meeting at his Kensington church to inform the congregation that Clark had forced Miss Bedford against her will to "kick the Bible out of her classroom." Word spread rapidly throughout the city's nativist network, and Philadelphia's American Republican leaders and evangelical Protestant clergymen convened a series of mass rallies in mid-March to protest Catholic attempts to "trample our free Protestant institutions in the dust." At one rally more than 3,000 protestors gathered to hear an American Republican spokesman remind those who would "remove the Bible from the public schools" that, "when we remember that our Pilgrim Fathers landed on Plymouth Rock to establish the Protestant religion, free from persecution, we must contend that this was and always will be a Protestant country."

Their enthusiastic reception at the city-wide rallies encouraged the American Republicans to carry their crusade right to the lair of the beast, the very neighborhood that symbolized Irish Catholic solidarity in Philadelphia: Third Ward, Kensington. The community was long and widely recognized as immigrant Irish "turf." It was dominated by Irish handloom weavers, dock laborers, teamsters, and other semiskilled workers who held little love for their native Protestant neighbors in adjoining wards. The neighborhood had been the scene of several riots in recent years, including a series of attacks on railroad construction workers trying to lay tracks down Front Street and some violent attacks on nonunion weavers who were failing to honor a strike by their fellow "brothers of the loom." Perhaps the most notorious incident had occurred a few months earlier, when the striking weavers attacked and dispersed a sheriff's posse, beat the sheriff soundly, and had to be quelled by the state militia troops. It was in this neighborhood of militant and aggressive Irish immigrants that the American Republicans chose to hold a rally on Friday afternoon, May 3, 1844, and invite the general public to attend.

That Friday meeting might well have been calculated to provoke a fateful confrontation with Kensington's immigrant Irish. The American Republicans chose to hold their rally in a schoolyard at Second and Master streets. When the American Republican spokesmen began their speeches, they were heckled, booed, and pelted with rocks and garbage by a crowd of several hundred, and eventually driven from the speaker's platform they had erected earlier in the afternoon. Undaunted (and quite self-righteously), the party decided to reconvene the meeting in the schoolyard on Monday, May 6, and placarded the city with notices urging every American Republican loyalist to attend. This time a large crowd of 3,000 turned out. Around 3:00 P.M., while noted temperance lecturer and political nativist Lewis C. Levin was arousing the crowd's interest, a sudden rainstorm erupted and the crowd moved spontaneously in search of shelter toward the Nanny Goat Market.

Relocating the rally in the market proved catastrophic. The Nanny Goat Market was the hub of the Third Ward Irish community. An open-sided, block-long covered shed at Third and Master streets, the market house served as a shopping center, a meeting place, and a social center for local residents. When the noisy but peaceable nativists arrived, a group of thirty or so Irish locals was waiting there to greet them. One Irishman was heard to proclaim, "Keep the damned natives out of our market house; this ground don't belong to them, it's ours!" Lewis Levin tried to continue his speech from a vendor's stand but hecklers drowned him out. Pushing and shoving began, someone pulled a pistol, a rival dared him to shoot, he did, and panic erupted under the shed. The Irish residents fled to their nearby homes, but the nativists were trapped in the open-sided shed with few places to hide. A rain of gunfire poured down on them from surrounding buildings, most of it from the Hibernia Hose House, the headquarters of an Irish volunteer fire company. The first nativist killed in the shooting, nineteen-year-old George Schiffler, became a martyr to the cause. His name was soon immortalized when a nativist militia company, a volunteer fire company, and a fighting street gang each took his name as their own. In subsequent years the street gang known as the Schifflers would fight many battles with Philadelphia's Irish and Democratic street gangs and volunteer fire companies.

The initial advantage possessed by the Irish snipers was soon balanced by the arrival of approximately eighteen nativist reinforcements who brought rifles and shotguns with them. Protected by the fire of their own sharpshooters, nativists began making forays out of the Nanny Goat Market, breaking windows and doors of the houses from which gunfire had been coming and scattering the inhabitants. Several Irishmen were badly beaten and left for dead as others saw their homes and furniture wrecked by the furious nativists. Finally, after two hours of heavy fighting, Sheriff Morton McMichael and a posse of two hundred deputies arrived and the fighting subsided.

That night, when darkness descended on Kensington, nativists from every corner of Philadelphia found their way to the neighborhood around the Nanny Goat Market. Around 10:00 P.M. a crowd "collected in the vicinity of Franklin and Second streets," marched toward the Nanny Goat Market, and on the way "commenced breaking into the houses on both sides of the street, destroying the furniture, demolishing the windows, and rendering the houses completely uninhabitable." The crowd then arrived at the gates of the seminary of the Catholic Sisters of Charity and were threatening to burn it down when a group of Irish defenders "advanced from above and fired a volley of ball and buckshot into the crowd." One nativist attacker died instantly, a second lingered for a month before dying of a chest wound, and several others were injured. On this note, Monday night's fighting in Kensington drew to a close.

Philadelphians awakened Tuesday morning, May 7, to find their city plastered with printed calls to a rally protesting the murder of George Schiffler. The message ended with the inflammatory words, "LET EVERY MAN COME PREPARED TO DEFEND HIMSELF." That morning, the nativist press was filled with militant cries for revenge. The daily *Native American* proclaimed:

> Another St. Bartholomew's day has begun in the streets of Philadelphia. The bloody hand of the Pope has stretched forth to our destruction. Now we call on our fellow-citizens, who regard free institutions, whether they be native or adopted, to arm. Our liberties are to be fought for — let us not be slack in our preparation.

By 3:30 P.M. that Tuesday afternoon, more than 3,000 persons had gathered behind Independence Hall to hear speeches condemning Kensington's Irish. . . .

When the speeches were finished and the American Republicans called for the meeting to adjourn, a voice in the crowd shouted, "Adjourn to Kensington right now!" The crowd took up the call, marched in loose military fashion out of the meeting ground, and turned northward to Kensington. When they arrived in the neighborhood of Second and Master, the marchers found that many of Kensington's Irish had fled the neighborhood and taken their belongings with them. Other inhabitants simply waited at home with their loaded guns. This time, the nativist procession did not pause to convene a meeting and hear speeches, but immediately attacked the Hibernia Hose House. Armed defenders there and in some of the houses along the street immediately opened fire, and in the few moments of shooting four nativists lay dead and eleven others fell wounded. The remaining nativists with a stomach for a fight retreated to the Nanny Goat Market for shelter, and it seemed that the pattern of the day before would repeat itself. This time, however, the nativists changed their tactics. Rather than try to shoot it out with the well-concealed Irish, the nativists snuck out of the market building and set fire to each of the houses from which gunfire had been coming. This tactic proved successful as hidden Irish snipers came tumbling out of the flaming buildings. They made easy targets for nativist gunners, and only poor nativist marksmanship explains why no Irishmen were killed. It was not until 5:00 P.M., nearly an hour after the shooting started, that General [George] Cadwalader, previously unprepared, arrived with several militia companies to restore order in the neighborhood.

The use of fire struck panic in the hearts of the remaining Kensington Irish, and by Wednesday morning most of them had packed their possessions and gone elsewhere to stay with friends and relatives, or to camp in the woods on the outskirts of Philadelphia. The militia was left to guard their abandoned homes, but the outnumbered soldiers were inadequate for the task. Roving bands of nativists snuck from house to house in the vicinity of the Nanny Goat Market and set each on fire. The city's volunteer firefighters, mostly native-born Americans, had little enthusiasm for fighting the flames. In addition, after setting up a diversion to draw the militia away, a group of arsonists gained access to St. Michael's Roman Catholic Church, whose priest had been an outspoken foe of nativism, and set it to the torch. Flames rapidly devoured the wooden structure, and as the cross fell from the toppling steeple the crowd cheered loudly. Volunteer firefighters, arriving on the scene, determined that the gathering would never permit them to extinguish the fire, so they contented themselves with hosing down nearby buildings to keep the flames from spreading. Other rioters completed the day's work by ransacking two stores that had been selling ammunition to Irish marksmen, and eventually they invaded the home of Hugh Clark, the man whose decision to suspend Bible reading in Louisa Bedford's class had provided the pretext for the fighting. The invaders threw Clark's valuable books and furniture into the street and used them to start a bonfire. Finally, several hours after the arson had begun in Kensington, General Cadwalader and Sheriff McMichael arrived with reinforcements and brought the wandering rioters under control.

Thus blocked, the angry nativists simply transferred their field of activity to downtown Philadelphia. By 10:30 that Wednesday night, a huge crowd had gathered in front of St. Augustine's Roman Catholic Church in the heart of that city. Although the mayor stood on the building's front steps and pleaded with the crowd to disperse, his appeals went unheard. Someone knocked him down by heaving a stone against his chest, and a young boy managed to sneak past the constables at a rear door and set the church afire. Within half an hour the $45,000 brick structure was a total loss. As the steeple fell, the crowd cheered as it had done at St. Michael's. Again the volunteer fireman dared only hose down nearby buildings.

The burning of St. Augustine's marked the last major violence in the Kensington phase of the Native American Riots. Governor David R. Porter placed Philadelphia under martial law, and the chief commander of the Pennsylvania militia, General Robert Patterson, took complete command of the city's government. More than 2,000 soldiers from across the state patrolled the streets of Philadelphia, and General Patterson banned all meetings and demonstrations. . . .

Martial law remained in effect for a week without a serious confrontation between troops and civilians, after which civilian government was restored to Philadelphia. Thus ended the Kensington phase of the 1844 Native American Riots.

The Kensington Riots had been the worst in Philadelphia's history. At least six persons had been killed, and as many as fifty had been seriously injured. Property losses in the three days of violence were conservatively estimated at $250,000, not counting the cost of medical bills and lost time from work.

While unusually destructive, the Kensington riots were in other ways typical of collective violence in the Jacksonian period. First, despite the fact that there was gunfire and killing in the first two days of fighting, it appears that only a relatively small portion of combatants on either side was armed. There is no way for us to know how many Philadelphians owned firearms in 1844, although rifles for hunting seem to have been quite common, and ammunition was widely sold in shops around the city. One of the stores set aflame by the crowd in Kensington, Corr's Grocery, was burned because its proprietor had been supplying bullets to his Irish compatriots. Jacksonian cities seem to have had no legal regulations about who could own, sell, or distribute guns or ammunition. Yet the use of guns by rioters was rarely reported in contemporary newspaper accounts. Crowds usually fought by hurling rocks, paving stones, bricks, and garbage, or by wielding clubs, knives, and slingshots. As a result, it was the exception rather than the rule for pre–Civil War rioting to claim the lives of its victims, or for more than one or two persons to be killed in the course of even the most serious fighting. During the three days and nights of the Kensington riots, for example, only one Irishman was killed, and he was an innocent bystander.

Second, the pattern of damage to property in Kensington indicates that, like most Jacksonian crowds, the nativist rioters exercised a good deal of restraint in their attacks. Despite their anger over the school Bible issue, the ambush at the Nanny Goat Market, and the murders of Schiffler and the others, it was not until Wednesday, two days after the outbreak of fighting, that widespread destruction was inflicted on Irish property. Before then only a few houses that had served as shelters for Irish snipers were targeted for burning. Other houses were stoned or damaged, but these two were suspected of harboring Irish marksmen. Even the choice of targets on Wednesday, when widespread arson was employed, was hardly random: Hugh Clark's house, his brother's tavern, Corr's Grocery, and two Catholic churches. Some additional homes may have been deliberately burned, especially in the area around the Nanny Goat Market, but many others fell unintended victim to the spreading flames. Rioters even bypassed the home of one elderly Irishman when they found him inside, too ill to make his escape. However much their anger had been provoked, the nativist rioters never rampaged through Kensington randomly destroying property or retaliating against whoever fell to hand. There was, in short, no orgy of irrational nativist fury. The rioters possessed clearly defined notions of what and who their targets ought to have been and why those targets deserved to suffer violence. While no one would argue that either the nativist or Irish rioters were acting dispassionately during the fighting, neither can one say that the rioters were insane, deranged, animalistic, or totally without sense or reason.

Third, the social composition of both sides in the Kensington riots was characteristic of that in many other Jacksonian riots. Contrary to many current stereotypes of rioters and looters, the Kensington combatants were not drawn from the poorest or most oppressed strata of Jacksonian society. The names of those injured or arrested, when traced to city directories, indicate that the rioters, frequently boys and young men in their twenties, were often employed as apprentice artisans, weavers, or laborers. They were not poverty-stricken outcasts, nor were they without a permanent residence. Many of the older men and women who participated on both sides were established members of their communities. Among the Irish there were property-owners, landlords, and employers who became as caught up in the heat of battle as their less affluent fellow immigrants. On the nativist side there were respectable American Republican lawyers, doctors, and dentists, as well as some constables and other elected officials. They fought alongside the youthful working-class members of nativist street gangs and volunteer fire companies notorious for their rowdy and combative behavior. What motivated rioters on both sides was not alienation, a sense of economic oppression, or a feeling of having "nothing to lose," but rather a deep commitment to their ethnic heritage and their political cause, intensified by their anger over the course of events that unfolded at the Nanny Goat Market. Tellingly, in three days of fighting and destruction, there was only one reported instance of looting. When rioters removed property from an Irish shop or Hugh Clark's home, it was to destroy it, not to keep it.

Fourth, the Kensington riots illustrate the intertwining of Jacksonian era collective violence with other, more peaceable forms of political and social behavior. The competition between immigrant Irish Catholics and native Protestant American Republicans began as a cultural controversy over the use of the Bible as a reading text in the public schools. It became a political issue when Hugh Clark convinced Louisa Bedford to remove the King James version from her class's daily lesson. After that, American Republicans began campaigning over the issue of "foreign interference" in the public schools, and when they carried this political campaign to Third Ward, Kensington, the debate changed from a clash of words to a clash of arms. . . . [T]he transition from cultural conflict to political conflict to physical conflict was all too frequent in Jacksonian group relations.

That the school Bible controversy shifted from a battle of petitions before the School Controllers to a battle of weapons in the streets of Kensington is stark testimony to the power of ethnic and religious issues to stir the passions of Philadelphians in 1844. It is also indicative, however, of the fifth and final factor common to most Jacksonian riots: the inability of public officials to prevent or suppress riots before they required the intervention of military troops. How strange it would seem today if, like Philadelphians on May 7, 1844, we awoke to find the walls, lampposts, and fences of our city or town plastered with calls for us to arm ourselves and attend a rally in order to seek revenge for the death of one of our fellow citizens. Then, once we arrived, we would find *no police officers* present to control the crowd or disarm its members. The current form of urban policing, in which uniformed officers actively patrol the streets searching out crime and disorder, and in which the police routinely patrol any political or protest rally prepared to disperse the crowd at the first sign of violence, was simply unknown in Jacksonian America.

"Preventive policing," as Jacksonians came to call it, was not introduced in Philadelphia until the 1850s. Like its sister cities Boston and New York, Philadelphia in 1844 still maintained public order through a system of constables, watchmen, and sheriff's posses whose origins dated back to the Middle Ages. . . .

. . . In the pre–Civil War era, city governments suffered from a shortage of manpower to police their citizens effectively. For various reasons, the majority of urban residents was not yet ready to surrender to local governments the tax monies or the authority needed to repress disorder and anti-social behavior. Jacksonian Americans seemed to possess a certain fatalism about the inevitability of periodic rioting — "intestine disorder," as it was known — and so cities and their residents simply learned to live with collective violence.

But neither the fatalistic outlook nor the weakness of public authorities was to survive the 1850s. By the eve of the Civil War, most of the nation's major cities had established preventive peacekeeping systems along lines still recognizable in today's urban police departments. With their introduction, collective disorder declined steadily in the 1850s and 1860s, and the 1870s was marked by a higher standard of urban public order than Jacksonians had ever imagined possible.

However dramatic their introduction, the police were not the only innovation that helped to pacify American cities by the time of the Civil War. By 1860, the northern industrial states had made public-school attendance compulsory for their youth. Public schools were meant to serve as nurseries for moral training and good citizenship. At the same time, the temperance movement stepped up its legal efforts to curb or eliminate liquor sales to the urban masses. In addition, having fought to a stalemate in the street, nativists and immigrants both channeled their competitive efforts into electoral politics, further diminishing the level of collective violence in the 1850s. Finally, other events such as the Mexican War of 1846–47 permitted a significant portion of America's urban street-fighting populations to vent their aggressive feelings on a common foreign foe, rather than each other. When reinforced by determined and street-wise police forces willing and able to carry out a mandate for civic order, these developments helped to make the 1850s a far less violent period than the 1830s and 1840s.

STUDY GUIDE

1. In the colonial period, many crowd demonstrations and riots were to *support* local government, such as the Boston selectmen or colonial legislature, against British policies. In our time, many demonstrations are *against* constituted authority, as in black protests against police arrests or antiwar and antinuclear sit-ins. How would you characterize the Philadelphia riots in this respect?

2. Feldberg mentions several causes of collective violence: religious prejudice; ethnic hostility; job competition; threats to an established group's wealth, power, or status; and a struggle for political power. Which causes seem to you to have been the key factors in the riots he describes? Why was the violence directed against the Irish, but not against the German immigrants?

3. The riots took place largely on "Irish turf" in Kensington and Southwark, and in the relatively good weather of May. What might have been different if the nativists had held their rallies in their own neighborhoods,

and in January? Were these factors of locale and timing also important in the riots of 1960s and the Miami riots of the 1980s?

4. Feldberg concludes that "the nativist rioters exercised a good deal of restraint in their attacks." In view of his description of the riots, do you agree with this conclusion? What does he mean by restraint in this context?

5. Do you see any differences between the kinds of people involved in riots in the 1840s and those involved in our time? Can one argue that rioting in the 1840s was provoked by the majority group in society, and that rioting today is more likely to be instigated by minority groups?

BIBLIOGRAPHY

Like many words in our language, the word "urban" is derived from the Latin *"urbanus"* (city) a fact that suggests the long, influential role of cities in European civilization. Though the colonists were largely farmers, they came from countries where government, culture, and commerce were centered in large cities such as London and Paris. Through much of our history, Americans have had a kind of love–hate relationship with cities, with the pastoral life of the farmer being held up as the ideal by adults and the big-city life being seen as an escape by many farm children. The attitudes of intellectuals are traced in Morton and Lucia White, *The Intellectual Versus the City* (1962). The sizeable towns of the colonial period were mostly seaports, the history of which is traced in books by Carl Bridenbaugh: *Cities in the Wilderness* (1938) and *Cities in Revolt* (1955). The growth of cities has been closely related to the development of transportation, commerce, and manufacturing. David T. Gilchrist, ed., *The Growth of the Seaport Cities, 1790–1825* (1967) examines developments along the Atlantic seaboard in the first decades of the new republic.

The history of particular cities can serve as case studies that illustrate general patterns of urban development. A great many "biographies" of cities have been published; two illustrative works are Bayrd Still, *Milwaukee*, rev. ed. (1965) and Bessie L. Pierce, *A History of Chicago*, 3 vols. (1937–1957). Allen F. Davis and Mark H. Haller, eds., *The Peoples of Philadelphia: A History of Ethnic Groups and Lower-Class Life, 1790–1940* (1973) examines poverty, housing for the poor, violence, and several of the ethnic groups of Philadelphia. In this edition of *The Social Fabric*, Feldberg's essay replaces one by David R. Johnson, whose book *Policing the Urban Underworld* (1979) is a fuller account of the development of modern policing. The study of some other urban problems can be followed in Charles E. Rosenberg, *The Cholera Years* (1962) and Nelson M. Blake, *Water for the Cities* (1956). Demography, the study of population trends, is used in much research in urban history: a fine example of this type of study is Stephan Thernstrom, *Poverty and Progress: Social Mobility in a Nineteenth-Century City* (1964).

There is a growing body of writing on the role of crowds and violence in the different periods of American history, some of which may be cited in the bibliography of your textbook. Much of this writing reflects the influence of the outstanding scholar of the crowd, a student of European history named George Rudé. An excellent introduction to the whole subject is his book *The Crowd in History, 1730–1848* (1964).

Some broader works treat cities of a particular type or of one region, as indicated in the following two titles: Robert R. Dykstra, *The Cattle Towns* (1968) and Richard C. Wade, *The Urban Frontier: The Rise of Western Cities, 1790–1830* (1959). Two general surveys of urban history are Constance Green, *The Rise of Urban America* (1965) and Charles N. Glaab and Theodore Brown, *A History of Urban America* (1967). Some excellent writing on urban history has been in the form of articles in historical magazines; Alexander B. Callow, Jr., *American Urban History*, 2nd ed. (1973) is one of several collections of such articles.

V WESTERN EXPANSION AND CIVIL WAR

At the time of the Treaty of Paris of 1783, the boundaries of the United States had been set at the Mississippi River on the west and along the 31st parallel on the south. By 1853, the country had added the huge territory of the Louisiana Purchase, acquired Florida from Spain, and swept westward over Texas, California, and Oregon into every square mile of territory that was to make up the continental United States. This breathtaking acquisition of territory had involved American intrigue in Florida, revolution in Texas, a blustering threat of force in Oregon, and full-scale war against Mexico. Generally, however, the American people were in advance of their government. Rather than gold, land — to settle on or to speculate in — was the chief lure that drew Americans westward into lands beyond the borders of their own country.

The acquisition of millions of acres of land beyond the Mississippi was one of the crucial factors in accentuating the sectional conflict that had begun in the 1830s. During the 1850s, the morality of slavery was the overriding issue in the minds of abolitionists. But for most people of both the North and the South, a matter of more immediate concern was whether or not slavery would expand into the western territories. The slogan of the Free Soil party of the North embodied the several aspects of sectional conflict: "Free Soil, Free Speech, Free Labor, and Free Men." This party's concern that labor and soil in the West be free points up the economic division of North and South. But the other parts of the slogan — free speech and free men — suggest that the country was also divided by psychological and social differences.

By 1861, many national social institutions, including the major religious denominations, had broken apart along sectional lines. And by that time, many thousands of Southerners saw the triumph of the northern Republican party in the 1860 election as not simply a political defeat but a threat to all southern institutions and to the southern way of life.

When we think of the westward movement, we usually imagine small parties struggling, in near starvation and haunting loneliness, across the Great Plains. The first reading describes the crowded conditions on the trails at the height of the migration and the cooperation that eased the hardships. The second and third readings describe the abolitionist movement that led to the Civil War and the astounding costs of that great conflict, both in casualties and in social and psychological destruction. American society had been torn asunder, and the reweaving of the disparate threads into a new social fabric was to prove a long and trying process. Some of the difficulties that were involved are described in the essay on the Reconstruction period that concludes this volume.

This photograph of pioneers on the trail west illustrates their mode of travel and the way they clung to the fashions they were used to back East.

18

JOHN D. UNRUH, JR.

The Way West

Few movements in all of our history have captured the imagination as has the settlement of the great American West. The image of the sturdy pioneer, plodding beside a lumbering covered wagon, fighting off Indian attacks, fording swift streams, and finally looking out upon the blue Pacific, has become enshrined in American folklore and on Hollywood celluloid. There is much in all of this that is sheer myth, but there is also much that is true.

The earliest openings of some American frontiers were accomplished by lone trappers and hunters who, because the game was there or because they weren't comfortable in more settled communities, turned their paths westward. Such men served as guides and added to the scant geographical knowledge of nineteenth-century America. But even in the fur trade, the single hunter was rapidly supplanted by the business organization, and it was John Jacob Astor's Pacific Fur Company that led thousands of other Americans to dream of the Oregon country.

In fact, settlement of the West in large numbers required careful planning, substantial equipment and supplies, organization, and community effort. Whether seeking gold in California, land in Oregon, or a religious Eden in Utah, the pioneers usually went west in a group. Leaders were chosen, supplies carefully assembled, and laws of the trail set down. But the fact that pioneer life primarily involved organized communities rather than lone scouts does not mean that struggle and hardship were any less a part of the frontier experience.

Americans today are still a migratory people, and until very recently California was the chief lodestar. But as we speed on interstate highways alongside the Platte River or fly over the Rocky Mountains in jet comfort, we have little idea of life on the trail in 1848. For this we must turn to the diaries of the men and women who made the long trek, who gave birth to infants on the wooden beds of wagons and pushed on the next day, and who buried children and parents in unmarked graves to which they would never return.

The view of western migration provided in the following selection, from John D. Unruh's book *The Plains Across*, is rather different from that of most writings on the subject. The author indicates how crowded the trails were during the height of the westward movement, and emphasizes the cooperation of the migrants with one another and with the Plains Indians.

[Between 1840 and 1860] approximately a quarter of a million overlanders had worn the trails to Oregon and California so deeply that in places the ruts are still visible. In that same period over 40,000 Latter-Day Saints traveled portions of those same trails to their Salt Lake Valley refuge, and by 1860 thousands of expectant gold seekers were penetrating the Pike's Peak region. . . .

These masses of westering overlanders do not coincide with the popular media image of widely scattered wagon trains traveling in relative isolation. Indeed, particularly between 1849 and 1853, most overlanders longed for privacy instead of the congested trails, crowded campsites, and overgrazed grasses they were experiencing. So many overlanders, for example, set forth from near St. Joseph on the same day in 1852 that teams traveled twelve abreast. Franklin Langworthy reported in 1850, from near South Pass, "The road, from morning till night, is crowded like Pearl Streat or Broadway," noting also that fathers had actually become separated from their sons in the "endless throng" and did not meet again until their arrival in California. Bennett C. Clark's company, in 1849, traveled late into the night near Ash Hollow in a desperate search for a vacant campsite.

Statistically inclined emigrants kept track of trail traffic during noon stops, on rare rest days, early in the mornings, and on particularly dusty days. James B. Persinger reported that their company passed 200 wagons early one 1850 morning, were passed by 100 another noon, and passed at least 500 more another day. Joseph Price wrote to his wife from Pacific Springs the same year that the 160 wagons which passed that point on June 27 was a smaller number than usual. . . .

Reprinted by permission from John D. Unruh, Jr., *The Plains Across: The Overland Emigrants and the Trans-Mississippi West, 1840–1860* (Urbana, Chicago, and London: University of Illinois Press). © 1979 by the Board of Trustees of the University of Illinois.

Not anticipating this trail congestion, emigrants during the gold rush consciously endeavored to travel in companies, formally or informally organized, just as they had in previous years when the trails had not been so crowded. The emigrant goal was always to insure that sufficient manpower would be available for whatever contingencies might arise: bridging or fording a stream, climbing a mountain, rounding up stampeded stock, resisting Indian attack. This vast armada of overlanders swarming together along the trails, especially during the gold rush, often created friction; tempers periodically flared as drivers jockeyed for position on the dusty main trail, and on occasion one traveling company passed another only after an actual race.

Such frustrations, however, were much overshadowed by the omnipresent emigrant interaction, which contributed so significantly to the success of the overland migrations. It is this cooperative quality of the migrations which scholars have so largely overlooked. Two neglected phases of emigrant interchange revolve around travelers who began the westbound journey only to turn back, and overlanders who traveled the trails eastward from the Pacific Coast to the Missouri and Iowa frontiers. For many westbound emigrants, the significant exchanges deriving from interaction with west-to-east trail travelers proved an unexpected bonus.

Although most of the turn-arounds were products of the gold rush years, a few overlanders had reconsidered the wisdom of their proposed venture ever since the overland movement had begun. In 1841, in fact, nearly 10 percent of the departing caravan of California- and Oregon-bound overlanders, Jesuit missionaries heading for the Flathead Indian territory, and other tourists and trappers made their way back to the Missouri settlements. . . .

. . . Since many of them had gone at least as far as Fort Kearny, and some to Fort Laramie and even beyond, their knowledge and advice were helpful to those pressing on. Indeed, the oncoming hordes so desired information — even if it was slightly exaggerated — that they pestered all returnees they met, unless there was serious sickness among them. . . .

Through information and mail service (one "goback" forty-niner brought back several letters), the turn-arounds provided their major assistance. But numbers of westbound overlanders who had suffered losses or had discovered outfitting errors or omissions were also much aided by this unexpected opportunity to purchase draft animals, wagons, tents, provisions, and other needed materials, since turn-arounds were usually willing to part with much of their outfit which they would not now be needing. On the other hand, a few returnees, having lost their draft animals, were forced to rely completely upon the charity of westbound emigrants in order to return to the frontier settlements. It is difficult to estimate the actual numbers of overlanders who retraced their steps, but in 1849, 1850, and 1852 there were certainly hundreds, and the yearly total probably approached and may even have surpassed 1,000 in 1850 and 1852.

Hasty conversations on the trail or at noon and evening encampments with eastbound overlanders direct from Oregon or California provided the most helpful and reliable sources of information to westbound emigrants. Such returning travelers were able to provide accurate — and sometimes disheartening — data on how far it really was to the mines, rumors notwithstanding, and whether the Indians evidenced hostile or friendly intentions. They also furnished advice regarding the various cutoffs, the availability of supplies at forts and trading posts, the presence of ferries at the various river crossings, the prices being charged there, and the location of buffalo herds. On occasion these eastbound parties also served as escorts for turn-arounds. . . .

Because west-to-east travelers were able to answer questions on the two matters of most interest and concern to overland emigrants — conditions on the trail and in California and Oregon — they were plied with questions by oncoming overlanders even more persistently than were the turn-arounds. And since eastbound travelers encountered almost the entire westbound migration this could become extremely frustrating, especially in years when 50,000 overlanders were trailing west. One 1850 party simply kept their mules going at a rapid pace, never stopping to entertain the "hundreds" of queries with which they were peppered, although they did shout back answers until they could no longer be heard. . . .

There was cause for eastbound overlanders being circumspect, especially those coming from California with gold dust in their possession. Enoch Conyers, while riding some distance from the main trail in 1852, encountered a solitary eastbound traveler encamped for the night. Upon first questioning, the man claimed to be a discouraged turn-around. When Conyers recognized him as his uncle, however, the solitary traveler admitted to be returning from California with considerable gold in his possession. He explained that he frequently camped far from the main trail and if seen claimed to be a turn-around. He had adopted this strategy because he feared robbers — especially "white Indians" — although he had barely survived a harrowing attack from real Indians shortly after crossing the Sierra Nevada Mountains.

Conyers's uncle had been more fortunate than a number of eastbound overlanders who fell victim to Indians and "highwaymen." . . . A particularly dangerous year for eastbound travelers was 1856, when the bodies of at least eight returning Californians were found along the Humboldt River after apparent robbery-murders. . . .

Although the impact of turn-arounds and eastbound overland travelers upon the overland emigrations was significant, the most important cooperation and interaction obviously prevailed among the much greater number of westbound overlanders. Because attrition, traveling company splits, combinations, and recombinations were so common to the overland emigrating experience, the matter of conveying advice, progress reports, and other newsworthy information to relatives, friends, and former traveling companions was extremely important. The "roadside telegraph" which the overlanders devised was a crude but surprisingly effective means of communication. Anyone wishing to leave a message would write a short note and place it conspicuously alongside the trail so that those following behind would be certain not to pass it by. . . . Even human skulls were used. With surfaces which had been smoothed and whitened by the elements, these skulls and bones were strikingly visible, especially when hung on a stick by the side of the trail. The inscriptions, when not purposely rubbed out, lasted a long time. Lodisa Frizzell in 1852 was still able to read penciled messages written in 1849.

Most overlanders were careful not to disturb these precious sources of information. Messages specifically directed to individual emigrants or particular companies were removed, but most others, after having been studiously read, were not otherwise disturbed. . . .

The roadside messages frequently communicated advice and information reflective of the cooperative concern most overlanders had for each other's safety and progress. The advice was often especially helpful to the many greenhorn travelers of the gold rush period. For example, forty-niner James Wilkins's outfit gratefully followed the recommendation on a trailside notice for avoiding a twenty-mile desert. The notice, according to Wilkins, had been posted "by a philanthropic Kentuckian" who had backtracked specifically to share his discovery of the alternate route for the benefit of those behind. Alonzo Delano found a signboard beyond Fort Laramie which read, "Look at this — look at this! The water here is poison, and we have lost six of our cattle. Do not let your cattle drink on this bottom." At a poisonous waterhole the next year James Evans commented, "Happy is the man who can read!" after observing a myriad of signs warning against tasting the water in phrases such as "He drank of this water and died" and "For God's sake do not taste this water." In addition to cautioning against bad water and grass, overlanders erected signs directing their comrades to fresh-water springs some distance off the road, or admonishing that this was the last available water or the last good grass before a desert stretch was to be crossed. So-called "cutoffs" which saved neither time nor energy were forcefully denounced. Harriet Ward spoke for many grateful overlanders after following a signpost's directions to reach a refreshingly cool spring some distance off the road in 1853: "Oh! what a pleasure to meet with such little mementoes of disinterested benevolence from strangers!"

A great many roadside communications dealt with Indian depredations, warning oncoming overlanders that losses of stock and human life had occurred at a particular location. Such announcements probably served the dual purpose of alerting emigrants to potential dangers as well as reporting the loss of animals, so that if any were subsequently found by other overlanders, the initial owner could claim the animal. Forty-niner John Edwin Banks even saw a notice offering a 200-dollar reward for five stolen horses and the persons who had committed the theft. . . .

. . . In 1849 some overlanders who had gone via Salt Lake changed their minds and traveled the southern trail to California in lieu of the usual Humboldt River route, having been influenced by rumors that Missouri packers had coldbloodedly killed three Indians and burned the grass for 200 miles to impede the progress of overlanders. As a result the trails were reportedly aswarm with revenge-minded Indians and completely unsafe. . . .

Most unplanned route changes, however, stemmed from the favorable accounts about shortcuts and cutoffs which wishful overlanders helped propagate. Emigrant diaries reveal much animated discussion and debate, and occasionally votes, as to whether an unknown cutoff should be attempted. Alonzo Delano, recording the deliberations of his company in 1849 regarding the Lassen Cutoff possibility, noted that emigrants from several traveling companies consulted together and that one man even went out thirty miles on horseback to check the new route. Delano's company, prompted by the urgings of its adventurous young men, took the supposed shortcut. Some of the various cutoff rumors were promulgated by interested parties, but there is ample evidence that many of the stories about how much time and distance cutoffs would save were freely circulated by and among emigrants eager for the trip to end but quite ignorant of any definite facts which would corroborate their roseate assertions. . . .

There were numerous other ways in which westbound overlanders cooperated to lessen the demands of the journey, almost always in a cheerful spirit of cooperation without seeking personal gain. Seasoned plains travelers advised novice overlanders of safe places to ford rivers so that expensive tolls could be avoided. Emigrant wagons bogged down in mudholes were pulled out by passing overlanders. Ropes, chains, boats, and bridge-building equipment were shared among different traveling groups. Overland companies encamping close together occasionally set out a mutual guard during the night. Following a rainstorm or stampede it was sometimes necessary for several traveling companies to cooperate in sorting out cattle which had milled together.

Also, emigrants on occasion volunteered to help strangers search for stock which had been stolen by Indians. This was emigrant cooperation at its best, for such errands of mercy could be dangerous. In 1857 one group of forty-two men from seven or eight different trains spent two fruitless days seeking sixty-one head of cattle stolen from an Arkansas train along the Humboldt River. Upon their return a second company was mustered from some of the trains which had come up in the interim, and this second group finally recovered thirty-six head of cattle and killed one Indian — seventy miles distant from where they had begun their search. Emigrant hunting parties killing more buffalo, deer, or other prairie game than needed often shared surplus meats with fellow overlanders.

A less joyous cooperative task was the burial of deceased overlanders. Passing emigrants were often asked to assist members of other traveling companies in digging graves and constructing coffins and grave markers. Most overlanders also stopped to rebury any deceased overlander whom they discovered, as Heinrich Leinhard's company did along the Humboldt River in 1846, after finding a man whose body had not only been dug up (presumably by wolves) but stripped of clothing and mutilated as well.

One of the most prevalent forms of interaction among westering overlanders was the inadvertent visit paid to another group of emigrants. Most frequently this was for the night, but it often occurred at mealtimes as well. While traveling westward, overlanders persistently rode ahead, lagged behind, or wandered off from their traveling company to hunt, explore, fix a wagon, read, sketch a picture, visit, and sometimes sleep. Often they did not conclude their activity quickly enough to be able to reach their own outfit that same day, and gladly accepted the hospitality and protection their fellow travelers readily extended in such circumstances. Captains and other traveling luminaries were also periodically invited to share a meal with captains of trains they were passing — Edwin Bryant in 1846 and J. Goldsborough Bruff in 1849 were frequent guests at other campfires during the course of their respective overland trips.

There was always considerable visiting among overlanders who had chosen to halt for a day of rest and recuperation and who were encamped in fairly close proximity. When the rest day was on Sunday, as it usually was, emigrants from various companies frequently assembled for a religious service. Gregarious overlanders, of course, needed no excuse to stop, chat, and make new friends. Some occasionally went to great lengths to do so, as with the young 1853 overlander who swam the Platte River to visit a company of emigrants traveling on the other side of that waterway. In addition to the interaction between trains on opposite sides of the Platte, on occasion ladies functioned as nurses among the sick in other trains. And, as proof that the amenities of civilized life were not neglected on the plains, Charlotte Pengra reported in 1853 that she gave her sunbonnet pattern to another lady who had admired it while passing by. . . .

Opportunities for purchasing additional oxen to pull an overloaded wagon, an extra wagon tongue, a new or extra wagon or riding horse regularly presented themselves somewhere along the trail. Numerous trades of cattle, horses, and mules were also recorded in emigrant diaries.

Particularly in 1849, when most overlanders took too much along and had to lighten their loads for the sake of their draft animals, fantastic bargains in clothing, revolvers, ammunition, foodstuffs, and almost everything else were available at many encampments. As the trip stretched out, many overlanders chose to sell their cumbersome wagons and most of their supplies in order to pack in to California by mule or horse. Some gold rushers made this change very early in the journey, retaining just as little in the way of provisions and supplies as they calculated would be necessary to complete the trip. This meant that mules and horses came to be increasingly valuable in the buying, selling, and trading among the overlanders, while oxen, wagons, and many other supplies and foodstuffs were sold at ridiculously low prices, if they could be sold at all.

An additional problem loomed toward the end of the journey, when overworked animals gave out or fell victim to Indian theft or arrow. Emigrants thus left with no way to transport their belongings sometimes were able to arrange with more fortunate overlanders to have their baggage carried through to the end of the journey, usually for some monetary or equivalent consideration. A few munificent overlanders asked nothing. These were real acts of compassion, since almost everyone's team was considerably worn down toward the journey's end. Along the Humboldt River in 1850, after traveling with his goods on his back for a day, Hugh Skinner secured accommodations in an Illinois wagon, thanks to a lady whose kindness led Skinner to remark, "I have uniformly found the women on the road more alive to the sufferings of their fellow creatures than the men." The bargain made, the emigrant usually traveled with his benefactor, but on occasion forged ahead on foot or with pack animal, planning to retrieve his goods later in California.

Clothing, blankets, and other personal belongings were important to overlanders, but food was crucial. The most significant assistance overlanders rendered to one another was certainly in sharing and selling provisions. A few gold rushers had even begun the journey with virtually no food supply, frankly planning to "sponge" off their better-prepared colleagues. One such 1849 foot traveler from Maine had reached Fort Kearny by such tactics, and figured that he would continue to find enough "Christians" on the route to supply his needs. . . .

In 1850 food was at a premium, especially on the later portions of the overland route. The rapidly increasing number of packers and other gold rushers running perilously low on rations frantically searched for overlanders well enough supplied to part with some of their provisions. The rapidly diminishing number of overlanders retaining surplus provisions happily watched prices skyrocket. Flour commanded up to $2 per pound; one overlander reported a man going from wagon to wagon unsuccessfully offering $50 for three pounds of flour. Hard bread sold at $1 a pound.

One small group of hungry emigrants immediately slaughtered the worn-out ox they had chipped in to purchase for $65 from a passing train. . . .

In such precarious circumstances, desperate overlanders resorted to tactics both clever and violent to induce their fellows to offer up precious provisions. . . . After Oliver Goldsmith had been refused foodstuffs by some southern overlanders, his companion, John Root, who possessed a strong southern accent, managed to get some food from the same group. Root apparently used his accent to good advantage on other occasions.

But ruses seem not to have been as much used as force. Goldsmith and four friends, after being told by one emigrant that they could have all the provisions they wanted, but at the steep price of $2 per pound, "marched up to him and said there were five of us to his one and that we intended to take what we needed at our own price, twenty-five cents a pound, which we did." When 1850 emigrant James Campbell encountered begging overlanders who had eaten nothing but frogs for four days, he prudently began sleeping in his wagon to prevent possible thievery. . . .

Often too, westering overlanders took up collections to provide unfortunate emigrants with the means to replace stock, wagons, or provisions. Thus, forty-niner Bernard Reid came upon a seventeen-year-old girl all alone save for her younger brother, who lay in their wagon sick with cholera. Both the mother and father had already died of the dread disease. The oxen were gone, and so was the faithless company with which the family had been traveling. Reid and others immediately took up a collection so that oxen might be purchased, two passing doctors prescribed medicine for the boy, and a Missouri group volunteered to take care of the orphans for the rest of the trip. Another 1850 gold seeker had been left by the trail after having been accidentally shot by one of his company. A passing physician attended to him, and westbound overlanders contributed money for his continuing care. When overlanders fording Thomas' Fork of the Bear River witnessed the drowning of one of the two horses an old man was relying on to take his family to California, they immediately took up a collection so the father could purchase another horse. And at the Green River ferry, in 1854, westbound emigrants again contributed funds to forward on to California the widow of a man who had just drowned.

Another common act of compassion was the attempt to ease the ordeal of desert crossings with "water wagons" manned and financed by overlanders having just completed the trip. Thirst-crazed overlanders were known to offer astronomical sums for a single drink of water during desert crossings. In 1850 on the desert beyond the Humboldt Sink, $5 was offered for a drink of water, and five gallons of water sold for $50. Henry Bloom reported that on the Hastings Cutoff desperate 1850 overlanders offered $10, $20, and up to $500 for a single drink of water. Fortunately for Bloom and his friends, the water wagon arrived before thirst elicited similar offers from them. This humane venture was especially prominent in 1850, when a wagonload of water was sent back every day by the emigrants who had crossed the preceding day. Not only water for the men but grass for draft animals was included, the effort being financed by contributions from the emigrants encamped at the spring which marked the welcome end of the treacherous long drive. An 1850 physician noted that their group had sent two relief loads back at a cost of $25 per wagon, the funds having been generously subscribed by passing overlanders. The wagon drivers gave the water free of charge to destitute overlanders, but those with money were charged from $1 to $5 per gallon. . . .

An additional legacy of the gold rush contributing considerably to emigrant interchange, albeit in a strange manner, was the trail of debris the greatest "litterbugs" of American history left in the wake of their transit across the West. Some traces had remained of the westward march of the overlanders of the 1840s, but since almost twice as many overlanders trailed westward in 1849 as in the entire previous decade, it was only natural that their residue would be greater. Further, their leavings were compounded by the overloaded wagons with which they had begun. They soon realized that the basic question was what they could do without, since their draft animals could never survive pulling such heavy loads. . . .

Many forty-niners began disposal operations as soon as they launched out onto the prairies. In the long run theirs was the wisest decision, providing they did not throw away too much. So much was abandoned within fifty miles of St. Joseph in 1849 that one emigrant indicated he would never go to California if he could have all that had been sacrificed that early in the journey. Persons went out from the outfitting points to collect the usable debris and brought back wagonloads of bacon, ham, flour, bread, beans, stoves, tools, medicines, extra wagon wheels and axletrees, clothing, and similar items, which were presumably resold or used by the scavengers. After viewing the perfectly good food and other materials along the trail, one forty-niner wrote: "If I was going to start again, I would get a light wagon for mules, and gather up the rest of my outfit along the road."

While debris accumulated everywhere, much of the abandoned merchandise was concentrated in the Fort Laramie vicinity. Many overloaded forty-niners had endeavored to persevere as far as the fort, where they anticipated profitable sales of their excess supplies. Upon discovering that the traders there needed none of their surplus commodities — which could be picked up along the trail for nothing in any case — the overlanders had no alternative but to begin dumping. Joseph Berrien reached the fort on May 30, well in the forefront of the 1849 migration, and dubbed the area "Camp Sacrifice" because of all that had already been left there. More than 20,000 pounds of bacon alone had been abandoned near the fort before June 1, and the great masses of overloaded emigrants were still to come. Howard Stansbury, en route to an exploration of the Great

Salt Lake Valley, enumerated some of the debris he saw in the Deer Creek area: "The road has been literally strewn with articles that have been thrown away. Bar-iron and steel, large blacksmiths' anvils and bellows, crow-bars, drills, augers, gold-washers, chisels, axes, lead, trunks, spades, ploughs, large grind-stones, baking-ovens, cooking-stoves without number, kegs, barrels, harness, clothing, bacon, and beans, were found along the road in pretty much the order in which they have been here enumerated." Virtually everything imaginable was found at least once somewhere along the overland trail: weapons, ammunition, tobacco, an iron safe, a Gothic bookcase, law and medical books — even a diving bell and accompanying apparatus.

If anything expendable remained in the wagons, it rarely lasted beyond the desert crossing to either the Carson or Truckee rivers. Here not only supplies but wagons and draft animals were left behind in ever-increasing numbers. Estimates of the number of abandoned wagons on the forty-mile desert ranged as high as 2,000 in 1850. Overlanders had already been passing and bemoaning the foul-smelling carcasses of dead animals — the victims of overwork and alkali poisoning — ever since leaving the Upper Platte ferry; what they witnessed on the desert crossings was merely the culmination. Though such tribulations were by no means unique to California gold seekers (Oregon-bound Maria Belshaw counted 190 dead animals along a 321-mile stretch of the Snake River in 1853), the debris, destruction, and stink reached their most astounding proportions on the deserts beyond the Humboldt Sink during the gold rush. . . .

A few gold rushers attempted a count. One 1850 traveler counted 2,381 horses and mules, 433 oxen, and 787 wagons, estimating the value of this and all other property left on the Carson Desert at $100,000. A subsequent tabulation of 4,960 dead horses, 3,750 dead oxen, and 1,061 dead mules led another observer to appraise the value of the abandoned property at $1 million. . . .

"The Dalles at present form a kind of masquerading thoroughfare, where emigrants and Indians meet, it appears, for the purpose of affording mutual aid." Jesuit missionary Pierre-Jean De Smet thus described, in 1846, a scene near the end of the overland route into Oregon's Willamette Valley. He could have written similarly of a multitude of other places along the Oregon-California Trail where overland emigrants and Indians met for purposes of aid and trade. That such beneficial interaction occurred, frequently and with considerable significance, contradicts the widely disseminated myth of incessant warfare between brave overlanders and treacherous Indians. The mass media view is not, of course, completely erroneous: Indians did kill hundreds of overlanders on the trails before the Civil War. The preoccupation with Indian depredations, however, has resulted in radical distortion of the historical record. Moreover, the depredations which did occur can be understood only in the context of the number and nature of Indian–emigrant encounters along the overland trails. . . .

While a relatively small number of overlanders relied upon Indians for route information or trail guidance, many overlanders willingly entrusted their stock, wagons, belongings, and even their families to Indian swimmers and boatmen at dangerous river crossings all along the trail. . . .

. . . [I]t was the Oregon overlanders during the 1840s and the early 1850s who relied most extensively on this form of Indian assistance. In doing so they were presumably following the advice of writers such as J. M. Shively, who had explicitly stated in his 1846 guidebook that "you must hire an Indian to pilot you at the crossings of Snake river, it being dangerous if not perfectly understood." Elizabeth Wood secured an Indian pilot after first attempting to ford the Snake River without one, perceiving, "It is best in fording this river to engage a pilot." Amelia Stewart Knight obviously agreed in 1853, remarking that there were many droves of cattle that could not be gotten across the Snake River without Indian help. Emigrant provisions, personal belongings, and wagons were also often put into Indian canoes to be rowed across raging rivers.

Payment was generally made in articles of clothing or in ammunition. James Longmire discovered on two occasions in 1853 that Indians were by no means devoid of effective bargaining techniques. At the Salmon Falls crossing an Indian, after swimming a few horses over the Snake River, mounted one of the best horses and rode off, while his employers remained helpless on the other side of the river. Later, in crossing horses over the Columbia River, Chinook Indians suddenly halted their exertions in midstream, demanding more money to complete the project. They got it, since any further delay would likely have been disastrous. Usually, however, the bargain, once made, was lived up to by both parties. . . .

Some of the 1843 overlanders who avoided Indian pilots and boats fared disastrously. The Applegate company constructed their own canoes, which they manned themselves with such lack of skill and luck that three in their party drowned and another was crippled for life. Sarah Cummins praised the Indians who helped their party portage around the Cascades in 1845 as "careful and considerate helpers. Not one deserted the ranks." She also stated that not a single dishonest act had been noticed. Mary Jane Long recalled how the Indians taking their party down the Columbia in 1852 had caught fish, built campfires, and brought up spring water while encamped. Once they even went back to a previous encampment to retrieve a gun which her father had inadvertently left behind but had not yet missed. Of course not everyone who took passage in Indian canoes was ecstatic about the experience. David Maynard, for instance, grumped in 1850, "We had a hard time, in consequence of the Indian being so damned lazy." Most emigrants, however, made the trip safely and with considerable respect for the skill of the native boatmen.

Indians aided overlanders in numerous other ways. Always eager to find ways of getting letters back to family and friends in the States, emigrants periodically negotiated with passing natives to transport letters back to the eastern settlements. At least some of these messengers faithfully fulfilled their trust, since many of the letters reached their destination. Forty-niner William Wells, for example, wrote to his wife from along the Kansas River: "This probably is the last chance I shall have to write to you and I do not know that you will even get this one. We have hired an Indian to take our letters to Independence — he may take them and he may not." One 1849 episode revealed both the shrewdness and trustworthiness of some Indian entrepreneurs. Although some of the forty-niners were dubious about the project, Reuben Shaw's company negotiated with three Sioux braves to carry numerous letters back to Council Bluffs. The Indians sagely refused a package deal for all the letters but instead bargained with each individual sender, thereby securing far more clothing, notions, tobacco, and jewelry. Shaw bartered a calico shirt for his letter and wrote, "The Indians got the shirt, and several months later I had the satisfaction of knowing that my wife received the letter." . . .

Even more astonishing to overlanders normally approaching all Indians with considerable suspicion, at least at the beginning of their overland trek, were the occasional acts of kindness and compassion by the Indians. Seeing William Johnston's difficulty in getting his mule-drawn wagons up the steep banks of Wakarusa Creek, a Shawnee Indian brought his pair of oxen to help pull the wagons up. An Indian with an extra horse overtook John Minto, who was walking ahead of his traveling company to Fort Hall, offered him a ride, and even gave Minto a saddle when he had trouble riding bareback. Another Indian brought wood and kindled a fire for John Zeiber's family at the Elkhorn River crossing in 1851 while Zeiber was occupied with fording wagons. . . .

James Evans was involved in a touching encounter on the Humboldt Desert in 1850. Exhausted and struggling on foot toward the Truckee River, Evans met a nearly naked Indian carrying a little tin bucket filled with water for thirsty emigrants — "When we met he offered me the bucket exclaiming, 'Watty, Watty, Oh! white man — watty!'" Evans declined because he was not in as dire straits as some he had passed, and urged the Indian to minister to them instead. "He went on, and I afterwards learned that he came up to the famishing man and after giving him two or 3 drinks of water brought up an Indian poney, put the white man on him and took him on until he came to Trucky River! Oh! such generosoty! and pray, why do not those Emigrants who are ahead have the same feelings of humanity?" Even the much-despised Digger Indians had their moments: Silas Miller reported a daring 1852 rescue of a drowning emigrant by two Digger braves. The Indians were rewarded for their heroics with suits of clothing and a two-month supply of provisions. . . .

. . . [D]uring the course of their trip virtually every overlander met at least a few Indians anxious to "swap." Most encountered a great many. Though some emigrants did manage to purchase certain items outright from native entrepreneurs, almost all the trading was conducted on the barter principle, since specie had little appeal for most prairie or mountain tribes. Many emigrants quickly learned, much to their surprise, that Indians were not easy marks in the bargaining process. Indeed, the traditional stereotype of the easygoing Indian, victimized in his every dealing with the white man, is simply not accurate. Finley McDiarmid, for example, found the Snake Indians to be "very sharp traders not easily cheated"; Cecelia Adams portrayed the Walla Wallas as "pretty shrewd fellows for money"; William Kelly suggested that the crafty Sioux compared favorably with wily British merchants; and Ansel McCall stated that the Sioux "in every case get the best of the bargain." . . .

Trade and aid were extremely significant aspects of the almost infinite variety of emigrant–Indian encounters. But they have been too often bypassed in the usual concentration upon pitched battles, scalps, and massacres. Initially the westbound emigrant wagons were strange curiosities to the natives in the same way that the overlanders were fascinated by the Indian life-style and customs. Accordingly, interaction, trading, and mutual aid prevailed throughout most of these crucial two decades of overland travel.

An analysis of the type and pattern of emigrant–Indian interaction during the antebellum era does suggest, however, that the overland emigrations quickened and perhaps made inevitable the military conquest of the western Indians. Almost from the very first, the perceptive plains Indians had recognized the threat the overland caravans represented to their way of life. Therefore, one of their first responses was to demand tribute of the passing trains. This tactic was employed at least as early as 1843. An 1845 overlander, speculating on the origin of this Indian tax, believed the practice to have begun with frightened emigrants willing to promise almost anything to travel safely. But it seems clear that tribute demands, which were most widely experienced by overlanders during the gold rush period, were grounded in more than simple repetition of a previous chance success. Emigrants continually reported that the Indians who came to demand tribute explained also why they were requesting the payments. The natives explicitly emphasized that the throngs of overlanders were killing and scaring away buffalo and other wild game, overgrazing prairie grasses, exhausting the small quantity of available timber, and depleting water resources.

STUDY GUIDE

1. Consider the preparations for a journey from Independence, Missouri, to Oregon or California. What would be essential in terms of food, clothing, housing, transportation, medicine, and tools? What mistakes in planning seem to have been the most common?

2. Gold was important in the great migration described by Unruh, but millions of people stayed home in the settled communities of the East, and many went to Oregon and other areas rather than responding to the lure of gold in California. In social and psychological terms, rather than in terms of striking it rich, how do you explain the motivation of the people who left their homes and went west?

3. How do the activities and behavior of the migrants along the trail, and the things they brought with them, indicate an attempt to preserve the life and values they had known in the East?

4. Suppose you were a contemporary Hollywood screenwriter-director with a knowledge of Unruh's work and an interest in doing a different kind of motion picture of the migration. How would it differ from the classic Western saga?

5. For some states entry into the Union depended on special circumstances, such as whether or not slavery would be allowed. But, in general, the date of admission indicates that the area had become fairly well populated with a settled society. Explain why California (1850), Oregon (1859), Nevada (1864), and Colorado (1876) were developed to the point of statehood well before the Dakotas, Montana, Washington, Idaho, and Wyoming, which were admitted in 1889–1890.

BIBLIOGRAPHY

As mentioned in the introduction to the preceding selection, the West and the great migration have a special place in the American imagination. A substantial number of diaries were kept by the overlanders, and both amateur and professional historians, as well as novelists and poets, have created a large body of literature on these subjects. Some have been interested in tracing the California and Oregon trails, others in depicting the life of the cowboy on the Plains or the miner in the camp. Some have romanticized the qualities of the pioneers, and some have created distorted pictures of the "savage" Indian. The first historian to call attention to the great significance of the frontier in American history was Frederick Jackson Turner; see especially his book *The Frontier in American History* (1920). Another great historian, Francis Parkman, gave his own account of a trip west in *The Oregon*

Trail (1849). In *The Great Plains* (1931), Walter Prescott Webb examined the unique natural environment of the area and how it affected the life of the settlers there.

Various aspects of the "Turner thesis" have been elaborated or subjected to severe criticism in the decades since its publication. A number of essays on the subject have been collected in Ray A. Billington, ed., *The Frontier Thesis: Valid Interpretation of American History?* (1966). Billington, a student of Turner, carried forward his teacher's work in a number of studies, especially *Westward Expansion: A History of the American Frontier*, 3rd ed. (1967). The deep symbolic and psychological significance of the West for Americans is set forth in Henry Nash Smith, *Virgin Land: The American West as Symbol and Myth* (1950).

In his many volumes on the frontier, Everett Dick discussed virtually every aspect of life in the American West; two volumes that are marvelous reading are *Vanguards of the Frontier* (1941) and *Tales of the Frontier from Lewis and Clark to the Last Roundup* (1964). The ultimate peril, being trapped in a mountain blizzard, is described in George R. Stewart, *Ordeal by Hunger: The Story of the Donner Party*, rev. ed. (1960). Recently a large number of excellent studies of the westward movement have been publised; John M. Faragher, *Women and Men on the Overland Trail* (1979) ranks with Unruh's book as one of the most important. Faragher's text places much greater emphasis on pioneer women, who are the subject of three other books as well: Julie R. Jeffrey, *Frontier Women: The Trans-Mississippi West, 1840–1880* (1979); Sandra L. Myres, *Westering Women and the Frontier Experience, 1800–1915* (1982); and Glenda Riley, *Frontierswomen: The Iowa Experience* (1981).

There are special studies of the mining frontier, the cattle frontier, and particular groups such as the Mormons. The following books are especially interesting: Rodman W. Paul, *Mining Frontiers of the Far West, 1848–1880* (1963) and Wallace Stegner, *The Gathering of Zion: The Story of the Mormon Trail* (1964). Daniel J. Boorstin, in his book *The Americans: The National Experience* (1965), argues persuasively that community cooperation, rather than individual effort, was the key to western settlement.

Wood engraving after an 1844 daguerreotype of Theodore Dwight Weld (1803–95), abolitionist crusader.

19

ROBERT ABZUG

The Abolitionist Impulse

Studying the American Revolution, the War of 1812, and the Mexican War has made you aware of the difficulties involved in understanding the causes of wars. As is the case with these earlier conflicts, so it is with the American Civil War — different historians have come to different conclusions as to the most important causes of the conflict. The distinguished historian Charles A. Beard, for example, suggested that the Civil War represented an economic conflict between an agricultural South and an industrializing North. Some historians have seen the cause as a breakdown of established political procedures, while others have suggested that the issue of control of the western territories was at the root of the struggle.

Whatever their interpretation might be, most historians would agree that slavery was deeply involved in the development of sectional feelings and the disruption of the Union. The Republican Party platform of 1860 conceded the rights of the states to control domestic institutions, which included slavery, and Lincoln tried to reassure the South that his election was not a threat to black slavery. Yet the South Carolina convention that voted secession from the Union saw the Republican triumph as a clear threat to slavery. In part, this was because many Southerners equated Republicanism with abolitionism.

Actually, abolitionists were highly unpopular in the North until after the passage of the Fugitive Slave Act of 1850. In the first decades of the nineteenth century, Benjamin Lundy had been a very lonely crusader, publishing his newspaper and walking the land to talk about the evils of slavery. With the exciting upsurge of social reform after 1830, people from many different backgrounds joined the antislavery crusade. The radical from New England, William Lloyd Garrison, called for the immediate abolition of slavery; two South Carolina sisters, Angelina and Sarah Grimké, became preachers in the cause; the ex-slaves Frederick Douglass and Harriet Tubman spoke against slavery and worked to help slaves escape; and the southern politician and editor James G. Birney ran for president of the United States on the Liberty Party ticket, which advocated abolition. Many historians consider the midwestern wing of abolitionism to have been the most important, and Theodore Dwight Weld was the most influential of several leaders in Ohio, Indiana, and neighboring states. Working through the churches and other social institutions, rather than denouncing them for their compromises on the slavery question, as others had done, Weld was remarkably successful in persuading people to join the abolition movement in the face of bitter denunciation and physical violence. The following essay from Robert Abzug's study of Weld gives a good picture of the courage of the abolitionists and the strong sense of a Protestant mission and moral reformation that underlay this and other reforms of the period.

Theodore [Weld]'s assignment for the Manual Labor Society included the task of finding the best location for a National Manual Labor Institution, one that would be the model school for training a millennial ministry. Though some in the manual labor camp favored Rochester, New York, voices from over the mountains turned Weld's attention toward Cincinnati. J. L. Tracy, a fellow Oneidan who now taught school in Kentucky, reminded Theodore that the Ohio Valley was "to be the great battlefield between the powers of light and darkness," and asked, "Why not train the soldiers of the Cross within sight of the enemies' camp?" At the same time, F. Y. Vail, a Cincinnati educator, offered his fledgling Lane Seminary as a site for the great experiment.

Tracy's argument was particularly compelling to Weld, who had long stressed the importance of the West. As early as 1827 he had urged [Charles G.] Finney to work in the hinterland rather than in eastern cities. . . . By 1832, as Finney preached in New York City, Weld argued ever more urgently that the "battlefield of the world," "Satan's seat," could not be won "by working the lever in Boston, New York, or Philadelphia." Only in the West could Finney "electrify the whole mass."

Weld's advice was well within one important tradition in Christian thought. As the scholar George H. Williams has argued, the wilderness, whether existing in the mind or in the world, symbolized to the Christian a "moral waste but a potential paradise," a ground upon which to fight one's personal battle for salvation or mankind's struggle for the Second Coming. . . .

In the end, Weld chose Lane for the experiment and his backers concurred. Unable to lure Finney from his New York activities, the manual laborites turned to Lyman Beecher as their choice for president of Lane. The peppery minister had moved strongly toward the Finneyite camp in the years after the Oneida revival, and he gladly accepted this position of leadership in the Christian vanguard. "If we gain the West," he wrote to his daughter, "all is safe; if we lose it, all is lost." . . .

Lyman Beecher was the kind of man who felt that the world depended on him for ultimate salvation; his hyperbolic prose spilled over with notions of disaster if his own way were blocked. Beecher's defensive tone — protection of American destiny from ignorant Catholics and infidels — rarely admitted a note of self-questioning. He concentrated on the defense of institutions and the defeat of external enemies. His Truths were embodied in the church and its auxiliaries. Debates over what constituted the true Christian life mattered less than solidarity in the larger battle. Weld and those who followed him from Oneida to Lane held a somewhat different view. To them victory in the millennial cause depended upon discovering the Truth and then acting in accord with its dictates; such an attitude called for scrupulous self-cleansing by both individuals and institutions as the first order of business. Purging oneself of sin was a prerequisite to dealing with Satan's legions. Still, as the Beecher family, Weld and his Oneida boys, and a miscellany of new students and faculty marched toward Lane, implicit differences could be ignored for awhile in the glow of Christian mission. . . .

. . . [T]hough the Oneida boys who followed Weld to Lane were enthusiastic about the prospects, they harbored a vigorous skepticism about the motives and qualifications of those outside their group. Men like Henry B. Stanton, Sereno W. Streeter, Calvin Waterbury, and John Alvord had learned too much about human fallibility at Oneida to allow a more charitable view, especially when the Millennium was at stake. . . . Streeter criticized a Mr. Grant, for instance, because he refused to be an example for the rest: "His influence was not a straw. He walked among the students like a speechless ghost. He gave no compositions nor declamations, lay abed late in the mor[ning], drank tea and coffee stoutly and his manual labor consisted in journeying from his room to the backhouse."

Fearing repetition of such mistakes at Lane, the Oneidans promoted their own nominees for faculty and criticized others whose names had been suggested. They were desperately afraid that antimanual labor men would "crush us by their caresses when they find they can't ever shin us by their kicks." More galling were the rumors that some trustees "were of the opinion that the Oneida boys had conspired to overthrow Lane Seminary." In fact, the image that the Oneidans presented might have inspired such fear. They flaunted their power, referred to Lane as their "ship," and at least one of them nicknamed the group "Illuminati." . . .

At the center was Weld. Beecher thought him a genius; he noted that the students considered him "a god." All could admire his hardy but saintlike presence. One story told how most of the students could not decide on room assignments; arguments became heated, and finally a lottery was decided upon. Weld drew second choice, but in a grand gesture said he would wait until the end; the act shamed the rest and they came to an "amicable adjustment" — all except, that is, for finding quarters for a particularly "slovenly and unsavory" fellow. Weld promptly offered part of his own room to him. According to another legend, a deep and dangerous well once had to be cleaned; only Theodore cheerfully volunteered and did the job all by himself. His physical courage, studied selflessness, and willingness to take command made him a model, a leader, a father. . . .

Weld took his role as "master-spirit" with full confidence. "I have a fine class," he boasted to his brother, "and have never been placed in circumstances by any means so *imposing*. When I came here matters were getting at loose ends." Presumably matters had been tightened up. Nor was the administration unappreciative; though leader of the students, Weld seemed far more responsible than his fellows. Professor Biggs, later a particular target of the Oneidans' contempt, wrote to Vail on the occasion of Theodore's return to school in July 1833: "Weld is here and we are glad." A year later he would change his mind.

As long as issues between students and administration were not clear, as long as tensions lay in the realm of personal suspicion and fear, of complaints about the lack of exemplary behavior on the part of either students or faculty — as long as the vying concepts of a millennial strategy had not squared off on some important issue — then Lane Seminary could proceed with its educational tasks and keep private resentments private. In fact, it was the strategy of men like Beecher to make sure that disputes between Christians did not obscure the larger shared task of defending against infidelity. Men like Weld, however, once sure of the moral worth and importance of a particular stance, could not help but enter it into the millennial equation and demand the loyalty of all good Christians. It was Lane's and Beecher's bad luck that the issue Weld chose was that of slavery. Slavery and the question of the rights of black freemen had vexed Americans of conscience for years. Yet for Theodore, who pressed the issue of slavery and the condition of free blacks on Lane and Cincinnati, the very intractability of the problem inspired forthrightness.

It had to be dealt with if America was to be saved and the Millennium achieved. By introducing the issue, Weld supplied Lane's uneasy populace with a cause over which to battle, a topic around which each side could mold a position against the other. The end result was that faculty and administration, despite their professed admiration for the theological class, asserted a belief in their own absolute authority. The students, for their part, left Lane, renouncing their commitment to an institution in favor of commitment to a set of ideals. Easy compliments faded as one found out the truth about the other.

The story of the Lane rebellion really begins with the saga of Weld's own conversion to abolition. The process was a long and subtle one, far more complex than indicated by Weld's own simple explanation of 1850, when he claimed that on the mnemonics tour he had seen "slavery at home, and became a radical abolitionist." The truth was that he became no instant abolitionist in the early 1820s — hardly an American in those years came close to such a position — but rather that a combination of experiences, coincidences, and personal traits slowly built a web of thought that in late 1832 led to Theodore's conversion to the cause. . . .

. . . Before 1831 the best solution Christians could offer was colonization: the shipping of slaves and free blacks back to Africa.

Colonizationists assumed that the black man was inferior and could not prosper alongside whites in America; he would of necessity sink to the bottom of society, creating problems of crime and saddling white America with an unproductive and undesirable population. In addition, many colonizationists feared retribution from these inferior beings, retribution for slavery and its excesses. If slaves remained enslaved, they would revolt; if freed on American soil, they would use their freedom for revenge. The logical solution was colonization, which would gradually remove the festering sore of black presence without causing undue tumult in white society.

Giving up colonization meant giving up these assumptions. In Weld's case the bases for rejection of black inferiority had been building in the 1820s. In the revival he found and embraced an egalitarian concept of men at odds with hierarchical structures and deferential attitudes. His advocacy of manual labor was, in part, a call for respect between classes and, in part, a romantic, personal urge to bring men of all walks of life together. In fact, Weld's emphasis on the physiological aspects of man focused on the human body all men shared rather than on the distinctions of class, color, or sex that divided them. Although Weld's emerging egalitarian vision did not yet include the black man it was compatible with basic assumptions of abolition thought. . . .

Such influences can only be considered preparatory in Weld's changing consciousness, very important preconditions that sensitized him to the plight of the slave or the free black but that did not immediately suggest the doctrine of abolition. First of all, issues like manual labor and temperance and Theodore's own shaky plans for completing his theological education stood in the forefront of his mind. Second, no one had yet presented him with some concrete argument and plan that might replace colonization as the solution to slavery. As late as September 27, 1832, Weld could write to his new friend James G. Birney, "I am ripe in the conviction that if the Colonization Society does not dissipate the horror of darkness which overhangs the southern country, we are undone. Light breaks *in from no other quarter.*" . . .

   The first major direct influence turning Theodore toward a new position on slavery probably was Charles Stuart, who had become extremely active in British antislavery and anticolonization efforts. "Pray for me, my beloved Theodore," Stuart wrote from England in March 1831; "I am traversing the country, holding meetings wherever I can, and endeavoring to awaken the conscience of the Nation, that Negro Slavery may be put off." He wrote again in June, "long[ing] to hear of [Theodore] being engaged in the Sacred cause of Negro emancipation"; Stuart enclosed ten copies of his latest pamphlet on the subject. The following spring he sent more material. At the same time, Tappan and his circle in New York began to take a more active interest in the slavery issue. Weld carried the influence of Stuart's probings and antislavery interest among his reform cohorts as he entered the South for manual labor and temperance lectures. In Huntsville, Alabama, he engaged in long discussions with James G. Birney, a slaveholder who had begun to consider taking on an agency with the American Colonization Society. Weld encouraged him in this course and hoped that he would find it in his heart to emancipate his own slaves.

   Theodore's increased interest in the slavery question presented a crucial dilemma. Stuart had argued for immediate emancipation without colonization, but, with no slaves on English soil, it was relatively easy for an Englishman to advocate such a position. For an American it was different. Slavery had seeped into every aspect of politics, economics, and social custom in the United States; fear of blacks had pervaded the white consciousness. It was a working assumption among the citizenry that emancipation on American soil would cause a race war unmatched in history. They had before them the examples of Santo Domingo, Nat Turner, and the images of their own irrepressible fantasies. And so it was that a troubled Theodore Weld could endorse Birney's work for colonization, sensing that "light breaks *in from no other quarter.*"

   Soon new light shone in the small college town of Hudson, Ohio, where three members of the Western Reserve community — Beriah Green, Elizur Wright, and Charles B. Storrs — were already spreading Garrisonian doctrine. Weld had come to speak on manual labor and temperance; by the time he left he had been converted to immediate emancipation. What exactly transpired is not known, but it is clear from what followed that two key points were stressed upon Weld's agitated conscience. The Hudson Garrisonians must have demonstrated that even by their own standards the colonizationists were doomed to failure, that they could not remove enough free blacks and newly freed slaves to reduce the black population to the point of safety. More important, however, they must have shown Weld that colonization doctrine itself avoided the central moral question of the black man's humanity and that not recognizing his humanity was a sin. Slavery and race discrimination were no mere misfortunes but sinful acts, whether engaged in actively or passively countenanced.

. . . Thus colonization, which sought to avoid rather than foster a change of heart, lulled America into a sleep of self-satisfaction while God's wrath continued to mount. The only answer was to convert slaveholders to immediate recognition of their sin and then to immediate emancipation, and to bring all Americans to a full recognition of the black man as a man. Then there would be no reason to fear freedom for the slave, for the attitudes that might have fostered contempt and rage would have begun to encourage love.

These doctrines cleared Theodore's mind on this most difficult of issues. By December, Elizur Wright was corresponding with Weld as an abolitionist comrade-in-arms. Arthur Tappan, informed of Theodore's conversion to the cause, promptly informed William Lloyd Garrison. Garrison invited Weld to an organizing session for the proposed American Anti-Slavery Society. Theodore declined because of "engagements quite indispensable," but affirmed to Garrison what he had learned at Hudson. Endorsing the "expressive name" of the New England Anti-Slavery Society, he wrote:

> From that I infer that the Society is based upon the great bottom law of human right, that *nothing but crime* can forfeit liberty. That no condition of birth, no shade of color, no mere misfortune of circumstances, can annul that birth-right charter, which God has bequeathed to every being upon whom he has stamped his own image, by making him *a free moral agent*, and that he who robs his fellow man of this tramples upon right, subverts justice, outrages humanity, unsettles the foundations of human safety, and sacrilegiously assumes the prerogative of God.

Thus Theodore conjoined antislavery with the egalitarian principles of the revival, of manual labor, and the broadest interpretation of the Declaration of Independence, leaving behind the dictates of "expediency or necessity." . . .

"I hardly know how to contain myself," Theodore exclaimed to Wright in January 1833. "If I was not positively pledged for two or three years to come, and if I had finished my education, I would devote myself to the holy work, come life or death." Nonetheless antislavery work edged into his life. He engaged in "many pitched battles" over slavery, sometimes even debating colonization agents. . . .

It was inevitable that Theodore should bring the cause to Lane, though his policy at first was to wait for just the right moment to strike. He could hardly do otherwise. "This Institution stands fiercely committed for Colonization and *against* Abolition," Weld wrote to Amos Phelps. "*Our Theological Professors* are exceedingly anxious to keep us from bringing up the subject for discussion." One reason was geography. "The proximity of Cincinnati and the whole eastern line of Ohio to slaveholding states," explained Theodore, "has thus far muzzled men both in public and private upon the subject of slavery. A universal paralysis pervades — tongues, pens, and presses." He promised Phelps, however, that "in due time you may expect to hear from this Institution — a more favorable Report."

In fact, Theodore had already begun to make plans for open discussion of immediate emancipation and colonization. After meeting with faculty and fellow students of colonization persuasion, he agreed not to "push" a debate for the fall 1833 term so that each side might have time "to prepare for a thorough discussion." Still, he was sure that a public meeting in the winter term might quadruple the small number of abolition advocates at Lane. These original supporters were among "the very first fellows in the Seminary," and included Asa Mahan of the Trustees and Professor John Morgan on the faculty. Other sympathetic hearts in the Cincinnati area included Weld's old Oneida friend, Horace Bushnell, then minister at a nearby town, and Thomas Cole, a Newport, Kentucky pastor. All told, the numbers were paltry; only faith in "changeless eternal right" buoyed their spirits.

It was with this faith that Theodore and his abolitionist fellows planned what were to become known as the Lane Debates. They were scheduled for February 1834, but months earlier preparations commenced in the revival style. "We early began to inculcate our views," Weld remembered, "by conversation, upon our fellow-students. Those of us who sympathized together in our abhorrence of slavery selected each his man to instruct, convince, and enlist in the cause. Thus we carried one after another, and, before ever we came to public debate, knew pretty well where we stood." In other words, the meetings were hardly debates at all. Asking two questions — "Ought the people of the Slaveholding States to abolish Slavery immediately?" and "Are the doctrines, tendencies, and measures of the American Colonization Society, and the influence of its principal supporters, such as render it worthy of the patronage of the Christian public?" — they were conceived of as conversion-oriented educational barrages. Despite doubts about the wisdom of such public meetings, President Beecher agreed not to stand in the way.

The debates lasted eighteen days, each question being discussed two and a half hours each of nine evenings. Weld held forth on the first two days; he introduced the topic of immediate emancipation through "facts ... gathered from various authentic documents" and drew appropriate conclusions. The most dramatic moments of the series came not from Weld, but rather from Southerners who gave firsthand testimony concerning the "peculiar institution." James Bradley, an ex-slave, countered notions that emancipation would be "unsafe to the community" and that "the condition of the emancipated negroes would be worse than it now is." Bradley himself had worked for five years to buy his freedom; having done so, he left Arkansas for a free state and finally enrolled at Lane for an education.

White Southerners, however, made the greatest impact. The audience could witness the sin of slavery as it acted in men's consciences; they could watch the process by which heartfelt recognition of sin would, if allowed to be spread, sweep the South and emancipate both master and slave. None of their speeches was recorded, but James A. Thome, a southern Lane student converted during the debates, described his experience to the first anniversary meeting of the American Anti-Slavery Society in May 1834. As Thome recounted it, he had always harbored uneasy feelings about slavery, but these sentiments had led him to colonization. Colonization's only effect, Thome now conceded, had been to "lessen [his] conviction of the evil of slavery, and to deepen and sanctify [his] prejudice against the colored race."

The debates showed to him that the true evil of slavery lay in the denial of black men's God-given rights and in the cruelty that enforced that denial. He described the burning sense of sin this realization brought: "Sin revived and I died." Thus the debates were something of a special form of revival. Slavery's sin "seize[d] the conscience with an authoritative grasp; it [ran] across every path of the guilty, haunt[ed] him, goad[ed] him, and [rang] in his ear the cry of blood. . . . It [wrote] 'thou art the man,' upon the forehead of every oppressor." But the conviction of sin also brought in the sinner "every susceptibility to compassionate outraged humanity" and found him "pledged to do its work." . . .

With the debates at an end, Theodore took a prominent role in galvanizing excited feeling into an Anti-Slavery Society. Its constitution summarized the meaning of immediate emancipation doctrine — what it was and what it was not. The society's object? "Immediate emancipation of the whole colored race, within the United States" — slave from master and "free colored man from the oppression of public sentiment" — "and the elevation of both to an intellectual, moral, and political equality with the whites." Why? Because the black man was created by God as "a moral agent, the keeper of his own happiness, the executive of his own powers, the accountable arbiter of his own choice." . . .

In acting on such propositions, the society promised to abide by the "law of love." It ruled out instigating slave rebellion as well as forcible intervention by the free states — one meant murder and the other meant war. Nor would it seek congressional interference. Rather the Lane abolitionists hoped to "induce [the slaveholder] to forsake *this*, as every other sin, by speaking the truth in love." They would demonstrate the advantage of emancipation by showing its "pecuniary interest," its safety, and by encouraging religious and secular public sentiment against slavery.

Moreover, the constitution of Lane's Anti-Slavery Society attempted to dispel the terror that the very phrase "immediate emancipation" seemed to provoke. It defined the term first by excluding the intention of "turn[ing] loose [slaves] upon the nation, to roam as vagabonds and aliens," denying that "they would be instantly invested with all political rights and privileges," but also refusing to allow "that they shall be expelled from their native land to foreign clime, as the price and condition of their freedom." In positive terms "immediate emancipation" meant that slaves would receive protection of the law instead of being at the mercy of unbridled passions, they they should be employed as free laborers, "fairly compensated and protected in their earnings," and that "they shall be placed under a benevolent and disinterested supervision, which shall secure them the right to obtain secular and religious knowledge, to worship God according to the dictates of their consciences, and to seek an intellectual and moral equality with the whites." While none of the sentiments expressed at Lane was new — William Lloyd Garrison and his followers had been espousing them since 1831 — those at Lane propounded them as if they had just invented them. Yet it was not so much the doctrines as the wondrous process of conversion that made the Lane Debates a momentous eighteen days.

Forming an Anti-Slavery Society was only one way of working out the millennial mission in relation to blacks. With a zeal typical of Oneida men, Weld, Huntington Lyman, Augustus Wattles, and others began to promote religious and secular schools in Cincinnati's black community. "We believe that faith without *works* is dead," Weld wrote to Lewis Tappan in March 1834. "We have formed a large and efficient organization for elevating the colored people in Cincinnati — have established a Lyceum among them, and lecture three or four evenings a week, on grammar, geography, arithmetic, natural philosophy, etc." Other activities included an evening school for reading skills, a library and a new reading room, three Sabbath schools and a number of Bible classes, all run or participated in by Lane students. Weld also suggested a plan for a "SELECT FEMALE SCHOOL." Two students, Augustus Wattles and Marius Robinson, became so committed to these projects that they dropped out of Lane to devote themselves full time to running a school for blacks. . . .

Theodore's enthusiasm over the Lane Debates and subsequent work in Cincinnati's "Little Africa" was further strengthened by the news of James G. Birney's conversion to abolition. Since Weld's meetings and correspondence with Birney in 1832, the troubled slaveholder had become a star in the colonization galaxy. An exemplary agent, he also had fired well-reasoned salvos at the upstart immediate emancipationists in various newspapers and finally in the Colonization Society's *African Repository*. It must have come as something of a shock to Weld when he received a letter from Birney announcing his turn to abolition and promising an open letter that would explain his position in full. Theodore assured him that the news would be "ringing in the public ears within a few days, from different papers on both sides of the Alleghany, but of course *only as something* REPORTED *not definitely known*." . . .

Even as Weld welcomed Birney to abolitionism, however, the citizens of Cincinnati were beginning to show their displeasure with antislavery activities at Lane and with the entry of Lane students into the black quarter of town. The confrontation that resulted became a major turning point in the history of abolition in America.

Theodore resolved one major question when he left Lane Seminary. Since early youth he had ostensibly been following a path to the ministry. No matter what the detours — a breakdown at Andover, the mnemonics tour, conversion by Finney, revival and temperance work, and finally the manual labor agency — he had returned to seminary. Yet upon leaving Lane, he gave up school and a career within the church forever. Instead he chose the life of an antislavery orator. Others among the Lane rebels, his closest comrades, had decided to continue their educations. They first set up a school of their own in Cumminsville, Ohio, and later flocked to Oberlin when Finney himself became head of its theological department. In June 1834, however, Weld made his own commitments clear in a letter declining a professorship at Oberlin. "The Providence of God has for some time made it plain to me," he wrote, "that the Abolition of Slavery and the elevation of the free colored race have intrinsic demands upon me superior to every other cause."

Theodore accepted an antislavery agency for Ohio and by late fall was in action. Hearing of Weld's decision, James G. Birney wrote in his diary, "I give him one year to abolitionize Ohio." Lewis Tappan made the same prediction. In the year and eight months that followed, Weld would become an antislavery legend. Theodore began his campaign at Ripley, an Ohio River town across the water from Kentucky. There he lectured eleven times and formed an antislavery society with little fuss. He then moved on to West Union, "one of the most hopeless places for anti-slavery effort," where he thought he had done some good. For the balance of December, he canvassed Hillsborough and Greenfield, and in January penetrated the Ross County towns of Concord and Frankfort. In February and March, Weld concentrated on the Circleville and Bloomingsberg areas. In April he led the planning of the Ohio State Antislavery Society's first meeting, which took place at Putnam on April 22–24. After this convention he continued his tour, moving south to Marietta and on to Pittsburgh, Pennsylvania, for the Presbyterian Church's General Assembly, then back to Ohio and into the Western Reserve — to Cleveland, Ravenna, Elyria, and Oberlin. Late in the year Weld moved back into Pennsylvania; by then the American Anti-Slavery Society had persuaded him to break new ground in New York State.

In preaching the antislavery cause Theodore followed a routine reminiscent of his prior agencies and illustrative of his ambivalence about authority. As in the past, he chose to work in the West, far from what in his mind were those oppressive centers of authority, the cities of the East. Some years earlier, he had assured Lewis Tappan that God had marked out for him a "diocese" in "the highways and hedges of the West." He dressed simply, in what he termed a "John the Baptist attire," emphasizing again his direct responsibility to God rather than to some earthly church or organization. Normally Weld stayed with a local minister or other sympathetic townsman, sought a hall or church, and then lectured on antislavery anywhere from six to twenty-five times. He then left town, expecting that local supporters would build upon the interest in abolition he had sparked. . . .

Opposition varied from town to town. Sometimes, as at West Union, Weld's enemies displayed no more than "a good deal of squirming and some noise and blustering threats, etc." Other towns, like Circleville, were not quite so hospitable. Mobs pelted him with stones through the open windows; one missile struck Weld on the head and stunned him for a few minutes. In typically heroic fashion, however, he finished the lecture. Theodore remembered another incident when a mob tramped four abreast into the courtroom where he was speaking and pushed his audience out into the night. The meeting reconvened at a schoolhouse, but the mob soon returned, this time brining sleigh bells, tin pans, tin trumpets, and a dog. As Weld commenced, horns tooted, pans rattled, bells rang, and one man pulled the dog's ears to make it bark.

Despite the mobs, Weld was optimistic. In February 1836, after almost a year and a half of lecturing, he predicted to Tappan that within five years half a million slaves would be free, one million and a half within the decade. Such a view necessitated an extraordinary reading of abolitionist power and public reactions. In all, the world view and strategy of Weld and his comrades require close examination, for they were beliefs that allowed these men and women to struggle against seemingly impossible odds.

Theirs was first of all a religious vision, one based upon the evangelical notion of converting the world to bring on the Millennium. Weld, in fact, described his antislavery efforts in terms reminiscent of a classic revival meeting. First he met "coldness, suspicion, opposition, and threats of personal violence and *thin* attendance." Gradually, interest and "anxious inquiry" increased. Finally, victory came — conversions, contributions, and perhaps a local antislavery society. "In each place the opposition has been strong, in two instances rising to absolute ferocity," Weld reported in February 1835, "but the Lord enabled me to move deliberately onward until the truth triumphed gloriously." A year later he reported the same pattern of triumph from Utica, New York: "I lectured for the eleventh time in the Bleecker Street Church tonight — great crowd. The Lord is with us — truth *tells*. Mob dead, buried, and rotten." . . .

Thus abolition, with its daring commitment to freedom and coexistence with blacks, engendered ardent support in a way colonization never could with its easily supported doctrine of expatriation. Abolitionism did not appeal to many people, but those most attracted to it were young men and women with the explosive, rebellious energy to get things done. Abolitionists tapped the same vein of discontent that sparked earlier and contemporaneous revivals of religion. Indeed, one colonizationist surmised with dismay, "I find that where New Measures flourish there Abolition (and kindred fanaticisms), flourishes." Colonizationists asked men to contribute time or money to solve what they considered an unfortunate moral, political, and economic problem, one open to solution without a basic change of heart on the part of the white man. Such a lukewarm appeal could only inspire a lukewarm response. But abolition asked men, dared men to confront the sins of slavery and racism as their own and demanded a regenerative commitment to the cause. Such an appeal was bound to infuriate most and inspire zealous devotion in a chosen few.

STUDY GUIDE

1. Weld apparently was a remarkable man who exercised a powerful influence upon acquaintances. One purpose of a biography is to give the reader a sense of the subject's personality. Where in the preceding pages do you get a sense of Weld's motivation, courage, and power as a speaker?

2. Some abolitionists devoted their efforts to assisting fugitive slaves, some to speaking against slavery, others to writing propaganda or working through churches or politics. They also differed in their views on how emancipation would be achieved. In your textbook or in *The Dictionary of American Biography* in your library, find information that will help you understand the differences among Weld, William Lloyd Garrison, Lyman Beecher, and James G. Birney.

3. How did Weld's strong Christian revivalist background influence his decision to take up the abolitionist cause, his crusading techniques, and his break with Beecher and Lane Seminary?

4. Southerners frequently claimed that the abolitionist program would deny

slaveholders their constitutional rights. On the other hand, some Northerners came to support the antislavery movement because they felt that the civil rights of abolitionists were being violated. How much truth was there in each of these arguments? How might the following clauses of the Constitution be relevant: Article IV, Section 2; Amendment I; Amendment V; and Amendment X?

BIBLIOGRAPHY

At the time of John Brown's execution, Ralph Waldo Emerson referred to him as a saint who had made the gallows as glorious as the cross. But a good many Americans of the pre–Civil War period thought of abolitionists as the devil incarnate. The attitudes of historians on the abolitionists have varied, as have their views of the relationship of abolitionism to the coming of the Civil War. Dwight L. Dumond provided a sympathetic view of the abolitionists in *Antislavery: The Crusade for Freedom in America* (1961) and argued that the slavery question was an important cause of war in *Antislavery Origins of the Civil War in the United States* (1939). Other historians have denounced the reformers, and agreed with Avery O. Craven, *The Repressible Conflict, 1830–1861* (1939), that it was a needless war.

There has been a great deal of study of abolitionism in the last two decades. An earlier work by Gilbert Barnes, *The Antislavery Impulse, 1830–1844* (1933), first pointed out the great significance of Weld and the midwestern wing of the movement. There are several good studies of blacks in the antislavery movement, including Benjamin Quarles, *Black Abolitionists* (1969) and Jane and William Pease, *They Who Would Be Free: Blacks' Search for Freedom* (1974). In another volume, *Bound with Them in Chains* (1972), the Peases provide biographical sketches of various types of abolitionists. There are also biographies of most of the leading abolitionists, including John L. Thomas, *The Liberator: A Biography of William Lloyd Garrison* (1963) and Benjamin Quarles, *Frederick Douglass* (1948). Women were an extremely important force in most aspects of nineteenth-century reform; their role in abolitionism is studied in Alma Lutz, *Crusade for Freedom: Women of the Antislavery Movement* (1968). Blanche G. Hersh, *The Slavery of Sex: Feminist-Abolitionists in America* (1978) is more recent and innovative.

Rather than approaching the subject through a study of the leaders, some historians have examined a particular phase of the antislavery crusade or the thought of people on the relationship of race and slavery. Larry Gara, *The Liberty Line* (1961) is one of several works on the underground railroad. Lorman Ratner, *Powder Keg: Northern Opposition to the Antislavery Movement, 1831–1840* (1968) is a full study of the animosity toward abolitionists. The attacks upon the abolitionists and upon the rights of free Negroes led to a concern about civil liberties, a subject that is examined in Russel Nye, *Fettered Freedom* (1949). Few free blacks, even those in northern states, were in an enviable position, as Leon Litwack indicates in *North of Slavery: The Negro in the Free States, 1790–1860* (1967). Another theme that has received much less attention than has abolitionism is the defense of slavery in pre-war thought. William Jenkins, *Pro-Slavery Thought in the Old South* (1935) dealt with this subject some years ago. Most writing on the abolitionists follows their activities only to 1860, but recently James McPherson carried their story through the Civil War and Reconstruction period in *The Struggle for Equality* (1964). Martin B. Duberman, *Antislavery Vanguard* (1965) is a collection of essays by several different scholars, as is Lewis Perry and Michael Fellman, eds., *Antislavery Reconsidered: New Perspectives on the Abolitionists* (1979).

These wounded troops near Fredericksburg, some perhaps maimed for life, were at least luckier than the 600,000 people who died in America's bloodiest war.

20

ALLAN NEVINS

The Price of War

The selections in this volume have illustrated the exceptional variety of American life in different parts of the country from the founding of the British settlements to the Civil War. The editors hope that you have received some impression of the actual working conditions in early American factories, of the life of Indians and slaves, of family life and social reform. The two selections on the American Revolution touched upon certain aspects of what has been called the age of limited warfare. The following selection, from Allan Nevins's article "The Glorious and the Terrible," gives a chilling picture of modern war.

In the twentieth century, there is little about war that is glamorous or chivalric. Those who fought in World War II, the Korean War, or the long war in Southeast Asia know the full import of General William T. Sherman's famous phrase, "War is hell." Massive bombings of civilian areas, atomic weaponry, napalm, massacres, and pushbutton slaughter have made a grim mockery of wartime heroism. The American Civil War has been described as the first modern war — partly because of tactical and logistic innovations and partly because of the astounding casualties, the use of scorched-earth policies, and a number of other grim forecasts of the future.

Yet, there are common elements in nearly all wars — elements that connect the Civil War and our modern warfare with the so-called gentlemanly wars of the seventeenth and eighteenth centuries. Death, cruelty, callousness, cowardice, and bravery are a part of the human condition in wartime, and they know no special period. In some wars, the devastation and dehumanization have been borne largely by the armies engaged. But where a civil war is fought in one's own country, the destruction and the psychological scars extend beyond the battlefield. In the sectional split of the United States that led brother to fight brother, wartime life assumed a very special poignancy, and the scars took a very long time to heal.

Every great war has two sides, the glorious and the terrible. The glorious is perpetuated in multitudinous pictures, poems, novels, statues: in Meissonier's canvases of Friedland and Austerlitz, Byron's stanzas on Waterloo and Tennyson's on the Light and Heavy brigades, St. Gaudens's Sherman riding forward victory-crowned, Freeman's "Lee." The terrible is given us in a much slighter body of memorabilia: Jacques Callot's gruesome etchings of the Thirty Years War, Goya's paintings of French atrocities in Spain, Zola's "The Debacle," Walt Whitman's hospital sketches, and the thousand-page novels that drearily emerged from the Second World War.

The two aspects do exist side by side. Every student of war comes upon hundreds of veracious descriptions of its pomp and pageantry, innumerable tales of devotion and heroism. They exalt the spirit. Yet every such student falls back from this exaltation upon a sombre remembrance of the butchery, the bereavement, and the long bequest of poverty, exhaustion, and despair. In observing the centenary of the Civil War, every sensible man should keep in mind that the conflict was a terrible reproach to American civilization and a source of poison and debilities still to be felt. . . .

. . . Who wishes to while away an idle hour by looking at the harrowing pictures in the "Medical and Surgical History" of the war? It is a trick of human memories to forget, little by little, what is painful, and remember what is pleasant, and that tendency appertains to the folk memory as well. One of the finest descriptive pieces of the war was written by the true-hearted Theodore Winthrop, novelist and poet, just after his regiment crossed the Potomac on a spring night in 1861 to encamp on the Virginia side. It is rapturous in its depiction of the golden moon lighting a path over the river, the merry files of soldiers, the white tents being pitched in the dewy dawn. But ere long Winthrop was slain at Big Bethel in an engagement too blundering, shabby, and piteous for any pen. We remember the happy march but forget the death.

Or take two contrasting scenes later in the war, of the same day — the day of Malvern Hill, July 1, 1862. That battle of Lee and McClellan reached its climax in the gathering dusk of a lustrous summer evening, no breath of wind stirring the air. The Union army had placed its ranks

From Allan Nevins, "The Glorious and the Terrible," *Saturday Review*, September 2, 1961. © 1961 Saturday Review Magazine. Reprinted by permission.

and its artillery on the slope of a great hill, a natural amphitheatre, which the Southerners assaulted. Participants never forgot the magnificence of the spectacle. From the Confederate and Union guns stately columns of black smoke towered high in the blue sky. The crash of musketry and deeper thud of artillery; the thunder of gunboat mortars from the James River, their shells curving in fiery golden lines; the cavalry on either flank, galloping to attack; the foaming horses flying from point to point with aides carrying dispatches; the steady advance of the Confederate columns and the unyielding resistance of the dense Union lines; then as darkness gathered, the varicolored signal lights flashing back and forth their messages — all this made an unforgettable panorama.

But the sequel! The troops on both sides sank exhausted on their arms. From the field the shrieking and moaning of the wounded were heart-rending, yet nothing could be done to succor them. The sky grew overcast; intense darkness shut down; and at dawn came a fierce downpour. "Such rain, and such howling set up by the wounded," wrote one Southern soldier; "such ugly wounds, sickening to the sight even of the most hardened as the rain beat upon them, washing them to a pale purple; such long-fingered corpses, and in piles, too, like cordwood — may I never see the like again!"

Both novelist and poet almost instinctively turn to the heroic aspects and picturesque incidents of war. Lowell's "Commemoration Ode," one of the half-dozen finest pieces of literature born from the conflict, necessarily eulogizes the heroes; Mary Johnston's "The Long Roll," perhaps the best Southern war novel, celebrates the ardors, not the anguishes, of Stonewall Jackson's foot-cavalry; St. Gaudens's monument on Boston Common to Robert Gould Shaw and his black infantry — the men whose dauntless hearts beat a charge right up the red rampart's slippery swell — shows the fighters, not the fallen. The historian assists in falsifying the picture. Cold, objective, he assumes that both the glorious and horrible sides exist, and need no special emphasis. He thus tends to equate the two, although the pains and penalties of war far outweigh its gleams of grandeur.

Then, too, a problem of expression impedes the realistic writer. It is not difficult to describe the pageantry of Pickett's charge. But when we come to the costs, what can we say except that the casualties were 3,000 killed, 5,000 wounded? It is impossible to describe the agony of even one soldier dying of a gangrened wound, or the heartache of one mother losing her first born; what of 10,000 such soldiers and mothers? Moreover, most historians, like the novelists and poets, have an instinctive preference for the bright side of the coin. Henry Steele Commager's otherwise fine introduction to his valuable compilation "The Blue and The Gray" has much to say about gallantry and bravery, but nothing about the squalor, the stench, and the agony.

If we protest against the prettification of the Civil War, the thoughtless glorification of what was essentially a temporary breakdown of American civilization, we must do so with an acknowledgment that it did call forth many manifestations of an admirable spirit. The pomp and circumstance, the parade and pageantry, we may dismiss as essentially empty. The valor of the host of young men who streamed to the colors we may deeply admire, but as valor we may fortunately take it for granted, for most men are brave. The patriotic ardor displayed in the first months of the war may also be taken for granted. What was highly impressive was the serious, sustained conviction, the long-enduring dedication, of countless thousands on both sides for their chosen cause. This went far beyond the transient enthusiasms of Sumter and Bull Run; far beyond ordinary battlefield courage. Lecky was correct in writing: "That which invests war with a certain grandeur is the heroic self-sacrifice which it elicits." All life is in a real sense a conflict between good and evil, in which every man or woman plays a part. A host of young Americans felt that they were enlisted in this large struggle, and regarded their service to the North or South as part of a lifetime service to the right.

Those who seek examples of this dedication can find them scattered throughout the war records. Lincoln specially admired his young friend Elmer Ellsworth, who had endured poverty and hardship with monastic devotion to train himself for service; Lee specially admired John Pelham, the daring artillerist. Both gave their lives. Some fine illustrations of the consecrated spirit can be found in the two volumes of the "Harvard Memorial Biographies" edited by Thomas Wentworth Higginson just after the war. The ninety-eight Harvard dead were no better than the farm lads from Iowa or Alabama, the clerks from New Orleans or New York, but some of them had special gifts of self-expression. Hearken, for example, to Colonel Peter A. Porter, who wrote in his last will and testament:

> I can say, with truth, that I have entered on the course of danger with no ambitious aspirations, nor with the idea that I am fitted, by nature, or experience, to be of any important service to the government; but in obedience to the call of duty, demanding every citizen to contribute what he could, in means, labor, or life, to sustain the government of his country — a sacrifice made the more willingly by me when I consider how singularly benefitted I have been, by the institutions of the land. . . .

As we distinguish between the shining glory of the war — this readiness of countless thousands to die for an enduring moral conviction — and the false or unimportant glories, so we must distinguish between the major and the lesser debits of the conflict. Some evils and mischiefs which seemed tremendous at the time have grown less in the perspective of years; some which at first appeared small now loom large.

It was one of the bloodiest of all wars; the total deaths in the Union and Confederate armies have been computed at about 620,000; and one of the facts which appalls any careful student is the enormous amount of suffering on the field and in the hospitals. The evidence of this, while not within the view of general readers, is incontrovertible. Armies the world over in 1860 were *worse* provided with medical and surgical facilities than in Napoleon's day. The United States, after its long peace, began the war with practically no medical service whatever. Surgical application of the ideas of Pasteur and Lister lay in the future. Almost every abdominal wound meant death. Any severe laceration of a limb entailed amputation, with a good chance of mortal gangrene or erysipelas. The North systematically prevented shipments of drugs and surgical instruments to the South, a measure which did not shorten the conflict by a day, but cost the Southern troops untold agony. Had it not been for the Sanitary Commission, a body privately organized and supported, Northern armies would have duplicated the experience of British forces in the Crimea; yet Secretary of War Stanton at first deliberately impeded the Commission's work.

The story of battle after battle was the same. Night descended on a field ringing with cries of agony: Water! Water! Help! — if in winter, Blankets! Cover! All too frequently no help whatever was forthcoming. After some great conflicts the wounded lay for days, and sometimes a week, without rescue. Shiloh was fought on a Sunday and Monday. Rain set in on Sunday night, and the cold April drizzle continued through Tuesday night. On Tuesday morning nine-tenths of the wounded still lay where they fell; many had been there forty-eight hours without attention; numbers had died of shock or exhaustion; some had even drowned as the rain filled depressions from which they could not crawl. Every house in the area was converted into a hospital, where the floors were covered with wretches heavily wounded, sometimes with arms or legs torn off, who after the first bandages, got no nursing, medical care, or even nourishment. "The first day or two," wrote a newspaper reporter, "the air was filled with groans, sobs, and frenzied curses, but now the sufferers are quiet; not from cessation of pain, but mere exhaustion." Yet at this time the war was a year old.

Still more poignant versions of the same story might be given. Lee and Pope fought Second Manassas on the last Friday and Saturday in August, 1862, so near Washington that groups standing on housetops in the capital heard the rumble of artillery. The battleground, five miles long and three wide, was thickly strewn with dead and wounded. Pope retreated in confusion; many in Washington feared the city might be taken. In these circumstances, as late as the following Wednesday one member of the inadequate body of surgeons estimated that 2,000 wounded had received no attention. Many had not tasted food for four days; some were dying of hunger and thirst. A reporter for the Washington *Republican* wrote on Thursday that some dying men could yet be saved by prompt help. And on Friday, a week after the battle began, a correspondent of the New York *Tribune* told of heart-rending scenes as the doctors searched among heaps of putrefying dead men for men yet clinging to life — men who, when anyone approached, would cry, "Doctor, come to *me*; you look like a kind man; for God's sake come to *me*."

Anyone who is tempted to think of Gettysburg only in terms of its heroic episodes, its color and drama, should turn to the pages in "Battles and Leaders" in which General John D. Imboden describes the transport of the Confederate wounded, after their defeat, back into Maryland. He was ordered to ride to the head of the long wagon column as, in darkness and storm, it moved south:

> For four hours I hurried forward on my way to the front, and in all that time I was never out of hearing of the groans and cries of the wounded and dying. Scarcely one in a hundred had received adequate surgical aid, owing to the demands on the hard-working surgeons from still worse cases that had to be left behind. Many of the wounded in their wagons had been without food for thirty-six hours. Their torn and bloody clothing, matted and hardened, was rasping the tender, inflamed, and still oozing wounds. Very few of the wagons had even a layer of straw in them, and all were without springs. The road was rough and rocky from the heavy washings of the preceding day. The jolting was enough to have killed strong men, if long exposed to it. From nearly every wagon as the teams trotted on, urged by whip and shout, came such cries and shrieks as these:
> "My God! Why can't I die?"
> "My God! Will no one have mercy and kill me?"
> "Stop! Oh, for God's sake stop just for one minute; take me out and leave me to die on the roadside."
> Occasionally a wagon would be passed from which only low, deep moans could be heard. No help could be rendered to any of the sufferers. No heed could be given to any of their appeals. Mercy and duty to the many forbade the loss of a moment in the vain effort then and there to comply with the prayers of the few. On! On! We must move on. The storm continued and the darkness was appalling. There was no time even to fill a canteen with water for a dying man; for, except the drivers and the guards, all were wounded and utterly helpless in that vast procession of misery. During this one night I realized more of the horrors of war than I had in all the preceding two years. . . .

Yet *this* was far from being the ugliest side of war. Nor was the suffering in the huge prison camps, South and North, part of the worst side of war;

the suffering which MacKinlay Kantor describes in his novel and to which Benét briefly adverts in "John Brown's Body":

> The triple stockade of Andersonville the damned,
> Where men corrupted like flies in their own dung
> And the gangrened sick were black with smoke and their filth.

What maims the bodies of men is less significant than what maims their spirit.

One ugly aspect of the Civil War too generally ignored is the devastation, more and more systematic, that accompanied it. For three reasons too little has been said of this devastation; the facts were kept out of official reports, the tale is too painful, and the recital easily becomes monotonous. Yet by 1862 the war in the South had become one of general depredation; by 1863, of wanton destruction; and by 1864, of an organized devastation which in terms of property anticipated the worst chapters of the two world wars. Georgia and the Shenandoah suffered in 1864 almost precisely as Belgium and Serbia suffered in 1914 — the executions omitted. It was barbaric, and the only excuse to be made is that war is barbarism.

The turning point in the attitude of Northern military men was reached when General John Pope on July 18, 1862, issued from Washington headquarters a set of Draconian general orders. Order No. 5 directed that the army should subsist as far as practicable upon the country, giving vouchers for supplies seized. Order No. 7 decreed the summary execution of persons caught firing upon Union troops from houses. Order No. 11 (five days later) required officers to arrest immediately all disloyal males within reach, to make them take the oath of allegiance or go South, and to shoot all who violated their oath or who returned from the Confederacy. The order for living on the country, widely publicized East and West, changed the attitude of troops, and inspired private looting as well as public seizures of property. Pope was soon ousted, but the moral effect of his orders persisted.

Though most of the facts were excluded from official reports, their sum total, insofar as one shrewd observer could arrive at it, may be found in John T. Trowbridge's graphic volume written in 1866, "A Picture of the Desolated States." In his preface Trowbridge speaks of the Union forces not as our heroic armies but our destroying armies. Even this practiced reporter is less graphic, however, than the people who suffered under the onslaught and wrote while their emotions, like their property, still burned. Hear a lady of Louisiana tell what occurred when N. P. Banks's army passed:

> I was watching from my window the apparently orderly march of the first Yankees that appeared in view and passed up the road, when, suddenly, as if by magic, the whole plantation was covered with men, like bees from an overthrown hive; and, as far as my vision extended, an inextricable medley

of men and animals met my eye. In one place, excited troopers were firing into the flock of sheep; in another, officers and men were in pursuit of the boys' ponies, and in another, a crowd were in excited chase of the work animals. The kitchen was soon filled with some, carrying off the cooking utensils and the provisions of the day; the yard with others, pursuing the poultry. . . . They penetrated under the house, into the outbuildings, and into the garden, stripping it in a moment of all its vegetables. . . . This continued during the day . . . and amid a bewildering sound of oaths and imprecations. . . . When the army had passed, we were left destitute.

Sherman believed in total war; that is, in waging war not only against the Southern armies, but the Southern people. His theory was that every man, woman, and child was "armed and at war." He wrote his wife in the summer of 1862 that the North might fall into bankruptcy, "but if they can hold on the war will soon assume a turn to extermination, not of soldiers alone, that is the least part of the trouble, but the people." He denied, in effect, that Southerners had a right to resist invasion. When Union steamers were fired on near Randolph, Mississippi, in the fall of 1862, he destroyed Randolph, and a little later had all houses, farms, and cornfields devastated for fifteen miles along the banks.

When he drove his red plowshare across Georgia and the Carolinas, his object was to leave only scorched earth behind. He had already written of his Western operations: "Not a man is to be seen; nothing but women with houses plundered, fields open to the cattle and horses, pickets lounging on every porch, and desolation sown broadcast; servants all gone, and women and children bred in luxury . . . begging . . . for soldiers' rations." His aim was that which Phil Sheridan avowed: to leave them nothing but their eyes to weep with.

The final devastation of half the South was horrible to behold, and it was distressing to think that these savage losses had been inflicted by Americans upon fellow Americans. Yet this was far from being the worst aspect of the conflict, or the least easily reparable. Damages on which we can fix the dollar sign are important not in themselves, but as they become translated into cultural and spiritual losses; into the intellectual retardation caused by poverty, for example. The physical recovery of the South was rapid. As it was primarily an agricultural section, a few good crops at fair prices did much to restore it; and the swiftness with which housing, railroads, bridges, and public facilities were rebuilt astonished observers of the 1870s just as the swift postwar recovery of Germany and Poland has astonished observers of our day.

Infinitely worse were the biological losses — the racial hurts — inflicted by the Civil War. The killing of between 600,000 and 700,000 young men in a nation of 33,000,000 and the maiming or permanent debilitation of as many more had evil consequences projected into the far-distant future.

We lost not only these men, but their children, and their children's children. Here, indeed, was a loss that proved highly cumulative. . . .

. . . [T]he multitude of Civil War dead represent hundreds of thousands of homes, and hundreds of thousands of families, that might have been, and never were. They represent millions of people who might have been part of our population today and are not. We have lost the books they might have written, the scientific discoveries they might have made, the inventions they might have perfected. Such a loss defies measurement.

The only noteworthy attempt to measure the biological losses was made by David Starr Jordan and his son Harvey in a volume called "War's Aftermath" (1914). The authors circulated carefully drawn questionnaires in Spottsylvania and Rockbridge Counties in Virginia, and in Cobb County in Georgia, inquiring particularly into the eugenic effects of the conflict. One of their queries brought out evidence that by no means all casualties were among the men; numerous girls and women succumbed to the hardships and anxieties of the conflict in the South. Another question elicited unanimous agreement that "the flower of the people" went into the war at the beginning, and of these a large part died before the end. President Jordan, weighing all the responses, reached two conclusions: first, that the evidence "leaves a decided evidence in favor of grave racial hurt," and second, that "the war has seriously impoverished this country of its best human values."

Even the terrible loss of young, productive lives, the grave biological injury to the nation, however, did not constitute the worst side of the war. One aspect of the conflict was still more serious. It was the aspect to which Lowell referred in lines written a few years after Appomattox:

> I looked to see an ampler atmosphere
> By that electric passion-gust blown clear
> I looked for this; consider what I hear. . . .
>
> Murmur of many voices in the air
> Denounces us degenerate,
> Unfaithful guardians of a noble fate. . . .

The war, as Walt Whitman truly said, had grown out of defects in the American character; of American faults it cured few, accentuated a number, and gave some a violently dangerous trend. Far behind the lines, it added to the already discreditable total of violence in American life. Applying to industry a great forcing-draft, the bellows of huge wartime appropriations, it strengthened the materialistic forces in our civilization. Its state and federal contracts, its bounty system, its innumerable opportunities for battening on the nation's woes, made speculation fashionable, and corruption almost too common for comment. Its inflation bred extravagance and dissipation.

Every month heightened the intolerance of war; it began with mobs in New York threatening newspaper offices, a mob in Philadelphia trying to lynch Senator James A. Bayard, and mobs in the South flogging and exiling Union men; as it went on, freedom of speech almost disappeared over broad areas. The atmosphere of war fostered immorality; Richmond and Washington alike became filled with saloons, brothels, and gambling dens, and such occupied cities as Memphis and Nashville were sinks of iniquity. For every knightly martyr like James Wadsworth or Albert Sidney Johnston there arose two such coarse, aggressive, selfish careerists as Ben Butler and Dan Sickles. Wadsworth and Johnston died in battle, but Butler and Sickles remained to follow postwar political careers. Seen in perspective, the war was a gigantic engine for coarsening and lowering the American character even while it quickened certain of our energies.

Parson Brownlow, a Tennessee Unionist, went from city to city in the North in 1862 demanding "grape for the Rebel masses, and hemp for their leaders"; saying that he himself would tie the rope about the necks of some rebel generals; calling for the confiscation of all Southern property; proclaiming that he would be glad to arm every wolf, bear, catamount, and crocodile, every devil in hell, to defeat the South; and declaring he would put down the rebellion "if it exterminates from God's green earth every man, woman, and child south of Mason and Dixon's Line."

In the South two famous leaders, Robert Toombs and Howell Cobb, united that year in an address to their people just as vitriolic. "The foot of the oppressor is on the soil of Georgia," it began. "He comes with lust in his eye, poverty in his purse, and hell in his heart. How shall you meet him? . . . With death for him or for yourself!" Better the charnel house for every Southerner, they continued, than "loathsome vassalage to a nation already sunk below the contempt of the civilized world." Thaddeus Stevens nursed his hatred until he spoke of "exterminating" or driving into exile all Southerners, just as Sherman declared he would "slay millions" to assure the safety of the Mississippi. Women of the South meanwhile expressed the most vindictive detestation of all Yankees. "I hate them," wrote one Mississippi woman after a raid on her community, "more now than I did the evening I saw them sneaking off with all we cared for, and so it will be every day I live."

Hatred was seen in its most naked form in those communities divided against themselves and racked by guerrilla war; in Missouri, Arkansas, parts of Kentucky, and East Tennessee. Writes Charles D. Drake, a distinguished Missouri leader, of his state: "Falsehood, treachery, and perjury pervaded the whole social fabric." He went on: "Could there be written a full account of all the crimes of the rebels of Missouri, and the outrages and wrongs inflicted by them upon her loyal inhabitants, during the four years of the rebellion, the world would shrink aghast from a picture which has no parallel in the previous history of any portion of the

Anglo-Saxon race." Confederate sympathizers in Missouri would have said the same of Union irregulars. One atrocity provoked another. These hatreds long survived the conflict, and indeed in some spots the embers still smoulder. Typifying the whole range of spiritual injuries wrought by the war, they justify the poet Blake's cry:

> The soldier, armed with sword and gun,
> Palsied strikes the summer sun.

The historian Mendelssohn Bartholdy, in his volume entitled "War and German Society," written as part of the Carnegie Endowment's huge economic history of World War I, concluded that the moral effects of war are much worse than the material effects. He also concluded that they are radically bad, for they strike at the very heart of a country's character: "modern war, with its robot-like disregard of individual values, is bound to make the peculiar virtue of a nation an object of attack." As respects the Civil War, we can agree. If it was necessary for preserving the Union and extinguishing slavery, it was of course worth more than it cost; but should it have been necessary? Could not better leadership from 1830 to 1860 have averted it? This is a bootless question. But it is certain that the conflict, so much the greatest convulsion in our history, so tremendous in its impact on our national life, so fascinating in its drama, was in spite of all compensating elements, all the heroism, all the high example we find in Lee's character and Lincoln's wisdom, materially a disaster and morally a tragedy.

It is unfortunate that of the flood of books on the war ninety-nine in a hundred are on military topics and leaders, and that a great majority fasten attention on the floating banners, the high-ringing cheers, the humors of the camp, the ardors of the charge; the whole undeniable fascination and romance of the first true *volkskrieg* in history. It is right, within measure, to let them lift our hearts. But the long commemoration will pass essentially unimproved if it does not give us a deeper, sterner, more scientific study of the collision of two creeds and two ways of life as related to an examination of war in general.

We should probe more deeply into its roots, a process that will expose some of the weaknesses of our social fabric and governmental system. We should pay fuller attention to its darker aspects, and examine more honestly such misrepresentations as the statement it was distinguished by its generosity of spirit, the magnanimity with which the combatants treated each other; a statement absurd on its face, for no war which lasts four years and costs 600,000 lives leaves much magnanimity in its later phases. We should above all examine more closely the effects of the great and terrible war not on the nation's politics — we know that; not on its economy — we also know that; but on its character, the vital element of national life.

This examination will lead into unpleasant paths, and bring us to unhappy conclusions; but it will profit us far more than stirring battle canvases. All nations must be schooled in such studies if the world is ever to find an answer to a question uttered just after World War I by William E. Borah, a question that still rings in men's ears: "When shall we escape from war? When shall we loosen the grip of the monster?"

STUDY GUIDE

1. Nevins raises the question as to whether the Civil War was necessary to abolish slavery. Some historians feel that slavery would have died out because it was becoming economically unprofitable; others argue that only conflict could have eliminated a system so deeply embedded in American life as was slavery. Is this a question that can be answered by historical study? What kind of evidence might be relevant if one attempted to do so?

2. Generally, historians simply study and try to *explain* wars, rather than make moral judgments on them. Do you see any special limitations to historical study or training that makes this sensible; or are historians in a better position than most people to judge, and in failing to do so are they abdicating their responsibility to inform society? How would you approach the question of judging the relative justness of the American Revolution and the Civil War or World War II and the Vietnam War?

3. Consider the following aspects of warfare, and indicate how wars in our time differ from the Civil War in each respect: treatment of civilian populations, individual atrocities, personal confrontations of infantry soldiers in battle and in picket-line duty, ways in which soldiers are killed, and the degree of personal responsibility and concern that higher officers feel for their armies.

4. Compare the feelings described by Nevins with the animosities that are described by Wallace Brown in his essay on the Loyalists during the American Revolution (Reading No. 6). What differences and similarities can you think of in the relations of the two opposing forces during these two wars? Why were the Loyalists in a more difficult position with respect to confiscation of property and such personal abuse as tarring and feathering than were the enemy forces during the Civil War?

BIBLIOGRAPHY

There are more books and articles on the American Civil War than on any other aspect of American history. Much of this material deals with the causes of the war and the military campaigns; to discover some of this literature, you can examine James G. Randall and David Donald, *The Civil War and*

Reconstruction, 2nd ed. (1961) and Thomas J. Pressly, *Americans Interpret Their Civil War* (1954). Many aspects of army life are treated in Bell I. Wiley, *Johnny Reb* (1943) and its companion volume by the same author, *The Life of Billy Yank* (1952). The attitudes of contemporaries toward the war are described in Henry S. Commager, ed., *The Blue and the Gray: The Story of the Civil War as Told by Participants*, 2 vols. (1940). Among the many general treatments of the war, the best are Allan Nevins, *The War for the Union*, 3 vols. (1959–1971); Bruce Catton, *This Hallowed Ground: The Story of the Union Side of the Civil War* (1956); and a three-volume series by Catton, of which the best volume is *A Stillness at Appomattox* (1953). George W. Smith and Charles Judah, eds., *Life in the North during the Civil War: A Source History* (1966) is a collection of writings from the period of the Civil War that will give you an idea of life behind the lines. One of the best secondary works on the same subject, but limited to the northern capital, is Margaret Leech, *Reveille in Washington, 1860–1865* (1941). Conditions there, of course, were considerably different from life in the Confederate capital, which is studied in Alfred H. Bill, *The Beleaguered City: Richmond, 1861–1865* (1946).

For a number of reasons, there are more good works on social conditions in the Confederacy than on wartime life in the North. A general work on the Confederacy, with several chapters on economic and social conditions, is E. Merton Coulter, *The Confederate States of America, 1861–1865* (1950). Charles W. Ramsdell, *Behind the Lines in the Southern Confederacy* (1944) is an excellent work more strictly confined to the home front, while Mary E. Massey, *Ersatz in the Confederacy* (1952) is a fascinating study of the substitutes that were used for food, clothing, and other necessities of life.

Bell I. Wiley also has works on southern whites and blacks in the Confederacy: *The Plain People of the Confederacy* (1943) and *Southern Negroes, 1861–1865* (1938). The latter work should be read in conjunction with the study of Negroes in the North by Benjamin Quarles, *The Negro in the Civil War* (1953). Chapters 7 and 8 of Quarles's book give an interesting picture of the reaction of blacks to emancipation. If you would like to supplement Nevins's general essay with a detailed account of the devastation in one campaign, see Burke Davis, *Sherman's March* (1980).

Southern blacks in the post–Civil War South soon learned that emancipation did not bring social equality.

21

JOEL WILLIAMSON

After Slavery

Few dreams in the history of the United States have been so cruelly
unrealized as the hope that with the end of the Civil War and the
destruction of the institution of slavery, black Americans would be
accorded some measure of equality and opportunity in American life.
With the end of the war in 1865, reform-minded Republicans, known
as Radical Republicans, sought to make this dream a reality. Through
their control of Congress they initiated Reconstruction, a program designed to restructure the social and political relations between whites
and blacks in the defeated South. In 1865 and 1866, Congress funded
the Freedmen's Bureau to feed, clothe, and protect the ex-slaves; civil
rights legislation was passed in 1866 and reinforced by the Civil Rights
Act of 1875, intended to outlaw varied forms of segregation; and three
amendments were added to the Constitution. The Thirteenth Amendment (1865) outlawed slavery, the Fourteenth Amendment (1868) extended federal citizenship to blacks and made illegal many parts of
the black codes, and the Fifteenth Amendment (1870) protected the
black man's right to vote.

Despite this and other legislation, and despite the ascension to
power of Reconstruction governments in the southern states — state
governments in which political power was shared by a combination
of southern scalawags, northern carpetbaggers, and emancipated
blacks — the Radical Republican effort to reconstruct the relations
between the races in the South ended in failure. The first stage of that
failure, what one historian has so aptly called "darkness at noon,"
came with the end of Reconstruction. Reconstruction was ended by
the disputed election of Republican Rutherford B. Hayes over Democrat Samuel J. Tilden in 1876 and by the Compromise of 1877, in

which the rights of black Americans were made secondary to the economic opportunities and social privileges of white Americans, both Democrats and Republicans. The second stage in the disfranchisement and segregation of American blacks came between the end of Reconstruction and the American entry into World War I in 1914. The caste system created in these decades paralleled, to a degree, the relations between the races in parts of southern Africa today.

The selection that follows tells us about the origins of the southern caste system. In his book *After Slavery: The Negro in South Carolina during Reconstruction, 1861–1877*, Joel Williamson finds that patterns of segregation came to South Carolina in the Reconstruction period. Williamson thus refutes a cardinal assumption made by C. Vann Woodward, the dean of southern historians. Woodward contends that until the 1890s, southern whites still held open options in their treatment of southern blacks and that "Jim Crow," the disfranchisement and the segregation of blacks, was a product of decisions made by southern whites *after* Reconstruction, closer to the turn of the century. Williamson's essay, taken from his study of the Reconstruction in South Carolina, demonstrates that in South Carolina this was not so.

The physical separation of the races was the most revolutionary change in relations between whites and Negroes in South Carolina during Reconstruction.

Separation had, of course, marked the Negro in slavery; yet the very nature of slavery necessitated a constant, physical intimacy between the races. In the peculiar institution, the white man had constantly and closely to oversee the labor of the Negro, preserve order in domestic arrangements within the slave quarters, and minister to the physical, medical, and moral needs of his laborers. In brief, slavery enforced its own special brand of interracial associations; in a sense, it married the interests of white to black at birth and the union followed both to the grave. Slavery watched the great mass of Negroes in South Carolina, but those Negroes who lived outside of the slave system were not exempt from the scrutiny of the whites. Even in Charleston, the free Negro community was never large enough to establish its economic and racial independence. In the mid-nineteenth century, as the bonds of slavery tightened, the whites were

From *After Slavery: The Negro in South Carolina during Reconstruction, 1861–1877*, by Joel Williamson. Copyright 1965 The University of North Carolina Press. By permission of the publisher.

forced to bring free Negroes under ever more stringent controls and to subject their lives to the closest surveillance.

During the spring and summer of 1865, as the centripetal force of slavery melted rapidly away, each race clearly tended to disassociate itself from the other. The trend was evident in every phase of human endeavor: agriculture, business, occupations, schools and churches, in every aspect of social intercourse and politics. As early as July of 1865, a Bostonian in Charleston reported that "the worst sign here . . . is the growth of a bitter and hostile spirit between blacks and whites — a gap opening between the races which, it would seem may at some time result seriously." Well before the end of Reconstruction, separation had crystallized into a comprehensive pattern which, in its essence, remained unaltered until the middle of the twentieth century.

There is no clear, concise answer to the question of why separation occurred. Certainly, it was not simply a response of Negroes to the prejudiced fiat of dominant whites; nor was it a totally rationalized reaction on the part of either race. Actually, articulate whites and Negroes seldom attempted to explain their behavior. Yet, the philosophies and attitudes each race adopted toward the other lend a certain rationality to separation, and, if we are always mindful that this analysis presumes a unity which they never expressed, can be applied to promote an understanding of the phenomenon.

For the native white community, separation was a means of avoiding or minimizing problems which, they felt, would inevitably arise from the inherent inferiority of the Negro, problems which the North, in eradicating slavery and disallowing the Black Code, would not allow them to control by overt political means. In this limited sense, segregation was a substitute for slavery.

Thus, first, total separation was essential to racial purity, and racial purity was necessary to the preservation of a superior civilization which the whites had labored so arduously to construct, and suffered a long and bloody war to defend. After the war, that civilization was embattled, but not necessarily lost. Unguarded association with an inferior caste would obviously endanger white culture. In this view, children were peculiarly susceptible to damage. "Don't imagine that I allow my children to be with negroes out of my presence," wrote the mistress of a lowcountry plantation in 1868, "on one occasion only have they been so with my knowledge." Even the Negro wet nurse, that quintessence of maternalism upon which the slave period paternalist so often turned his case, emerged as the incubus of Southern infancy. "We gave our infants to the black wenches to suckle," lamented an elderly white, "and thus poisoned the blood of our children, and made them *cowards* . . . the Character of the people of the state was ruined by slavery and it will take 500 years, if not longer, by the infusion of new blood to eradicate the hereditary vices imbibed with the blood (milk is blood) of black wet nurses." . . .

Separation also facilitated the subordination of the inferior race by constantly reminding the Negro that he lived in a world in which the white man was dominant, and in which the non-white was steadfastly denied access to the higher caste. Further, the impression of Negro inferiority would be constantly re-enforced by relegating the baser element, whenever possible, to the use of inferior facilities. The sheer totality of the display alone might well serve to convince members of the lower caste that such, indeed, was in the natural order of things.

Many whites had envisioned the early elimination of the freedman from the Southern scene, and many had eagerly anticipated this event. In time, however, it became evident to all that the Negro would be neither dissolved nor transported to Africa. In a sense, separation was a means of securing the quasi elimination of Negroes at home. It was, perhaps, a more satisfactory solution than their demise or emigration, since it might produce many of the benefits of their disappearance without losing an advantageous, indeed, a necessary supply of labor.

Finally, separation was a logical solution to the problem posed by the widespread conviction that the races were inherently incompatible outside of the master-slave relationship. If the white man could not exist in contentment in the proximity of Negroes, then partial satisfaction might be achieved by withdrawal from associations with members of the inferior caste. This spirit was evident among some of the wealthier whites who voluntarily dispensed entirely with the services of Negro domestics. Elderly William Heyward, in 1868 still second to none in the ranks of the rice aristocracy, stopped taking his meals at the Charleston Hotel because, as he said, he found "the negro waiters so defiant and so familiar in their attentions." "A part of the satisfaction is," he explained to a friend, "that I am perfectly independent of having negroes about me; if I cannot have them as they used to be, I have no desire to see them except in the field." Planters were often manifesting precisely the same sentiment when they deserted their land and turned to grain culture, or to the use of immigrant labor. Separation was also a way of avoiding interracial violence. B. O. Duncan and James L. Orr, both native white Republicans, argued against mixing in the public schools because they were convinced that minor irritations between children would generate major altercations between parents of different races. Conceived as a means of avoiding violence, separation, ironically, was subsequently enforced by the use of violence. . . .

Contrary to common belief, the separation of the races was not entirely the work of the whites. Suspicious, resentful, and sometimes hateful toward the whites, chafed by white attitudes of superiority, and irritated by individual contacts with supercilious whites, Negroes, too, sought relief in withdrawal from association with the other race. In many instances, the disassociation was complete — that is, many Negroes left the state. During the war, Corporal Simon Crum of the First South Carolina declared his intention of leaving South Carolina after the capitulation because, as he phrased it, "dese yer Secesh [secessionists] will neber be cibilized in my time." For those who could not or would not leave, alternative forms of withdrawal were possible. A major facet in the new pattern of agriculture was the removal of Negro labor from the immediate supervision of white men. As the Negro agriculturalist moved his labor away from the eye of the white man, so also did he move his family and his home. Plantation villages became increasingly rare as Negro landowners and renters either built new houses on their plots or, in a rather graphic symbolic display, laboriously dragged their cabins away from the "Negro street." Negroes in the trades and in domestic service followed similar trends. Furthermore, Negroes chose to withdraw from white-dominated churches, though they were often urged to stay, and they attended racially separated schools in spite of the legal fact that all schools were open to all races. Negroes also tended to withdraw from political association with members of the white community.

Finally, on those few occasions when Negroes entered into polite social situations with whites, Northern as well as Southern, they were often ill at ease. For instance, while driving along a road near Columbia, a planter and his wife met William, "a fine looking light mulatto" who had been their stableboy as a slave. William was driving a buggy and seated beside him was a young white woman, elegantly attired. The woman was a "Yankee school marm," probably one of the new teachers in Columbia's Negro school. As he passed his late master and mistress, the Negro averted his gaze and did not speak. The following day, he approached the planter and apologized for having been escort to a "white woman." He had met the teacher at a celebration, he explained, and she had insisted on his taking her to see the countryside.

During Reconstruction, the Negro's withdrawal was never a categorical rejection of the white man and his society. In the early days of freedom, it was primarily a reaction against slavery, an attempt to escape the unpleasant associations of his previous condition and the derogatory implications of human bondage. However, as the memory of slavery faded, a more persistent reason for withdrawal emerged. Essentially, it was the Negro's answer to discrimination. Almost invariably, attempts by individual Negroes to establish satisfactory relations across the race line were unsuccessful, and, all too often, the pain of the experience was greater than the reward for having stood for principle. During Reconstruction and afterward, only a few were willing to undergo such pain without the certainty of success. It was much easier, after all, simply to withdraw.

Withdrawal as a solution to the race problem was by no means satisfactory to the Negro leadership. Implicit in the behavior of Negro leaders during Reconstruction was a yearning for complete and unreserved acceptance for members of their race by the white community. However, overtly, and rather politically, they carefully distinguished between "social equality" and what might be appropriately termed "public equality." For themselves, they claimed only the latter. "Our race do not demand social equality," declared W. J. Whipper, a member from Beaufort, on the floor of the house of representatives in Columbia. . . .

What the Negro leadership did insist upon was public equality, that is, absolute civil and political parity with whites and full and free access to most public facilities. These latter included restaurants, bars, saloons, railway and street cars, shipboard accommodations, the theater, and other such places of public amusement. Once they gained political power, Negro leaders hastened to embody this attitude in legislation. Within a week after the first sitting of the Constitutional Convention of 1868, a Negro delegate introduced a resolution which was eventually included in the state's bill of rights: "Distinction on account of race or color, in any case whatever, shall be prohibited, and all classes of citizens shall enjoy equally all common, public, legal and political privileges." Similarly, one of the first bills passed by the Republican legislature prohibited licensed businesses from discriminating "between persons, on account of race, color, or previous condition, who shall make lawful application for the benefit of such business, calling or pursuit." Convicted violators were liable to a fine of not less than $1,000 or imprisonment for not less than a year. During the debate on the measure in the house, not a single Negro member spoke against the bill, and only five of the twenty-four votes registered against it were cast by Negroes, while fifty-three of the sixty-one votes which secured its passage were those of Negro legislators.

Negro Congressmen were no less ardent in championing the same cause in Washington, particularly in 1874, when a federal civil rights bill was up for consideration. "Is it pretended anywhere," asked Congressman R. B. Elliott, who had only recently been denied service in the restaurant of a railway station in North Carolina on his journey to the capital, "that the evils of which we complain, our exclusion from the public inn, from the saloon and the table of the steamboat, from the sleeping-coach on the railway, from the right of sepulture in the public burial-ground, are an exercise of the police power of the State? . . . Are the colored people to be assimilated to an unwholesome trade or to combustible materials, to be interdicted, to be shut up within prescribed limits?" Several days later, in the same place, Congressman R. H. Cain declared, "We do not want any discrimination to be made. I do not ask any legislation for the colored people of this country that is not applied to the white people of this country. All that we seek is equal laws, equal legislation, and equal rights throughout the length and breadth of this land."

It was upon this emotional, uneven ground that an essentially new color line was drawn. It was established in a kind of racial warfare, of assaults and withdrawals, of attacks and counterattacks. Nevertheless, well before the end of Reconstruction, both forces had been fully engaged and the line was unmistakably formed.

Even before the Radicals came into power in South Carolina in 1868, native whites had already defined a color line in government-supported institutions, on common carriers, in places of public accommodation and amusement, and, of course, in private social organizations. The degree of separation in each of these areas varied. In many instances, obviously, some compromise between expense and the desire for complete separation had to be made. Usually, the compromise involved the division of available facilities in some manner. If this was thought to be inconvenient, Negroes were totally excluded.

Typical was the treatment of Negro and white prisoners in the state penitentiary under the James L. Orr regime [1865–68; South Carolina]. Criminals of both races were confined in the same institution but were quartered in separate cells. Ironically, the racial concepts of white prison officials sometimes redounded to the benefit of Negro inmates. Minor violations of prison rules were punished every Sunday by the offenders being tied closely together, blindfolded, and forced to work their way over a series of obstacles in the prison yard. The chief guard explained that the white offenders were placed in the most difficult middle positions of the "blind gang" because "they have more intelligence than the colored ones and are better able to understand the rules of the institution."

It is paradoxical that the Negro leadership, once in office, pressed vigorously for an end to separation in privately-owned facilities open to the public but they allowed a very distinct separation to prevail in every major governmental facility. The most obvious instance was the schools, but the distinction also stretched into the furthermost reaches of guber-natorial activity. For example, a visitor to the state insane asylum in Columbia in 1874 found that "The Negro female inmates occupy a separate part of the same building" in which the white women were housed.

On the other side, within a month after they had gained the vote, Negroes in South Carolina opened a frontal attack against racial discrim-ination on common carriers. Typical was their assault on the Charleston Street Car Company. At the time of its inauguration, the facilities of the company consisted of double tracks running the length of the peninsula with a spur branching off near the mid-point. Horse-drawn cars, each manned by a driver and a conductor, ran along the tracks at regular intervals. The cars contained seats in a compartment, and front and rear platforms. Before the cars began to run in December, 1866, the question of the accommodation of Negro passengers was thoroughly canvassed. "Proper arrangements will in due time be made to allow persons of color to avail themselves of the benefits of the railway," the management assured the Negro community, but it had not then decided between providing "special cars" for the Negroes as was done in New Orleans, or "assigning to them a portion of the ordinary cars as is more usual in other cities." Negro leaders rejected both alternatives. As a Northerner wrote from Charleston in January, 1867, "Every scheme that could be devised that did not contemplate the promiscuous use of the cars by whites and negroes alike, was scouted by the Negro paper here; and the result is that negroes are now debarred the use of the cars altogether, unless they choose to ride upon the platform." . . .

After the Negro gained political power, the battle against discrimination became more intense and assumed a wider front. The so-called antidiscrimination bill, passed in the summer of 1868, on paper was a most formidable weapon. In essence, it imposed severe penalties upon the owners of public accommodations who were convicted of discrimination. Burden of proof of innocence lay on the accused, and state solicitors (public prosecutors) who failed to prosecute suspected violators were themselves threatened with heavy punishments.

The effect of the new legislation on common carriers was immediate. A Northern teacher returning to Beaufort in the fall of 1868, after a few months' absence in the North, observed a portion of the results:

> We took a small steamer from Charleston for Beaufort. Here we found a decided change since we went North. Then no colored person was allowed on the upper deck, now there were no restrictions — there could be none, for a law had been passed in favor of the negroes. They were everywhere, choosing the best staterooms and best seats at the table. Two prominent colored members of the State Legislature were on board with their families. There were also several well-known Southerners, still uncompromising rebels. It was a curious scene and full of significance. An interesting study to watch the exultant faces of the negroes, and the scowling faces of the rebels . . .

The same legislation applied to railway facilities; and, apparently, it was applied without a great amount of dissent. Adjustment was made easier, perhaps, by the acquisition of some of the railroad companies by Radical politicians within the state, or by Northern capitalists, and by the close understanding which usually prevailed between Republican officeholders and those Conservatives who managed to retain control of their railroads. While formal discrimination was not practiced by railway operators, unofficial racial separation did occur on a large scale. On all of the major lines first- and second-class cars were available. Most Negroes apparently deliberately chose to ride in the more economical second-class accommodations, and virtually all of the whites — particularly white women — took passage on the first-class cars. The separation thus achieved was so nearly complete that the first-class car was often referred to as the "ladies' car." It is highly relevant that the first Jim Crow legislation affecting railroads in South Carolina provided for the separation of the races only in the first-class cars, because, of course, this was the only place on the railroads where there was any possibility of a significant degree of mixing. . . .

In the winter of 1869–1870 and through the summer which followed, a concerted attempt was made by the Negro leadership to win the full acceptance of Negroes into all places of public amusement, eating, drinking, and sleeping. Special provisions for the accommodation of Negroes at public entertainments had been made in ante-bellum times, but physical separation of the races was invariably the rule. In December, 1868, Charles Minort, a mulatto restaurateur and lesser political figure, nearly provoked a riot in a Columbia theater by presuming to seat his wife and himself in the front row, a section traditionally reserved for tardy white ladies. Presumably, he should have chosen seats among the other Negroes present who "had taken their seats, as has always been the custom, in the rear." Minort yielded to the clamor of the whites in the audience, but, a year later, the Negroes of Charleston instituted judicial proceedings against the manager of the Academy of Music for refusing to mix the races in the boxes of the theater. The management barely succeeded in winning a postponement but was able to complete the season before the case came to trial.

In the spring of 1870, Negro leaders in Charleston launched an attack against discrimination in restaurants, bars, and saloons. On March 25, for instance, Louis Kenake, accused of violating the antidiscrimination act, was brought before Magistrate T. J. Mackey and put on a bond of one thousand dollars while awaiting trial. Other white restaurant keepers of Charleston united to oppose and test the validity of the act, but, in the week which followed, at least six additional charges were lodged against operators of such businesses. The assault was not confined to Charleston and demonstrations by Radical politicians were frequent during the campaign of 1870. In April, a Laurens woman wrote to her son in Missouri that "On Monday the yankees & some negroes went to Hayne Williams' and asked for drink, which 'Ward' refused them, that is, to drink at the gentlemans bar. They quietly marched him off to jail, & locked the doors, putting the keys in their pockets. The family are all at Spartanburg, we look for H. Williams to night, and I am afraid of a fuss, for he is a great bully." In the same month, during a Radical meeting in Lancaster, a Negro was refused service in a local bar with the comment that no "nigger" could buy a drink there. Lucius Wimbush, a Negro senator, hearing of the incident, went to the bar, ordered a drink, and was refused. He immediately had the barkeeper arrested and placed under bail. . . .

Negroes were also ambitious to open sleeping accommodations to their race. In the summer of 1868, as the first Negro legislators gathered in Columbia, native whites had been extremely apprehensive that they would attempt to occupy rooms in the city's hotels. Even *The Nation*, which had applauded the opening of common carriers to both races, declared that hotels were another and "delicate" matter, where separation was everywhere observed. The white community was vastly relieved to find that no such invasion was attempted, one upcountry newspaper having sent a special correspondent to Columbia to ascertain the fact. Nevertheless, when Negro legislators debated the antidiscrimination bill early in the session, they made it very clear that hotels were included. William E. Johnson, the African Methodist Minister then representing Sumter County in the statehouse, noting that the management of Nickerson's Hotel was concerned lest Negroes apply for rooms, declared that if he found private accommodations filled he would want to know that this resort was open to him. George Lee, a Negro member from Berkeley, observed that a group of junketing legislators had recently failed to find lodging in Greenville and that this law was desired to prevent that sort of occurrence. "Equal and exact justice to all," he demanded, ". . . it is what we must have." Negroes were subsequently allowed to attend meetings in Columbia hotels, but it is apparent that none were ever given lodging.

Negroes also decried the fact that places of permanent rest occupied by whites, as well as those of a more temporary variety, were denied to their race. For instance, S. G. W. Dill, the native white Radical who was assassinated in Kershaw in the summer of 1868, and Nestor Peavy, his Negro guard who was killed in the same assault, were buried in racially separated cemeteries.

Thus, from 1868 until 1889, when the antidiscrimination law was repealed, Negroes in South Carolina could legally use all public facilities which were open to whites. However, in actual practice, they seldom chose to do so. "The naturally docile negro makes no effort at unnecessary self-assertion," a Northern visitor in Charleston explained in 1870, "unless under the immediate instigation of some dangerous *friends* belonging to the other race, who undertake to manage his destiny." This particular reporter was certainly prejudiced against the race; but four years later another Northern observer congratulated the Negroes of South Carolina on the "moderation and good sense" which they exhibited in their "intercourse with the whites." He concluded, "They seldom intrude themselves into places frequented by the whites, and considering that in South Carolina they have a voting majority of some thirty thousand and control the entire State Government, it is somewhat remarkable that they conduct themselves with so much propriety." Indeed, after 1870, even the Negro leadership hardly seemed inclined to press further their political and legal advantage to end separation. Of the numerous charges lodged under the antidiscrimination law, not a single conviction was ever recorded.

Even when Negroes pressed themselves in upon the prejudice of whites, the latter adjusted by total or partial withdrawal, so that a high degree of separation was always and everywhere maintained.

Some whites responded to the pressure by total withdrawal, that is, by leaving the state entirely. Of course, many of those who left South Carolina did so primarily for economic reasons, but many also departed from purely racial motives. A Winnsboro lawyer and pre-war fire-eater revealed the thinking of many emigrants when he asked William Porcher Miles, in April, 1867, how he could live in a land where "Every 'mulatto' is your Equal & every 'Nigger' is your Superior." Pronouncing the Negro majority "revolting," he advised Miles to go to England. ". . . I have no doubt you could succeed & at any rate w[oul]d not have as many Negro Clients & negro witnesses to offend y[ou]r nostrils as in these USA. I can't conceive of any ones remaining here who can possibly get away — Suppose, it were certain, wh[ich]. it is not, that no U S Congress will ever pass a Law requiring that your Daughter & mine shall either marry Negroes or die unmarried. Still the Negro is already superior to them politically & to their Fathers also, & must ever be so henceforth." . . .

After Negroes were firmly entrenched in official positions in government, native whites evinced a distinct tendency to refrain from associations which recognized the authority of Negro officers over white citizens. For instance, in the heavily Negro county of Abbeville, in 1870, a distressed guardian asked one of the magistrates, who happened to be a Democrat, to dispatch a constable to return an orphan girl stolen away from his house. "When you send for Laura," he begged, "please send a white man, as she is a white girl under my charge, and I would not like to subject her to the mortification of being brought back by a colored man. Besides that I would be censured by the community as they would know nothing of the circumstances of the case." . . .

Withdrawal was also the means by which native whites combatted attempts by Republican officials to end separation in institutions supported by the government. The withdrawal of native whites from the University and the State School for the Deaf and Blind at the prospect of Negro admissions are illustrations of white determination either to maintain separation or to dispense with the services afforded by related state institutions. If the Radicals had attempted to end separation in the common schools, it is virtually certain that the whites would have removed their children from these schools too. As one post-Redemption [post-Recon-struction] proponent of universal education argued, separation was essential to academic progress. Only by this means, he explained to Governor [Wade] Hampton, could it be achieved "without any danger of social equality — *and this is the great bug bear.*" Doubtless, it was the threat of withdrawal by the whites which dissuaded the Radical leadership from further attempts to end separation in institutions over which they had, by political means, absolute control.

Whites also refused to engage in normal civic activities in which the color line was not distinctly drawn. Thus, native whites chose not to join militia companies in which Negroes participated and were reported to be extremely apprehensive of being forced to undergo the "humiliation" of joining a mixed company. Too, whites were reluctant to sit with Negroes in the jury box. An elderly Spartanburg farmer verbalized his feelings on this point in the summer of 1869: "When I go to court & see negroes on the jury & on the stand for witnesses it makes me glad that I am so near the end of my race to sit on a jury with them I dont intend to do it we have a law that exempt a man at 65 & I take the advantage of it." This kind of withdrawal often reached odd extremes. In the spring of 1870, at the peak of the Negro leadership's drive for admission to privately owned public accommodations, the white Democrats of the Charleston Fire Department refused to decorate their engines and join in the annual parade because Negro fire companies were being allowed to march in the procession. . . .

Native whites also tended to withdraw from public places where the color line could not be firmly fixed and the Negro could easily assert his equality. "The whites have, to a great extent — greater than ever before — yielded the streets to the negroes," wrote a Columbian on Christmas Day, 1868. Similarly, in Charleston, in the late spring of 1866, a young aristocrat noted that the battery with its music and strollers had been yielded to the ladies and gentlemen of non-noble lineage on Saturdays, and by all whites to the Negroes on Sundays. On Saturdays, he declared, "the battery is quite full of gentlemen and ladies but it is not much patronized by the elite. . . . On Sunday afternoon the ethiops spread themselves on the Battery."

The same reaction was manifested by the whites wherever the Negro leadership succeeded by legal means in ending separation. For instance, when Negroes won admission to the street cars of Charleston, the whites simply withdrew. "On Sunday I counted five Cars successively near the Battery crowded [with] negroes, with but one white man, the Conductor," wrote a native white in May, 1867. "The ladies are practically excluded." When the Academy of Music was threatened with a discrimination suit in 1870, the white community replied with a counterthreat to withdraw its patronage and thus close the theater. Adjustment which fell short of complete separation remained unsatisfactory to whites. "Even the Theatre is an uncertain pleasure," complained a Charleston lady in 1873, "no matter how attractive the program, for you know that you may have a negro next to you." Probably many of her contemporaries found the exposure too damaging and stayed home.

The social lives of native whites were, of course, absolutely closed to

Negroes. Access to the homes of the whites was gained by Negroes only when they clearly acquiesced in the superior–inferior relationship dictated by the owners, and even then entrance was often denied. "I told him I would never allow negroes to go in it while I owned it," wrote a Laurenville woman, incensed that a man who had bought her former home had rented it to Negroes. In spite of the fact that some Negro domestics lived in quarters behind the houses of their employers, whites were already rejecting Negroes as neighbors. A real estate agent in Aiken in 1871 responded to this sentiment when he refused offers from Negroes for city lots at triple prices because, as he explained to the owner, "purchasers among the whites will not settle among the Negroes, and I am afraid to sell to only a few of the latter." Negroes were also not permitted to join any of the numerous social organizations in which native whites participated. The Patrons of Husbandry (the Grange), waxing strong in the state in the early 1870s, was not only exclusively white in membership, but was accused of widening the racial gap by its attitudes and actions toward Negroes. Of course, such separation had been practiced before, but the exclusion of the Negro in freedom from the social organizations of the whites was not so much tradition as it was deliberate decision. . . .

Separation is, of course, a relative term. It was obviously not possible for Negroes and whites to withdraw entirely from association with each other. If intimate contact led to irritation and violence, it also led to warm personal friendships — often with the superior–inferior, paternal bias, but no less real for all of that. Cordiality could and did breach the barrier of race. Yet the fact remained that it was difficult to establish a human bond across the color chasm and, once established, the tie had to be assiduously maintained against the constant erosion induced by a thousand and one external forces of social pressure.

That there was sometimes tenderness between individuals of different races is abundantly evident. On the Elmore plantation near Columbia, in the fall of 1865, the young white master was nightly importuned by the Negro children to get out his fiddle and play. Frequently he did so, the dozen or so Negro boys and girls dancing around the fire, begging for more after the fiddler had exhausted himself in a two-hour concert. The concern of many late masters for their ex-slaves was matched by the interest of individual Negroes in the welfare of their recent owners. A freedman seeking relief for a white family from a Bureau officer explained his motivation: "I used to belong to one branch of that family, and so I takes an interest in 'em." Occasionally, ex-slaveowners retained the friendship and assistance of their erstwhile bondsmen when all others had deserted them. . . .

Sometimes, intimacy became miscegenation. The census reports are uncertain witnesses and contemporaries are typically mute on the point;

but scattered references suggest that racial interbreeding was markedly less common after emancipation than before. "Miscegenation between white men and negro women diminished under the new order of things," a Bureau officer later wrote. "Emancipation broke up the close family contact in which slavery held the two races, and, moreover young gentlemen did not want mulatto children sworn to them at a cost of three hundred dollars apiece. In short, the new relations of the two stocks tended to separation rather than to fusion." A Northern traveler visiting the state in 1870 concurred: "From all I could see and learn, there are far fewer half-breed children born now than before the Rebellion. There seems, indeed, a chance that the production of original half-breeds may be almost done away with. . . ."

Legal, moral, and social pressures exercised by the white community upon its members, as well as the physical separation of the races suggest that these were valid observations. The Black Code pointedly declared that "Marriage between a white person and a person of color shall be illegal and void," and when the code was revised in 1866 this portion emphatically remained in force. Children born of Negro mothers and white fathers, so recently especially prized for their pecuniary value, became simply illegitimate issue and a liability to the community. In addition, the laws of bastardy came to be applied against the fathers of mulatto children. Perhaps most important was the fact that, in the minds of the native whites, children of mixed blood personified the adulteration of the superior race and embodied in living form the failure of Southern civilization. Many whites, turned to soul-searching by their defeat, fixed upon miscegenation as their great sin. "It does seem strange that so lovely a climate, and country, with a people in every way superior to the Yankees, should be overrun and destroyed by them," wrote a rice aristocrat in 1868. "But I believe that God has ordered it all, and I am firmly of opinion with Ariel that it is the judgement of the Almighty because the human and brute blood have mingled to the degree it has in the slave states. Was it not so in the French and British Islands and see what has become of them."

Just as complete separation of the races was physically impossible, there was little possibility that miscegenation might entirely cease. One does not have to travel far into contemporary sources to discover instances in which white men had children by Negro women. In 1867, a lowcountry planter, accused of fathering the mulatto child of his Negro house servant, wrote plaintively to his mother: "This child was begotten during my absence in Charlotte & Charleston, from the middle of December until nearly the middle of January, & the Father of it was seen night after night in Emma's house, this I heard on my return, but as it was no concern of mine I did not give it a thought. She was *free*, the Mother of 5 Children & could have a dozen lovers if she liked. I had no control over her virtue." In 1874, a planter on the Cooper River in St. John's noted the existence of circumstances on his plantation which might have led to similar results. "Found a white man staying with one of the colored people on the place," ran the laconic note in his journal. "He being engaged in rebuilding Mayrents Bridge." Some of these liaisons were of prolonged duration. In 1870, Maria Middleton, a Negro woman, brought suit against a Pineville physician for failure to support her three children which he had allegedly fathered. Strangely, the defendant's lawyer did not deny the paternity, but sought dismissal on the plea that the plaintiff had no legal grounds for suit.

Once in power, the Radicals hastened to repeal the prohibition against interracial marriage. Thereafter, informal arrangements were sometimes legalized. In the spring of 1869, a reporter stated that three such marriages had occurred within the state — a Massachusetts man had married a Beaufort mulatto woman, and two white women had married Negro men. In 1872, the legislature explicitly recognized interracial unions by declaring that the "children of white fathers and negro mothers may inherit from the father if he did not marry another woman but continued to live with their mother."

There were a surprisingly large number of cases in which white women gave birth to children by Negro fathers. During his stay in Greenville, Bureau officer John De Forest heard of two such births and noted other instances in which white women were supported by Negro men. Such situations, he believed, were largely the result of the loss of husbands and fathers in the war and the destitution of the country generally. In 1866, in neighboring Pickens District, a case came into the courts in which Sally Calhoun, "a white woman of low birth," and a Negro man were brought to trial for the murder of their child. Ironically, the Negro was freed, though obviously implicated, and the woman was convicted and imprisoned. Apparently, some of these liaisons were far from casual as a Spartanburg farmer rather painfully suggested to his brother in Alabama: "My dear Brother as you have made several Enquiries of me and desiring me to answer them I will attempt and endeavor to do So to the best information that I have on the Various Subjects alluded to by you the first Interrogatory is Relative to John H. Lipscomb's daughter haveing Negro Children, I am forced to answer in the affirmative no doubt but she has had two; and no hopes of her Stopping. . . ."

By the end of Reconstruction, Negroes had won the legal right to enjoy, along with whites, accommodations in all public places. In reality, however, they seldom did so. On the opposite side of the racial frontier, the pattern of separation was fixed in the minds of the whites almost simultaneously with the emancipation of the Negro. By 1868, the physical color line had, for the most part, already crystallized. During the Republican regime, it was breached only in minor ways. Once the whites regained political power, there was little need to establish legally a separation which already existed in fact. Moreover, to have done so would have been contrary to federal civil rights legislation and would have given needless offense to influential elements in the North. Finally, retention of the act had a certain propaganda value for use against liberals in the North and against Republican politicians at home. Again and again, the dead letter of the law was held up as exhibit "A" in South Carolina's case that she was being fair to the Negro in the Hampton tradition [a reference to the relatively mild and paternalistic forms of racism practiced by upper-class whites, who, for many years, were led by governor, and later senator, Wade Hampton]. After the federal statute was vitiated in the courts, after racial liberalism had become all but extinct in the North, and as the Negro was totally disfranchised in South Carolina, the white community was ready and able to close the few gaps which did exist in the color line, and to codify a social order which custom had already decreed.

Ultimately, the physical separation of the races is the least important portion of the story. The real separation was not that duo-chromatic order that prevailed on streetcars and trains, or in restaurants, saloons, and cemeteries. The real color line lived in the minds of individuals of each race, and it had achieved full growth even before freedom for the Negro was born. Physical separation merely symbolized and reinforced mental separation. It is true that vigorous assaults by one side or the other forced the enemy to yield his forward trenches and to alter slightly the precise line of the color front. It is also true that material changes in post-Reconstruction Southern society pushed the trenches into areas which had not existed before. This often gave the illusion of basic change, of a breakthrough by the dominant whites in the war of races, whereas, actually, it merely represented the extension of the old attitudinal conflict onto new ground, only to bring with it the stalemate that marked the struggle elsewhere. Viewed in relation to the total geography of race relations, the frontier hardly changed; and the rigidity of the physical situation, set as it was like a mosaic in black and white, itself suggested the intransigence of spirit which lay behind it. Well before the end of Reconstruction, this mental pattern was fixed; the heartland of racial exclusiveness remained inviolate; and South Carolina had become, in reality, two communities — one white and the other Negro.

STUDY GUIDE

1. What motives, according to the author, led southern whites to seek segregation from their ex-slaves? Does Williamson consider these motives to be entirely rational?

2. What were the basic demands of the black leadership?

3. List the various institutions of the South in which segregation took place, and explain how.

4. Williamson draws a distinction between separation by segregation and separation by withdrawal. When did southern whites tend to practice one and when the other?

5. Intimacy between the races does not appear to have ceased after emancipation. What evidence does the author have for this, and how does he account for it?

6. Would you, on the basic of this selection, agree that segregation began in the immediate postwar years? If so, why; if not, why not?

BIBLIOGRAPHY

The Reconstruction experience is dealt with in a number of volumes. James G. Randall and David Donald, *The Civil War and Reconstruction* (1969) is basic. More specialized are the following: Kenneth M. Stampp, *The Era of Reconstruction* (1965); John Hope Franklin, *Reconstruction: After the Civil War* (1961); and Rembert W. Patrick, *The Reconstruction of the Nation* (1967). Studies of race relations in individual states will be found in Joel Williamson, *After Slavery: The Negro in South Carolina during Reconstruction, 1861–1877* (1965), from which the above selection was taken; Vernon C. Wharton, *The Negro in Mississippi* (1965); Herman Belz, *Emancipation and Equal Rights* (1978); and Howard Rabinowitz, *Race Relations in the Urban South* (1978). White resistance to black freedom and equality is dealt with in Allen W. Trelease, *White Terror: The Ku Klux Klan Conspiracy and Southern Reconstruction* (1971) and in Michael Perman, *Reunion without Compromise: The South and Reconstruction, 1865–1868* (1973). The institutionalization of white racism before the turn of the century is traced in the following: C. Vann Woodward, *The Strange Career of Jim Crow* (1974); Hortense Powdermaker, *After Freedom: A Cultural Study in the Deep South* (1930); John Dollard, *Caste and Class in a Southern Town* (1937); and Allison Davis, Burleigh B. Gardner, and Mary R. Gardner, *Deep South: A Social Anthropological Study of Caste and Class* (1941).

To the student:

We, as publishers, realize that one way to improve education is to improve textbooks. We also realize that you, the student, have a large role in the success or failure of textbooks. Although teachers choose books to be used in the classroom, if the students do not buy and use books, those books are failures.

Usually only the teacher is asked about the quality of a text; his opinion alone is considered as revisions are written or as new books are planned. Now, Little, Brown would like to ask you about this book: how you liked or disliked it; why it was successful or dull; if it taught you anything. Would you fill in this form and return it to us at: Little, Brown and Co., College Division, 34 Beacon St., Boston, Mass. 02106. It is your chance to directly affect the publication of future textbooks.

_____

Book title: _____ School: _____

Course title: _____ Course enrollment: _____

Instructor's name: _____

1. Did you like the book? _____

2. Was it too easy? _____

   Did you read all the selections? _____

   Which did you like most? _____

   Which did you like least? _____

3. Did you like the cover? _____

   Did you like the size? _____

   Did you like the illustrations? _____

   Did you like the type size? _____

(over)

4. Were the study questions and bibliographies useful? _____

   How should they be changed? _____

   _____

5. Are the introductions useful? _____

   How might they be improved? _____

   _____

6. Do you feel the professor should continue to assign this book next
   year? _____

7. Will you keep this book for your library? _____

8. Please add any comments or suggestions on how we might improve
   this book, in either content or format.

   _____

   _____

   _____

   _____

   _____

9. May we quote you, either in promotion for this book, or in future
   publishing ventures? _____ yes _____ no

_____   _____
date   signature